D0068147

Eschatology

Hans Schwarz

WILLIAM B. EERDMANS PUBLISHING COMPANY
GRAND RAPIDS, MICHIGAN / CAMBRIDGE, U.K.

Wm. B. Eerdmans Publishing Co.
255 Jefferson Ave. S.E., Grand Rapids, Michigan 49503 /
P.O. Box 163, Cambridge CB3 9PU U.K.

Printed in the United States of America

05 04 03 02 01 00   7 6 5 4 3 2 1

Library of Congress Cataloging-in-Publication Data

Schwarz, Hans.
  Eschatology / Hans Schwarz.
    p.   cm.
  ISBN 0-8028-4733-1 (pbk.: alk. paper)
    1. Eschatology. I. Title.

  BT821.2.S353 2000
  291.2'3 — dc21   00-041729

www.eerdmans.com

Contents

Preface   xi

Abbreviations   xiv

Introduction: Who Still Cares about the Future?   1

Biblical Eschatology contra the Obsession
   with the Present   2

Idea of Progress Is Grounded in Christian Eschatology   6

Estrangement between Eschatology and Progress   14

For the Sake of Sanity: Recovery of an
   Eschatological Outlook   17

PART I:
THE DISCOVERY OF THE FUTURE

Expecting Life Beyond as a Primal Human Phenomenon   24

The Scope and Shape of Eschatology   26

Chapter 1: The Old Testament View of Eschatology   31

1. Developing an Eschatological Consciousness   31

2. The Human Destiny   35

    a. Emphasis on the This-Worldly Aspect of Life   36

    b. Translation and Resurrection   38

  3. The Last Judgment   41

    a. Responding to a Holy and Gracious God   41

    b. The Day of the Lord   43

    c. Universal Scope of Salvation   45

  4. The Coming of a Messiah   47

    a. The Significance of the Term "Messiah"   48

    b. Main Sources for the Concept of a Messiah   49

    c. Expansion of the Messianic Hopes in the Apocalyptic Period   51

  5. The Iranian Connection   55

**Chapter 2: The Eschatological Proclamation
of the New Testament**   61

  1. The Jewish Context   61

  2. The Eschatological Figure of Jesus   68

    a. Jesus' Eschatological Message of the Kingdom of God   69

    b. Jesus' Self-Understanding   73

    c. Jesus and the Question of the Future   79

  3. The Eschatological Proclamation of the Gospel Writers   82

    a. The Interim in the View of the Synoptics   83

    b. The Emphasis on the Present in the Gospel of John   88

  4. The Eschatological Message of Paul   91

    a. Paul's Eschatological Call   91

    b. Our Life as a Life between the Aeons   93

    c. Eschatology beyond Spiritualism and Disappointment   95

  5. The Eschatological Scope of the Early Church   97

PART II:
THE MANIFOLD FACES OF ESCHATOLOGY

Chapter 3: Present Discussion of Christian Eschatology   107

   1. The Rediscovery of the Eschatological Perspective   108

     a. The Kingdom of God as an Eschatological Concept   108

     b. The Consistent or Consequent Eschatology   111

     c. A Noneschatological Jesus   115

   2. Present-Oriented Approach to Eschatology   120

     a. Existential and Ethical Approaches   120

     b. Transcendentalistic Approaches   129

   3. The Future-Directedness of Eschatology   135

     a. Exegetical Considerations   135

       Eschatology as Fulfillment and Promise   136

       Delay of the Parousia   139

     b. Systematic Proposals   142

       Prolepsis of Eschatology   143

       Theology of Hope   146

   4. The Liberating Power of Eschatology   152

     a. Eschatology from the Underside   152

       Problematic and Legitimation of Liberation Theology   153

       Eschatology in the Context of Liberation   157

     b. Feminist Perspectives   162

   5. Christian Eschatology in a Universal Context   166

     a. Process Theology   166

     b. Eschatology among the World's Religions   170

Chapter 4: Confronting Secular Varieties of Hope   173

   1. The Impact of Science   173

     a. The Option of Scientific Materialism   175

    b. The Evolutionary Perspective   185

    c. Facing a Possible Ecological Holocaust   194

         World Come of Age or an Aging World?   195

         Greenhouse Effect   196

         Pleonexia   199

         Overpopulation   201

         The Eschatological Context of Ecology   203

         Future-Directedness of Eschatology   207

  2. The Impact of Philosophy   209

    a. The Option of Secular Existentialism   210

         Life Bounded by Death   210

         Humanity Thrown upon Itself   214

    b. Utopia from the Left   217

         A New World through Revolution   217

         Concrete Utopia   222

         The Right to Be Lazy   224

  3. The Impact of Religiosity   227

    a. A Homespun Eschatology   227

    b. Ambivalence of Secular Humanism   237

         Faith in Human Reason *(Humanist Manifesto I* and *II)*   237

         A Modest Assessment of the Future   240

PART III:
WHAT CAN WE HOPE FOR?

Chapter 5: Approaching the New World   247

  1. Death   249

    a. The Ambiguity of Death   249

    b. Death as the Gate to the Eschaton   256

  2. Immortality – Yes or No?   261

a. *Immortality and Occultism*   262

b. *Immortality and Near-Death Experiences*   263

c. *Immortality and Greek Philosophy*   269

d. *Immortality and Christian Faith*   272

3. Resurrection   280

    a. *Decisive Character of Christ's Resurrection*   280

    b. *Creative Newness of Christ's Resurrection*   283

    c. *Christ's Resurrection and Our Resurrection*   286

    d. *Resurrection of the Body*   287

    e. *"Between" Death and Resurrection*   290

       Time as a This-Wordly Entity   291

       The Eternity of God as Fulfillment of Time   293

       Death as Finality and Transition   296

Excursus: Reincarnation and Transmigration of the Soul   301

Chapter 6: Controversial Areas of Eschatological Hopes   309

1. Setting a Date for the End   309

    a. *A Fertile Tradition*   310

    b. *Bringing About the End by Force*   314

2. Hope for the Millennium   322

    a. *Origin and Growth of an Idea*   322

    b. *Joachim of Fiore and the Rise of Millennialism*   325

    c. *Keeping the Fervor*   330

       Historic Premillennialism   331

       Postmillennialism   332

       Amillennialism   332

       Dispensational Premillennialism   332

3. Universal Salvation *(Apokatastasis Panton)*   337

    a. *Origen and the Origins of the Apokatastasis Idea*   338

    b. *The Apokatastasis Idea in More Recent Theological Reflection*   341 *c. Apokatastasis or "Christ's Descent into Hell"?* 346

4. Purgatory 352
   a. A Narrow Biblical Basis 353
   b. The Human Component to Salvation 356

Chapter 7: The New World to Come 365
    Beyond Resignation and Futurist Activism 368

1. Proleptic Anticipation of the New World 370
   a. The Church as Reminder of God's Future 370
       The Symbol of the Future 371
       The Whole People of God 374
       The Anticipation of the Heavenly City 377
   b. The Signs of the End 381
       Anticipating the End 381
       The Birth Pangs of the New World 383
       The Antichrist 385

2. Entry to the New World 387
   a. Consummation of the World 387
   b. Final Judgment 390
   c. Paradox between Justice and Love of God 394

3. Disclosure of the New World 397
   a. Disclosure of the Kingdom of God 397
   b. Heaven and Hell 398
   c. Completion 404

Index of Names 409
Index of Subjects 417
Index of Scripture References 427

Preface

The crows croak
and move to town in whirring flight:
Soon it is snowing, —
fortunate is the one who still now — has a place called home!

These are the opening lines of a poem entitled "Lonesome" written by the nineteenth-century German philosopher Friedrich Nietzsche (1844-1900). Perhaps it is just my nostalgic mood as an aging seminary and university professor that makes me believe, as Nietzsche did in the nineteenth century, that the world has grown colder, that more solitary figures, from unwed mothers to career-driven individuals, and from left-out and leftover old folks to preschoolers, are making up our societies. Downsizing, revenue maximizing, and globalizing are adding to increasingly frigid temperatures. In 1997, for instance, the unword of the year in Germany was "affluence garbage" *(Wohlstandsmüll)*, denoting those who were victims of other people's prosperity. We do not need much imagination to realize that in such a climate life has become cheap. We have precious little time to care for other people's lives, and perhaps we do not even want to care. Yet with our own lives it is not that much different. A young doctor in our university hospital once told me: "Unless you volunteer for weekend and evening duties, your contract will not be renewed, and before you know it, you are old." It is not that people are mindless and uncaring, but that we have developed a system that produces mindless and uncaring people, either by the demands of the workweek or by the seduction of the leisure business.

It is not surprising that in this situation the classical symbiosis between Christianity and culture, as portrayed, for instance, by the method of correlation between world and word in the theology of Paul Tillich (1886-1965), is no longer tenable. "The synthesis of Christianity and culture becomes more and more questionable," we are told by Frederick Herzog (1925-1996).[1] Of course, we have witnessed the decline of the mainline churches and the growth of the more evangelically minded denominations. Yet this shift is deceiving, since the overall percentage of people with a religious affiliation in the USA has remained remarkably constant throughout the last thirty or forty years. Moreover, in other countries, such as Germany, even free churches and sects are not making inroads in a largely secularized society. With this diminished interest in religious matters, the coming of the new millennium will attract theological reflection only among the more conservative church members — if at all. The larger populace will mark it as an occasion for celebration and self-aggrandizement, but not for reflection.

Would it not be wiser simply to pass over the issue of eschatology, meaning the Christian reflection on the end of our lives and of the world in general? I would respond with a loud "No!" and that for two reasons:

1. At the beginning of another millennium, it is important for us as Christians to reflect on what we can still believe. Of course, we must keep in mind that we are no longer a young religion looking forward to the imminent coming of Christ, as the members of the nascent church did in the first centuries. By and large, our denominations have become institutions and churches and congregations that are run by annual budgets and trustworthy programs and that bear little witness to any eschatological urgency.

2. At the beginning of this new millennium we realize that there is, on the one hand, an ever larger number of people lacking the bare necessities of life and, on the other hand, an affluent club enjoying luxuries beyond imagination. Many of us are caught between the two, and we are tempted more than ever to simply shrug our shoul-

1. Frederick Herzog, "Vom Ende der Systematischen Theologie," in *Gottes Zukunft — Zukunft der Welt: Festschrift für Jürgen Moltmann zum 60. Geburtstag*, ed. Hermann Deuser et al. (Munich: Chr. Kaiser, 1986), 502 (translation mine).

ders in resignation, claiming that we cannot change things. There is also another segment of society that could not care less about organized religion and that attempts to find its own way out of the quagmire of the world's problems, perhaps still dreaming that at the end we will reach Utopia.

We owe the liberating vision of Christian eschatology to those tempted by passive resignation as well as those lured by wishful utopia. We owe them the confident affirmation that there is an answer to our troubles and our questions, an answer, however, not provided by us but by God. Christian eschatology is needed today, perhaps even more than ever, to provide for us both a perspective of the future and, even more importantly, a guiding light showing us how to pursue life meaningfully in the present. It is out of this sense of responsibility that this book is written. I do not pretend to know all the answers. But I do believe that I know *who is the answer*. This answer, God in Christ, is spelled out in its eschatological implications; it is for some perhaps too far away, and for others not far enough away, but hopefully it will be presented in a way that is always true to the Judeo-Christian tradition which allows us insight into this all-decisive facet of our faith.

That this treatment of eschatology can finally appear, I owe first of all to the efforts of Hildegard Ferme, who tirelessly and effectively produced the various versions of this manuscript. Then I owe a big thank you to Dr. David Ratke for many improvements in style and content. My graduate research assistant Anna Madsen deserves thanks for proofreading and compiling the indices, as does Alexander Lisse for checking the biblical references, and to my wife, Hildegard, I am in debt again for putting up with a husband who finished another book-length manuscript. All shortcomings that the text might still contain remain my responsibility.

Regensburg, July 1999   HANS SCHWARZ

Abbreviations

ANF   *Ante-Nicene Fathers,* ed. Alexander Roberts and James Donaldson. 10 vols. Grand Rapids: Eerdmans, reprint of 1884-86 edition.

DS   Heinrich Denziger and Adolf Schönmetzer, *Enchiridion. Symbolorum.* 34th edition. Freiburg: Herder, 1967.

FaCh   *The Fathers of the Church: A New Translation.* Washington, D.C.: Catholic University of America Press, 1947- .

LW   *Luther's Works, American Edition.* Vols. 1-30, ed. Jaroslav Pelikan. St. Louis: Concordia Publishing House, 1955-67. Vols. 31-55, ed. Helmut T. Lehmann. Philadelphia: Fortress Press, 1955-67.

NPNF FS   *Nicene and Post-Nicene Fathers of the Christian Church,* first series. Ed. Philip Schaff. Grand Rapids: Eerdmans, 1983 reprint edition.

NPNF SS   *Nicene and Post-Nicene Fathers of the Christian Church,* second series. Ed. Philip Schaff. Grand Rapids: Eerdmans, 1983 reprint edition.

PL   *Patrologiae Cursus Completus.* Series Latina. Ed. Jacques-Paul Migne. 221 vols. Paris, 1841-64.

TDNT   *Theological Dictionary of the New Testament,* ed. Gerhard Kittel and Gerhard Friedrich. Trans. Geoffrey W. Bromiley. 10 vols. Grand Rapids: Eerdmans, 1964-76.

TDOT   *Theological Dictionary of the Old Testament,* ed. G. Johannes Botterweck, Helmer Ringgren, and Heinz-Josef Fabry. Trans. John T. Willis et al. Grand Rapids: Eerdmans, 1977- .

TRE	*Theologische Realenzyklopädie.* Vols. 1- . Ed. Gerhard Krause and Gerhard Müller. Berlin and New York: Walter de Gruyter, 1977- .
WA	*D. Martin Luthers Werke: Kritische Gesamtausgabe.* Vols. 1- . Weimar: Hermann Böhlau, 1883- .
WA.TR	*D. Martin Luthers Werke: Kritische Gesamtausgabe.* Tischreden. Weimar, 1912- .

Introduction: Who Still Cares about the Future?

"This is the end — for me the beginning of life." These are the last words of Dietrich Bonhoeffer (1906-45), handed down to us before he was executed by the Nazis during the last days of World War II.[1] Bonhoeffer was not an otherworldly person. If he were, he would not have been accused by the Nazis of being part of the resistance movement. As we can glean from the letters he wrote when he realized the Nazis were not going to release him from prison, he had a passion for this life and agonized about wasting it behind bars. His last words show us, however, that this life was not everything for him. There was something else to come, something to long for, to trust and to rejoice in. In this way he stands in strong contrast to many people today.

In many European countries such as France, Great Britain, and Germany, the majority of people do not believe in life after death and even fewer believe in a final judgment. The USA is different in this respect, because people there are believers. Surveys show that most Americans believe in the Bible as the inspired word of God; they believe in the divinity of Jesus of Nazareth and in eternal life. Yet the appalling fact is that most of these so-called believers are very ignorant when it comes to content. Most cannot even enumerate four of the ten commandments. They seem to follow one of the great American heroes of World War II, and later president, Dwight D. Eisenhower (1890-1969),

---

1. Dietrich Bonhoeffer, *Letters and Papers from Prison,* ed. Eberhard Bethge, rev. ed. (New York: Macmillan, 1967), 225.

1

who reportedly once said: "Everybody must believe in something and I do not care what it is." Yet if we do not care, we do not put that much emphasis in it either. It is not surprising that our lifestyles run counter to what the Bible expects from us.

Biblical Eschatology contra the Obsession with the Present

The evangelist Billy Graham (b. 1918) once wrote:

> That's the way a Christian should live his life, in constant anticipation of the return of Christ! If we could live every day as though it might be the very last one, before the final judgment, what a difference it would make here on earth!
>
> But we don't like to think that way! We don't like to think that our carefully made plans, our long-range schemes may be interrupted by the trumpets of God! We're so engrossed in our own little activities that we can't bear the thought of having anything spoil them! Too many people would rather say, "Oh well, the end of the world hasn't come yet, so why think about it — it's probably a thousand years away!"[2]

This quotation shows in a nutshell the contrast in which most of us live. I have occasionally jokingly said that church executives and bishops have their date books filled so far in advance that if Christ were to come they would probably plead with him for a different date, because they already have an appointment for that date. Most of us are little empire builders who resemble the rich fool who decided to pull down his barns after a good crop and build larger ones. Jesus said to the rich man, "You fool! This very night your life is being demanded of you. And the things you have prepared, whose will they be?" (Luke 12:20). We conduct our lives as if we would live forever. But this is no surprise.

When do we ever have the luxury of sitting down in solitude and thinking — about our own life, about our family, or about anything of ultimate concern? We are too busy to think. The academy of Plato (427-347 B.C.) and Aristotle (384-322 B.C.) was a place where one could enjoy a leisurely walk or simply sit there, exchanging views with others or fo-

---

2. Billy Graham, *Peace with God* (Westwood, N.J.: Revell, 1968), 228-29.

cusing on one's own thoughts. Yet today a professional academy, such as
the American Academy of Religion, is as different from those of antiquity as day is from night. When it convenes its annual meeting, thousands of people gather for three or four days of what could very well be
the busiest days of their whole year, with one important event joining
another or running parallel to it from early morning to late night.

We have been accustomed to think from date to date. A politician
plans from one election to the next, and a salesperson from the spring to
the fall collection. We are like the factory workers on the assembly line
who never get the full picture, but just small segments of the whole work
process. We encounter only segments of time. We are glad to know that
we end the year in the black, that we have not been laid off, or even got a
raise. In the same way as lifelong allegiance to one job and one company is
a thing of the distant past, we are never confronted with the question of
what the whole thing is for. Only occasionally, when something severely
interferes with our mindless rushing through the present — when we are
confronted with a divorce or a heart attack, for instance — do we take
stock of our lives. For a moment we come to our senses. Perhaps then we
tell ourselves that if we would have to do things over again, we would do
them differently. But life must go on, and soon we are pushed back into
"reality" and its demands of the immediate present.

Many of us are church people, and we sing from our hymnals, "Re-
fresh your people on their tiresome way; / lead us from night to never-
ending day."[3] But once we leave the church service, our thoroughly
commercialized world quickly takes hold of us again, telling us where
we can get a special bargain. Life is not supposed to be a vale of toil and
tears. It is supposed to be fun, and emotional upsets are cured through
psychiatric treatment, pills, or, less expensively, through our pastor. If
we do not have enough money to enjoy life, we can get an instant loan
and instant credit. While people of past generations had to hope for a
life beyond, because life here was short and filled with drudgery, for the
majority of us there is no such need. The claim of Karl Marx (1818-83),
that "religion is only the illusory sun which revolves round man as long
as he does not revolve round himself" and that "*the task of history*, therefore, once the *world beyond the truth* has disappeared, is to establish the
truth of this world," is already an historical fact for us when applied to es-

3. *Lutheran Book of Worship*, "God of Our Fathers," Hymn 567, stanza 4.

3

chatology.[4] We have almost succeeded in forgetting the last things and instead devote exclusive attention to the present, meaning to life here on earth.

Our noneschatological lifestyle also shows in our trivialization of death. Decades ago, news reporters were excited when they could report about a murder. But in our metropolitan areas, so many murders and violent deaths occur that only in very exceptional cases do they make headlines. Death simply belongs to our modern society as part of urban violence, the drug culture, and the traffic conditions. We are used to these daily death reports in the same way we have become accustomed to violent movies and the daily death toll on TV. Sudden death has not just become a by-product of modern living, it is also a term in sports language. It is hardly understood as something leading up to the last things, to life eternal or to judgment.

Even when death hits us personally — for instance, when one of our loved ones dies — things remain under control thanks to the comprehensive care of funeral homes. A special color for mourning (usually white or black) that is worn by the immediate relatives for one year or longer disappeared long ago. Moreover, hardly anybody dies at home. Even when hit by a fatal heart attack within our own four walls, we are rushed to the hospital and "pronounced dead on arrival." We have managed to shut away death into the sterile white walls of the hospital room and the intensive care unit. What was normal for the patriarchs of the Old Testament — dying in the midst of their families, with both parties saying farewell to each other — is hardly any longer a possibility for us. We have no immediate encounter with death, except through its trivialization in TV programs, its facticity in news services, or in the euphemistic version offered by the funeral home, where the diseased often look better than they did during their lifetime. Thanks to cosmetology and embalming practices, perpetual care will be extended to the dead in our cemeteries.

Until very recently many women died in childbirth or shortly thereafter. Diseases during infancy, such as measles and smallpox, heavily affected infant mortality rates until virtually the end of the nineteenth century. It was normal that people died, young and old, and

4. Karl Marx, "Contribution to the Critique of Hegel's Philosophy of Right," in *On Religion* (New York: Schocken Books, 1964), 42.

usually they died at home. Death had an impact on everyone. In some countries the bride was given a shroud as a wedding gift, reminding her how precarious her future life would be. When people such as Martin Luther (1483-1546) asked in the medieval period, "How can I find a gracious God?" his question was certainly not unrelated to the general outlook of that time. Life was precarious, threatened by natural disasters and diseases of all sorts. One wanted to make sure that at least at the gate of death a gracious God was awaiting the deceased. When Luther discovered by studying Scripture that Judgment Day did not need to be conceived as a day of wrath, but as one of joy, this was a great liberating move. One need not be afraid of death. One no longer needed to do all kinds of penitential rituals to placate a God of wrath. In the letters of his later years, Luther showed that he was longing for death and for a better hereafter, and that the craving for life had no attraction for him.[5]

Yet we do not want to look that far. Actuarial tables tell us how many years we can expect to live. At the same time, we are aware more than ever of the sudden possibility of death. We know that a heart attack can terminate our life in the blink of an eye, and we are still consciously bothered by the possibility of a nuclear disaster. Nonetheless, outlook on life is neither positively nor negatively determined by the uncontrollable fact of death. We would prefer to shut out death completely. Therefore, the possibility of cloning humans has received immense attention. It is not so much the medical angle that fascinates us (for instance, that we could develop spare parts for an aging population), but the hope that we could duplicate ourselves and in this way live forever. The possibility of removing the death barrier seems to emerge, and we are again hoping for eternal life here on earth. Medical doctors are already doing their best to prolong life and would rather "pull the plug" too late than too soon. Many people sacrifice the pleasures of gourmet cooking and try through dietary asceticism to escape from threatening heart attacks or from shortening their lives, while politicians spend billions of dollars each year to save us from the conceivable attacks of other nations.

We have made ourselves so much at home here that the last things are no longer appealing. The Bible frequently describes eternal life and heaven in the picturesque language of a celestial banquet. Such imagery

---

5. Cf. Martin Luther, in a letter to James Probst [Wittenberg], December 5, 1544, in *LW,* 50:246; cf. also "To Mrs. Martin Luther. Halle, January 25, 1546," in *LW,* 50:284-85.

has little attraction for people who watch their daily diets. And the prospect of streets paved with gold, gates of pearls, and celestial choirs does not mean much in an affluent society. They would be interesting museum pieces or something you could visit while touring Disney World or other amusement parks. But to live there would be a different matter. We prefer to enjoy our own modern amenities.

Our life here is in stark contrast to any life beyond. While life beyond should be devoted to eternal worship and service to God, we tell ourselves that we enjoy our busy lives, and even good church members hardly find time for daily devotions. We read in the New Testament that in heaven there will be neither male nor female, while our life here is hardly worth anything if sexuality is excluded, whether through impotence or some disease. In heaven, we are told, we will mostly sing hymns and adore God, while here, as anybody who has been active in a church choir knows, one of the most frustrating jobs is to recruit new choir members. Above that, Sunday school attendance is declining and agnosticism and self-made religions are increasing all over the world. While access to life beyond death depends on God's grace, access to life here on earth depends on our own success; and while forgiveness of sins is the essential prerequisite of heavenly bliss, earthly blessing is determined by our own efforts. We have become mature, we have taken our time into our own hands and no longer rely on what many consider the vague promises of a life hereafter.

Idea of Progress Is Grounded in Christian Eschatology

The Jewish Christian philosopher Eugen Rosenstock-Huessy (1888-1973) wrote: "Christianity is the founder and trustee of the future, the very process of finding and securing it, and without the Christian spirit there is no real future for man. Future means novelty, surprise; it means outgrowing past habits and attainments. When a job, a movement, an institution promises nothing but treadmill repetition of a given routine in thought and action, we say correctly, 'There is no future in it.'"[6]

Rosenstock-Huessy claims the obvious here: to understand any-

---

6. Eugen Rosenstock-Huessy, *The Christian Future; or, The Modern Mind Outrun* (New York: Harper Torchbooks, 1966), 61.

thing we must consider its context. The context for modern life, at least in the West, and through our global civilization even beyond that, is the Judeo-Christian tradition. As any calendar, sales chart, or bank account statement shows, our modern life and its progressiveness presupposes a linear concept of time, a time arrow that has a definite starting point and a definite goal. This linear understanding of time originated in the Judeo-Christian religion. As far as we know, all other worldviews and religions, with the exception perhaps of Zoroastrianism, a religion not unrelated to the Judeo-Christian tradition, are confined to a cyclical understanding of time.

For instance, in the Canaanite religion of Israel's neighbors, the most important active figure of their pantheon was Baal, a weather and fertility god. The local differentiations of his name and his being notwithstanding, he is *the* Canaanite god "with whom the nomadic tribes of Israel who confessed Yahweh came into contact from their emigration from Egypt till after the exile."[7] We can still discern several festivals in which Baal played a prominent role. The most important was the new year festival in the fall, where most likely the return of Baal from the underworld and his enthronement on Mount Sapan, at the Orontes River near Ugarit, was celebrated. In spring there was the feast of mourning for Baal, and finally in June the feast of the destruction of Mot, the death god. Baal battled with the god of death until Mot (death) conquered him and took him down to the underworld, from which his sister and sometime consort Anath freed him by destroying Mot after a violent struggle. As William F. Albright (1891-1971) writes:

> In the Baal epic it is recorded that at the beginning there was a victory of Death over Baal, which was later followed by a triumph of Baal over Death, at the end of which the sad refrain,
>
>> Truly I know that Triumphant Baal is dead,
>> That the Lord of the Earth has perished,
>
> is changed to
>
>> Truly I know that Triumphant Baal lives,
>> That the Lord of the Earth exists.[8]

7. So M. J. Mulder, "Baal," in *TDOT,* 2:199.

8. William Foxwell Albright, *Yahweh and the Gods of Canaan: A Historical Analysis of Two Contrasting Faiths* (Garden City, N.Y.: Doubleday, Anchor Books, 1969), 126.

The cult of Baal reflected the cyclical events of nature, which had great significance for the agrarian society in Canaan. "The Canaanite could explain the change from one season to another and the differences between good and bad years only by believing that sometimes Baal was weak, sick, or even dead. This was a basic assumption of their religion. But such ideas were foreign to monotheistic Yahwism."[9] In the beginning of summer, the people lamented the death of Baal and the triumph of the death god Mot, because in the summer drought vegetation dried out and perished through the merciless rays of the sun and the scorching winds of the desert. Later in the season people rejoiced and celebrated the death of Mot and the "resurrection" of the fertility god Baal when the fall or winter rains drenched the dry ground and promised a good crop.

Such a seasonal rhythm between "life and death" does not provide much incentive for long-range planning, because humanity feels subjected to the power of nature. The Indian religions of Buddhism and Hinduism provide even less stimulus to engage in intensive planning for the future. Again, they portray a cyclical worldview and advocate as one of the main goals of this life the negation of all craving for life in order to break out of the fatal *samsara* (wheel of life) of birth, death, and reincarnation. Any interest in the future and any appreciation of life here on earth would only jeopardize the release from this world and its troubles. While there are significant differences between these various traditions, "the dominant trend is towards a belief that the true self *(Atman)* is unborn and never dies, and that the ultimate goal of the human spirit is to escape a continual cycle of birth, death, and rebirth, and attain either absorption into the Absolute or union with God."[10]

One might argue that the Greeks are an exception, because they reached a very high cultural level without a linear concept of time. There may be some truth in this. But when we penetrate the cultural facade, we realize very quickly that the Greek view of life, similar to that of Rome, was quite pessimistic. Indicative of this is the fate of the two *kouroi,* Cleobis and Biton, whose statues we can admire in the Museum

9. Mulder, 2:200.
10. So Paul Badham and Linda Badham, "Death and Immortality in the Religions of the World: An Editorial Survey," in *Death and Immortality in the Religions of the World,* ed. Paul Badham and Linda Badham (New York: Paragon, 1987), 3.

of Delphi. The ancient historiographer Herodotus (ca. 484–ca. 425 B.C.) tells us the myth connected with them. They were two well-liked young men. Their mother was a priestess of Hera and had to drive into the Heraeum for the Hera festival at the ancient city of Argos, south of Corinth. When the oxen were late in coming from the fields and time was running out, the two sons took the place of the oxen and pulled their mother in the cart to the Heraeum, which was five miles away. They were praised by everyone for this deed, and their mother prayed to Hera that they should receive the best that is available in this world. The reward was that on that day "the two youth fell asleep in the temple. They never woke more, but so passed from the earth."[11]

This world and the life connected with it have no actual value. Even Aristotle despised manual labor, which was left to the slaves, and preferred to concentrate on eternal issues. Plato, too, recognized this world as only a reflection of the eternal and unchanging world. He postulated a release from this earthly prison by which the eternal soul could return to its origin and destiny. The Greeks "were primarily concerned with the *logos* of the *cosmos,* not with the *Lord* and the meaning of history."[12] The *logos* was wisdom and the eternally unchanging; history, however, was singular and accidental. Only in Christianity did the *logos* become flesh and was understood as the Lord of history (John 1:14). During the classical period of Greek history, however, the gods of Homer (eighth century B.C.) looked like deified people and were themselves subject to the destiny of the world. In later Hellenism the mystery religions indicate an unfulfilled yearning for immortality in which the Christian hope of the resurrection of the dead easily found open ears. Friedrich Nietzsche, in his *Birth of Tragedy: Hellenism and Pessimism,* detected a pervasive pessimism through which any optimism eventually "suffers shipwreck."[13]

The British historian Arnold Toynbee (1889-1975) even suggested that the "cyclic view of the process of history was taken so entirely for

11. Herodotus, *The History of Herodotus* 1.31, trans. George Rawlinson, ed. Manuel Komroff (New York: Tudor, 1932), 11.

12. Karl Löwith, *Meaning in History: The Theological Implications of the Philosophy of History* (Chicago: University of Chicago Press, 1949), 4.

13. Friedrich Nietzsche, *The Birth of Tragedy: Hellenism and Pessimism* 15, in Friedrich Nietzsche, *"The Birth of Tragedy" and "The Case of Wagner,"* translated with a commentary by Walter Kaufmann (New York: Random House, Vintage Books, 1967), 97.

granted by even the greatest Greek and Indian souls and intellects — by Aristotle, for instance, and by the Buddha — that they simply assumed that it was true without thinking it necessary to prove it."[14] Yet Toynbee himself opted for a "cyclic movement of civilizations round the cycle of birth, death, birth."[15] One civilization emerges, attains its height, and provokes another civilization to originate. The latter conflicts with the former, gains strength while fighting it, and finally prevails until a third emerges. Like the waves of the sea crashing against the shore and receding, one civilization after the other is doomed to death without any evident progress.

Why is the Judeo-Christian religion so different that it can provide the ground for the modern emphasis on this world and the concern for the future? The reason can be found in two basic convictions: (1) the belief in one God and (2) the identification of this one God as the creator and redeemer of everything that is. Often the people of Israel were attracted to the polytheism of their neighbors, but their religious leaders always brought them back to Yahweh, the only God. Though Yahweh was, in a special sense, regarded as the divine head of the Hebrew community, this theocracy tended to be universalistic. Especially under the influence of the prophetic movement, that is, from about the middle of the eighth century B.C. onward, the Israelites thought of Yahweh more and more as the divine head of all humanity, while the neighboring nations still worshiped their respective particularistic gods.

How decisive this monotheistic and universalistic view of God is, can be shown by comparing the Judeo-Christian religion with Zoroastrianism. Both conceive history as a forward movement, but the strict dualism between the two main gods, Ormuzd and Ahriman, while finally resolved in the eschaton, prevented Zoroastrianism from pursuing the idea of progress. The Judeo-Christian belief in historic progression is largely due to the understanding of history as salvation history *(Heilsgeschichte)*. The God of Israel is not a God of the past but of the future. This is already indicated in the Old Testament covenant concept,

14. Arnold J. Toynbee, *Civilization on Trial* (London: Oxford University Press, 1946), 14. However, Toynbee conceded the possibility that our present civilization may survive because this cyclic movement is no inescapable fate and leaves room for freedom of choice to give history "some new and unprecedented turn" (39).

15. Toynbee, 236.

and is emphasized further in the apocalyptic periodization of history in the intertestamental period.

Greco-Roman thinking was past oriented and mainly interested in the eternal laws beyond and above history out of which historical events flowed in eternal occurrence and recurrence. Thus the Greeks were not concerned about the Lord of history, but about the regularity and steadiness of the cosmos which they first perceived in the movements of the heavenly bodies. In the Judeo-Christian religion God was conceived as the agent of history, who works in and with history. Though the God of Israel was undoubtedly first understood as the redeemer of Israel, the consequent development of the universalistic view of God led to the understanding of God as the creator of everything that is. One should realize, however, that the gradual understanding of Yahweh as the creator of the world did not evolve to replace other creation stories that might have been prevalent within the Israelite community. As soon as the concept of creation emerged, the Israelites assumed Yahweh as the creator.

When the Israelites moved into Canaan, they encountered a religion which had much to say about creation. We notice this, for instance, when Abraham returned from rescuing Lot from the hand of the four kings and met King Melchizedek of Salem, probably the ancient name of Jerusalem.[16] Melchizedek is called a priest of God Most High (in Hebrew, *El Elyon*). He blessed Abraham and said to him:

> Blessed be Abram by God Most High,
>   maker of heaven and earth;
> and blessed be God Most High,
>   who has delivered your enemies into your hand!
>
> (Gen. 14:19-20)

In this city a god with the name of *El Elyon* was worshiped, who was said to have created heaven and earth. When Israel was confronted with such a godhead in the land they had occupied, the question was inescapable: How should they respond to such a claim?

Was *El Elyon* the creator of heaven and earth and Yahweh only the rescuer from Egypt, meaning the God of history? Such specialization of

---

16. For the following, cf. Walther Zimmerli, *Die Weltlichkeit des Alten Testaments* (Göttingen: Vandenhoeck & Ruprecht, 1971), 20-21.

11

gods was quite common in the environment of Israel. Fertility statues of Astarte and many other symbols of the worship of gods and goddesses in Israel have been discovered in archaeological excavations. From these discoveries we may conclude that the Israelites were not immune to worshiping other gods. Yet the official line was different. Abraham responded to Melchizedek: "I have sworn to the LORD [Yahweh], God Most High [*El Elyon*], maker of heaven and earth, that I would not take a thread or a sandal-thong or anything that is yours" (Gen. 14:22-23). Abraham immediately identifies Yahweh with *El Elyon,* the creator of heaven and earth, because it was inconceivable for him that any god but Yahweh could be the creator of heaven and earth.

The understanding of a creator god did not develop as a separate belief system parallel to the notion of Yahweh as the redeemer. The Israelites were practical people, even in their religion. If Yahweh had brought them out of Egypt into the Promised Land, then he had also provided them with the goods of the Promised Land. Yahweh was its creator. As the Old Testament scholar Gerhard von Rad (1901-71) said: "From the earliest times this was Israel's view of Yahweh's relationship to the land, and to its way of life. This was the blessed plot given to the nation by the saving activity of Yahweh, the mighty Lord of history, and it still remained Yahweh's land."[17] Yahweh provided the origin of the world; he is active in it and will provide its redemption. This latter part came to its fulfillment in the Christian faith when the history of Jesus of Nazareth was understood as the decisive redemptive act of God. Thus history had a definite beginning (its creation), a definite course (the present acts of God), and a definite goal (redemption in and through Christ). History had a goal worth living for, and the present gained its well-deserved recognition too because it was the arena in which the faithful could prove themselves eligible for that final goal.

There was no emphasis on humanity, though. In the Judeo-Christian tradition, it was clearly understood that humanity could never reach the final goal without the saving grace of God. This emphasis on the grace of God is already expressed in the covenant concept. According to Jewish thinking, a covenant is always offered by a stronger power (Yahweh) to a

---

17. Gerhard von Rad, "The Theological Problem of the Old Testament Doctrine of Creation" (1936), in *The Problem of the Hexateuch and Other Essays,* trans. E. W. Trueman Dicken (Edinburgh: Oliver & Boyd, 1966), 132.

weaker power (the Israelite community) and not vice versa. When the Christian church saw itself in continuance with the Old Testament community, the church found it impossible to accept the prevailing humanistic anthropology of the Greco-Roman world. In the Greco-Roman world, history was seen as a record of human deeds, purposes, successes, and failures. "The gods have no plan of their own for the development of human affairs; they only grant success or decree failure for the plans of men."[18] Christianity, however, rejected such optimistic ideas of human nature. The inability to achieve clearly planned goals was no longer understood as accidental but as a permanent element in human nature, arising out of the condition of humanity as a fallen creature. Especially Augustine, with his concept of a corrupt humanity, influenced the thinking of the Western world for at least a thousand years.

At the same time, this did not indicate a rejection of humanity. Admittedly, the historical process is not the working out of humanity's purposes, but of God's, because it is basically salvation history. We do not determine the course of history — God does. But God's purpose is not self-gratifying. It is a purpose intended for us, embodied in human life, and achieved through the activity of human wills. God predetermines the final goal, and he sees to it that everything will eventually move in this direction. But each human being is an historically important and responsible agent. We know what we want and pursue it, though we often do not know why we want it and therefore might stand in the way of obtaining it.

God still works through us, even when we resist his purpose. We receive ultimate dignity and importance only as vehicles of God's redemptive purpose. All hope is founded and centered in God, and not in the belief in progress or in humanity. The acting and active God who provided the beginning, who controls the present, and who will provide the future is the decisive center of all Christian and Jewish hope. Even now Christian churches still emphasize human unworthiness, though sometimes more out of tradition than conviction, and it is questionable whether the hope in an active and gracious God still determines the life orientation of most church members.

18. R. G. Collingwood, *The Idea of History* (London: Oxford University Press, 1967), 41.

Estrangement between Eschatology and Progress

During the Middle Ages God-confidence prevailed over self-confidence. The pope ranked higher than the emperor, and everything was done to the glory of God and through God's grace. Gradually, however, humanity became more confident in itself.

One of the first documents that shows that self-confidence prevailed over God-confidence is René Descartes's (1596-1650) *Discourse concerning the Method* (1637). He writes that, while in Germany at the beginning of winter, he was put up in a place where he had no conversation partner. "I remained all day near a stove, where I had complete freedom to weigh my thoughts."[19] The result was the introduction of radical doubt into modern philosophy and Western thought. He realized that it is possible to doubt everything except the fact that he was doubting. If that were denied too, there would be nothing. Consequently, the starting point for reestablishing reality was *"I think therefore I am"* because "from the very fact that I was thinking of doubting the truth of other things, it followed very evidently and very certainly that I was."[20] Consequently, the "I" of the solitary human being became the foundation of all reality. Though Descartes still needed God to guarantee for him the reality of the world outside him, the decisive point was made.

One hundred fifty years later Immanuel Kant (1724-1804) went a decisive step further in his essay "Answer to the Question: What Is Enlightenment?" (1783) by saying: "Enlightenment is man's leaving his self-caused immaturity. Immaturity is the incapacity to use one's intelligence without guidance of another. Such immaturity is self-caused if it is not caused by lack of intelligence, but by lack of determination and courage to use one's intelligence without being guided by another. *Sapere Aude!* 'Have the courage to use your own intelligence!' is therefore the motto of the enlightenment."[21]

19. René Descartes, *Discourse concerning the Method* 2.19, in *René Descartes: The Essential Writings,* translated with an introduction and concordance by John J. Blom (New York: Harper Torchbooks, 1977), 120, where he also refers to the Thirty Years' War, during which this treatise was written.

20. Descartes, *Discourse concerning the Method* 4.40-41, 134-35.

21. Immanuel Kant, "What Is Enlightenment?" in *The Philosophy of Kant: Immanuel Kant's Moral and Political Writings,* edited with an introduction by Carl J. Friedrich (New York: Random House, 1949), 132.

Kant is advocating human freedom in political and religious matters and the dominance of human intellect and reason over any outside force. Humanity should no longer be dependent on someone or something else. Kant calls such dependence immaturity. We have become mature and are capable of determining our own destiny. This optimistic attitude prevailed throughout the Enlightenment era.

Gotthold Ephraim Lessing (1729-81), in *The Education of the Human Race* (1780), draws an important analogy between education and revelation. Education is revelation made to the individual, while revelation is an education which has come and still continues to come to the whole human race. Nevertheless, education does not give a person anything one might not have derived from "within oneself," but one merely obtains it more quickly and easily. By the same token, "revelation gives nothing to the human race which human reason could not arrive at on its own; only it has given, and still gives to it, the most important of these things sooner."[22] Thus, according to Lessing, the goal of human progress is no longer found beyond humanity, but in humanity itself. But Lessing did not yet realize that his insistence on the rediscovery of "innate ideas" as the goal of progress must necessarily exclude true progress in the sense of creative novelty. Still, the optimistic trust in the newly established self-confidence continued.

Charles Darwin's (1809-82) theory of evolution in the nineteenth century made humanity even more optimistic, because now the door seemed to be open for new and unprecedented human progress. If we had evolved so high above the animal world, we could evolve much higher. While Kant emphasized human autonomy, that we should have enough self-confidence to determine our own views, here the next step was taken with the implicit hope that we are able to evolve beyond our present state.

Herbert Spencer (1820-1903) shaped the outlook of North America in the second half of the nineteenth century unlike any other writer by converting the theory of evolution into "an instrument of unbridled optimism."[23] Development was for him a cosmic principle that pertains especially to the human species. Universal development has to be made

---

22. Gotthold Ephraim Lessing, *The Education of the Human Race*, in *Lessing's Theological Writings*, selections in translation (London: Adam & Charles Black, 1956), 83.

23. John Baillie, *The Belief in Progress* (New York: Scribner, 1951), 144-45.

fruitful for humanity to drive it to further progress. Nothing can be excluded from this progress: no knowledge, no value systems, and no feelings. Humanity is in control of its future; it can determine its own progress and need no longer rely on an active God.

Along with the change from God-confidence to self-confidence, another important shift emerged which contributed to the belief in progress induced by humanity: the secularization of the kingdom of God. The root for this shift lies in the Calvinistic theory of double predestination. We are predestined at birth either to be received into heaven after life on earth or to be condemned to eternal damnation. Of course, we want to find out as early as possible what our destiny is. In popular understanding the fact of election could be seen in earthly success. Thus Calvinists worked tirelessly in an ascetic manner to prove to themselves and to others that they were on the right side. The results of this work, of course, could not be enjoyed but had to be added to the constant increase of the employed capital. Max Weber (1864-1920) and Ernst Troeltsch (1865-1923) rightly called Calvinism the forerunner of modern capitalism.[24]

Surprisingly, Pietism played a similar role with its radical orientation toward otherworldliness. Their otherworldliness, by necessity, led Pietists to responsible use of their time here on earth. Time was not to be spent in worldly joy and amusement, but in self-crucifying work. The housefather who presided over devotional meetings is at the same time the forerunner of many industrial endeavors. In the nineteenth century, the centers of the Pietistic movement in Germany, namely, Rhineland-Westphalia and Württemberg, became centers of industrial develop-

24. Ernst Troeltsch, *Protestantism and Progress: A Historical Study of the Relation of Protestantism to the Modern World*, trans. W. Montgomery (Boston: Beacon Press, 1958), 131-33. Whereas Max Weber sees at this point a close affinity between Calvinism and Judaism, Troeltsch rejects this idea, since the Calvinistic use of Jewish ethical teaching cannot sufficiently explain the phenomenon of modern capitalism (Max Weber, *The Protestant Ethic and the Spirit of Capitalism*, trans. T. Parsons [London: Allen & Unwin, 1948], 270 l. 58, and Troeltsch, 141-42 n. 1). Though Weber's thesis certainly needs modification (cf. Robert W. Green, ed., *Protestantism and Capitalism: The Weber Thesis and Its Critics* [Boston: Heath, 1959; 2nd ed., 1973]), the stimulus that Pietism and Calvinism provided for the development of modern capitalism and industrialization is undeniable (cf. Ernst Benz, *Evolution and Christian Hope: Man's Concept of the Future from the Early Fathers to Teilhard de Chardin*, trans. H. G. Frank [Garden City, N.Y.: Doubleday, Anchor, 1968], esp. 129-31).

ment. The religious convictions of the Pietists led to the splendid material success of their grandchildren, most of whom long ago discarded the religious convictions of their forebears.

In America the development was similar, partly in direct connection with the immigration of German Pietists. One of the best-known American steel companies, the Bethlehem Steel Company in Bethlehem, Pennsylvania, was begun by a blacksmith who had emigrated from Herrnhut, Germany, at the beginning of the eighteenth century.[25] He settled in Bethlehem, a Moravian missionary settlement in the forests of Pennsylvania, and started a small blacksmith shop there. Quality and industriousness helped to develop his workshop into a huge enterprise. Though the name Bethlehem still points to the pietistic and pacifist origin of what was once one of the largest steel companies in the United States, it was turned into a huge conglomerate without regard to its religious premise.

In his book *The Kingdom of God in America,* H. Richard Niebuhr (1894-1962) pointed to an important factor that caused this loss of the religious premise. He claimed that the spiritualistic and Calvinistic groups favored a heaven of their own design. They considered humanity to be virtuous enough to acquire such a heaven. Also, the radical transformation of life on earth eventually undermined the expectation of heavenly bliss. Through hard work, conditions on earth became attractive enough to cause them to forget life in heaven, especially when they felt that humanity was on its way to bringing about the kingdom on earth.[26]

For the Sake of Sanity: Recovery of an Eschatological Outlook

Is secular progress sustainable? A few years ago I was dumbfounded when I saw a divorced woman student on campus carrying a coffee mug with the logo: "Life is a bitch. And then you die." The philosopher Karl Löwith (1897-1973) phrased the same insight less crassly when he

25. Benz, 130, provides this striking example.
26. H. Richard Niebuhr, *The Kingdom of God in America* (New York: Harper Torchbooks, 1959), 150-52.

wrote: "Neither antiquity nor Christianity indulged in the modern illusion that history can be conceived as a progressive evolution which solves the problem of evil by way of elimination."[27] As the psalmist realized, life is short.

> The days of our life are seventy years,
>   or perhaps eighty, if we are strong;
> even then their span is only toil and trouble;
>   they are soon gone, and we fly away.
>
> (Ps. 90:10)

While marketing and advertising agencies tell us that we will enjoy perpetual youth and that everything is within our reach, the terms "rat race" and "making ends meet" speak a different language. There is hardly a student who has not confessed that he or she does not have enough time to do all the assignments properly and to be adequately prepared for exams. And many people mutter in surprise at the end of the year: "I don't know where the year has gone!" We have ceaselessly segmented time into terms, quarters, and semesters, or into months and years, that seep past us in quick succession. As Eugen Rosenstock-Huessy reminds us: "Meaningful history depends upon having one beginning, one middle, and one end. If our data are not oriented by single pillars of time in this way, history becomes a mere catalogue of changes."[28] By secularizing life we have stripped time, and therewith history, of its creator on the one hand, and of its fulfiller on the other. Even the present is no longer supported by God, but by our own efforts. Therefore, similar to cyclical thought, we are only confronted with changes without beginning and end.[29] Yet, as Buddhists tell us, such running in circles is unbearable. We need to break out of it to attain true fulfillment.

Our rushing toward the future would be more bearable if we could discern true progress. Yet, as anybody realizes, the vision of self-perpet-

---

27. Löwith, 3.

28. Rosenstock-Huessy, 71.

29. Löwith, 205-7, observes that modern trust in the continuity of history is irreconcilable with a linear view of history and is actually much closer to the classic theory of a cyclic movement. Thus the modern view of history is an eclectic and inconsistent combination of the Greco-Roman and the Judeo-Christian views of history.

uating progress is an illusion. We cannot obtain larger and larger pieces of a pie that is not increasing in size. Since we are finite creatures living on a finite earth, we will sooner or later encounter boundaries; in some areas we have already. For instance, as our population increases, land is becoming more and more precious. With California being the most populated state in the USA, the old slogan "Go west" no longer makes sense. If we go far enough west, we either drown or, avoiding that fate, are confronted with other human beings on the other side of the Pacific Rim. Humanity is basically thrown in upon itself.

We have abandoned God-confidence to gain self-confidence. Yet this hard-won autonomy stands on shaky ground. How can we as finite beings be true granters of time and history as God had been when he was understood as creator, sustainer, and redeemer? Either we must pretend to be infinite, something we are not, or we must endow time itself with the attribute of infinity and thereby divinize it. Our immense attention to everything which seems to point to the future, such as the stock market or other economic indicators, seems to show that we have taken the latter option. Since they are, however, derived from our finite world, they are finite too and cannot grant us true future and ultimate meaning. They are, at the most, temporary pointers to a precarious temporary future. Moreover, the undue attention on them makes us oblivious to our actual situation, a situation without an ultimate goal and unaware of the true meaning of history.

The loss of a meaningful goal makes more and more people push the panic button. They ask to what end we are progressing and if there is anything worthwhile to hope for except uncertainty. The slogan that anything goes as long as it makes you happy or, even worse, the wide acceptance of a pervasive nihilism are indicative of a vacuum that could easily be filled with new ideologies and even totalitarianism. As long as God provided the goal at the end of history and beyond it, progress had a definite goal. This focal point was understood to determine the destiny of our life but could not be reached within it. Once this God-provided destiny is denied, the goal must be found within time. However, it can never be reached, because then there would be nothing left to hope for. It has to recede within the ever farther progressing horizons of history, and the speed of its recession must be at least equivalent to the speed of our own progress. The idea of never ending progress is already indicated in Lessing's remark that if God offered him a choice between the possession of truth and the quest of it, he would unhesitatingly prefer the latter. Kant went along similar lines in interpreting life immortal as the endless advance toward a perfection that can never actually be attained.

But what happens when the god of progress falters? What happens when the clouds on the horizon of history darken more and more the bright prospects of the future? It should at least arouse our suspicion when we notice the increasing number of people of all ages who resort to alcohol and to drugs, whether illegal narcotics or prescribed tranquilizers, to escape from an uncertain and progress-demanding future. Perhaps we have created a world of standards without meaning and goals without ultimate direction. Though we are transitory beings, we do not receive our identity from transitoriness and steady change, even if they might allure us to an ever better future, but from something beyond change and transitoriness. Humanists readily admit this too when they refer to the infinite (i.e., unchangeable) value of a human being. But what are we doing? Are we trying to catch our own shadow that the idea of progress is projecting in front of us? It might even be that we shall some day discover that there is no ultimate hope for us as long as we try to provide it (penultimately) for ourselves, because it is constantly superseded by our own rushing into the future.

At this point Christian eschatology gains new significance.

1. It shows us that the modern idea of progress alienated itself from its Christian foundation. Though it maintained a linear view of history, it deprived history of its God-promised goal. Consequently, the progressive character of history became an end in itself. At the same time, we promoted ourselves from God-alienated and God-endowed actors *in history* to deified agents *of history*. Then we slipped into the dilemma of how to assert convincingly a linear progression of history while still denying the metaphysical origin and goal of this progression. Our present situation of environmental exploitation, human deprivation, and the threatening meaninglessness of life seems to indicate that we are unable to achieve self-redemption, a goal that the pursuit of steady progress demands.

2. It provides a hope and a promise that we are unable to attain through our own efforts. Eschatology is not obsolete, nor can it be replaced by any secular or religiously colored idea of progress or self-fulfillment. But it endows our life and even the idea of progress with

new meaning. Secular endeavors for progress have to be related to and based on Christian eschatology. On the basis of the Christ event, they can be understood as the proleptic anticipation of the God-promised eschaton which at the same time is their incentive, their directive, and their judgment. Secular endeavors for progress and a social and ethical transformation of the world are legitimate and necessary, but they are preliminary and inadequate, and they yearn for their final completion through God's redemptive power. Apart from Christian eschatology, they miss not only God, but humanity too. Instead of leading to freedom and new humanity, they lead to new slavery and potential self-destruction. This is the reason eschatology is crucial in our time.

Part I
The Discovery of the Future

Animals and young infants have no awareness of the future. They live in the present. As infants grow up their awareness increases, of tomorrow, the day after, and the next year. Humans can extend themselves into three spheres. Their memory reaches into the past; their activities are focused on the present; and their planning aims at the future. While the past can be pushed back almost endlessly into the timelessness of the primordial myth, by its very nature the present undergoes steady change. What was still present in one moment is past in the next and something new emerges in the present. We experience the present like a movie that is continuously moving past us. We could say that the future is also continuously moving. It approaches us and moves ever nearer till it is present. Yet it is significant that we cannot push the future in front of us at will. At one point our future, our earth, and the universe at large will no longer recede. We will have reached the limits of our life, of the earth, and of the universe. But with this discovery of the boundary, our encounter with the future is not over. In virtually every society and religion there is some intimation, however dimly present or fully developed, that there is something beyond these limits, either another life through another revolution of the wheel of life or a new life in another form and perhaps on another plateau.

Expecting Life Beyond
as a Primal Human Phenomenon

As far as we know, humanity has always thought about life after death. The paleontologist Karl J. Narr (b. 1921) writes:

> It is only from the Middle Paleolithicum onward that we know about funerals which, in their way, partly testify to the protection of the dead and, most likely, also to the provisions of food and tools offered for the dead and partly also for binding the deceased. Regardless of what the case may have been, loving care for the deceased or fear of the dead, it witnesses to the faith in a continuance of life after death in some form or other.... But even in earlier times (e.g. the Peking Man) there are indications that skulls or parts of skulls were separately preserved which we may explain by the idea of a further connection and a continuation of action after (for our conceptuality, physical) death in some form or other.[1]

Narr says the human beings he is talking about are *"in principle fully developed human beings,"* which means the transition must have been made from animal to humanity. In a similar way the paleo-historian Jakob Ozols (b. 1922) states: "Though it may sound surprising, the oldest religious expression of early humanity accessible to us is the faith in a nonmaterial form of soul indwelling in him."[2]

Behind the customs Narr tells us about is perhaps the belief in some kind of general animism which developed in the last Ice Age to a shamanism which, at least in northeast Asia, continued into the beginning of this century. According to shamans, there is a little figure of shadowy existence which can neither be grasped nor wounded with common weapons. This is the actual life of a person. Without this little figure the person is helpless and sick. "After death, this shape of the soul separates

---

1. Karl J. Narr, "Beiträge der Urgeschichte zur Kenntnis der Menschennatur," in *Neue Anthropologie*, ed. Hans-Georg Gadamer and Paul Vogler (Stuttgart: dtv, 1973), 4:31-32 and 37. Cf. also John Hick, *Death and Eternal Life* (New York: Harper & Row, 1976), 55-56, in his section on "primitive man." Hick states that humanity is unique in knowing that it is going to die but at the same time denies it and hopes for a life beyond (cf. 55).

2. Jakob Ozols, "Über die Jenseitsvorstellungen des vorgeschichtlichen Menschen," in *Tod und Jenseits im Glauben der Völker*, ed. Hans-Joachim Klimkeit (Wiesbaden: Otto Harrassowitz, 1978), 14.

from the body and leads its own life largely independent of the body. Yet it continues to return to the skeleton, especially to the skull, to rest there. When a person is alive it leaves the body only at night or in extraordinary situations, such as sudden fright, severe disease or in special conditions such as trance or ecstasy. This shape of the soul should not remain absent for long. If it does not return soon, the person falls sick, it is exposed to many dangers and with a longer absence of this shape of the soul the person must even die."[3]

There is an actual duplicate of every person which resides in the body. Ozols also explains that drilling small holes into skulls of persons who are still alive may have been attempts to help this shape of the soul enter and leave the skull without problems. For the same purpose there exist holes in coffins made of stone.

We can see from Stone Age paintings that the souls of the dead no longer belong to this world. They have their own realm of life in the beyond, a shadowy world that was already a matter of fact for people living in the Ice Age. Since the skull is so important, we need not be surprised that we have burials of skulls only, and since animals were not thought to be that different from people, even the skulls of some animals were ritually buried. For prehistoric persons the concept of life after death was determined primarily by the conviction of an immortal figure of the soul. "This conviction has remained the most important part of religions until the most recent times. It is evidently shaped by the concept of events in dreams, but also by other events. The state without protection and participation during sleep has led to the assumption that this figure of the soul is the actual life and the protective power of the person."[4]

The recognition of an *anima* (spirit) residing in the human person that can move to different places, especially during sleep, as we may naively assume when we dream about things that are far away, was then expanded to the conclusion that this *anima* leaves the body forever at death and continues to exist somewhere else. This primal human concept of a soul or spirit led to an eschatology, meaning a concept of the *eschata*, the last things. For these early human beings it was clear that the *eschata* are not simply things that occur at the end, but in a decisive way

3. Ozols, 15.
4. Ozols, 35.

they influence present people and their well-being. Eschatology therefore is a comprehensive concept extending to this life and beyond.

The Scope and Shape of Eschatology

In its broadest sense the term "eschatology" includes all concepts of life beyond death and everything connected with it such as heaven and hell, paradise and immortality, resurrection and transmigration of the soul, rebirth and reincarnation, and last judgment and doomsday. Eschatology also is determined by and determines our understanding of humanity, of body and soul, and of value systems and worldviews. A naturalistic concept of the human species will result in a different concept of eschatology than will a spiritualistic one, and a dualistic concept of body and soul will result in yet a different outlook on eschatology. Eschatology is also related to funeral, burial, and mourning customs. When the Egyptians left certain presents in the tombs of the dead, it showed their understanding of the life beyond and how to reach it (e.g., that the dead need food on their journey to the hereafter and servants to serve them over there). Or let us remember that our Christian custom of burying the dead emphasizes in a symbolic way the preservation of the unity of the person contained in the expectation of a "bodily" resurrection. Hindu mourners, however, burn the dead and strew the ashes into the holy Ganges River, since they do not believe in a resurrection of the body, but that only the *spirit* of the cremated person will be wafted to higher worlds.

Eschatology always influences and shapes the conduct of life and vice versa. In an individual eschatology the conduct of this life will determine the destiny of the individual after death, whereas in a collective eschatology the destiny of all humanity is taken into consideration. A cosmic eschatology even goes beyond the scope of humanity and includes the destiny of this earth or of the whole cosmos. Cosmic eschatology often reckons with recurrent world periods: first a golden age, then a decline in a period of crises, and finally a return to the conditions of the golden age in the period of cleansing or renewal. Of course, this is based on a cyclical concept of time. In Jewish apocalyptic a different periodization was reached. Here the distinction was made between the present aeon of turmoil and anxiety and the future aeon of the final end of all history and the coming of the Savior. Resistance against political and religious oppression contributed to an intensified expectation of the end, which provided the context for the proclamation of Jesus of Nazareth.

Historical catastrophes and crises often influence eschatological expectations. For instance, the catastrophe of World War II in Europe brought many estranged people back to the churches, and the proclamation of the Word of God gained renewed attention. In a similar way the rise of dialectical theology, which pronounced the immediacy of God, cannot be properly understood without considering the political and economic turmoil after World War I. The present intense expectations which erupt occasionally — for instance, in the Templer movement in Switzerland and among the Branch Davidians in Texas, leading to disasters and even mass suicide — are not unrelated to the mood of uncertainty and despair to which many people are subjected. Also the turn of a millennium has always intensified eschatological expectations. Even disasters, such as the great earthquake in Lisbon, Portugal, in 1755, which leveled two-thirds of the city, can cause a reorientation in eschatological thinking. It decisively thwarted the notion of our world as the best possible one.

But eschatological time is not only a time of crisis. It is also a time of salvation. The coming of the redeemer and of the Messiah is expected and celebrated. The cargo cult in Melanesia and the messianic movements in Africa both expect a time of redemption, though in a mostly secularized, political, and economic manner. Political freedom fighters, such as Nelson Mandela in Africa and Fidel Castro in Latin America, are at times regarded as messianic leaders who initiate an era of secular salvation. Similarly, in many countries, especially in the United States, we experience the emergence of saints and pseudosaints who promise their devout followers new spiritual insights and often also redemption from anxieties and physical ailments.

The eschaton is often regarded as a repetition of the primeval time. For instance, in the Pauline letters in the New Testament, Christ is seen as the new Adam and the new creation is understood in contrast to the first creation. For Paul, however, there is a progressive movement from the first creation to the new creation, while in most religions the movement is not conceived as linear and singular but as cyclical and periodic. Very often the seasonal rhythm influences the cultic calendar, and the

27

changes of the seasons provide the pattern for cultic periods of expectation and fulfillment. Sigmund Mowinckel (1884-1965) and S. H. Hooke (1874-1968) attempted to understand the earliest Old Testament eschatology in a similar rhythmic pattern.[5]

The enthronement of Yahweh was considered the central festival in Israel. It celebrated Yahweh's arrival in Jerusalem and his occupation of the throne there. Psalms 47, 93, 97, and others that use the term "Yahweh has become king" allude to this occasion. The festival of the enthronement of Yahweh was at the same time the New Year's festival and was celebrated in the fall prior to the beginning of the rainy season which "created the world anew."[6] Since Yahweh promised the advent of the rainy season, this was a time of expectation. It was also a time of remembrance, because Yahweh, who had once conquered the powers of chaos, would now conquer all evil powers and all enemies of Israel and secure his kingship. "At this festival the congregation has most vividly experienced the personal coming of the Lord to save his people — his

5. Cf. Sigmund Mowinckel, *The Psalms in Israel's Worship*, trans. D. R. Ap-Thomas (Nashville: Abingdon, 1967), 1:111-14, 130; and S. H. Hooke, "Myth and Ritual: Past and Present," in *Myth, Ritual, and Kingship: Essays on the Theory and Practice of Kingship in the Ancient Near East and in Israel*, ed. S. H. Hooke (Oxford: Clarendon, 1958), 13-20. While Mowinckel attempted to show how Israel adopted the cultic pattern of the vegetational Canaanite religion to the point where the cyclical pattern was historicized in view of the salvational activity of Yahweh, Hooke was more interested in trying to show the similarity between the Israelite religion and the vegetational religions of its environment. According to Hooke, there was never a "pure" Israelite religion that did not share much in common with the religions of its neighbors. On the contrary, the cultic pattern of the divine kingship, an essential part of Israelite worship, was prevalent throughout the ancient Near East.

Ivan Engnell must at least be mentioned here as one of the most fervent advocates of the idea of an enthronement festival of Yahweh. In his doctoral dissertation *Studies in Divine Kingship in the Ancient Near East* (Oxford: Blackwell [1943], 1967), he confines himself to establishing the theory of a divine kingship prevalent throughout the ancient Near East. In later writings, however, he suggests that the enthronement festival in its Canaanite version lays the groundwork for the Israelite understanding of Passover, the Feast of Booths, the belief in the resurrection, messianism, and even essential features of the idea of God (cf. his essay "Old Testament Religion," in *Critical Essays on the Old Testament*, trans. and ed. J. T. Willis with the collaboration of H. Ringgren [London: SPCK, 1970], 35-49). It seems that the history of Israelite religion is more complicated and multifaceted than Engnell suggests.

6. Mowinckel, *Religion and Cult*, trans. John F. X. Sheehan (Milwaukee: Marquette University Press, 1981), 109.

epiphany. In the cultic festival, past, present and future are welded into one."[7] This idea of Yahweh's final victory outlived the destruction of the Israelite nation and laid the foundation for the new cosmic enthronement of Yahweh when he will establish his kingdom at his "day." "From the experiences of the enthronement festival and its ideas, Judaism's eschatology received its concrete notions."[8]

We agree with Mowinckel that the harvest festival as an agricultural feast may have been taken over from the Canaanites after their settlement, along with the conception of their deity as king and the annual celebration of his ascension and enthronement.[9] Yet there are decisive differences. While in the Canaanite religion the god Baal gained his final victory and ascension after defeat, death, and resurrection, this was an impossible thought for the Israelites. Yahweh the Lord has always lived and always lives; he is the holy God who does not die (Hab. 1:12). This means that the basic rhythmic and thus cyclical pattern had to be abandoned in favor of the God who everlastingly creates and sustains

---

7. Mowinckel, *Psalms in Israel's Worship*, 1:112-13.

8. Mowinckel, *Religion and Cult*, 110.

9. It has to be mentioned here that many scholars deny that such an enthronement festival of Yahweh ever existed. For instance, Georg Fohrer, *History of Israelite Religion*, trans. David E. Green (Nashville: Abingdon, 1972), 143-44, rejects the idea of such a festival and points out that an identification of God and king, which such a festival presupposes, is an unacceptable thought for Israel. Th. C. Vriezen, *An Outline of Old Testament Theology* (Newton, Mass.: Bradford, 1958), 183, says that "the so-called feast of the ascension of Yahweh to the throne is an unfounded modern hypothetical construction which is confusing rather than clarifying. Yahweh's life is not renewed, neither is His Kingship." For Vriezen the New Year's festival, which, according to the advocates of this idea is supposed to be identical with the enthronement festival of Yahweh, is the occasion on which Yahweh is *glorified* as Creator and King (285). Cf. also the excellent study of Hans-Joachim Kraus, *Worship in Israel: A Cultic History of the Old Testament*, trans. A. W. Heathcote and Ph. J. Allcock (London: Hodder & Stoughton, 1958), 18, who concurs with Martin Noth's position advanced in his essay "God, King, and Nation in the Old Testament," in *The Law in the Pentateuch and Other Studies*, trans. D. R. Ap-Thomas (Philadelphia: Fortress, 1967), 145-78, in saying that the historical foundations of Israelite kingship rule out "a mythical interpretation." Horst Dietrich Preuss also states succinctly: "One cannot derive from the Old Testament passages that tell of the sovereignty of YHWH evidence for an enthronement festival of YHWH. An enthronement festival could have been only an aspect of the Autumn Festival or the New Year's Festival" (*Old Testament Theology*, trans. Leo G. Perdue [Louisville: Westminster John Knox, 1996], 2:232).

life. Of course, in many places the worship of vegetational gods did make inroads into Israel without these fundamental modifications, as we can see from finds of figurines connected with the worship of Baal. But whenever the Old Testament, the official document of Israelite religion, refers to this worship, it condemns it as paganism. In the Israelite faith the enthronement festival was removed from the pattern of the cyclical vegetational religion to the world of historical reality. It served to emphasize the coming presence of Yahweh, who is active and discloses himself in living history.

This brief survey shows both the antiquity of eschatological thinking and also the multitude of concepts connected with it.[10] We have also noticed that single motifs (enthronement of a god, dying and rising of a god) never exist independently. A single root explanation will not do justice to eschatology. Although there is a basic structure to eschatology, there is always a complexity of motifs embedded in it which is expressive of and influential for the religious and cultic life of the people.

10. We have not yet made mention of apocalyptic thought, though it is closely associated with eschatology. We will refer to it in the context of Judaism, since that was the prime seedbed for apocalypticism.

1. The Old Testament View of Eschatology

The Old Testament spans a history of many centuries. It was written by various people who reflected on God's self-disclosure as they had encountered it or heard about it through other people. The oldest verifiable historical events to which the Old Testament refers go back beyond 1000 B.C., while the most recent occurred barely before 150 B.C. This is the approximate time span we have to cover when we talk about eschatological awareness as encountered in the Old Testament. Three main areas are decisive for eschatological thinking in the Old Testament: human destiny, the last judgment, and the promise of and hope for a Messiah. These themes also indicate a historical progression.[1] The promise of and hope for a Messiah emerged fairly late, while human destiny is one of the earliest topics in the Old Testament. Yet how did the eschatological consciousness emerge in the Old Testament?

1. Developing an Eschatological Consciousness

Since Israel as a country was tucked in between the superpowers of Mesopotamia in the north and Egypt in the south, it would not be sur-

---

1. To find the center of Old Testament eschatology in Jerusalem, as claimed by Donald E. Gowan, *Eschatology in the Old Testament* (Philadelphia: Fortress, 1986), 3, seems unwarranted. While Zion is undoubtedly important for Israel, the eschatological hopes are not focused on a particular location but eventually on individual human destiny and on the renewal, or rather re-creation, of nature.

prising if Israel's eschatology were to be heavily influenced by political, cultural, and religious forces emanating from these countries. Yet surprisingly, the documentary evidence shows precious little influence. Unlike in Egypt and Mesopotamia, there are no Old Testament writings that are exclusively concerned with death and the hereafter. Nor do any Old Testament myths describe the journey into the netherworld.[2] In Egypt, though, there is much literature concerning the hereafter — the Pyramid Texts from the third millennium, the Coffin Texts from around 2000 B.C., and the Book of the Dead from around 1500 B.C., for instance. This literature served as a guide for both the dead on their journey into the hereafter, allowing them to withstand the dangers which threatened there, and the living, so they would know what to expect once they died. In some cases, for instance in Assyria and Babylonia, the texts concerning the hereafter are parts of larger works — the twelfth table of the Gilgamesh Epic and Ishtar's journey into the netherworld, for example.

Egypt, we notice, was basically a "death-driven culture." For the Egyptian, death "was an ever-present menace throughout his life and impinged to a greater or lesser extent upon his earthly existence. Its presence . . . was driven home upon him by the surrounding landscape. This oasis of culture was embedded in a lifeless waste, and his tombs were located on the edge of the hostile desert."[3] The narrow, fertile strip of land along the Nile River was surrounded by the immense, life-threatening desert. The intense preoccupation with death is documented by elaborate funeral customs. First, the dead body was embalmed so that it could continue to exist in a lifelike state. Second, the tombs were, to a large extent, patterned according to housing conditions in this life. Provisions for the deceased were enclosed in the tombs, and the walls and ceilings were elaborately decorated. Even the great pyramids show this obsession with death. As funerary monuments, they were expected to withstand the tides of time and witness to the immortality of their builders.

---

2. Cf. Werner Berg, "Jenseitsvorstellungen im Alten Testament mit Hinweisen auf das frühe Judentum," in *Die grössere Hoffnung der Christen: Eschatologische Vorstellungen im Wandel*, ed. Albert Gerhards (Freiburg: Herder, 1990), 28-29, especially the literature cited there.

3. Siegfried Morenz, *Egyptian Religion*, trans. Ann E. Keep (Ithaca, N.Y.: Cornell University Press, 1973), 192.

This cult of the dead, in which the corpses were prepared for eternity by mummification and by the regular supply of provisions and gifts by which they could continue to participate in this earthly life in perpetuity, should have precluded any thought of life in some other realm, in heaven or in the realm of the dead, for instance. Yet the opposite is true. Because of his godlike status, heaven was at first accessible "only to the deceased king, but then became 'democratized,' as it were, and opened up to the commoners."[4] Initially only the king had a soul *(ba)*, as distinct from the vital life force *(ka)*. But the Coffin Texts, which date from the First Intermediate Period (ca. 2134-2040 B.C.) and the Middle Kingdom (ca. 2040-1780), show that private persons too acquired what had previously been reserved for the king — they also had a soul. With this there were two possibilities open for them: either the soul was separated from the body and went to heaven while the dead body went to the netherworld, or both of them stayed together for the ascent to heaven. "In this way the preservation of the body in the tomb became the prerequisite for ascent to heaven."[5] To arrive at heaven one first had to pass through judgment. This was again a frightening experience, since the verdict did not depend on one's moral rectitude. One sought to avoid a negative decision by magical means, as we can gather from the Coffin Texts and the Book of the Dead. According to Egyptologist Siegfried Morenz (1914-70), the reason for reliance on magic in order to avoid the judgment of the dead "was the belief in equation with Osiris, the king of the gods and god of vegetation, the first to rise from the dead, who encompassed with himself every person buried with the proper ritual."[6] The dead wanted to become like Osiris, who was brought back to life with the help of his consort Isis.

How tenuous such hope for something positive beyond death was, however, is shown by the Greek historian Herodotus, who relates an incident he himself observed. "When the Egyptians are seated at a banquet," he writes, "they pass around a deceased person in a container [i.e., no doubt a mummylike statuette] so as to remind themselves of death and to encourage each other to enjoy life: 'Gaze here, and drink and be merry; for when you die, such will you be.'"[7] Life was not just focused

---

4. Morenz, 204.

5. Morenz, 206.

6. Morenz, 210.

7. Morenz, 195, and cf. *The History of Herodotus* 2.78, trans. George Rawlinson, ed. Manuel Komroff (New York: Tudor, 1932), 107.

on this world and the present existence, but on living well and enjoying whatever one could, because one never knew when life would be over.

In Mesopotamia we also encounter a fairly gloomy outlook. For instance, in the epic of Ishtar's journey to the netherworld we read:

> To the land without return, the realm of [Ereshkigal(?)],
> Ishtar, the daughter of Sin [meaning the moon god] [turned]
>   her attention;
> Yea, the daughter of Sin turned [her] attention
> To the dark house, the dwelling of Irkal[la] [= Ereshkigal];
> To the house from which he who enters never goes forth;
> To the road whose path does not lead back;
> To the house in which he who enters is bereft of li[ght];
> Where dust is their food (and), clay their sustenance;
> (Where) they see no light (and) dwell in darkness.[8]

Once one is down there, life as we know it is gone. There is no return unless one returns as a spirit of the dead to help or to haunt the living. The grave was seen as a transitional place, and therefore one wanted to give the dead the means for the journey in terms of food, servants, and other supplies. "The journey to the nether world was an unavoidable and irrevocable conclusion of human earthly existence, a temporary escape from the nether world was only possible in the form of the spirit of a dead person."[9] Even of Gilgamesh we hear:

> The life thou seekest thou wilt not find;
> (For) when the gods created mankind,
> They allotted death to mankind,
> (But) life they retained in their keeping.[10]

Death was the final destiny for humanity, and there was no notion of a life everlasting or a life in a hereafter. Death meant a highly reduced shadowy existence as some kind of spirit in the netherworld. Therefore

---

8. As printed in Alexander Heidel, *The Gilgamesh Epic and Old Testament Parallels* (Chicago: University of Chicago Press, 1963), 121.

9. Heinrich Schützinger, "Tod und ewiges Leben im Glauben des Alten Zweistromlandes," in *Tod und Jenseits im Glauben der Völker*, ed. Hans-Joachim Klimkeit (Wiesbaden: Otto Harrassowitz, 1978), 58.

10. *The Gilgamesh-Epic* (table X, col. III), in *The Gilgamesh Epic,* 70.

attention was focused on the present, on a good life with all the pleasantries one could afford. If one was careful in one's life attitude and had the favor of the gods, one could hope for a long and full life as the most valuable result possible.

Initially at least, the focus on this world can also be seen in the Old Testament. Yet for Israel the emphasis on this life was also connected with their understanding of God, who had shown his power when he rescued Israel from Egypt and established a covenant with that people. When God introduced himself to Moses as "I am who I am" (Exod. 3:14), this did not imply a static vision; rather God was pointing to his future actions in the sense of "I will be the one as the one whom I will prove myself."[11] Yet this kind of promise was initially directed to the Israelite community, not to the individual, and it was also directed to the future of history within that community.

2. The Human Destiny

While the writings of the Old Testament which reflect on the beginning of the Israelite nation are not oblivious to the destiny of the individual, they show little or no concern about a life or destiny after death. As we hear in the story about Abraham, God's blessing was for this life: "I will make of you a great nation, and I will bless you, and make your name great, so that you will be a blessing" (Gen. 12:2). During the nomadic period of the Israelite tribes, the dead were either left behind in a foreign environment (23:19-20) or carried with the tribes (50:5-6). When the Israelites settled down in the Promised Land, they could no longer leave their dead behind, but encountered their corpses whenever they had to bury someone else. They had to open the stone-hewn family tombs and make room for the newly deceased. The expression "gathered to his people" (25:8) refers to the custom of using a tomb over and over again.[12] In contrast to the elaborate myths and epics of other na-

11. Cf. Horst Dietrich Preuss, *Old Testament Theology*, trans. Leo G. Perdue (Louisville: Westminster John Knox, 1996), 2:257-59, who points to the Israelite faith in this history-making God as the foundation of Old Testament eschatology.

12. Walther Eichrodt, *Theology of the Old Testament*, trans. J. A. Baker, 2 vols. (Philadelphia: Westminster, 1961-67), 2:213, states rightly that the concern to be united with one's father and the other members of the family is clearly derived from a belief that the

tions, the Israelites did not waste much thought on a life beyond. Of course, they knew that death was not the end of human existence, but they did not understand it as the transition to a better hereafter or to a netherworldly torture chamber. It was at best a shadowy existence that they envisioned. But it was not the survival of a soul that one expected. It was rather a diminished existence of the whole person that vegetates in the netherworld and in some way or other is not unconnected with the corpse and, after its decay, with the bones. "For this reason, cremation was unknown, the burning of bones was considered a sacrilege" (Amos 2:1).[13] Since there was no spirit of the dead roaming around, the dead had no power over the living, and no cult of the dead developed. In contrast to other Near Eastern religions, the resting places of the dead were forbidden ground for the Israelites. If one encountered a death in the family or had touched a dead person, one was considered unclean and was excluded from the worship of Yahweh. The Lord is a God of life, and the emphasis was upon life here on earth.

a. Emphasis on the This-Worldly Aspect of Life

The Israelite faith emphasized, from its very beginning, life in this world, since it is there that Yahweh proved his power and faithfulness.[14] Their almost exclusively corporate thinking seemed to make it unnecessary for them to reflect on individual "survival." One continued to live on in one's sons and through them in the community. It was one of the most devastat-

---

dead still survive in some way or other in the grave. "This is, in fact, the oldest form of belief in survival." Eichrodt, however, does not admit a development from the belief of a survival in the grave to the belief of a survival in sheol, since the custom of giving food to the dead continued in Israel up to the very latest period.

Though it is likely that both forms of conceptualization (survival in the grave and survival in sheol) coexisted for some time, spiritualization (survival in sheol) seems to have prevailed in the long run. This would also be analogous to the changing conceptualization of God (from picturesque anthropomorphism [Gen. 3] to a more spiritualized and transcendent understanding [Isa. 6 or Ezek. 11]). We also must remember that the younger parts of the Old Testament are undeniably more interested in the final destiny of the dead than the older parts — a fact which seems to indicate a development.

13. Georg Fohrer, *History of Israelite Religion*, trans. David E. Green (Nashville: Abingdon, 1972), 219.

14. Fohrer, *History of Israelite Religion*, 215.

ing fates to die without a male heir, for then there was no hope. The end that the Israelites desired was a death in old age with their sons assembled around them (Gen. 49:33). The Bible says that Abraham died as "an old man and full of years" (Gen. 25:8), that Job died "old and full of days" (Job 42:17), and that many of the other great figures of the Old Testament died in similar fashion. To die at a ripe old age is understood as a blessing, and the Proverbs pronounce this very definitely:

> The fear of the LORD prolongs life,
> but the years of the wicked will be short.

(Prov. 10:27)

An early death was understood as punishment for godlessness (1 Sam. 2:32). This is why even a king may pray in fervent words to Yahweh for temporary deliverance from death (Isa. 38:3). Later, when the Israelites wrestled with the concept of salvation, this was initially understood in strictly this-worldly terms. Life will then be prolonged to an amazing degree, "for one who dies at a hundred years will be considered a youth" (Isa. 65:20).

This does not mean that the Israelites accepted death as a natural phenomenon. As we can gather from the first chapters of the Bible, humanity in its rebellion against God had brought death upon itself.[15] But even in its death-prone existence it was sustained by God (cf. Gen. 3:21). Life and death were ultimately understood as ordered and destined by Yahweh; in a sovereign and yet merciful manner he provides both. Death, however, was not yet conceived as the transitional stage which leads to life eternal. King Hezekiah expresses very well why he wants to be saved from the pit, the place in the tomb where the remains of the decayed corpse are preserved:

> For Sheol cannot thank you,
> death cannot praise you;
> those who go down to the Pit cannot hope
> for your faithfulness.

(Isa. 38:18)

15. Cf. Walther Zimmerli, *Man and His Hope in the Old Testament* (Naperville, Ill.: Allenson, 1968), 48-49, where he writes: "This is how the Yahwist describes the primitive history of the human species: subjected to death by his own guilt before God, characterized by hopelessness, and yet in the midst of this ruin still sustained by God."

God is a God of the living, but not of the dead. That Hezekiah's sickness can be connected with death and sheol shows that both terms are also used in a metaphoric sense. They can denote hostile and threatening powers and the anxiety they produce.

The cultic laws express clearly that the dead are "off limits" for the living.[16] Saul's attempt to communicate with the dead does not end in failure but in personal catastrophe. He is finally rejected by Yahweh (1 Sam. 28). This also shows that from their earliest days onward the Israelites knew that death was not the final end. The dead existed beyond death in the shadowy sphere of Sheol (Isa. 14:9-11). Such an existence beyond death is also indicated by the gifts, such as lamps, pots with food, and water, which were put into the tomb.[17] Later these gifts were only of a symbolic nature, as can be seen from the use of broken pottery.

b. Translation and Resurrection

Parallel to the understanding of death destined by God are some rare exceptions mentioned in the Old Testament where people were exempted from this destiny. First, there is the exceptional occurrence of translation. Enoch was faithful to God, and thus God received him into his immediate presence (Gen. 5:24). A chariot of fire and horses separated Elijah from Elisha, and Elijah was taken up into heaven by a whirlwind (2 Kings 2:11). These are the only two instances in the Old Testament of a translation from life here on earth to a life beyond, but the Old Testament Apocrypha tells of a translation of Ezra and Baruch (2 Esd. 4:9-49; 2 Bar. 46:7; 76:2). Even a person like Moses had to die, although God himself buried him so that nobody could find his tomb (Deut. 34:5-6). This kind of translation in the immediacy of God seems to show an exceptional privilege on account of an outstanding life with God already here on earth. "In principle at least the possibility is shown

16. Th. C. Vriezen, *An Outline of Old Testament Theology* (Newton, Mass.: Bradford, 1958), 204, suggests that this attitude may be due to the fact that the belief in Yahweh as the giver of life always had to combat the ancient Eastern belief in spirits, the worship of the dead, and the rising of the spirits. According to Vriezen, this conflict also accounts for the fact that the Old Testament speaks very little about life after death.

17. Cf. Leonhard Rost, "Grab," in *Biblisch-Historisches Handwörterbuch*, ed. Bo Reicke and Leonhard Rost, 3 vols. (Göttingen: Vandenhoeck & Ruprecht, 1962-66), 1:605-6.

here that the general rule of death can be broken and the bitter way into the desolation of *sheol* can be avoided."[18] While this does not indicate a hope for everyone, at least a way beyond sheol is opened up.

Death, though, is not the all-decisive event. In different parts of the Old Testament there is also the expectation of a kind of resurrection. Traditionally quoted passages, such as Job 19:25-26 ("For I know that my Redeemer lives . . .") or Psalm 73:24 ("You guide me with your counsel, / and afterward you will receive me with honor"), hardly fit here.[19] They either point to an expectancy that lies strictly within the realm of life here on earth or rely on an ambiguous Hebrew text. But then we read in Isaiah 26:14,

> The dead do not live;
>> shades do not rise,

and later in the same chapter,

> Your dead shall live, their corpses shall rise.
>> O dwellers in the dust, awake and sing for joy!

(v. 19)

Similarly we hear in Psalm 49:15:

> But God will ransom my soul from the power of Sheol,
>> for he will receive me.[20]

---

18. Friedrich Nötscher, *Altorientalischer und alttestamentlicher Auferstehungsglauben* (Darmstadt: Wissenschaftliche Buchgesellschaft, 1970 [1926]), 126.

19. Christoph Barth in his instructive book, *Die Errettung vom Tode in den individuellen Klage- und Dankliedern des Alten Testaments* (Zollikon: Evangelischer Verlag, 1947), 163, mentions: "So far nobody has convincingly stated that Psalm 73 contains a proof passage for the idea of an eternal life after death. Such a proof cannot be built on verse 24, since the text seems to be ambiguous." He also asserts that, according to the Psalms, salvation from death is not conceived of as a bodily resurrection of the decayed corpse or as a continuation of life beyond death. The realm of the dead is "a land of no return" (165). Salvation from death means salvation from a hostile, threatening, and judging death. God will take the bitterness of death from the pious and let them die in peace.

We do not consider here resuscitations as they are related in 1 Kings 17:17-24 (the widow's son), 2 Kings 4:20-37 (the Shunammite's son), and 2 Kings 13:20-21 (the buried man), since these passages tell about resuscitations, meaning a return to this life, and not about a resurrection to new life.

20. The argument of Hans-Joachim Kraus, *Psalms 1–59: A Commentary*, trans.

In later parts of the Old Testament we even hear about resurrection with a twofold outcome: "Many of those who sleep in the dust of the earth shall awake, some to everlasting life, and some to shame and everlasting contempt" (Dan. 12:2).[21]

Can we discard these passages as indicating a personal pagan piety that is alien to corporate trust in Yahweh? Or shall we try to harmonize them with passages that seem to know nothing about a *life* after death? Neither solution seems to do justice to the fact that most passages that indicate such a hope are of a later date. It seems to be a gross oversimplification to say that in the Old Testament "death follows on life and in the providence of God death is the end," so that only this world is open to the faithful.[22]

To read the whole New Testament understanding of an individual and a universal resurrection back into the Old Testament would be equally unjustified. Though the Old Testament understanding of human destiny had not yet risen to the clarity of New Testament perceptions, death was not the end for the Israelites. But God's revelation does

Hilton C. Oswald (Minneapolis: Augsburg, 1988), 484, that Ps. 49:15 could be understood as testimony to the belief in the resurrection seems to be convincing.

21. Fohrer, *History of Israelite Religion*, 389-90, claims that Dan. 12:2 is the only Old Testament passage that supports the hope for a resurrection. At the beginning of the end time Yahweh's power will extend over the living *and* the dead, so that the dead will no longer be excluded forever from the reign of God. Fohrer leaves no doubt that he much more appreciates a different train of thought: to find fulfillment of life in the reign of God and communion with God in this life so that the hereafter becomes irrelevant. According to Fohrer, this view is dominant throughout the Old Testament.

Other scholars think differently. Vriezen, *An Outline*, 204, for instance, claims that faith in God as the Lord of life who performs miracles and who rules everywhere, even in sheol, "was the root from which afterwards the belief in the resurrection of man could spring." This seems to indicate that the hope for the resurrection is a consequent conclusion from the emerging belief in Yahweh's dominion over all the world, Israelite and non-Israelite, and visible and invisible. And if Eichrodt, 2:512, is right in claiming that the belief in the resurrection attested by the book of Daniel is "clearly both much more strongly developed and indeed already a fixed dogma," this again suggests that such belief did not just originate around 200 B.C., but had its roots much earlier in history.

22. Cf. Ludwig Köhler, *Old Testament Theology*, trans. A. S. Todd (Philadelphia: Westminster, 1957), 150. The German original says it even more drastically: "Nach Gottes Ordnung ist der Tod das Ende. Es gibt nur ein Diesseits" (*Theologie des Alten Testaments*, 3rd ed. [Tübingen: Mohr, 1953], 137). But even Köhler concedes that the belief in the resurrection is at least "vaguely hinted at in the Old Testament" (137).

not occur in a single day. It occurs according to the human needs and questions that have to be met and answered. When Israel's corporate existence collapsed and most of the people were led into the Babylonian exile, the almost exclusive focus on corporate fulfillment no longer sufficed. That there is outside help to clarify burning issues, as the Canaanite and Parsistic influences indicate (Dan. 12:2), shows that non-Israelite terms and concepts were not despised in explaining and clarifying Yahweh's plan of salvation for his people.

3. The Last Judgment

In analogy to the Israelite emphasis on life here on earth, God's judgment was first conceived as a judgment here on earth and during our lifetime. God judges all misdeeds here on earth, because

> vengeance is mine, and recompense,
> for the time when their foot shall slip.
>
> (Deut. 32:35)

Within the covenant community one should fear and trust God. Fear results from the awareness that he is mighty and powerful, whereas trust is the appropriate reaction to the One who is a powerful God and who has chosen Israel as his people.

a. Responding to a Holy and Gracious God

God is not understood as a capricious power who plays dice with the world. He is a faithful God who sticks to his orders and promises and who in turn wants us to be like-minded. The Old Testament cult is grounded in the knowledge that God is trustworthy and reliable. Yahweh is the God who brought the Israelites from Egypt into the Promised Land. He is holy, and therefore Israel should be holy too (Exod. 19:6; Lev. 11:44). He has given his law to Israel and, as a righteous God, is always connected with the law.[23] This law expresses God's gra-

---

23. While the law in the sense of the Torah or the cultic law is of a relatively late date, there is no doubt that from the very beginning the relationship of Yahweh presup-

cious ordering of and caring for life, and as such is unquestionable, un-changeable, and reliable. The delight of the righteous is in the law of the Lord (Ps. 1:2), and he is pleased with the law (Ps. 119:13-14). Such a positive understanding of the law expresses the response of the Israel-ites to the covenant God made with Israel, and it corresponds with the faithfulness and trustworthiness of Yahweh expressed in the covenant.

God judges those who do not adequately respond to his gracious care and therefore ignore his law. Nathan and Elijah had to remind their kings of the law of the Lord, and beginning with Amos, the prophets frequently reminded the whole Israelite nation of its obligation to the Lord and his law. Of course, this is not a unilateral process. Especially the Psalms show us that, knowing about God's covenant with Israel and God's past history with Israel, individuals could also remind God of his obligations. But the Old Testament usually shows that God observes his part of the covenant, so that Israel could address him in the polarity of praise and petition.[24] Yet most stories of the Old Testament show the people of Israel in a different light. While Yahweh keeps his obligations and his promises, the people do not live up to theirs. Then Yahweh be-comes the judge of his people.

Not only Israel was included in the judgment of God. Amos an-nounced that other nations are included also. Often the judgment oc-curred because these nations had offended Israel (Isa. 34:8), and some-times Yahweh gave them directly into the hands of Israel. Arrogance, pride (Isa. 16:6-7), or disobedience (Mic. 5:15) was the cause for God's judgment. Not even the mightiest powers at that time, Egypt and As-syria, were excluded from the rule of God. Finally, toward the close of the Old Testament, the empires were compared with wild and ferocious animals that have to concede the final victory to God when he will erect his kingdom.

---

posed some specific ways of conduct which always included obeying Yahweh's word (of law or obligation). For the complexity of the Old Testament law, cf. Klaus Koch, "Gesetz XI: Altes Testament," in *TRE,* esp. 13:42-45.

24. Cf. Claus Westermann, *Praise and Lament in the Psalms,* trans. K. R. Crim and Richard N. Soulen (Atlanta: John Knox, 1981), 153-54.

b. The Day of the Lord

God is not just a God of promise and threat. He brings his promises and threats into reality. They can often be seen as occurring within history. The exodus from Egypt and the occupation of the Promised Land (Palestine) were crucial fulfillments of God's promises. In a similar way, the coming of judgment was initially conceived as an event within history. The destruction of Jerusalem was still understood as judgment over Israel (Lam. 1:4-5). But, similar to the promises of God that were modified and expanded (although they were always fulfilled), the day of judgment too was eventually understood to include more than the immediate historical event.[25]

Already the royal psalms (Pss. 2; 20; 21; etc.) expressed a hope in the Lord who will destroy all enemies of Israel. Yet they did not speak of a future, eschatological judgment, but of an "earthly king of David's line, who has just been enthroned" and whom Yahweh will assist.[26]

As early as the eighth century, however, the Day of the Lord, the Judgment Day, "was a familiar theologoumenon [object] taken over from an earlier time."[27] This day was thought to be a day of light and the

---

25. Cf. Fohrer, *History of Israelite Religion*, 269-71, in his treatment of the concepts of the Day of the Lord and the remnant; and Jürgen Moltmann, *Theology of Hope: On the Ground and the Implications of a Christian Eschatology*, trans. J. W. Leitch (New York: Harper & Row, 1967), 104-5, who convincingly demonstrates how God's promises were constantly being modified and expanded. Cf. also, to the whole issue of faith in Yahweh and the prospect of the future, the excellent study by Horst Dietrich Preuss, *Jahweglaube und Zukunftserwartung* (Stuttgart: W. Kohlhammer, 1968).

26. Sigmund Mowinckel, *He That Cometh*, trans. G. W. Anderson (Oxford: Basil Blackwell, 1959), 11.

27. So Köhler, *Old Testament Theology*, 219-20. Vriezen, "Prophecy and Eschatology," in *Supplements to Vetus Testamentum*, vol. 1, *Congress Volume: Copenhagen 1953* (Leiden: Brill, 1953), 199-229, advocates a very interesting development of Israel's understanding of eschatology which seems to have some merit (225-27):

    1. Pre-eschatological period (before the classical prophets): The future is seen to a great extent in the light of the past, the idealized age of David. Israel's hopes are mainly political-national.

    2. Proto-eschatological period (Isaiah and his contemporaries): this is the period in which the vision of a new people and a new kingdom is beginning to play a part, a kingdom that will embrace the whole world and that rests on the spiritual forces that spring from God.

    3. Actual-eschatological (Deutero-Isaiah and his contemporaries): the kingdom

43

great day of salvation. Popular expectations also went in the direction of historical, political, and cosmic changes. Sometimes the expectation of catastrophes in nature was part of this idea of the judgment on all nations and the salvation of Israel (Zech. 14:5-15). But the prophets turned these nationalistic eschatological expectations into a pronouncement of calamity and disaster. Especially Amos emphasized the Day of the Lord as a day of darkness and not of light, as a day of gloom with no brightness in it (Amos 5:19-20). It would be a day of the sword, of hunger and pestilence, a day of great slaughter (Isa. 30:25), a day of fright and anxiety. God would destroy the whole world (Isa. 13:5), and great changes would occur in nature, such as earthquakes, darkness, drought, and fire (Mal. 4:1). The judgment that the Lord executes when his great and fearful day comes is one of the main themes of the prophetic proclamation.[28]

But God's judgment is not his last word. Terms like "the end of the days," "in the latter days," "in those days," "in this time" (Isa. 2:2; Jer. 23:20; 30:24; 48:47; Ezek. 38:16; Hos. 3:5; and many others) are common for most prophets and point to the Day of the Lord, to the coming of his kingdom. Yet the prophets did not share the naive and popular hope that "Israel as a state and a people would always and in all respects be victorious without more ado."[29] They eventually realized that a new creation and a full salvation could only be reached through defeat and absolute destruction. This did not impair their confidence in the dominance and kingship of Yahweh over all nations, but they were less confident than their audience in the dignity and power of their own nation. For instance, in the context of announcing the Day of the Lord, Amos pronounces total destruction over Israel unless they immediately return to

---

of God is not only seen as coming in visions, but is experienced as coming, and the world is going to be changed.

4. Transcendental-eschatological period of apocalyptic: salvation is not expected to come in this world, but either spiritually in heaven or after a cosmic catastrophe in a new world.

Of course, Vriezen is aware of the danger of such a periodization, and he states that many of these lines run parallel to each other and extend their influence for centuries afterward in various movements (e.g., the pre-eschatological period and the development of the concept of the Messiah).

28. Cf. Köhler, *Old Testament Theology*, 220-21.

29. Vriezen, *An Outline*, 351.

Yahweh. And even if they would return, Yahweh is free to grant them forgiveness or to withhold it (Amos 5:14-15).[30]

c. Universal Scope of Salvation

Judgment does not result in the ultimate destruction of Israel and the other nations. "Foundational is the *sequence of doom and salvation*. The emphasis is on salvation, it is the clue, the actual content of expectation, even if by necessity usually not the only one."[31] There is a redirection to something new that, it is hoped, will come. Even in the book of Amos, after long and serious threats of impending judgment, all of a sudden we find an affirmation of salvation (9:11-15). Of course, one can suggest that these are additions to Amos by a later editor, but already in Amos's own announcement of judgment we find the possibility of a new future (5:4b). With Isaiah the hope for a new future is so intensified and expanded that we can call him *"the first preacher of the eschatological expectation."*[32] Isaiah expects complete destruction and, afterward, universal salvation. Salvation is no longer confined to Israel, but is open for the whole world. In picturesque language this is expressed in Isaiah 2:2-4: Mount Zion will tower over all other mountains, and all nations and tribes shall flock to it to hear the ordinances of God. When Isaiah employs mythical imagery, this shows that the expected new order of salvation reaches out beyond historical reality. God will also be judge of all nations; all wars will cease and there will be everlasting peace. This peace will affect the realm of nature. Everybody will have plenty of food and will enjoy a long life (cf. Isa. 7:21-25 and 11:6-9). Salvation in the picture of Isaiah still comes via Israel, and even Jesus did not change this. But this understanding is not one of nationalistic prejudice, because the "house of the *Lord*" is in the center, and the beginning of God's kingdom presupposes the destruction of Israel.

The prophets after Isaiah stand in continuity with this picture. Yet the immense and hopeless struggle of the Israelite nation for survival lets them express the hopes of salvation in a more spiritualistic and indi-

---

30. Cf. Fohrer, *History of Israelite Religion,* 246.
31. So Rudolf Smend, "Eschatologie II: Altes Testament," in *TRE,* 10:262.
32. Vriezen, *An Outline,* 360.

vidualistic way. God will create something new in forgiving the sins of the past and burying them in the depths of the sea (Jer. 31:34; Ezek. 16:63; Mic. 7:18-19). He will take the old heart of stone out of his people and give them a new heart of flesh so that they can do his will and be his people (Ezek. 11:19-20). In contrast to Isaiah, a hope for all nations is missing here. This is not surprising when we remember that Ezekiel spoke to Israel at a time when the nation had collapsed. Still, the theocentric emphasis is maintained: "Then they shall be my people, and I will be their God" (Ezek. 11:20b). It may be noteworthy to mention that Ezekiel uses the metaphor of the resurrection of the dead to stress the miraculous aspect of God's restitutive action (Ezek. 37:1-14).[33]

With Deutero-Isaiah the picture changes, since the destruction of Jerusalem is already past history. The prophet has experienced the judgment to which Isaiah still pointed, and now he proclaims the immediate future as the time of salvation. He even draws a parallel between the impending time of salvation, the creation in the beginning, and the exodus from Egypt (Isa. 51:9-10). God created the earth, he provided land for Israel, and now the time of salvation will be like a new creation. In describing salvation Deutero-Isaiah uses the same word, *bara'* (to create), that is used in the creation stories in Genesis. In so doing he indicates that salvation is a creative act of God in the same sense as the creation in the beginning.[34]

The time of salvation also causes a change in nature. In paradisiac fertility the land will yield good crops (Isa. 41:18-19), and everything and everybody will praise the Lord (43:21). The Lord will now make an everlasting covenant with Israel that will fulfill God's gracious faithfulness once promised to David (55:3). Israel has the missionary task to be the light to all nations and to serve as a covenant with the people (42:6-7). God will create a new heaven and a new earth; he will rejoice in Jerusalem and be glad in his people. After the exile, a late writer even adds

33. The vision in Ezek. 37 "concerns a picture of the people's restoration after the return from exile, but the elements of this symbolism leave it to be understood that the resurrection of the dead was envisaged as a possibility." So Edmond Jacob, *Theology of the Old Testament*, trans. A. W. Heathcote and Ph. J. Allcock (London: Hodder & Stoughton, 1958), 310.

34. Vriezen, *An Outline*, 361-62, mentions that Deutero-Isaiah uses the term *bara'* sixteen times. In Genesis, where the term is used with second-highest frequency, we find it nine times.

that now the former things will be forgotten and there will be no sorrow and distress as in bygone days (65:17-25).

If one were to elaborate only the positive eschatological side of Deutero-Isaiah's message, one might classify him as a universalistic utopian with a strong nationalistic tinge. But he knows that the message of impending salvation is preached to almost deaf ears. The Israelites in Babylon complain that their way is hidden from the Lord (40:27), that the Lord has forsaken and forgotten them (49:14). They hear the message but reject the content. And yet the prophet does not give in. He knows that the Israelites have always had a rebellious character (48:8) and do not hesitate to resort to physical resistance in rejecting the word of salvation (50:6). Finally, he understands that merely proclaiming the salvation of Israel does not change anybody. The only access to salvation for his people and for the whole world is through the substitutionary suffering of the innocent Servant of Yahweh (42:1-4; 49:1-6; 50:4-11a; 52:13–53:12). But who is that Servant of Yahweh whom Deutero-Isaiah introduced? It is difficult to prove convincingly that he symbolizes Israel in a collective way because Israel was never the innocent, willing, and faithfully suffering servant.[35] It must rather be a person with a universal, prophetic mission. Deutero-Isaiah was such a man, and reflections of his personal encounter with Israel may have colored the sections about the Servant of Yahweh. But would he describe his own future death? Perhaps we come closer to an answer when we associate the figure of the Servant of the Lord with the figure we meet in the last part of our survey of Old Testament eschatology.

4. The Coming of a Messiah

Christos, the Greek equivalent for the Hebrew word "messiah," is the title that is most frequently applied to Jesus of Nazareth in the New Testament. Most Christians therefore understand Jesus of Nazareth to be the Messiah and assume that title to have originated from promises con-

---

35. Cf. Gerhard von Rad, *Old Testament Theology,* vol. 2, *The Theology of Israel's Prophetic Traditions,* trans. D. M. G. Stalker (New York: Harper & Row, 1965), 259-61. Von Rad, in his careful yet brief discussion of the problem of who the Servant of Yahweh is supposed to be, comes to the conclusion that Deutero-Isaiah points to a prophetic figure of the future, "a prophet like Moses" (262).

tained in the Old Testament. But in looking for explicit references in the Old Testament, we discover hardly any messianic references that have eschatological significance.[36]

a. The Significance of the Term "Messiah"

The term "Messiah," or anointed one, can refer to the high priest (Lev. 4:5), but usually it denotes the king of Israel (2 Sam. 1:16), who was anointed when he was designated king. Yet the expected king of the final time, of the eschaton, is never called the Messiah.[37] The only exception is Isaiah 45:1, where a foreigner, the Persian king Cyrus (†529 B.C.), is called the Messiah to whom God speaks. This reference demonstrates the high expectations that had been connected with the edict of Cyrus that permitted the exiles to return to Jerusalem. But the Old Testament writers are not aware of a person called the Messiah who is to bring eschatological salvation. The eschatological fulfillment is too closely connected with God as the actor in history to be mediated by a messianic figure. This is different from the New Testament, in which Jesus is primarily understood as the Messiah, because he was believed to be returning to fulfill the eschatological expectations once pronounced to Israel. Though the title Messiah is not used in the Old Testament in an eschatological context, the hope is already present for a God-provided figure who will usher in the eschaton. We will see

36. Hans-Peter Müller, *Ursprünge und Strukturen alttestamentlicher Eschatologie* (Berlin: Töpelmann, 1969), 212, points out very convincingly that in the total context of Old Testament eschatology the hope for a Messiah plays only an unimportant role. The Messiah belongs mostly on the side of the people who are redeemed by Yahweh, and only seldom is he conceived of as the actual bringer of salvation or even its mediator. In the New Testament, however, the Messiah is usually understood as an eschatological figure, as a redeemer sent by and representing God who initiates the end time and brings salvation to the people.

37. Cf. A. S. van der Woude, "Messias," in *Biblisch-Historisches Handwörterbuch*, 2:1197. For the following, cf. also Hugo Gressmann, *Der Messias* (Göttingen: Vandenhoeck & Ruprecht, 1929), 1. Though the king was understood as viceroy and mandatory of Yahweh himself, as expressed in the royal psalms, the office of the king did not seem to exert much influence on the development of the idea of the Messiah. Cf. Gerhard von Rad, *Old Testament Theology*, vol. 1, *The Theology of Israel's Historical Traditions*, trans. D. M. G. Stalker (Edinburgh: Oliver & Boyd, 1962), 318-20.

later that this figure seems to have originated from a retrospective glorification of David and from the promise that was given to him through Nathan (2 Sam. 7:12-15).

b. Main Sources for the Concept of a Messiah

From the very beginning Israelite history is seen as a promissory history (Gen. 12:2-3). The messianic figure in this history who is expected to bring about eschatological salvation is usually associated with the house of David. The blessing Jacob gave to Judah (Gen. 49:8-12) can be considered the oldest of these "messianic" expectations. The one who is supposed to come is described as one who will bring about and live in an age of "paradisaical abundance."[38] He will bind his foal to the vine and wash his garments in wine. The oracle of Balaam (Num. 24:15-19) talks with a nationalistic and political tinge about the star that shall come forth out of Jacob and have dominion over the neighboring nations. The restoration of the fallen "booth of David," as indicated in the book of Amos, seems to go along similar lines (Amos 9:11-15). This restoration is expected as a dominion of Israel over all the nations. In recapitulating an idealized past as "the days of old" (9:11), Amos describes the messianic time as one of prosperity and peace ("The mountains shall drip sweet wine, / and . . . my people Israel . . . / shall rebuild the ruined cities and inhabit them" [9:13-14a]).

In Isaiah's proclamation the messianic references are expanded beyond the scope of the immediate national and historical reality (Isa. 7:10-17; 9:1-7; 11:1-8). Many exegetes hesitate to consider 7:10-17 a messianic reference, since the birth of a child with the name "Immanuel" by a young woman could easily refer to Isaiah's own wife.[39] But the other two announcements, in 9:1-7 and 11:1-8, clearly have a messianic

---

38. Gerhard von Rad, *Genesis: A Commentary*, trans. J. H. Marks (Philadelphia: Westminster, 1961), 419-20, however, does not call it a "messianic" passage.

39. Cf. Georg Fohrer, *Messiasfrage und Bibelverständnis* (Tübingen: Mohr, 1957), 11-14, who treats there all pertinent messianic references. Cf. also von Rad, *Old Testament Theology*, 2:173-74, who gives a good survey of the discussion on Isa. 7:10-17. Edward J. Young, *The Book of Isaiah*, 3 vols. (Grand Rapids: Eerdmans, 1965-72), 1:289, is somewhat too confident in his comments on this passage: "There can be only one of whom this can be predicated, namely, Mary, the mother of the Lord."

character. In the midst of the darkness of destruction a light is emerging (9:1-7). The Lord has broken the yoke that Assyria had imposed on Israel, and now his anointed will be enthroned. The child who was conceived and the son who was given is not a child in the physical sense but the anointed one who becomes the son of Yahweh through his enthronement (cf. Ps. 2:7). His names "Wonderful Counselor, Mighty God, Everlasting Father, Prince of Peace" indicate that his reign will be one of justice and peace. In Isaiah 11:1-8 the messianic peace is emphasized even more in stating that the "spirit of the Lord" will rest on the Messiah, and his reign now encompasses all of nature. Finally Micah proclaims that from Bethlehem, the village of David, the messianic ruler will come forth "whose origin is from of old" (Mic. 5:1-5). The return of the Israelites to their homes is presupposed, and the messianic peace and the magnitude of the kingdom are stressed.[40]

Toward the end of the Old Testament era, Haggai and Zechariah appear. For them the destruction of the Israelite nation and the return from exile are past events. They are aware that these events did not usher in the messianic kingdom. But God was present once in his temple in Jerusalem, so they emphasize the importance of rebuilding the temple as the prerequisite for the coming of Yahweh and of his kingdom (Hag. 1:7-8; Zech. 4:9). It is not enough to reoccupy the Promised Land; it is also necessary to reinstitute the place of worship as the cultic center of Israel and to be ready for the eschatological advent of Yahweh. Both prophets see themselves at the beginning of the time of salvation. The building of the temple initiates the time of salvation; the messianic prosperity starts (Hag. 2:19); and everybody will live in messianic peace (Zech. 8:12). Both see in Zerubbabel the anointed of the Lord, the coming Messiah (Hag. 2:20-23; Zech. 4:6-10).

But their high expectations end in disappointment. Zerubbabel is

---

40. We certainly agree with Georg Fohrer, "Die Struktur der alttestamentlichen Eschatologie," in *Studien zur alttestamentlichen Prophetie (1949-1965)* (Berlin: Töpelmann, 1967), 45-46, when he says the eschatological prophecy of the Old Testament usually does not refer to the end of the world or of history. It views the eschatological events as taking place within the framework of the nations, where political events or other historical incidents provide the starting point. But Fohrer also points out that nature and the cosmos are often included in these views. Especially toward the later parts of the Old Testament, the tendency is clearly universalistic in comprising the totality of world and history.

never enthroned, and the hope for the fulfillment of the Davidic promise has to be revised again. The exulting words:

> Lo, your king comes to you;
>   triumphant and victorious is he,
> humble and riding on a donkey,
>   on a colt, the foal of a donkey,
>
> (Zech. 9:9)

are too early. One generation before Zechariah, Deutero-Isaiah judged the situation much more realistically in the songs of the Servant of Yahweh. Confronted with the stubbornness and unbelief of his people, he realized that true deliverance and fulfillment of salvation could only be brought about through the vicarious suffering of the true Servant of Yahweh.

> We have all turned to our own way,
> and the LORD has laid on him
>   the iniquity of us all.
>
> (Isa. 53:6)

Though the messianic element of the victorious king is not lacking in Deutero-Isaiah's description of the suffering servant, he ultimately did not dare to identify him with an historic figure. The understanding that the bringer of salvation could not be identified with a figure of present or past history, but will be a figure acting in and through history, was more clearly conceived in the time of apocalyptic.

c. Expansion of the Messianic Hopes in the Apocalyptic Period

Two important changes occurred in eschatological thought during the time of apocalyptic. A different role was attributed to the Messiah and a new understanding of history was gained. In the apocalyptic visions of Daniel, God is still the ruler of the world. God brings about the cosmic and political changes and causes the eschatological time of salvation. In the apocalyptic books of 1 Enoch, 2 Esdras, and 2 Baruch, the Messiah enjoys a more independent position. He himself destroys the enemies and brings about the salvation of Israel. Together with his independence there is an increasing emphasis on his preexistence. He who existed before all worlds comes in the last time from heaven to initiate the time of salvation. To some degree this is already prefigured in the "son of man" imagery of Daniel 7. There the son of man (be he a corporate or an individual figure) signifies the final victory of God's power and greatness over the antigodly powers.[41] As a messianic figure, he ushers in the final triumph of God's people in God's kingdom in God's appointed time.[42]

While the prophets conceived of the enemies of Israel also as God's enemies who will either be converted or destroyed in the last time, in the apocalyptic period all antigodly powers were included in this picture. If God is to have dominion over the world, all powers have to succumb. For instance, according to *1 Enoch,* God smites the Gentiles in their final assault against Israel. Thereafter he sets up his throne, and the coming of the messianic kingdom is preceded by "the day of the great judgment" in which not only wicked people "but also Azazel, demons and fallen angels will be punished or destroyed."[43] All the Gentiles will become righteous and worship God, and Jerusalem with its holy temple will be the center of the kingdom. While in *1 Enoch* the kingdom is established on this earth, the tendency is to idealize this kingdom. Thus Jerusalem as its center is not the old Jerusalem, but a new Jerusalem which is either conceived as a purification of the old (*1 Enoch* 6–36) or as a replacement of it (*1 Enoch* 83–90).[44]

---

41. Cf. D. S. Russell, *The Method and Message of Jewish Apocalyptic: 200 BC–AD 100* (London: SCM, 1964), 327.

42. H. H. Rowley, *The Relevance of Apocalyptic: A Study of Jewish and Christian Apocalypses from Daniel to the Revelation,* rev. ed. (New York: Association, 1963), 29-30, mentions that "no member of the Davidic house headed the rising against Antiochus Epiphanes, and it would have been a sheer lack of realism to import a Davidic Messiah into the visions." On the other hand, the thought of a Levitic Messiah had not yet arisen. Rowley also gives good treatment to the question of whether the son of man in Daniel can be interpreted as the Messiah and comes to the conclusion that "there is no evidence that the Son of Man was identified with the Messiah until the time of Jesus" (32). Though literally speaking, Rowley is right, the son of man figure in Dan. 7 certainly cannot be regarded as totally unmessianic. We rather follow here von Rad, *Old Testament Theology,* 2:312, who says there can be no doubt "that the son of man described in Dan. VII.13 is initially presented as a Messianic figure in the wider sense of the term."

43. Russell, 287.

44. Cf. Russell, 290-91.

In the Similitudes of Enoch this view is expanded. The kingdom is now seen to be established not only on a transformed earth but also in a transformed heaven. In the *Testament of Moses,* a book which probably originated when Jesus was still in his teens, this tendency goes even further. We are told that God's kingdom "will appear throughout his whole creation" (10:1). The whole conception of the coming events of the end is no longer confined within nationalistic or this-worldly expectations. It is supramundane, and the kingdom is viewed as a kingdom of heaven.

The supranationalistic and supraworldly view of God's reign was only possible because the apocalyptists could view history as a unity. The unity of history, however, presupposed a monotheistic faith in the one God who shaped and destined the world to his purpose.[45] This was already part of the Israelite heritage when the intertestamental period began. But the apocalyptists believed that they stood so close to the end of the world that they were able to take in the whole history at one glance and declare its meaning in terms of the divine purpose. "Within this purpose the people of Israel had a very high destiny which they dared not evade."[46] God is the Lord of the whole earth; Judaism is the embodiment of religion for all humanity; and Israel is the instrument for the establishment of God's worldwide rule. From their vantage point the apocalyptists assumed they could see the past, present, and future in one continuous progression preordained by God. In this age all evil tendencies will grow until they culminate in the dominion of the political powers of this world. Then the end of this age will be near. The visible symptoms of the coming end are: utmost evil, unrest and wars, and disturbance in nature (especially in the stellar courses). These are, at the same time, the travails that indicate the birth of the new aeon. The new aeon will be the complete opposite of the old. It will be the unlimited dominion of the kingdom of God.

This theocentrically developed, systematic, and highly deterministic concept of history culminates in the promised reign of the kingdom of God. "This historifying of the world in the category of the universal eschatological future is of tremendous importance for theology, for indeed it makes eschatology the universal horizon of all theology as such. Without apocalyptic a theological eschatology remains bogged down in the

---

45. Cf. Russell, 218-20.
46. Russell, 221.

ethnic history of men or the existential history of the individual."[47] Apocalyptic, by including all powers and all nations, transcends the nationalistic eschatological expectations of Israel and opens the dimension of a new hope for the whole universe. Harold H. Rowley (1890-1969) captures this important deed of apocalyptic thinking very clearly when he says:

> They did not believe that God was indifferent to the world He had made; nor did they think He was impotent to take a hand in its course. They would have smiled at the idea so widespread in our day that God is of all beings the most helpless. . . . The apocalyptists believed in God, and believed that He had some purpose for the world He had made, and that His power was equal to its achievement. Their faith goes beyond the faith in divine control of history, indeed. It is a faith in the divine initiative in history for the attainment of its final goal. Such a belief is fundamental to the Christian view of God and the world. . . . Unless we believe in the eternity of human history in our world, we must expect that somehow, somewhere, the course of history will come to an end. We can look for it to peter out, or we can look for the world to be snuffed out ignominiously. But if we believe that it is God's world, and that He created it with some purpose, we must find some way of translating the faith of the apocalyptists that that purpose will be achieved.[48]

Gerhard von Rad (1901-71), to quote just one prominent representative of a very different evaluation of the apocalyptic movement, states that though apocalyptic cannot deny its relationship to prophecy, it exposed itself to the danger of teaching "a great cosmological gnosis."[49] Although in the fourth edition of his *Old Testament Theology* von Rad rewrote his entire chapter "Daniel and Apocalyptic," his tone was not much more positive. The concept of salvation history that had prevailed in the prophetic view of history is now abandoned in the period of

---

47. Moltmann, 137-38. One should note, however, that such a universalistic view has its problems. While there was a universal scope, what really mattered were the faithful in Israel. But even for those there was no salvational determinism. There was also widespread pessimism on account of human depravity and the overwhelming force of the political powers. Cf. Karlheinz Müller, "Apokalyptik/Apokalypsen IV," in *TRE*, 3:233, 243-44, who is very critical of some systematizing interpretations.

48. Rowley, 167-68 and 171.

49. Von Rad, *Old Testament Theology*, 2:308.

apocalyptic, according to von Rad, and history is conceived of in strictly deterministic terms.[50] (Such a view is, of course, clearly rejected by Rowley.) But even von Rad leaves open the question of whether the apocalyptic view of history is a detrimental alienation from the belief in Yahweh or "a breakthrough to new theological horizons."[51] This breakthrough, we must assert, has occurred in Jesus of Nazareth. For him the apocalyptic dimension of the kingdom of God has become the center of his eschatological message.

5. The Iranian Connection

Apocalyptic thinking did not suddenly emerge in postexilic Judaism through the events of the Babylonian exile when Israel was exposed to the influence of the Iranian religion (Parsism) and the Babylonian religion. Yet "anyone who has even a superficial knowledge of the Iranian religion cannot but be struck by the parallels that may be drawn between it on the one hand and Judaism and Christianity on the other. The ideas of God, angels and archangels, of Devil, demons and archfiends, as found in both, present so great a similarity that comparisons between the angelology and demonology of the two types of religion become inevitable."[52] We could also quote the German historian of religion Hans-Joachim Klimkeit (b. 1939), who writes: "There is hardly any other nation in the circle of the peoples in the ancient Orient that comes so close to Judaism and therewith the Old Testament roots of Christendom in its essential concepts as those communities of peoples in the Iranian language family. Next to the idea of one supreme god who cannot be depicted any further, there are especially two further concepts woven into each other that connected many Iranians of antiquity with the main stream of post-exilic Judaism: namely the hope in an end-time transfiguration and renewal of the world and the hope in the resurrection of the dead."[53] The Iranians were not a uniform community, ex-

---

50. Von Rad, *Theologie des Alten Testaments*, 4th ed. (Munich: Chr. Kaiser, 1965), 2:321.

51. Von Rad, *Theologie des Alten Testaments*, 2:322.

52. A. V. Williams Jackson, *Zoroastrian Studies: The Iranian Religion and Various Monographs* (New York: AMS, 1965), 205.

53. Hans-Joachim Klimkeit, "Der iranische Auferstehungsglaube," in *Tod und Jenseits*, 62.

cept for their language; they came from India and settled in Mesopotamia. Similar to that of late Israel, their religion was directed toward the end times. Unless the Israelites were totally deaf and blind during the Babylonian exile, there must have been some influence exerted on them by the spiritual world of Iran.[54] The Iranian religion in a narrower sense is documented in the Holy Book of the Avesta, which contains in its oldest passages the *gathas,* the songs of Zarathustra, which actually go back to him and his time.

The priest and prophet Zarathustra (Zoroaster, according to the Greek transcription) seems to have lived in eastern Iran probably in the sixth century before Christ.[55] At the center of his proclamation was the god Ahura Mazda, or Ormuzd. He was the creator of heaven and earth, without image, and the lawgiver of the whole cosmos. Loyalty to Ahura Mazda excluded the worship of any other old Iranian gods.

Their strict monotheism resembles that of the Israelite religion. However, Zoroaster emphasized the insurmountable opposition between almighty Ahura Mazda and Angra Mainyu, or Ahriman, the manifestation of everything evil. This cleavage seems to result in an antithetical dualism of an ethical and metaphysical nature, the strictest dualism "known in the history of religion."[56] Zarathustra expresses this dualism in the following way: "I will speak of the two spirits of whom the holier said unto the destroyer at the beginning of existence: 'Neither our thoughts nor our doctrines nor our minds' forces, neither our choices nor our words nor our deeds, neither our consciences nor our souls agree'" (Yasna 45:2).[57] Once these spirits or "gods" made their ini-

---

54. The impact of the Iranian religion on the development of Judeo-Christian eschatology is often emotionally debated. Preuss, *Old Testament Theology,* 2:256, who is very hesitant to admit any influences, concedes, for instance, that the influence of Parsism "can be indicated for the first time in Old Testament and early Jewish apocalyptic. However, Persian influence is not the deciding factor in solving the problem of the origins of Old Testament and early Jewish apocalyptic but only assists in this effort."

55. Friedrich Heiler, *Die Religionen der Menschheit in Vergangenheit und Gegenwart* (Stuttgart: Reclam, 1959), 423.

56. So Günter Lanczkowski, "Iranische Religionen," in *TRE,* 16:251.

57. The Yasnas are quoted according to Jacques Duchesne-Guillemin, *The Hymns of Zarathustra,* a translation of the Gathas together with introduction and commentary, preface by Richard N. Frye (Boston: Beacon Press, 1963).

tial ethical choice, they separated themselves and the world into a sphere of light and a sphere of darkness.[58]

The incompatibility of both gods is for Zarathustra the basis of his ethical demands. Though the ethical demands remain mostly in the realm of social ethics (the liberation of the suppressed peasants and herdsmen), the actual goal of ethical realization lies in the eschaton. Already here and now the village will prosper through righteousness, and those who adhere to good will obtain "integrity and immortality" (Yasna 48:11.14). Characteristic for Zoroaster's doctrine is a twofold outcome of history: an eternity of bliss and an eternity of woe, allotted respectively to good and evil people in another life beyond the grave. After death the soul of the deceased has to cross the Chinvat bridge, "the Bridge of the Separator" (Yasna 46:10), which stretches over hell, an abyss of molten metal and fire. For those who are good the bridge grows broader and broader for easier transit and subsequent ascent into heaven, where the pious soul will live in eternal joy. But for those who are wicked the bridge grows narrower until it is like the blade of a razor-sharp sword, and the soul falls into the abyss of hell, where there will be eternal torment and suffering. There is also some kind of intermediate state for those whose good and bad deeds are in strict balance.

Zoroastrian religion also knows of a judgment and completion of the whole world: "At the last turning-point of creation . . . where thou wilt come with thy Holy Spirit, with thy Dominion" (Yasna 43:5.6). Then the "sphere of lies" will collapse and the final judgment will take place. This judgment also results in a transformation of the world. The Saoshyans, or savior, will come and bring the present world to its end. The dead will be resurrected, and both the wicked and the good will have to pass through a flood of molten metal. The good will pass without harm and enter the new world. The wicked will either be purified or burned; and the evil spirits will be burned. After this worldwide purification in the last days of the present crisis, Ahura Mazda's sovereignty will be complete, and together with him the good will enjoy a new heaven and a new earth. Of course, not all ideas that we know from the Iranian religion go back to Zoroaster. Some are later developments of the Avesta, the sacred book of Zoroastrianism or Parsism, but most have their roots in his teachings.

58. Cf. Heiler, 428.

Since the individual person is not just part of a community but responsible for his or her own destiny, individual destiny gains stronger attention. Therefore the notion of the resurrection of the body is the result of Zarathustra's teaching in which the individual person and its own personality comes more into focus.[59] The resurrection of the dead is connected with a renewal of the world. Therefore Ahura Mazda, the great god, commands: "Let the dead arise (unhindered by these foes), and let bodily life be sustained in these now lifeless bodies."[60] Yet the preservation of the body is no presupposition for life beyond. The body can be intentionally given to decay because one knows about the further clothing of the soul or the new creation and resurrection. Both lines of thought are recognizable in Parsism: that corpse and soul are separated and the soul journeys to heaven, or that full life is given only when the powers of the "soul" are united with the body. Therefore there are the so-called "towers of silence" where the deceased are exposed to birds of prey because one does not want to contaminate the earth with corpses and the future one hopes for does not depend on a survival of the corpse.[61]

If we want to sum up the possible influence of Zoroaster's doctrines on the Judeo-Christian religion, we can conclude the following:

1. There are evident analogies between the relationship of good and evil in the Israelite religion and the relationship of good and evil in Zoroaster's system. This becomes especially clear in Qumran.[62] The sons of light and the sons of darkness, the realm of truth and the realm of lies, are important in Qumran theology. This seems to point to a direct borrowing on the Jewish side. However, the Qumran scrolls never found their way into the Old Testament corpus. Even the terminological dualism in the New Testament, as in the Gospel of John, bears only a very limited resemblance to Parsistic dualism.

2. The dramatic salvation-historical periodization of history as found

---

59. So Klimkeit, 70.

60. "Miscellaneous Fragments (IV)," in *The Zend-Avesta*, trans. L. H. Mills, vol. 31 of *The Sacred Books of the East*, ed. F. Max Müller (Delhi: Motilal Banarsidass, 1969 [1887]), 391.

61. Cf. Klimkeit, 74, for further details.

62. Cf. the lucid comments by Raymond E. Brown, *New Testament Essays* (Garden City, N.Y.: Doubleday, Image Books, 1968), 142-45, in his comments on the relationship between Zoroastrianism, the Old and New Testament Scriptures, and Qumran.

58

in the idea of the four empires in Daniel 2:1-47 and 7:1-28 comes close to the periodization of Parsism.

3. The expectation of the heavenly savior in the last time, as seen in Enoch, resembles the Zoroastrian idea of a Saoshyans, especially since he could be understood as a descendant of Zarathustra. It is difficult, however, to decide to whom we should attribute chronological priority because for Zoroaster, unlike later Zoroastrianism, the Saoshyans is not yet an eschatological figure and a final *new* existence is only vaguely indicated.

4. We are in a similar dilemma with the Zoroastrian idea of punishment of the ungodly through fire. Though there might be an influence on the development of these ideas in the later writings of Judaism (Dan. 7:10-11 and *1 Enoch* 67:4-7), the motif of a cosmic fire is also a well-known Greek and Stoic feature of eschatology.

5. The case of rewards and punishments, heaven and hell, is different, however.[63] The assumption of a direct Zoroastrian influence on postexilic Judaism makes it easy to understand why the Jews suddenly abandoned the idea of Sheol, as a shadowy and depersonalized existence which is the lot of people irrespective of what they had done on earth, and why they advanced, at exactly the time when they had made contact in exile with the Medes and Persians, an understanding of afterlife which paralleled Zoroaster's teachings.[64] For instance, Daniel, the alleged minister of Darius the Mede (521-485 B.C.), distinctly mentions everlasting life and eternal punishment in saying: "Many of those who sleep in the dust of the earth shall awake, some to everlasting life, and some to shame and everlasting contempt" (Dan. 12:2).[65]

---

63. So R. C. Zaehner in his excellent study, *The Dawn and Twilight of Zoroastrianism* (London: Weidenfeld & Nicolson, 1961), 57-58.

64. Geo Widengren, *Die Religionen Irans* (Stuttgart: Kohlhammer, 1965), 355, shows in his careful study that eschatology and apocalyptic have received their decisive impulses from Iran. The periodization of history and the resurrection of the body are specific Iranian doctrines that gained great significance. He also mentions the interesting fact that in pre-Islamic times there are only a few Semitic words found in the Iranian languages, while the Iranian influence on the Hebrew, Aramaic, and Syriac languages is truly impressive. A similar relationship can be established for the Iranian and the Greek languages (357). This seems to indicate in which direction the influence was exerted.

65. Although the book of Daniel is postexilic (ca. 150 B.C.), this passage seems to in-

It is remarkable that once the Jews had made contact with the Iranians, they took over the typical Zoroastrian doctrine of an individual afterlife in which rewards are to be enjoyed and punishments endured. Contrary to other "syncretistic" attempts, there seems to have been no objections made by their religious leaders.[66] This might indicate that in Israel the time was ripe for such beliefs. Moreover, the whole Near East seemed to wrestle during the sixth and fifth centuries before Christ with the destiny of the individual and of the world at large. This would cover the second half of what philosopher Karl Jaspers (1883-1969) termed the "Axial Period" of world history (from 800 to 200 B.C.), in which humanity as we know it today emerged.[67] Soteriological and eschatological systems were developed in Hellenistic Gnosticism, in apocalyptic Judaism, and finally in Christianity.

---

dividualize the metaphoric imagery of Ezek. 37 and expands it into a twofold outcome (for Israel). (Cf. Otto Plöger, *Das Buch Daniel* [Gütersloh: Gerd Mohn, 1965], 171-72, for this passage.) This means that the material used in this passage is certainly older than the book of Daniel, and thus the reference to Darius the Mede and his time is not totally unjustified.

66. Of course, we should not forget that at the time of Jesus the resurrection of the body was still a controversial subject in the eyes of the Sadducees.

67. Karl Jaspers, *Origin and Goal of History,* trans. M. Bullock (New Haven: Yale University Press, 1953), 24.

2. The Eschatological Proclamation of the New Testament

The Old Testament provides the historical background for the eschatological proclamation of Jesus of Nazareth and of the New Testament. The continuity between the two must be affirmed in a twofold way: (1) Yahweh, the God of Abraham, Isaac, and Jacob, the God of the Old Testament, is the father of Jesus of Nazareth; and (2) Jesus was a Jew. The New Testament is still concerned with the promises that are given by the same God to the same ethnic community in the same geographical area of our earth, but it shows that only the sameness of God is decisive while the ethnic and geographical boundaries are no longer valid. Everyone and everything will participate in the new future. This universalistic scope would be hard to explain without consideration of the context in which the eschatological proclamation of Jesus and the emergence of the New Testament Scriptures took place.

1. The Jewish Context

Trying to explain to his (Roman) readership the situation in Palestine, the Jewish historian Josephus (b. ca. A.D. 37) states: "There are three philosophical sects among the Jews. The followers of the first which are the Pharisees, the second the Sadducees, and the third sect, which pretends to be a severe discipline, are called Essenes."[1] He calls the Pharisees the first

---

1. Flavius Josephus, *The Great Roman-Jewish War: A.D. 66-70*, 2.8.2, trans. William

of the three sects or schools.[2] Its members are especially able in explaining the law, and they teach that the souls are immortal. After death the souls of the good people enter another body, while the souls of the wicked enter eternal punishment. The Sadducees, however, deny a continued existence of the soul as well as the idea of punishments or rewards in the netherworld. The Essenes, who he attests are very rigorous in their lifestyle, hold fast to the belief "that the bodies are corruptible, and that the matter they are made of is not permanent; but that the souls are immortal, and continue forever, and that they come out of the most subtile air, and are united to their bodies as to prisons, into which they are drawn by a certain natural enticement; but that when they are set free from the bonds of flesh, they then, as released from a long bondage, rejoice and mount upward. And their opinion is like that of the Greeks, that good souls have a habitation beyond the ocean. . . . While they allot to bad souls a dark and tempestuous destiny of never-ceasing punishments."[3]

While Josephus may make the Pharisees and Essenes more Greek in their view of the afterlife than they actually were, he is pointing to a decided difference between them and the Sadducees, who denied an afterlife altogether. He is also introducing us to three important groupings that were influential during Jesus' lifetime and the formation of the New Testament, two of them being the Pharisees and the Sadducees, who figured prominently in the Gospels. The Essenes are not mentioned in the Bible, and their name is presumably derived from the Aramaic, meaning "the pious."[4] In protest against the worldliness of the temple priests, they left for the desert and participated in the Jewish war (A.D. 66-70) against the Romans. They existed at least from 150 B.C. to A.D. 70 and lived mainly near Ein Gedi in the desert region of the Dead Sea. They formed a monastic community, studied the law and the prophets, kept the Sabbath holy, and had frequent ritual washings.

Since the Qumran community is located not far from the oasis of Ein Gedi, it is often seen as part of the Essene movement. In the Qumran texts

---

Whiston, edited with an introduction by William R. Farmer (New York: Harper Torchbooks, 1960), 76.

2. Josephus, *Great Roman-Jewish War* 2.8.14, 79.

3. Josephus, *Great Roman-Jewish War* 2.8.11, 79.

4. Cf. for the following, G. Baumbach, "Essener," in *Biblisch-Historisches Handwörterbuch*, ed. Bo Reicke and Leonhard Rost, 3 vols. (Göttingen: Vandenhoeck & Ruprecht, 1962-66), 1:443-44.

we read very little about the individual's destiny after death, since the individual person was so closely integrated into the community that personal destiny after death was rarely thematized.[5] Yet the whole lifestyle of the community was eschatological. Observing the rules of the community was the only way to face the imminent end time; doing so exhibited an attitude which assured that one belonged to the covenant of God with Israel. It was important for community members to repent of all evil ways in order to make the proper decision between the two superhuman powers, "the sons of light" and "the sons of darkness." The battle between these two continued in humanity itself. While everything depended on God's grace and his determining will, every member was, at the same time, summoned to the strictest observance of the law.

Others fought the battle against evil not within themselves, but turned toward the outside. Especially in Galilee, since the middle of the first century B.C., rebels arose against secular rulers. King Herod therefore persecuted the rebels as mere bandits.[6] When Herod the Great died in 4 B.C., there was widespread unrest. Later, after his son Archelaus lost his throne in A.D. 6, having ruled Judea, Idumaea, and Samaria since his father's death, there was disagreement among religious groups as to the consequences. Pharisaic groups pleaded for a hierocracy (a rule of the priests under Roman administration), while others, such as Judas the Galilean, who came from a rebellious tradition, wanted to fight Rome and demanded an immediate theocracy. This led to the emergence of the Zealots and the Sicarii.

"The Zealots proper, the group actually called by that name, far from being a long-standing resistance organization, was merely one among several groups from among the Judean or Idumean peasantry which emerged in the middle of the great revolt and continued the armed resistance against the Roman legions."[7] The Zealots were the first to enter Jerusalem and wanted to set up an alternative government there, but they were driven back by Simon bar Giora and his sizable messianic movement in the uprisings of A.D. 66. The Sicarii were "dagger men" who emerged in roughly 50 and inaugurated a program of

---

5. Cf. for the following, Johann Maier, *Zwischen den Testamenten: Geschichte und Religion in der Zeit des zweiten Tempels* (Würzburg: Echter, 1990), 281.

6. Cf. Maier, *Zwischen den Testamenten,* 283.

7. Richard A. Horsley with John S. Hanson, *Bandits, Prophets, and Messiahs: Popular Movements at the Time of Jesus* (San Francisco: Harper & Row, 1988), 247.

assassinations and kidnapping against key symbolic figures of the Jewish ruling circles who collaborated with the Romans. "After joining other groups who were battling against Jewish aristocratic leaders and Roman troops in Jerusalem at the outset of the great revolt in the summer of 66, they withdrew from the hostilities when their fellow Jewish insurgents turned on them — and sat out the rest of the revolt atop Masada."[8]

These few pointers indicate that there existed not just three main philosophical groups, as Josephus wants his readers to believe. The actual situation in Jewish Palestine was much more complex, indicating a diversity of social, political, and religious unrest. There were many popular messianic movements inspired by prophets who claimed that their course of action would lead to divinely sanctioned liberation from alien rule. Usually they were ended by swift and deadly Roman military intervention. These popular messianic movements were motivated by an eager yearning for deliverance and indicated a frustration over intolerable conditions. They occurred during a period of Jewish history in which apocalyptic thought patterns were apparently widespread. "The term 'apocalyptic' comes from the Greek language and means 'revelation.' Nowadays it is used primarily to denote a religious movement in which 'revelation' plays a special role, a movement within so-called late Judaism. This Judaism, whose religious documents in general were not accepted into the Hebrew canon of the Old Testament, is to be placed in the period from the third century B.C. down to the New Testament times."[9]

While in the older traditions of Israel the remembrance was nourished of what God had done for his people, now attention turns exclusively to the future.[10] It is God alone who knows when history will come to an end and when the new aeon will emerge in which, in its fullness, the universal dominion of God will appear, which up to now has been

---

8. Horsley, 248. To talk here about "social banditry" seems to downgrade the widespread liberation movement that Horsley accurately portrays. There were many forms of uprising and resistance against oppression in many countries throughout the centuries. Yet in Palestine their motivation was intensely religious.

9. Walter Schmithals, *The Apocalyptic Movement: Introduction and Interpretation*, trans. John E. Steely (New York: Abingdon, 1973), 13. "Movement" in this definition should be understood as a literary movement engendered by and reflective of a widespread and diverse sentiment.

10. For the following cf. Karlheinz Müller, *Studien zur frühjüdischen Apokalyptik* (Stuttgart: Katholisches Bibelwerk, 1991), 53.

hidden. The seer in the apocalyptic time is so close to the end of the first aeon that he seems to pre-vision the eruption of the new aeon. Therefore the imminent expectation of this new beginning in a new aeon is a fundamental ingredient of the apocalyptic confession.

"The Most High has made not one world but two," we read in 2 Esdras 7:50. Of these two worlds, or aeons, we only know the present one, which is full of troubles and anxieties. "God who is himself a single person, made a clear separation by way of pairs of opposites, . . . in that he has set before their eyes first the small and then the great, first the world and then eternity, this world being transitory, but the one to come eternal" (Pseudo-Clementines Hom. II 15:1-2). The new world is an eternal one which is the opposite of this world and will come when the time is fulfilled. "And when the whole of creation, visible and invisible, which the Lord has created, shall come to an end, then each person will go to the Lord's great judgment. And then all time will perish, and afterward there will be neither years nor months nor days nor hours. . . . And all the righteous, who escape from the Lord's great judgment, will be collected together in the great age" (*2 Enoch* 65:6ff.). This final judgment is not only pronounced about Israel but has universal significance. Israel's own history is embedded in the totality of history. When this universal history is brought to consummation, Israel and its destiny will have been completed.

In this universal vision the end is not brought about by the apocalyptic seer but by God himself. Therefore neither legions nor armies, neither kings nor potentates can thwart the course of history. Any doubt or resistance is seen as the work of powers that are hostile to God and, by extension, to Israel. All the powers of the world can do nothing against God's mighty arm, but still they are seen as becoming increasingly menacing. "The knowledge about the satanic threat through external powers only increases the internal confrontation, because the external enemy ultimately can do nothing against God as threatening as that enemy may be. The apocalypticist perceives the actual threat as coming from the internal enemy, those Jewish people who are not ready to join in the apocalyptic adventure and therefore seemingly miss the charge of election in the decisive phase of salvation history."[11] The apocalyptic seers have unyielding

---

11. Johann Maier, "Apokalyptik im Judentum," in *Apokalyptik und Eschatologie: Sinn und Ziel der Geschichte*, ed. Heinz Althaus (Freiburg: Herder, 1987), 53.

hope and immense optimism.[12] Since God is at the center of their thinking and is the all-powerful Lord, nothing will ultimately escape his will.
God has the last word, and the goal of everything will be his kingship.
Though God's plans are hidden and his ways are often inconclusive, the
seers are convinced that these ways will certainly lead to the predetermined goal for the faithful of God's people.

With this kind of conviction people influenced by apocalyptic
thought are ready to take on everything, all the evils of the end time and
the last onslaught of the godless powers. They are certain of their ultimate destruction, a precondition of the coming of the kingdom. Therefore they find new meaning in suffering, and comfort those who are disenfranchised. Others take their life into their own hands and follow the
call to ultimate rebellion. This means apocalypticists are on both sides
of the fence: those who passively await the coming of the kingdom and
others who join the rebellious forces.

Apocalyptic writings can either comfort in case the end is delayed
or increase the fervent expectations. In the latter case, Satan obtains
more and more prominence as the opponent of God. In a mythical way
he can become the monster or the dragon that is involved in the final eschatological battle through which the old aeon comes to its close.[13] He
can also assume historical features and be identified with threatening
rulers such as King Antiochus IV Epiphanes (who ruled from 175-164
B.C.), Herod the Great, or Nero (A.D. 54-68), as in the New Testament
book of Revelation. On the side of God there appears the preexistent
and transcendent eschatological figure of the Son of Man who "shall de-
pose the kings from their thrones and kingdoms" (*1 Enoch* 46:5). This
"Chosen One" who "was concealed in the presence of (the Lord of the
Spirits) prior to the creation of the world, and for eternity" (48:6), is also
"his Messiah" (48:10). We notice here that Jewish messianism has its origin in the conviction of the final catastrophe through which we arrive
from the historic present to the messianic future.[14] Yet this catastrophic

12. Cf. for the following, Josef Schreiner, *Alttestamentlich-jüdische Apokalyptik: Eine
Einführung* (Munich: Kösel, 1969), 195-96.

13. Cf. Schmithals, 23.

14. Cf. Gershom Scholem, "Zum Verständnis der messianischen Idee im Judentum" (1970), in *Apokalyptik,* ed. Klaus Koch and Johann Michael Schmidt (Darmstadt:
Wissenschaftliche Buchgesellschaft, 1982), 335, who emphasizes the revolutionary element in the transition from the historic present to the messianic future.

apocalyptic element was already emphasized in prophets such as Amos (Amos 9) and Isaiah (Isa. 3–4). Yet we must be careful not to overemphasize the position of the Messiah. While in Jewish apocalyptic the Messiah has heightened significance, in rabbinic literature he becomes almost peripheral, since eschatology is of little concern to the rabbis.[15]

For rabbis it was important to observe the law and to lead a pious life so that they would obtain the heavenly reward. Sheol was, for them, not eternal, but only a passing stage, for in due time the dead will be resurrected. Therefore *Mishna Sanhedrin* 10:1 reads: "All Israelites have a share in the world to come." But for apocalyptic thinkers and perhaps also for the large number of disenfranchised, a judgment day was needed "when all the arrogant and all evildoers will be stubble; the day that comes shall burn them up," and when the Lord "will send you the prophet Elijah before the great and terrible day" (Mal. 4:1-5). Elijah, who had not died but had ascended to heaven (2 Kings 2:11), became the center of countless legends and assumed the position of the forerunner of the Messiah and also of the great judgment.

In conclusion we notice that apocalyptic literature and thought forms contained many different elements gathered from different sources.[16] The elements mentioned, such as the Son of Man, the Messiah, the last judgment, Satan, this aeon and the coming aeon, and the cataclysms in history and nature, are familiar to those who read the New Testament and are aware of the proclamation of Jesus. The New Testament scholar Ernst Käsemann (1906-98) did not exaggerate when he stated that "apocalyptic was the mother of all Christian theology."[17] Having now sketched out the context in which the New Testament emerged, we must finally turn to that document. Though there is a legitimate interest in the New Testament, we first want to focus our at-

---

15. So Samuel Sandmel, *Judaism and Christian Beginnings* (New York: Oxford University Press, 1978), 206.

16. Cf. Maier, *Zwischen den Testamenten*, 264-66, who emphasized that Judaism before and during the time of Jesus did not simply longingly wait for a savior. There were many disparate elements of hope and eschatology present in Judaism.

17. Ernst Käsemann, "The Beginnings of Christian Theology" (1960), in Ernst Käsemann, *New Testament Questions of Today*, trans. W. J. Montague (Philadelphia: Fortress, 1969), 102; *Versuche und Besinnungen* (Göttingen: Vandenhoeck & Ruprecht, 1964), 2:100; and the discussion of this thesis in Klaus Koch, *The Rediscovery of Apocalyptic*, trans. Margaret Kohl (Naperville, Ill.: Allenson, 1972), 78-85.

tention on the one who gave rise to it, Jesus of Nazareth. While we are not interested in a biography of Jesus, we contend that his proclamation cannot just be regarded as a presupposition of New Testament theology, but as an integral part of it.[18] Any attempt to understand the New Testament meaning of eschatology without considering Jesus' own proclamation arrives at a book without its content.

2. The Eschatological Figure of Jesus

The relationship between Jesus and eschatology is significant in three areas: in his proclamation, in his self-understanding, and in his attitude toward the future. As far as we know, Jesus had a definite proclamation; he had a definite understanding of himself that is reflected in his conduct;[19] and he was not oblivious to the future.

New Testament research has shown us how difficult it is to penetrate beyond the reflections of the first Christian community and the writers of the New Testament texts to the historical Jesus. But the new quest and the continued quest have also shown us that such a task is not impossible. Yet the historical Jesus alone is not what matters. If it were, the New Testament would have missed its point, since it neither provides us nor wants to provide us with a biography of Jesus of Nazareth. But it is of fundamental theological relevance how the historical Jesus is reflected in the New Testament.[20] He is the starting point and the focus of the New Testament proclamation, and without an adequate understanding of him we cannot arrive at an adequate interpretation of the New Testament kerygma. Without a basic knowl-

18. Cf. the opposite position held by Rudolf Bultmann, *Theology of the New Testament*, trans. Kendrik Grobel (New York: Scribner, 1951), 1:3.

19. Ernst Fuchs, "The Quest of the Historical Jesus" (1956), in *Studies of the Historical Jesus*, trans. A. Scobie (Naperville, Ill.: Allenson, 1964), 21-22.

20. It is not only "the great enigma of New Testament theology, *how the proclaimer became the proclaimed*," as Bultmann had thought (cf. "The Christology of the New Testament," in *Faith and Understanding*, edited with an introduction by Robert W. Funk, trans. Louise Pettibone Smith [New York: Harper, 1969], 1:283). It is of decisive theological relevance whether and to what degree there is a continuity between Jesus and the New Testament kerygma in the midst of all discontinuity (cf. James M. Robinson, *A New Quest of the Historical Jesus* [Naperville, Ill.: Allenson, 1959], 90-91).

edge of Jesus and his message, we would be unable to determine whether the New Testament proclamation is in continuity or in discontinuity with Jesus' own teaching. This is one of the reasons why a strictly kerygmatic theology always seems somewhat abstract, lacking the dynamic power exhibited by Jesus.[21]

a. Jesus' Eschatological Message of the Kingdom of God

Jesus' proclamation was a wholly eschatological proclamation.[22] Jesus did not give his listeners a timetable and inform them in detail about things that were going to happen at some future point, but he addressed his audience in such a way that an immediate decision was implied.[23] He did not spell out certain eschatological doctrines, but confronted the people with a radical decision for or against God. This demand for a decision became at the same time a decision for or against Jesus and his actions. His proclamation, his own person, and his own actions form a unity that provoked and called for a decision. "Follow me, and let the dead bury their own dead" (Matt. 8:22); "No one who puts a hand to the plow and looks back is fit for the kingdom of God" (Luke 9:62); "And blessed is anyone who takes no offense at me" (Matt. 11:6) — these are only a few passages that show the urgency of an immediate decision here and now. The now is the decisive point of history and no longer the future, as it was in apocalyptic or in the promissory history of the Old Testament. This decisiveness of the present that Jesus proclaimed is illuminated by his own actions.

21. Cf. Karl Heim, *Ich gedenke der vorigen Zeiten: Erinnerungen aus acht Jahrzehnten* (Hamburg: Furche, 1960), 316-18, where he claims that the extreme dialectic of Bultmann dissolves the historic basis in which the kerygma is grounded.

22. A total eschatological understanding was first advocated by Albert Schweitzer. Dialectic theology, with its most prominent representatives in Karl Barth and Rudolf Bultmann, picked up this idea.

When Hans Conzelmann, *An Outline of the Theology of the New Testament*, trans. J. Bowden (New York: Harper & Row, 1969), 99, suggests that "Jesus' idea of God" can only in a qualified sense be called eschatological, he does have a point. Jesus certainly said many things that have no eschatological significance. The synoptic tradition has even preserved for us sayings that clearly go in a noneschatological direction. Still, the main and overwhelming intention of his proclamation is undeniably eschatological.

23. Bultmann, *Theology*, 1:9-11.

When John the Baptist sent two of his disciples to ask Jesus whether he was the promised one or whether they should wait for someone else, Jesus referred them to his actions. He did not refer to any titles that were conferred on him, but to his actions.[24] "The blind receive their sight, the lame walk, the lepers are cleansed, the deaf hear, the dead are raised, the poor have good news brought to them" (Luke 7:22) was his answer. With this remark he applied to himself the Old Testament imagery which was connected with the time of salvation (Isa. 35:5-6). When at the wedding in Cana he turned water into wine, this epiphanic miracle (John 2:11)[25] referred to the Old Testament understanding of wine as the symbol of the time of salvation. Jesus introduced himself here as the one in whom this salvation had become manifest. Jesus also talked about the new wine that should not be poured into old wineskins (Matt. 9:17). The old time is past; the time of salvation has been initiated. At one point Jesus stated it even more clearly: "But if it is by the finger of God that I cast out the demons, then the kingdom of God has come to you" (Luke 11:20). With Jesus of Nazareth the kingdom of God has already started. What had been expected for centuries, what had been projected into the future or into the present for so long, has now started. The kingdom of God is in the midst of you, said Jesus. It was not because he was such an important preacher, or because he had such an important message, that he called for an immediate decision. The kingdom of God has come with his appearance, and thus it is the time of decision. The today of Jesus is the goal of history.

Here we notice a decisive difference between Jesus' own proclamation and the apocalyptic environment in which he lived.[26] Apocalypticism

24. Many exegetes who are concerned about the historical Jesus also emphasize that only Jesus' actions can illuminate the significance of his person and his call for a decision. Ernst Fuchs, for instance, advocated this method in his programmatic essay "The Quest of the Historical Jesus," in *Studies of the Historical Jesus*, 11-31. This method seems to have been picked up by other students of Bultmann. But even Joachim Jeremias, coming from an entirely different direction, did extensive studies of the parables of Jesus in his quest for the *ipsissima vox Jesu* (original sayings of Jesus). Cf. Joachim Jeremias, *The Parables of Jesus*, trans. S. H. Hooke, 2nd rev. ed. (New York: Scribner, 1972).

25. Rudolf Bultmann, *The Gospel of John: A Commentary*, trans. G. R. Beasley-Murray et al. (Philadelphia: Westminster, 1971), 118-19. Though Bultmann recognizes this miracle as an epiphanic miracle, he wants to connect it with a Hellenistic environment (Dionysius cult) instead of with the Old Testament.

26. Cf. for the following, Eta Linnemann, "Zeitansage und Zeitvorstellung in der

had furthered a strong eschatological tension between the present conditions and the future expectations which partly resulted in an imminent expectation of the end Jesus announced that what had been expected with fervent hope. was already being fulfilled in the present. Yet both expectation and the tension connected with it made it possible that Jesus' proclamation of the coming of the kingdom of God was still related to the eschatological final disclosure. This means that Jesus pointed to the present in which the kingdom of God had been realized as well as also announcing the future dimension of the kingdom.[27] Yet that future was neither far off into the distance nor seen as immediately near.

As much as Jesus emphasized the inbreaking of the kingdom of God, he was just as reticent concerning future events or states. This is also true for setting a date for the expected end. About that day or hour nobody knows except the Father (cf. Mark 13:32). "The eschata are reserved for God and his decision; what the future of God will bring is withdrawn from human knowledge and human imagination."[28] This refusal to set any dates which would enable humans to prepare for the impending end shows that setting such a date is a divine prerogative. The kingdom of God is not to be realized by humans; they have no way of speeding it up or determining who gets the seats of honor. Yet the decisive battle has already been won and Satan has been thrown out of heaven, where he stood at God's right hand, accusing the righteous and bringing all their misdemeanors to God's attention.[29] Therefore Jesus can proclaim: "The time is fulfilled, and the kingdom of God has come near; repent, and believe in the good news" (Mark 1:15). With the announcement of the kingdom or the dominion of God, Jesus enforces a hope which since Deutero-Isaiah was part of the Judaic tradition (cf. Isa. 52:7).

But in contrast to the prophetic tradition as well as to apocalypticism, both of which looked toward the future as the time of salvation, though often the most imminent future, Jesus pointed to the present.

Verkündigung Jesu," in *Jesus Christus in Historie und Theologie: Neutestamentliche Festschrift für Hans Conzelmann zum 60. Geburtstag,* ed. Georg Strecker (Tübingen: Mohr, 1975), 262.

27. Cf. Linnemann, 254.

28. Rudolf Schnackenburg, "Das Neue und Besondere christlicher Eschatologie," in *Zukunft: Zur Eschatologie bei Juden und Christen,* ed. Rudolf Schnackenburg (Düsseldorf: Patmos, 1980), 67.

29. Cf. Helmut Merklein, "Eschatologie im Neuen Testament," in *Apokalyptik und Eschatologie,* 13.

This also shows the big difference between John the Baptist and Jesus. As we just heard, Jesus emphasized repentance, but unlike John the Baptist, he did not just issue a call to repentance and a warning about the impending judgment. Especially in addressing the individual he could point out the difference between doom and salvation with utmost severity. "If your hand causes you to stumble, cut it off; it is better for you to enter life maimed than to have two hands and to go to hell, to the unquenchable fire" (Mark 9:43). Still, for Jesus the time of salvation was now, and therefore he could show the graciousness of God, the acceptance of the sinner by grace alone. When we hear that Jesus heals the sick and that he accepts the outcast, such as Mary Magdalene or Zacchaeus, then "the expectations for the future time of salvation are already beginning to be fulfilled, not in its totality, not in its universality, but yet in such a way that already this presence stands under the sign of the kingdom of God."[30]

Although Jesus emphasized the decisiveness of his own person and of the present time, he did not point to an impending or immediate end of the world, except to reinforce the urgency of an immediate decision for or against God.[31] As far as we know, the oral tradition of the sayings of Jesus, sometimes called Q, contains no indication that Jesus was a "doomsday prophet" of the immediately approaching end of the world. If there are any authentic words of Jesus about such matters, they should be found in the Q source. But there is no evidence in Q. This coincides with another finding: neither the Jewish contemporaries of Jesus nor the Jewish polemics after Jesus accused him of announcing an immediate end of the world which did not come. We cannot imagine that they would not have exploited such false prophecy. Evidently Jesus was not interested in such prophecies. The Gospels tell us that he brushed aside John the Baptist, who fervently proclaimed the immediate coming of the end. Why was Jesus not interested in the immediate future and in prophecies of the immediate end of the world? Perhaps we may get a better understanding of this phenomenon if we investigate Jesus' self-understanding.

30. So with much detail Schnackenburg, 60-64; quote is on 60.

31. Cf. to the following, Ethelbert Stauffer, *Jesus and His Story*, trans. R. Winston and C. Winston (New York: Knopf, 1960), 155-56. Bultmann, *Theology*, 1:29, mentions too that "the synoptic tradition contains no sayings in which Jesus says that he will sometime (or soon) return."

b. Jesus' Self-Understanding

It was neither the task nor the intention of Jesus to proclaim a doctrine of the last things or a flawless doctrine of Christ. Nevertheless, if we correlate his assertions about the eschaton and especially about the kingdom of God with his person, we cannot but ask what kind of person he was. We get some clues about his self-understanding from the way he related himself to his message and from the few instances when he talked about himself. While Jesus did not make himself the focus of his teachings, it would be unrealistic to assume that he never said a word about himself. But can we distinguish clearly enough between the way people experienced him and reflected upon him and the way he actually talked about himself? The dilemma is most evident when we consider the titles of Jesus.

Most Christians would state without hesitation that Jesus was the Christ and that he called himself the Messiah. However, a careful analysis of the New Testament shows us that the title Messiah, or *Christos* in Greek, is used only 53 times in the Gospels but 280 times outside the Gospels. It is entirely missing in the oldest source, Q, as are the titles Son of David, King of Israel, and King of the Jews.[32] Mark, the oldest Gospel, does not give us clear evidence that Jesus used the term "Messiah" either. The Gospel of John, which uses the term quite frequently, never does so in such a way as to indicate that Jesus himself had used it. This shows that the term "Messiah" could not have played an important role in the life of Jesus.

Jesus probably refused the title Messiah whenever it was conferred on him.[33] He was not interested in the political and nationalistic aspira-

32. Cf. Stauffer, *Jesus and His Story*, 160-61; and Vincent Taylor, *The Names of Jesus* (New York: St. Martin's Press, 1953), 19, 24, 77.

33. So Ferdinand Hahn, *The Titles of Jesus in Christology: Their History in Early Christianity*, trans. H. Knight and G. Ogg (London: Lutterworth, 1969), 161. Hahn connects this possible repudiation of the messianic title with the fact that in Jesus' life any indication of a zealotic tendency in thought or action is entirely lacking. Taylor, *The Names of Jesus*, 20, also states that Jesus' unwillingness "to use the title must mean that He repudiated the current nationalistic expectations associated with it." Since this seems to be a commonly accepted position among exegetes, advocates of a "theology of rebellion" or of revolution will find it difficult to base their ideas on sound exegetical ground.

A very exceptional position is taken by S. G. F. Brandon, *Jesus and the Zealots: A Study of the Political Factor in Primitive Christianity* (New York: Scribner, 1969), who advo-

tions connected with the coming of the Messiah, and he did not want to be taken for a political liberator. Never do we hear that he conspired against the Roman occupation army or that he wanted to revolt against them. Though the charges against him were finally of a political nature, he clearly denied them. He did not want to be a Judas Maccabaeus or a Bar Kochba or any of the many other political and religious messiahs that emerged in Israel before or after him.

There was, however, another, less politically and nationalistically colored title Jesus seemingly used, the title "Son of Man." This title occurs about eighty times in the Gospels and only four times outside of them. It occurs in all four Gospels, including Q. But it is almost exclusively used in sayings of Jesus and hardly ever by people addressing Jesus. As indirect support for the thesis that Jesus could have used the title, we may note that it was never used in the Jewish apocalyptic literature after Christ. Only 2 Esdras uses the term, and Rabbi Abbahu (ca. 300) says in the Jerusalem Talmud: "If a man says to you: 'I am God,' then he lies; if 'I am the son of man,' he will finally regret it" (*J. Ta'an.* 2:1).[34]

Jesus and the first Christian community certainly did not invent the term "Son of Man." Already in Judaism it has a definite connotation in its apocalyptic context.[35] In later Judaism the main eschatological function of the Son of Man was judging.[36] Jesus, however, expanded and

---

cates the idea that Jesus sympathized with the Zealot movement, whereas the apostles wanted to present a pacifist Christ. For an evaluation of Brandon's ideas, cf. the review of *Jesus and the Zealots* by John T. Townsend in *Journal of Biblical Literature* 89 (June 1970): 246-47. Cf. also Oscar Cullmann, *Jesus and the Revolutionaries*, trans. G. Putnam (New York: Harper & Row, 1970), who states that Jesus' attitude was one of "radical obedience to the will of God, which is anchored in the most intimate communion with God and in the expectation of his kingdom and in his prevailing justice" (vii-viii). This led Jesus on the one hand to an unreserved criticism of the existing order, but on the other hand "also to a rejection of resistance movements, since these divert one's attention from the kingdom of God with their setting of goals, and violate by their use of violence the command of absolute justice and absolute love" (51-52).

34. Hermann L. Strack and Paul Billerbeck, *Kommentar zum Neuen Testament aus Talmud und Midrasch*, vol. 1, *Das Evangelium nach Matthäus* (Munich: Beck, 1922), 486-87. Cf. also Stauffer, *Jesus and His Story*, 163-64.

35. Cf. Hahn, 20.

36. Cf. for the following, Oscar Cullmann, *The Christology of the New Testament*, trans. S. C. Guthrie and Ch. A. M. Hall, rev. ed. (Philadelphia: Westminster, 1963), 157-59.

modified this picture of the Son of Man who is coming to judge all nations. For him this title is not just one of exaltation but of humiliation, and he connects it with the title of the suffering servant. Thus he who judges the world in the name of the Lord also suffers vicariously for it and reconciles it with God. In an almost classic way this is expressed in Mark 10:45 where Jesus says: "For the Son of Man came not to be served but to serve, and to give his life a ransom for many."

With this word we have already touched upon the first group of Son of Man sayings that speak about the Son of Man who is going to die and then will be resurrected. The second group deals with sayings of the Son of Man who has come to judge and to save. The third deals with the Son of Man who has power to forgive sins. All three have eminent eschatological significance but are not colored by popular nationalistic overtones. Jesus is the Son of Man who lives unknown among the people. But at the end of time he will appear openly to judge and to redeem. Though he does not live as the Son of Man in glory, his actions already show who he is. He is the master of the law, he can judge and forgive sins (Mark 2:10, 28), he can condemn and provide salvation. According to the Gospel of John, he even permits someone to fall down before him and adore him (John 9:35-38). This kind of adoration was strictly reserved for God, but Jesus as the Son of Man, the representative of God, is eligible for such cultic devotion.[37] The attitude toward him decides the future of the individual. Thus the present is decisive; it is the time of the Son of Man.

The deepest self-understanding of Jesus, however, cannot be captured in a title. It is a strictly singular phenomenon, namely, that Jesus is the final self-disclosure of God. The final self-disclosure of God and thus the end of all history in anticipation occurred in Jesus.[38] Jesus' confession that he was this direct and final self-disclosure of God led to his conviction as a heretic. But how did he express this self-understanding? We remember that at the trial of Jesus, the high priest concluded from the answer Jesus gave to the question, "Are you the Messiah, the Son of the Blessed One?" (Mark 14:61), that Jesus had committed blasphemy.

37. Cf. Bultmann, *The Gospel of John*, 339 n. 3.

38. Cf. Wolfhart Pannenberg, "Dogmatic Theses on the Doctrine of Revelation," in *Revelation as History*, ed. Wolfhart Pannenberg, trans. D. Granskou (New York: Macmillan, 1968), 134. The reader of this translation of Pannenberg's theses is well advised to check the German original over against the often very "free" translation.

But what is contained in Jesus' answer that would lead to such a devastating reaction? Jesus seemingly recited only Jewish eschatological expectations when he said:

> I am; and
>> "you will see the Son of Man seated at the right hand of the Power," and "coming with the clouds of heaven."
>
> (14:62)

The issue becomes clear when we consider the Old Testament use of the phrase *ego eimi* (I am). In the Septuagint we find this phrase several times, most prominently in Deutero-Isaiah, rendering the Hebrew *ani hu,* meaning "I [am] He," into Greek.[39] In Deutero-Isaiah the phrase *ani hu* is a solemn statement or assertion that is always attributed to Yahweh (cf. Isa. 41:4; 43:10; 46:4). Over against claims made by other gods, this phrase asserts polemically that only Yahweh is the Lord of history. It also seems to be a concise abbreviation of the longer form of divine self-predication, especially of "I am Yahweh." While the *ani hu* formula as divine self-predication of Yahweh occurs outside Deutero-Isaiah only in Deuteronomy 32:39, the self-predication "I am Yahweh" is rather widespread in the Old Testament. As Ethelbert Stauffer has pointed out, there is also some evidence that the *ani hu* was used liturgically in the worship of the Jerusalem temple, since the Levites presumably sang the Song of Moses, containing Deuteronomy 32:39, on the Sabbath of the Feast of Tabernacles.[40] The use of *ani hu* lived on in the worship service of the temple and of the synagogues, and was known even to the Qumran community.[41]

At a few decisive places in the Gospels Jesus uses the term *ego eimi* in a way analogous to the Old Testament theophany formula. For instance, according to Mark 13:6, Jesus says: "Many will come in my name and

---

39. Cf. for the following, the valuable comments by Philip B. Harner, *The "I Am" of the Fourth Gospel: A Study in Johannine Usage and Thought* (Philadelphia: Fortress, 1970), esp. 6-26. The absolute use of the *ego eimi,* i.e., with no object following, should not be confused with the *ego eimi* sayings that necessitate an object (e.g., John 6:35: "I am the bread of life"). For the latter cf. Eduard Schweizer, *Ego eimi: Die religionsgeschichtliche Herkunft und theologische Bedeutung der johanneischen Bildreden, zugleich ein Beitrag zur Quellenfrage des vierten Evangeliums,* 2nd ed. (Göttingen: Vandenhoeck & Ruprecht, 1965).

40. Stauffer, *Jesus and His Story,* 179.

41. So Harner, 23.

say, 'I am he!' and they will lead many astray."[42] In Matthew this theophanic self-predication is expanded into an explicitly christological statement which reads: "saying, 'I am the Messiah!'" (Matt. 24:5).

Returning to the answer that Jesus gave the high priest in Mark 14:62, we must admit that it could be interpreted without reference to the Old Testament revelational formula *ani hu* or to any of its variations. It could simply have been a solemn way of saying "yes," as Matthew, for instance, interprets it in 26:64. Philip B. Harner, for instance, arrives at the notion that "it is not likely that we can understand the *ego eimi* of Mk 14:62 and Lk 14:70 in an absolute sense."[43] This conclusion is surprising, however, considering that the corollary evidence seems to lead in the opposite direction, namely, that the *ego eimi* in Mark 14:62 is indeed used in an absolute sense as a divine self-predication. The matter becomes clearer if we look at the usage of *ego eimi* in other passages in Mark. The phrase appears first in 6:50 at the conclusion of the miracle of Jesus walking on water, where he tells his disciples: "Take heart, it is I; do not be afraid." Here the phrase functions almost in a titular sense and as a revelational formula. In 13:6 Jesus warns his disciples that "Many will come in my name and say, 'I am he!' and they will lead many astray." Again *ego eimi* is used as a formula of revelation or identification, since its misappropriation leads the believer astray.

We may conclude that Jesus' use of the *ego eimi* in Mark 14:62 is

---

42. Cf. Ernst Lohmeyer, *Das Evangelium des Markus* (Göttingen: Vandenhoeck & Ruprecht, 1954), 270-71; and Vincent Taylor, *The Gospel according to St. Mark* (London: Macmillan, 1957), 503-4, who is hesitant to see a theophanic formula contained in this passage.

43. Harner, 34, in his careful analysis of the *ego eimi* formula. Cf. also Ernst Haenchen, *Der Weg Jesu: Eine Erklärung des Markus-Evangeliums und der kanonischen Parallelen* (Berlin: Walter de Gruyter, 1968), 511-12, who, in his discussion with Stauffer, rejects the thesis that this passage dates back to Jesus. According to Haenchen, it simply reflects the expectation of the first Christian community. Since this expectation (the return of Christ before the death of the members of the Sanhedrin) was not fulfilled, the passage was changed in Matthew and Luke. Taylor, *St. Mark*, 568-69, also admits that this passage reflects the apocalyptic hopes of the church, but comes to the conclusion that it is probably actually the reply of Jesus to the challenge of the high priest. Its "emphasis lies on the enthronement, and on the enthronement as the symbol of triumph." For the following cf. the careful study by John Donahue, *Are You the Christ? The Trial Narrative in the Gospel of Mark* (Missoula: Society of Biblical Literature, 1973), 91-93, that arrives at similar conclusions to ours.

more than a simple affirmation. He uses a revelational formula to disclose himself and identify himself with God. As the words following the *ego eimi* show, the messianic secret is lifted and Jesus unashamedly admits his messianic sonship. "In Mk 14:62 therefore Jesus is making an explicit Messianic claim, the Messianic Secret is being formally disclosed."[44] Since the messianic secret was carefully hidden in Mark, we may wonder whether Jesus' response does not reflect the theology of the Evangelist more than Jesus' own words. We might be overestimating the historical value of this passage if we do not concede the possibility that this passage has been carefully edited to reflect the eschatological hopes of the nascent church. But there is another way of determining the historical probability of the *ego eimi* response of Jesus.

As Ernst Fuchs has pointed out, Jesus emphasized, in his proclamation, the will of God in a way that only someone who stood in God's place could.[45] For instance, in his parables Jesus did not simply tell us how God acts, he told us that God acts the way Jesus acts. We see this especially well in the parable of the lost sheep (Luke 15:3-7). Luke tells us that when the Pharisees and scribes remarked, "This fellow welcomes sinners and eats with them" (15:2), Jesus told them parables of God's concern for the lost and sinful, implying that God acts like Jesus. Mark 14:62 indicates that at the end of his career Jesus not only acted as if he stood in God's place, but evidently even told his audience that he stood in God's place and did so by using the revelational formula *ego eimi*. In all likelihood, *ego eimi* was Jesus' own response to the high priest. Since Jesus did not conform to the prevalent messianic expectations but nevertheless made claims that could only be understood in messianic terms, the high priest and most other people at that time concluded that Jesus had committed blasphemy.

Another similarly misunderstood theophanic self-predication occurs in Jesus' reply to the Samaritan woman. When she said to him in the traditional messianic expectation, "'I know that Messiah is coming' (who is called Christ). 'When he comes, he will proclaim all things to us,'" Jesus

44. So rightly states Norman Perrin in his careful study, "The High Priest's Question and Jesus' Answer (Mk 14:61-62)," in *The Passion in Mark: Studies in Mark 14–16,* ed. Werner H. Kelber (Philadelphia: Fortress, 1976), 82.

45. Fuchs, *Studies,* 154-55; cf. also Joachim Jeremias, *New Testament Theology,* vol. 1, *The Proclamation of Jesus,* trans. J. Bowden (London: SCM, 1971), 251-53, who makes the connection between the emphatic use of the word *ego* and Jesus' own conduct.

corrected her by saying, "I am he, the one who is speaking to you" (John 4:25-26). He thereby revealed himself as the full self-disclosure of God. But the woman did not understand him. She was too entangled in the traditional pattern of messianic thinking.

This is the overall impression that Jesus of Nazareth left: he emphasized his presence as the decisive hour, he emphasized himself as the full self-disclosure of God, and he emphasized that with him the kingdom of God had come.[46] Nobody really believed him until Easter. They were all caught up in the traditional thinking that the Messiah and the eschaton were close at hand. They shut their eyes to the present and expected everything in the near future. But what does Jesus' emphasis on the present mean? Is there no future to come? Did everything already happen in the life and death of Jesus of Nazareth?

c. Jesus and the Question of the Future

Jesus rejected any predictions of when the end of the world would occur. About that day nobody knows except God himself (Mark 13:32). Since God has entered this world in Jesus, we cannot postpone preparing for our encounter with God until we assume that this world will soon come to an end. We must always be ready.

Jesus emphasized the thatness of the rule of God. Introducing a time factor or speculating about its full realization would have only diminished the intensity of this emphasis. Yet the time aspect is not completely excluded, since the tension between present and future, meaning the already inaugurated turn of the aeons and the still outstanding

---

46. Of course, the singular character of Jesus can be asserted with other arguments. Rudolf Bultmann, for instance, who disclaims that Jesus' life had any messianic characteristics, asserts that, for Jesus, God became God at hand. This closeness finds its expression when Jesus addressed God simply as "Father" (*Theology*, 1:23). While Bultmann mentions the phrase "Father" only in passing, Joachim Jeremias has recognized the decisive character of this phrase: "His Father has granted him the revelation of himself as completely as only a father can disclose himself to his son. Therefore only Jesus can disclose to others the real knowledge of God" (*New Testament Theology*, 1:61). Though we cannot doubt that the address "Father" in the mouth of Jesus means something special, it emphasizes more the difference between God and Jesus, while the theophany formula *ego eimi* emphasizes more the unity.

full realization, is mirrored in Jesus' correlation between human and divine activity.[47] The full realization of the rule of God, God's kingdom, in the future is the sole prerogative of God. No human activity can accelerate or delay its coming. But Jesus' audience lives in the present, and this means in the time of salvation which is already anticipated. This kind of anticipation makes human activity relevant, since the present is the time of decision. Jesus asks his listeners whether they are willing to venture everything on that kingdom. Therefore Jesus emphasizes the necessity of unconditionally fulfilling God's will, as we see, for instance, in the Sermon on the Mount. While we can neither bring the kingdom about nor make ourselves eligible to enter that kingdom, our decision for or against it has eternal significance, as we can see from the kingdom parables (cf. Matt. 13).

Jesus wanted to prepare his contemporaries for the kingdom. But he neither delineated a chronology of life eternal nor a geography of the beyond. Even the resurrection of the dead was not a central theme of his proclamation, though he believed in it and therefore sided on this issue with the Pharisees and against the Sadducees (cf. Mark 12:18-27).[48] While we hear nothing about a new creation or a new heaven and a new earth, we still can gather that he advocated a "heavenly" concept of salvation which was thought to be even more different from our present condition than suggested by apocalyptic thought.

"Jesus showed little interest in speculating about what humans would find in restored paradisal conditions."[49] It was sufficient that God "is God not of the dead, but of the living" (Mark 12:27). While our present body was of little concern for life eternal, at death the individual would be

---

47. Cf. for the following, Ingrid Maisch, "Die Botschaft Jesu von der Gottesherrschaft," in *Gegenwart und kommendes Reich: Schülergabe Anton Vögtle zum 65. Geburtstag,* ed. Peter Fiedler and Dieter Zeller (Stuttgart: Katholisches Bibelwerk, 1975), 40-41.

48. Cf. for the following, the interesting comments by Jacques Schlosser, "Die Vollendung des Heils in der Sicht Jesu," in *Weltgericht und Weltvollendung: Zukunftsbilder im Neuen Testament,* ed. Hans-Josef Klauck (Freiburg: Herder, 1994), esp. 62, 74, and 83-84.

49. So Colleen McDannell and Bernhard Lang, *Heaven: A History* (New Haven: Yale University Press, 1988), 30. Yet they are too quick when they say: "At death the soul will pass into another world, while the body remains in the grave. No bodily resurrection is mentioned or expected" (28). And: "At death, the individual soul would be judged" (29). Jesus did not just focus on the soul but always on the individual person. Therefore salvation is for the person, not for the soul alone. Analogously he also did not reject the hope for a resurrection of the dead in whatever form and dimension that might take place.

judged and followers of Jesus would be granted eternal life in God's heavenly kingdom. Therefore Jesus was the decisive point in history. He did not comfort the one criminal on the cross with some future expectation, but assured him that today he would be with him in paradise (Luke 23:43). Jesus' person, his proclamation, and his action demanded an immediate decision, and this decision implied an immediate reward. This does not mean that the future will be insignificant. Quite the opposite! Only because of Jesus' presence will our future make any sense.

Jesus and his destiny are, symbolically speaking, the lens through which the rays of all history since the creation of the world are focused and projected into the future.[50] The future is predictable solely because it receives its future-directedness from Jesus Christ. In this way Jesus determined the future. He told his followers not to be worried about the future, because in him and in the attitude toward him the future was already irreversibly decided. Of course, this was contrary to most of the popular messianic hopes and expectations. People expected the total fulfillment of history in the present or in the immediate future. Some even saw in Jesus the political messianic leader who would once and for all redeem Israel from all its enemies. Even some of the disciples confessed after Jesus' death with bitter resignation: "But we had hoped that he was the one to redeem Israel" (Luke 24:21). One might even speculate that the reason Judas betrayed Jesus was so Jesus would then be forced to enter into the decisive battle with the Romans and other oppressors and openly inaugurate the kingdom.

When Jesus was finally resurrected, the question had to be decided again: Should the resurrection be interpreted in the strictly apocalyptic context as the first act of the final eschatological drama, or was it the ultimate event of the proleptic anticipatory history of Jesus? Many seem to have interpreted it as the first act of the eschatological drama, after which the other acts were to follow in rapid succession.[51] The hope that

50. This is especially well captured in the Gospel according to Luke. Cf. Hans Conzelmann, *The Theology of St. Luke*, trans. G. Buswell (Philadelphia: Fortress, 1982), 16-17.

51. Wolfhart Pannenberg, *Jesus — God and Man*, trans. L. L. Wilkins and D. A. Priebe (Philadelphia: Westminster, 1968), 66-67, has characterized this situation very appropriately. However, we wonder if the occurrence of the resurrection was so self-evident for Jesus' Jewish contemporaries that they knew exactly what it meant, even if they shared the common apocalyptic expectation.

the end should come soon is traceable in many places in the New Testament. Most of the books of the New Testament reflect this situation.

3. The Eschatological Proclamation of the Gospel Writers

The Evangelists faced the all-decisive question of how they should respond to the person and destiny of Jesus: (1) Should they interpret his resurrection as the first act of the final eschatological drama and intensify the eschatological fever of the expectation of an end of the world near at hand? Or (2) should they admit that the end did not come as soon as most of them had hoped and concentrate on a biographical report? Or (3) should they try to interpret future history in light of the final self-disclosure of God as it had occurred in and with Jesus of Nazareth? Regardless of their individual emphases and predilections, the Gospel writers seemed to work along one and the same line: in the life, destiny, and resurrection of Jesus there had occurred the final self-disclosure of God.[52] We live in an interim period between this self-disclosure and the universal transformation of the world.

Exegetical research shows more and more clearly that the Gospels differed considerably from each other in interpreting the interim period. The different emphases show that each of the Gospels has a different chronological distance from the life, death, and resurrection of Jesus and therefore faces a different situation. Moreover, the Gospels are confronted with their own particular communities to whom they attempt to convey the eschatological significance of Jesus. Regardless of how much we emphasize the differences in their respective proclamations, we should not overlook that they agree in their central assertions. They were not accepted into the New Testament canon because they disagreed with each other, but because they converged in their central message and complemented each other.

---

52. Cf. thesis 4 in Pannenberg's *Revelation as History*, 139.

a. The Interim in the View of the Synoptics

The synoptic writers sought to counter the apocalyptic fever of the impending end of the world and the resulting disenchantment when the final events did not occur by emphasizing the length of the interim before the final eschaton.[53] Statements that suggest an immediately approaching eschaton are balanced by passages that speak of it in the most distant future. The statement, for example, that "there are some standing here who will not taste death until they see that the kingdom of God has come with power" (Mark 9:1) is countered with the assurance that before Christ will finally return, the gospel must be preached to all nations (Mark 13:10). Or in a similar way, the words "Truly I tell you, this generation will not pass away until all these things have taken place" are immediately followed by the assertion, "heaven and earth will pass away, but my words will not pass away" (Mark 13:30-31; Matt. 24:34-35; cf. Luke 21:32-33). The first part of the verse seems to point clearly to the eschaton at hand, while the next sentence, in pointing to the trustworthiness of Jesus' word, seems to counteract any possible disappointment.[54]

The *Markan account*, as the oldest Gospel, stands closer than the other Gospels to the disturbing situation caused by Jesus' death and resurrection. Mark sees one way of combating all vain hopes in the impending end by asserting that Jesus did not want any outsiders to understand fully the secret of the kingdom of God. Only his disciples, in

---

53. For the view of the synoptics, cf. Hans Conzelmann, "Eschatologie IV. Im Urchristentum," in *Religion in Geschichte und Gegenwart*, 3rd ed. (Tübingen: J. C. B. Mohr [Paul Siebeck], 1957-65), 2:671-72. For a good survey for the different positions in redaction history (the different approaches to the kerygma by the composers of the Gospels), cf. Joachim Rohde, *Rediscovering the Teaching of the Evangelists*, trans. D. M. Barton (London: SCM, 1968).

54. Erich Grässer, *Das Problem der Parusieverzögerung in den synoptischen Evangelien und in der Apostelgeschichte* (Berlin: Töpelmann, 1960), 199-200. However, we wonder if Grässer is right in pointing already to Mark 3:30 and similarly to Mark 9:1 as words of comfort because of the delayed parousia. While most exegetes, Grässer included, admit a gradual weakening of impending eschatology, many do not check whether the idea of the impending eschaton is in continuity or in discontinuity with Jesus' own proclamation. It is interesting that Grässer, for instance, does not reach his conclusion that Jesus' expectation of the imminent eschaton was his only eschatological hope after a careful exegesis of pertinent New Testament passages, but after a review of positions that differ from his own view (16).

coming from the Easter event, have the privilege of understanding completely the life, destiny, and proclamation of Jesus (Mark 4:11-12).[55] Before Easter, even the disciples could not really understand him (6:52; 9:32). Because of the Easter experience, the interim period is no longer a time of frustrated waiting, but of intense activity. The period between the resurrection of Jesus Christ and his final coming is the time of world mission. However, unlike Matthew and Luke, Mark does not yet reflect on the activities of the exalted Christ during this time, and he mentions the emerging church only implicitly in connection with the task of world mission.

Mark imparts to his community hope in the world to come, eternal life, and the kingdom. The word sowed by the Evangelist falls on various kinds of soil. Yet at one point, perhaps during this generation, Christ will return and all will see the Son of Man. Those who had their eyes opened by the Son will be gathered by him, whereas the others will remain in the distance. For the elect there will be rich compensation for the calamities to which they had been exposed.[56] Yet he also tells his readers that the decision concerning salvation or doom is already occurring in the present, because those who have found their way to Jesus must now live out the consequences of their faith and follow the right path. There is only hope for the future if one is now faithful to Jesus and his word. This hope enables his followers to remain alert and faithful.

When we look at the approach of the Gospel of *Matthew*, we see a much more elaborate and clarified understanding of the interim period. This Gospel wants to show that the Old Testament promises have found their fulfillment in Jesus.[57] He did not come to abolish the law and the prophets, but to fulfill them (Matt. 5:17-18). He fulfilled the Immanuel promise (Isa. 7:14; Matt. 1:22-23), the Galilee promise (Isa. 9:1; Matt. 4:12-15), the Bethlehem promise (Mic. 5:2; Matt. 2:5-6), the servant of the Lord promise (Isa. 53:4; Matt. 8:17), and many others. Consequently

---

55. Cf. for the following, Conzelmann, *An Outline*, 141-42. Conzelmann also advances an interesting interpretation of the "parable theory" (Mark 4:10-12). He claims that it means that Jesus' work can be understood only from after Easter, i.e., through faith (139). Though there is certainly some validity in this statement, we wonder if this explains the "parable theory" sufficiently.

56. Johannes M. Nützel, "Hoffnung und Treue: Zur Eschatologie des Markusevangeliums," in *Gegenwart und kommendes Reich*, 90.

57. Cf. for the following, Conzelmann, *An Outline*, 145-46.

a multitude of Old Testament eschatological titles are bestowed upon him. He is the Messiah, the Son of David, the King of Israel, the Son of God, and the Son of Man, to name just a few. This is to show not so much that Jesus is the bringer of the eschaton, but that he stands in true continuity with the Old Testament.

This continuity is crucial for the interpretation of the interim period, since the church that Jesus founded is the true Israel because of his authority (Matt. 16:18). The historical nation of Israel has neglected and lost its commission to be the light to the nations. Thus the church replaces it and steps into continuity with the Israel of promise. Though there are specific orders and structures in the church (18:15-17), the church is not here to stay. It is only an interim community. It is also far from being a pure community of true believers. Not until the final judgment will the just be separated from the unjust (chap. 13). Yet the church is already on its way toward this final judgment when Christ will appear and select the chosen ones. The theme of the coming judgment is consistent throughout the Gospel. The Sermon on the Mount (chaps. 5–7), the sending out of the Twelve (chap. 10), and the apocalypse (chap. 24) all indicate the judgment as *the* coming event. Yet the emphasis is not on judgment. The Gospel of Matthew "concludes with the command for mission and not for drawing lines between believers and unbelievers. It is convinced that Jesus is the Messiah, the gateway to the kingdom, and also its inaugurator."[58]

Since Jesus is the promised one, the present age is the time of fulfillment. While this age commences with the birth of Jesus and concludes with his parousia as the Son of Man, there are two distinct periods denoted respectively by "the kingdom of heaven which is at hand" and the "gospel of the kingdom." Correspondingly, there is the ministry to Israel carried out by John the Baptist (3:1-2), Jesus (4:16), and the pre-Easter disciples (10:16). Then there is the ministry to the nations through the post-Easter disciples or the church (24:14-31 and 26:13). Yet these ministries are carried out under the commission of Jesus (10:5; 28:18-20; John the Baptist is also clearly designated as forerunner to Jesus). Consequently the time of Israel found its fulfillment in the time of Jesus. God has visited his people, gathered them, and made known to them his

---

58. Hans Schwarz, "The Significance of Matthew's Eschatology for Systematic Theology," in *1996 Seminar Papers*, ed. Society of Biblical Literature (Atlanta: Scholars Press, 1996), 186.

will. Now the church is the representative of the ethical demands, that is, of the conduct that corresponds to God's righteousness (6:33).[59] By proclaiming the ethical demands, the church preserves "the continuity between the then of the time of Jesus and the present up to the final goal of history which will occur in a near or a more distant future; it [the church] shows the individual Christians in times which are changing the way toward righteousness."[60]

Luke finally moved beyond the notion of a strict interim period by introducing a salvation-historical understanding of history. Already in the opening chapters of his Gospel, he placed Jesus in the context of world history (Luke 2:1-4 and 1:5-6). But the Evangelist does not want to convey the idea that the life and destiny of Jesus are subject to the course of history. Jesus is the focal point of history through whom all history receives its significance and proper valuation. Luke distinguishes three main epochs of history: (1) the time of Israel; (2) the time of Jesus as the center of history; and (3) the time of the church. John the Baptist is depicted as the last of the prophets and not as the forerunner of Jesus (16:16), since Jesus is without forerunner and without precedent.[61] The whole epoch of the law and the prophets leads up to Jesus and then, all of a sudden, Jesus appears as the center of time.

Luke does not seem to encounter the issue of impending eschatology, nor is he bothered with any other exuberant eschatological expectations. "When you hear of wars and insurrections, do not be terrified; for these things must take place first, but the end will not follow immediately" (21:9) seems to be his dominant theme. The decisive event has happened. Jesus has come, and some day he will usher in the final end of all history and judge the living and the dead. "But this end will not bring anything new with respect to salvation."[62] In analogy to his ascension,

---

59. Cf. Peter Fiedler, "Der Sohn Gottes über unserem Weg in die Gottesherrschaft," in *Gegenwart und kommendes Reich*, 97, to this passage, who speaks in this context about the transformation of the kingdom proclamation into an ethical program.

60. Georg Strecker, "Das Geschichtsverständnis des Matthäus" (1966), in Georg Strecker, *Eschaton und Historie: Aufsätze* (Göttingen: Vandenhoeck & Ruprecht, 1979), 106.

61. So Conzelmann, *Theology of St. Luke*, 101.

62. Ulrich Wilkens, "The Understanding of Revelation within the History of Primitive Christianity," in Pannenberg, *Revelation as History*, 97, in his review of the understanding of revelation in Luke.

Christ will only return as the exalted Lord. "The actual center of Lukan theology is neither eschatology nor salvation history, but christology. Luke announces Christ as the one who has come, as the one who will come, and as the one exalted in heaven who can be experienced in the activity of the church and in the Spirit during the present interim."[63] This means that for Luke eschatology becomes an essential and central aspect of Christology.

The Lukan view of history and of the future is not one of resignation or pessimism. God has provided the interim as the time of the church. Since the gospel is spread to ever new shores and Christians are given God's Holy Spirit, it is of no interest how long the church will last and when the end will come. In viewing the life and destiny of Jesus, we realize that he has announced the end times and the coming of his kingdom. The truth of what he stood for and the truth of his proclamation are guaranteed "by his miracles, his resurrection and ascension and the sending of the spirit."[64] Christians are not alone in the world. The exalted Christ in heaven is active in his word which is proclaimed in history. His people work in "his name" and in "his spirit." Christians live in this world without fear and without wild expectations, but with hope. The main concern of Luke, both in his Gospel and in the Acts of the Apostles, is to incorporate the Christian existence into the world, yet to keep it open for the final end of all history. To assure a meaningful Christian existence in the present, Luke maintains a future completion of salvation in the parousia.[65] While he never affirms an imminent return of Christ, he also does not say that the time of the church will last very long or almost indefinitely. Seen from his vantage point, he even seems to have expected the parousia in the near future.

63. Josef Ernst, *Herr der Geschichte: Perspektiven der lukanischen Eschatologie* (Stuttgart: Katholisches Bibelwerk, 1972), 112.

64. Conzelmann, *An Outline*, 150-51. It should be evident by our references to Conzelmann that he provides by far the most enlightening view of eschatology during the decisive period of the formation of the synoptic Gospels.

65. Cf. for the following, Hans-Joachim Michel, "Heilsgegenwart und Zukunft bei Lukas," in *Gegenwart und kommendes Reich*, 112. Ruthild Geiger, *Die Lukanischen Endzeitreden: Studien zur Eschatologie des Lukas-Evangeliums*, 2nd ed. (Frankfurt am Main: Peter Lang, 1976), 266-67, also shows that Luke did not eliminate the imminent expectation of the end but that it is of less urgency for him, considering the different situation of his time.

b. The Emphasis on the Present in the Gospel of John

For Martin Luther (1483-1546) the Gospel of John was the main Gospel, because it proclaimed Christ so clearly. In recent times, however, this Gospel has become more and more "the puzzle of the NT, both historically and literally, in theology and in the history of religion."[66] This is also true for its eschatological outlook. It replaces the eschatological terms of the synoptics with its own terminology. The standard synoptic term "the kingdom of God" is only used twice in John, and the term "this aeon" is replaced by "this cosmos," "the future aeon" by "the eternal life," and "the end of the aeon" by "in the last day," to list just a few changes. It is also the only Gospel that talks about the "ruler of this cosmos," and it has no specific apocalyptic passages in contrast to the synoptic Gospels (Mark 13; Matt. 24; Luke 17 and 21).

In the Gospel of John, Jesus talks about "my Father's house" instead of about "heaven" (John 14:2), and he says he "will come again" (14:3), a phrase not used in the synoptic Gospels. On the other hand, he assures those who believe in the One who sent him that they already have eternal life (5:24). They will not come into judgment, but have passed from death to life. When Martha says about her dead brother, "I know that he will rise again in the resurrection on the last day," Jesus replies in a similar way, "I am the resurrection and the life. Those who believe in me, even though they die, will live, and everyone who lives and believes in me will never die" (11:24-26). Does this mean that the now is so decisive as to devaluate the future? Or do we already have eternal life now and nothing else is to come?

It would be a serious misunderstanding to assume that John eliminated all future eschatology and concentrated strictly on the present as the time of salvation.[67] It is true that according to John, salvation is a

---

66. Ethelbert Stauffer, *New Testament Theology*, trans. J. Marsh (New York: Macmillan, 1959), 39.

67. We should note here that research into the Johannine literature and into the Gospel of John is very tricky and by no means uncontested. Some scholars distinguish three layers: (1) In the oldest one Jesus was simply claimed to be the Messiah with the full and final realization of salvation occurring in the future when Jesus will return as the Son of Man (cf. Georg Richter, "Präsentische und futurische Eschatologie im 4. Evangelium," in *Gegenwart und kommendes Reich*, 136). (2) For the second layer, that of the Evangelist, all that which in the first layer was expected in the future is already occur-

present reality for the believer.[68] While this presence of salvation has to be continually actualized, it is presupposed that there is a dimension of salvation after death in the life to come.[69] But the true future is actualized.[70] John wants to demonstrate that in Jesus Christ the exclusive opposition between God and the world is bridged. Jesus is the incarnate Word of God (1:14). One can see, by the authority Jesus claims and through the actions he performs, that God himself speaks and acts in and through him (14:9-11). In Jesus the opposition between the present life and the life beyond is bridged. Therefore the opposition between life and death, between time and eternity, and between present, past, and future is only a relative one.[71] Even the law of gravity is suspended when confronted with Jesus Christ (6:19). Because of the coming of the divine into the sphere of the created, the boundaries of this world have only relative, but not irrelevant, character. The main task is accomplished; the ruler of this world is already judged (16:11).

While in Jesus Christ the opposition between this life and the future one is bridged, for the believer a new dichotomy emerges. Jesus was not

---

ring in the here and now (136). (3) An anti-Docetic redactor then amended and corrected the present-oriented eschatology of the Evangelist by also announcing a future-apocalyptic eschatology, including the parousia of Christ (cf. 144). If such changes, from a future orientation to the present and then again to the future, took place, we must accept the final result. Perhaps the church realized that in the long run one cannot do without a future-directed eschatology, either because such an approach is true to the life and destiny of Jesus, or humanity cannot live without such orientation, or even because of both. Cf. here also the convincing argument of Wolfhart Pannenberg, "Redemptive Event and History" (1969), in *Basic Questions in Theology: Collected Essays*, trans. G. H. Kehm (Philadelphia: Fortress, 1970), 1:25.

68. Cf. C. H. Dodd, *The Interpretation of the Fourth Gospel* (Cambridge: Cambridge University Press, 1958), 147-48, who rightly mentions that the miracle of Lazarus's bodily resurrection anticipates the final resurrection.

69. So correctly Günter Klein, "Eschatologie IV," in *TRE*, 10:289, who refutes an enthusiastic elimination of the future as well as a narrowing down of the future to an "innerworldly future."

70. Cf. Conzelmann, *An Outline*, 356, who opposes here Bultmann's rather one-sided interpretation of a "present eschatology." Cf. also L. van Hartingsveld, *Die Eschatologie des Johannes-Evangeliums: Eine Auseinandersetzung mit Rudolf Bultmann* (Assen: Van Gorcum, 1962).

71. So Ethelbert Stauffer, "Agnostos Christos: Joh. XI.24 und die Eschatologie des vierten Evangeliums," in *The Background of the New Testament and Its Eschatology*, ed. W. D. Davies and D. Daube (Cambridge: Cambridge University Press, 1956), 299.

the Messiah everybody expected. "He came to what was his own, and his own people did not accept him" (1:11).[72] The Gospel of John is the Gospel of great misunderstandings. In fascinating style the Gospel writer managed to point out that unbelievers are confronted with Jesus like a color-blind person is confronted with traffic lights. One may know everything about it, but in the decisive moment one cannot grasp the exact meaning. Unbelievers constantly misunderstand Jesus. They exclude themselves from participation in the real future, because only believers can discern that Jesus opens up the real future for us. Believers have the promise of the Comforter, or the Holy Spirit (14:16-17, 25-26; 16:4b-11, 12-15), whom Jesus Christ will send to guide them into all truth. The Comforter bridges the gulf between the historical Jesus who is no longer among them and the proclamation of the gospel. He legitimizes the existence of the believers as a waiting existence, an existence of participation in a salvation which has been brought about through Jesus but is not commonly accessible.

The eschatological aspect of the Gospel of John shows less missionary character than that of the synoptics.[73] This is not surprising because by now the Jews had evicted the Christians from the synagogues (16:2). Thus the liberating and encouraging power of Jesus' coming gains renewed significance. The Gospel of John encourages a faithful eschatological existence of proleptic fulfillment and yet of expectation. "But these are written so that you may come to believe that Jesus is the Messiah, the Son of God, and that through believing you may have life in his name" (20:31). This characterizes the intention of the Gospel: to give witness to the eschatological significance of Jesus, and to bridge the gulf between Jesus' redemptive act and his second coming. Though the Gospel of John does not proclaim a dynamic message that incites one to action, but rather a comforting message that invites one to contemplation, its basic description of the Christian existence is very close to that of Paul.

---

72. Dodd, *Fourth Gospel*, 228-29, suggests that, unlike any other New Testament writer, the writer of the Fourth Gospel is fully aware of the Jewish ideas associated with the title "Messiah" but puts Jesus' messiahship, in part, in clear opposition to such ideas.

73. Cf. Conzelmann, *An Outline*, 332. It may be an overstatement to say with Conzelmann that the Gospel of John has no missionary character. When Bultmann, *The Gospel of John*, 698, mentions that the Gospel wants to "awaken the faith that Jesus is the Messiah, the Son of God," he seems to be closer to the truth.

4. The Eschatological Message of Paul

It is not for chronological reasons that we introduce Paul as the last important representative of New Testament eschatology. Paul's writings are the earliest we have in the New Testament. Thus he should be listed first. But of the writers mentioned so far, he is the only one who was not a disciple or follower of Jesus during Jesus' life on earth. Once a persecutor of the early Christian community, he became one of its most fervent advocates. He became a Christian late, as he himself admits (1 Cor. 15:8). Though it is safe to assume that he had some knowledge of Jesus and the Christian faith before he was converted, his knowledge was not extensive.[74] Soon after his conversion, however, he became one of the most influential Christians, and in considering his eschatological outlook we will notice that he probably comes closest to the eschatological message of Jesus of Nazareth. He also understood best how to incorporate the life, destiny, and resurrection of Jesus Christ into his eschatological picture. As Paul represents, so to speak, the most influential and the most developed eschatology within the New Testament, it is proper to present him at the conclusion of our survey of the New Testament.

a. Paul's Eschatological Call

The key to understanding Paul's eschatological message is his call. When Paul introduces himself to the Roman congregation, he says: "Paul, a servant of Jesus Christ, called to be an apostle, set apart for the gospel of God, which he promised beforehand through his prophets in the holy scriptures, the gospel concerning his Son, who was descended from David according to the flesh and was declared to be Son of God with power according to the spirit of holiness by resurrection from the dead, Jesus Christ our Lord, through whom we have received grace and apostleship to bring about the obedience of faith among all the Gentiles for the sake of his name, including yourselves who are called to belong to Jesus Christ" (Rom. 1:1-6). Paul does not introduce himself as a freelance, self-made missionary, but as one called to serve as an apostle. "He

---

74. Bultmann, "The Significance of the Historical Jesus for the Theology of Paul" (1929), in *Faith and Understanding*, 1:221-22; and Conzelmann, *An Outline*, 163.

is a man who has been appointed to a proper place and a peculiar task in the series of events to be accomplished in the final days of this world."[75] Those events have as their central figure the Messiah, Christ Jesus, crucified, risen, and returning to judgment and salvation. It is important for Paul that Jesus Christ is the fulfillment of the Old Testament prophecies and that he lived here on earth as a descendant of David.[76] This establishes the continuity between Paul's proclamation and the Old Testament faith. Similar to the Old Testament and Judaism, Paul emphasizes the end of the world and of humanity as a future event. Therefore he uses familiar terms such as "end," "day," and "revelation" to indicate that God will finally disclose "his eternal power and divine nature" (cf. Rom. 1:20).[77] On the other hand, it is also important that through his resurrection Jesus of Nazareth was exalted as our Lord Jesus Christ and designated Son of God. This establishes and emphasizes the continuity between the Old Testament promises and the resurrection of Jesus Christ. According to Old Testament expectations and promises, the series of final events had started with Jesus' coming and his death and resurrection.

Through his death and resurrection as the Messiah, Jesus had taken his place at the right hand of his Father in heaven. "What remained was *his parousia* and the coming of the Kingdom of Heaven in power and glory."[78] The ethnic particularity of salvation had become obsolete since Jesus, formerly the Messiah of the Jews, had been enthroned as Lord and Savior of the whole world. Our Savior is at the same time the Lord of the universe (Phil. 2:9-11): all humankind and all cosmic powers, the entire universe, belong to him. Through Christ's enthronement all people have access through faith to his kingdom and to salvation. This fact constitutes the gospel for the non-Jewish people. Paul was chosen to proclaim this gospel in the interim between the resurrection of Jesus Christ and his coming in power. The conviction that the gospel must be spread so that people can accept Christ and be saved gave Paul

---

75. Anton Fridrichsen, in his short but excellent study *The Apostle and His Message* — *Uppsala Universitets Årsskrift* (Uppsala: Lundequistska Bokhandeln, 1947), 3.

76. Cf. for the following, also C. H. Dodd, *The Epistle of Paul to the Romans* (New York: Harper, 1932), 4-5.

77. Cf. Franzjosef Froitzheim, *Christologie und Eschatologie bei Paulus* (Würzburg: Echter, 1979), 257.

78. Fridrichsen, 4.

the drive to proclaim it in an unknown and pagan environment. Paul did not want to deprive them of their choice just because he had not fully responded to his call in the eschatological time.

But Paul was no apocalyptist. The apocalyptic fulfillment was imminent, yet Paul realized that there is a tension between fulfillment and expectation. "Since Paul already lives consciously in the endtime, there is no theory about the coming messianic kingdom. The Messiah is Jesus who has died and has been resurrected. Christians live in the endtime."[79] What is still missing is the transformation of the world and the resurrection which is also understood as a transformation. In the parousia of Christ, the eschatological event of his death and resurrection comes to its conclusion: Christ becomes the final judgment and salvation of the world. Since apocalyptic ideas are not constitutive for Paul's eschatology, his missionary enterprise, though urgent, can be more relaxed and he can establish centers of mission which he most likely would have never done if the end was just around the corner.[80]

b. Our Life as a Life between the Aeons

Paul also sees the Christian life as a life between the aeons. He was convinced that we live in the final era.[81] The old aeon has passed away and the Messiah has come. But the new aeon is not fully here, because the Messiah has not yet returned in power. This "not yet" is no reason for bewilderment. The events of the final era will occur successively according to the preordained plan of God and will lead up to the definite goal, the destruction of the old world and the creation of the new and eternal aeon. The decisive events in this apocalyptic picture are the resurrection of the dead, which was made possible and initiated by Christ's resurrection (1 Cor. 15), and the surprising coming of the Day of the Lord (1 Thess. 5:2).

79. So Wolfgang Beilner, "Weltgericht und Weltvollendung bei Paulus," in *Weltgericht und Weltvollendung*, 103.

80. Cf. Klein, 280, who makes the connection between Paul's establishment of centers for mission and his practical disinterest in apocalyptic ideas.

81. Martin Dibelius, *Paul,* edited and completed by W. G. Kümmel, trans. F. Clarke (Philadelphia: Westminster, 1953), 62, emphasizes that for Paul "the whole life was regarded from the point of view of the end: this life was only an intermediate state."

Christ is the end of the law (Rom. 10:4) and the end of history. The old covenant no longer applies to us since a new covenant has been established (2 Cor. 3:6). But we still live in a transitional period, in a time of faith (2 Cor. 5:7) and of waiting (Rom. 8:23-25). This does not mean that the coming eschaton is totally beyond our consciousness. Our interim existence is determined by the future, because salvation is already active in us. We participate in the gifts of grace — in faith, love, and hope (1 Cor. 13). We are not like those who have no hope. We have died with Christ in our baptism, and we live in Christ and Christ lives in us (Gal. 2:20). This means that the Christian existence is a dialectical existence. It is lived in the world, but not from this world.[82] The power of existence is given to us from beyond, the beyond which will come to us in the eschaton.

The future was certainly important for Paul and cannot be eliminated from his expectations.[83] Though Paul actualized the future by saying that we already live with Christ, he was looking forward to being resurrected with him and living with him in a manifest way (2 Cor. 4:14; 1 Thess. 4:14). This expectation is both being actualized in the present and still to be fulfilled in the future. The final eschatological events and the fulfillment of our eschatological existence lie in the future. In spite of his emphasis on the dialectical character of existence between actualization in anticipation and the still outstanding fulfillment, he occasionally succumbed to the eschatological fever of impending eschatology. For instance, he was convinced that since his conversion the coming of the eschaton had already made progress (Rom. 13:11); he was sure that the Lord was close at hand (Phil. 4:5); and he assured the people in Thessalonica that the Lord would return in his lifetime (1 Thess. 4:15).

But suggesting an imminently impending apocalyptic cataclysm was peripheral to his faith. In this way Paul shared with all theologies their temporality. His context was that of the apocalyptic, a context

---

82. Cf. Bultmann, *Theology,* 1:308, where he explains this dialectic in pointing to the situation of the church. On the one hand the church belongs to the new aeon and is no longer a phenomenon of this world, but on the other hand it manifests itself in individual congregations which exist in this world.

83. Cf. the excellent exposition by Conzelmann, *An Outline,* 184-86. Bultmann, *Theology,* 1:306-7, emphasizes that such a cosmic "drama can only be the completion and confirmation of the eschatological occurrence that has already now begun."

from which he could not extricate himself.[84] But his hope was not bound to a fixed date, only to falter with the resulting delay. It was grounded in the gospel that pronounced the fulfillment of the Old Testament promises and asked at the same time for a faithful existence. Moreover, Paul knew that salvation is realized in us today in a paradoxical way (2 Cor. 4:7-12). While Jesus emphasized the present as the time of decision, Paul emphasized the present as the time of faithful and active waiting to enter into the fulfillment of the new creation. Paul included the Christ event in the kerygma and proclaimed it in a "Christian" time. For him the decisive turning point of history was already past.[85]

c. Eschatology beyond Spiritualism and Disappointment

Paul, the most influential writer of the New Testament, saved Christian eschatology from two blind alleys: unhistorical spiritualism and over-anxious disappointment.[86] Especially in his firm discussions with a gnostic group in Corinth, he emphasized the proleptic and preliminary eschatological character of Christian existence. The interim is not yet the time of fulfillment. The eschaton is still to come, and a faithful existence is the only way to be prepared for it. The interim is the time of the proclamation of the gospel and the time where we can and shall realize the (ethical) teachings of Christ. In our new allegiance to Christ, we enjoy an existence of freedom from the law but without libertinism.

84. Cf. Hans-Heinrich Schade, *Apokalyptische Christologie bei Paulus: Studien zum Zusammenhang von Christologie und Eschatologie in den Paulusbriefen* (Göttingen: Vandenhoeck & Ruprecht, 1981), 214, who emphasizes that Pauline theology shares the destiny of all theology: it is not free from elements of time-bound worldviews.

85. Cf. Günther Bornkamm, *Paul,* trans. D. M. G. Stalker (Minneapolis: Fortress, 1995), 232-34, in his discussion with Ernst Bloch, who depicts Jesus as the rebel and arch-heretic while claiming that Paul brought Jesus' gospel of the kingdom to nothing and robbed it of its power. Bornkamm, however, affirms rightly that "to a greater extent than any of his predecessors or successors" in the early church, Paul thought out and developed the implications of the change "brought about by Jesus' death on the cross and the presence in the Spirit of the living Lord" (236).

86. Cf. Conzelmann, *An Outline,* 185. Ulrich Luz, *Das Geschichtsverständnis des Paulus* (Munich: Chr. Kaiser, 1968), 396, claims that Paul used future eschatological assertions primarily in his proclamation to those in temptation, but usually did not use them directly to combat enthusiastic anticipation of the future. We wonder if such a distinction is possible. The arguments cited by Luz are not very convincing.

95

But Paul did not condone a body/soul dichotomy similar to Hellenism or gnostic ideas. The body is not inferior to the soul. It is not the prison of the soul, and salvation does not mean the release of the soul at death from the body and the return to God as its origin. Salvation pertains to the whole human being, and without Christ, humanity, in its totality, is a victim of sin and death. Salvation is not achieved in this life, but only through the resurrection from death when the whole human being will be renewed and the earthly body will be changed into a heavenly nonspiritual body. Therefore the disregard for this body by some people in Corinth is immediately countered with a reference to the resurrection (cf. 1 Cor. 6:12-20). Any continuation of the Christian believer after death is not simply an extension or continuation of our earthly way of existence. Resurrection from the dead does not mean that one obtains one's former earthly body again. We will enjoy a totally transformed body in the resurrection. Therefore "the completion of salvation for Paul is in the future."[87] Then community with Christ in faith, which already shapes this earthly life of the faithful, will find its fulfillment and cannot be destroyed by death.

While Paul rejects the utopian and enthusiastic idea that a completion of salvation is realized already in the present, he resonates with those Christians who are "longing to be clothed with our heavenly dwelling" (2 Cor. 5:2). Paul therefore emphasizes to those who are disappointed because the eschaton has not yet arrived that the eschatological fulfillment will not tarry. It is a future event affecting us, our earth, and the whole creation. Christ's resurrection was the first part of it, and, since we know that the resurrection of the dead is part of eschatological events, the end cannot wait indefinitely.[88] Jesus' resurrection has validated for us the apocalyptic idea of the resurrection of the dead. Christ anticipates the resurrection of the dead through his own resurrection, thus providing us with a foundation for hope.

87. Cf. Heinrich Zimmermann, "Tod und Auferstehung im neutestamentlichen Frühchristentum," in *Tod und Jenseits im Glauben der Völker,* ed. Hans-Joachim Klimkeit (Wiesbaden: Otto Harrassowitz, 1978), 94-95, who very convincingly shows the difference between Greek-Hellenistic thought and Paul's understanding of salvation as far as it pertains to body and soul.

88. Cf. Pannenberg, *Jesus — God and Man,* 106-8, in his enlightening treatment of the "delay of the parousia and the meaning of Jesus' resurrection."

5. The Eschatological Scope of the Early Church

The modernistic Roman Catholic theologian Alfred Loisy (1857-1940) once wrote: "Jesus foretold the kingdom, and it was the Church that came."[89] Like many of Loisy's opponents had done, one could interpret his statement to mean that there was a contradiction between the message of Jesus and the goal of the church. Yet this was not Loisy's intention, nor can we discern a drastic reorientation once the New Testament epoch concluded. This becomes immediately evident with the Revelation of John, one of the last writings in the New Testament.

In typical apocalyptic fashion Revelation addresses the issue of who will finally rule the world. The answer we glean from the assertion of the angel in 11:15 leaves no doubt:

> The kingdom of the world has become the kingdom of our Lord
> and of his Messiah,
> and he will reign forever and ever.

Yet at the same time that this cosmic rule of God and of the Messiah is announced, one is told that one-third of the cosmos has already been destroyed, that God's rule has started, and that the partial realization of this rule and the hope for its completion are joined together. While we can say that God's rule over the cosmos is *the* eschatological theme of the book of Revelation, it also includes the judgment over the world.[90] The place of God's rule is "a new heaven and a new earth" (21:1), and its center will be "the holy city Jerusalem coming down out of heaven from God" (21:10). Then again,

> the home of God is among mortals.
> He will dwell with them;
> they will be his peoples,
> and God himself will be with them.
>
> (21:3)

89. Alfred Loisy, *The Gospel and the Church*, trans. Christopher Home, ed. Bernard B. Scott (Philadelphia: Fortress, 1976 [1903]), 166, and the caution made by Peter Neuner, "Loisy, Alfred," in *TRE*, 21:454, concerning that statement by Loisy.

90. So rightly Franz Mußner, "'Weltherrschaft' als eschatologisches Thema der Johannesapokalypse," in *Glaube und Eschatologie*, ed. Erich Gräßer and Otto Merck (Tübingen: J. C. B. Mohr, 1985), 225.

The goal of the eschatological rule of the cosmos is not judgment but the communion of God with his people. Therefore we do not hear about the last judgment of both the faithful and the ungodly.[91] Even the cosmos seen by itself is of secondary interest. The only important thing is that God will overcome the resistance of all ungodly people and powers. This salvational confidence that God will be victorious over everybody and everything gave the Christian community the strength to survive as a small and quite often persecuted group.

The continuation of a millenarian hope based on 20:1-10 also served as an impetus to lift up and spread the Christian faith amid an often hostile environment.[92] Papias, a Christian of the third generation, is the first one we know who advocated millennial ideas. "Through unwritten tradition" he received "certain strange parables and teachings of the Savior, and some other more mythical things. To these belong his statement that there will be a period of some thousand years after the resurrection of the dead, and that the kingdom of Christ will be set up in material form on this very earth."[93] The church historian Eusebius (ca. 260–339/40) writes about this disapprovingly: "I suppose he got these ideas through a misunderstanding of the apostolic accounts, not perceiving that the things said by them were spoken mystically in figures. . . . But it was due to him that so many of the Church Fathers after him adopted a like opinion, urging in their own support the antiquity of the man; as for instance Irenaeus and any one else that may have proclaimed similar views."[94] Indeed, in his book *Against Heresies,* Irenaeus (ca. 130–ca. 200) refers to the Apocalypse of John and passages from Isaiah talking about the "times of the kingdom" and the "resurrection of the just, which takes place after the coming of the Antichrist, and the

---

91. Cf. for the following, Jürgen Roloff, "Weltgericht und Weltvollendung in der Offenbarung des Johannes," in *Weltgericht und Weltvollendung: Festschrift für Werner-Georg Kümmel zum 80. Geburtstag,* ed. Hans-Josef Klauck (Tübingen: Mohr [Paul Siebeck], 1985), 126, who points out that in contrast to other early Christian literature, we do not read anything in Revelation about a twofold judgment: "In particular, the function of the Christ of the parousia as judge over those who belong to him is missing."

92. Cf. Jaroslav Pelikan, *The Christian Tradition: A History of the Development of Doctrine,* vol. 1, *The Emergence of the Catholic Tradition (100-600)* (Chicago: University of Chicago Press, 1971), 124-25, who traces the transformation of this apocalyptic vision.

93. Eusebius, *History of the Church* 3.39.11-12, in *NPNF* SS, 1:172.

94. Eusebius, *History of the Church* 3.39.12-13, in *NPNF* SS, 1:172.

destruction of all nations under his rule." Then "the righteous shall reign in the earth."[95] "After the times of the kingdom," a new Jerusalem will descend upon a new earth.

The *Epistle of Barnabas,* which was written around 80-100, shows that the notion of a millennium actually originated from the Jewish interpretation of creation. Since God finished his creation in six days, Barnabas concludes that "this implies that the Lord will finish all things in six thousand years, for a day is with him a thousand years. And he himself testifies saying, 'behold, today will be as a thousand years.' Therefore, my children, in six days, that is, in six thousand years, all things will be finished. 'And He rested on the seventh day.' This means: When His Son, coming [again], shall destroy the time of the wicked man, and judge the ungodly, and change the sun, and the moon, and the stars, then shall He truly rest on the seventh day."[96] In this passage Barnabas concludes that six thousand years after the creation of the world, according to Jewish counting, the millennium will commence.

Since millennial ideas were so widespread in the early church, it is no surprise that they were neither a mark of orthodoxy nor of heterodoxy, meaning of heresy. Justin Martyr (ca. 100–ca. 165) explained to Trypho, a Jew who asked him whether he believed in a millennial rule of Christ: "I and many others are of this opinion, and [believe] that such will take place, as you assuredly are aware; but, on the other hand, I signified to you that many who belong to the pure and pious faith, and are true Christians, think otherwise."[97] Thus, the notion of a millennium arising as the end was ushered in was one permissible opinion among others.

Millenarian ideas received added impetus in a different way when Emperor Constantine officially sanctioned the Christian faith in 325. Though Eusebius was critical of the book of Revelation, he greeted nevertheless the Constantinian era as an eschatological time of salvation and peace. The reign of God was no longer outstanding but a present reality. Citing Psalm 46:8-9:

Come, behold the works of the LORD;
    see what desolations he has brought on the earth.
He makes wars cease to the end of the earth;

95. Irenaeus, *Against Heresies* 5.35.1-2, in *ANF,* 1:565-66.
96. *Barnabas* 15, in *ANF,* 1:146.
97. Justin Martyr, *Dialogue with Trypho* 80, in *ANF,* 1:239.

> he breaks the bow, and shatters the spear;
> he burns the shields with fire,

Eusebius rejoices "in these things which have been clearly fulfilled in our day."[98] Then he narrates: "The whole race of God's enemies was destroyed in the manner indicated, and was thus suddenly swept from the sight of men. So that again a divine utterance had its fulfillment: 'I have seen the wicked oppressing, and towering like a cedar of Lebanon. Again I passed by, and they were no more; though I sought them, they could not be found' (Ps 37:35f.). And finally a bright and splendid day, overshadowed by no cloud, illuminated with beams of heavenly light the churches of Christ throughout the entire world." World history, the history of the church, and the life of the faithful were seen as converging to one point, the manifestation of the reign of God over the whole world through the emperor. Yet the Arian controversies soon arose. The true Godhead of Christ and therefore a unilateral unfolding of the kingdom on earth was deemed unrealistic, as Eusebius himself realized.

Perhaps Augustine (354-430) was more realistic when he showed the continuing battle between two kingdoms or two cities till Judgment Day. He wrote: "In this way there are two communities — one of the ungodly, and another of the holy — which are carried down from the beginning of the human race even to the end of the world, which are at present commingled in respect of bodies, but separated in respect of wills, and which, moreover, are destined to be separated also in respect of bodily presence in the day of judgment."[99] This did not mean for him a status quo, since "five ages of the world, accordingly, [have] been now completed (there has entered the sixth)."[100] With the advent of Jesus "the sixth age has entered on its process; so that now the spiritual grace, which in previous times was known to a few patriarchs and prophets, may be made manifest to all nations ... in order that in this sixth age the mind of man may be renewed after the image of God, even as on the sixth day man was made after the image of God." In analogy to the six days of creation, the first five millennia were a preparation on the way

98. For this and the following quote, see Eusebius, *History of the Church* 10.1.6ff., in *NPNF* SS, 1:369.

99. Augustine, *On the Catechizing of the Uninstructed* 19.31, in *NPNF* FS, 3:303.

100. For this and the following quote, see Augustine, *On the Catechizing of the Uninstructed* 22.39, in *NPNF* FS, 3:307.

to salvation. In the present millennium humanity is being transformed into the image of God, first through Christ's incarnation and then through the mission enterprise of the church. As Justin Martyr said, after the world has lasted the 6,000 years, the first resurrection will take place and the just will rule the earth. Since it was common opinion in the early church that the world should last for 6,000 years and Christ had come after 5,500 years, this meant that history had almost completed its present course. Soon the Antichrist will emerge, a first resurrection will take place, and then a thousand-year reign of Christ with the faithful. Thereafter renewed struggles with the dark forces will commence, then comes a second resurrection, and a final judgment and eternity.

With this timetable in the background, certain turning points of history, such as the end of a millennium or the coming to power of an especially assertive emperor, intensified the eschatological hopes of the people. While the kingdom of God was only occasionally identified with the Christian community or the church, for the most part the hope in the millennium served to assert God's definite rule of the world. But the actual goal of Christians was not seen to lie in this world but beyond in a new world to come. "The church is earthly, the kingdom is heavenly and otherworldly."[101] The transcendent goal did not diminish eschatological urgency.

Since grace was already present in the sacraments, one yearned for its completion, as *The Teaching of the Twelve Apostles* shows: "Let grace come, and let this world pass away."[102] Therefore we are not surprised when Hermas receives the following answer in reply to his question of whether the end is present: "Foolish man! Do you not see the tower yet building? When the tower is finished and built, then comes the end; and I assure you it will be soon finished."[103] This meant that the Christian community was still living in the end time, and it was therefore necessary to be prepared for that end. This end comprised the whole person.

Here one had to remember the gnostics, who taught that matter was intrinsically evil and therefore only the immaterial soul, and not the

101. So correctly Reinhold Seeberg, *Lehrbuch der Dogmengeschichte,* 6th ed. (Darmstadt: Wissenschaftliche Buchgesellschaft, 1965), 1:664 (§19).
102. *The Teaching of the Twelve Apostles* 10.6, in *ANF,* 7:380, and Pelikan, 1:126, who sees in these words part of an ancient eucharistic liturgy.
103. Hermas, *Vision* 3.8, in *ANF,* 2:16.

bodily dimension of the person, could participate in salvation. Against this split between the material and the spiritual, Irenaeus objected vehemently, saying that if this were true, then Christ did not redeem us with his blood, "nor is the cup of the Eucharist the communion of his blood, nor the bread which we break the communion of his body."[104] The heretics, Irenaeus explained, despise "the handiwork of God" and do not admit the salvation of the flesh.[105] Therefore they "disallow a resurrection affecting the whole man." In opposition to those heretics who claim that, immediately upon his death on the cross Jesus departed on high, leaving his body to the earth, Irenaeus affirms that Jesus was resurrected on the third day. Similarly we must await the time of our resurrection and cannot expect to be immediately taken up to God.

In the same vein the Apostles' Creed and the Nicene Creed emphasized the resurrection of the body and life everlasting, thus not allowing a split between the material and the spiritual. Especially Gregory of Nyssa (ca. 331-95) advances a very elaborate argument concerning the resurrection of the whole being. Even if the body disintegrates, Gregory tells us, "he surely remains in the world; and the world . . . is held by the hand of God."[106] Therefore a body, whatever form or shape it takes, can never fall out of the realm of God. Moreover, even if we would take the soul as that which would survive, it must have some semblance of our material nature even after the dissolution of the body, as we gather from the story of the rich man who recognizes Lazarus in Hades (Luke 16:24-31). While there is always a change going on with our bodies, there are "tokens of identity in all the changes which the body undergoes."[107] The bodily dimension of the person takes on a variety of forms. But these forms necessarily remain "in the soul as in the impression of a seal," so that the soul can then receive back to itself "all those things which correspond to the stamp of the form." Therefore "it is not beyond probability that what properly belongs to the individual should once more return to it from the common source."

Gregory wants to establish the plausibility of a resurrection of the

104. Irenaeus, *Against Heresies* 5.2.2, in *ANF*, 1:528.

105. For this and the following quote, see Irenaeus, *Against Heresies* 5.31.1, in *ANF*, 1:560.

106. Gregory of Nyssa, *On the Making of Man* 26.2, in *NPNF* SS, 5:417.

107. For this and the following quotes, see Gregory of Nyssa, *On the Making of Man* 27.3ff., in *NPNF* SS, 5:418.

whole person. But the tendency is very clear, a tendency reiterated by virtually all the major theologians of the early church: there is a resurrection of the dead, meaning not only a survival of a soul but a re-creation, or rather a new creation, of the person in a resurrected state. The hope for the resurrection together with the notion that God's reign will eventually prevail throughout the world did not eliminate or make unnecessary the breaking in of the eschaton or the parousia of Christ. On the contrary, one expected the new world to come and saw the need to prepare oneself now for that new world.

Tertullian perhaps gave an accurate description of the Christian community when he wrote: "We are a body knit together as such by a common religious profession, by unity of discipline, and a bond of a common hope."[108] At the same time he wrote that Christians prayed, among other things, "for the delay of the final consummation." The Christians of the early church were a hoping and praying community expecting the breaking in of the eschaton. Yet in contrast to the apocalyptic seers who wished the final consummation upon themselves and especially upon the enemies of God, Tertullian at least witnesses to a different perspective. God has put us on this earth with a twofold mission, to prepare ourselves for the end and to be witnesses to the gospel. The execution of this twofold task has now become of primary importance, and the final consummation, though still unwaveringly hoped for, recedes into the background.

---

108. See Tertullian, *Apology* 39, in *ANF*, 3:46, for this and the following quote.

Part II
The Manifold Faces of Eschatology

In our present age we cannot confine our discussion to *Christian* eschatology, since even in those regions where the Judeo-Christian tradition is dominant, many secular varieties of hope have emerged. This is due to the impact of science, the appropriation of philosophical trends, and the various religious movements that have emerged either in opposition to the Judeo-Christian tradition or as an attempt to improve upon it. Even in the Judeo-Christian tradition eschatology should not be taken for granted as a dominant concept, though it decidedly shaped theological discourse throughout the twentieth century.

3. Present Discussion of Christian Eschatology

In our attempt to outline the biblical scope of eschatology, we have been aware that there are many other approaches to Old and New Testament eschatology.[1] Indeed, the quest for a proper understanding of New Testament eschatology has dominated twentieth-century theology more than any other topic. In previous centuries, while dogmatics always contained a concluding chapter on the so-called last things, meaning on death, resurrection, and the coming kingdom, that chapter was quite divorced from the rest of the theological discourse.

It was not until Albrecht Ritschl (1822-89) that the kingdom of God became a dominant theme. For instance, the first of four parts in his *Instruction in the Christian Religion,* which constitutes nearly one-third of the text, focuses on the doctrine of the kingdom of God. There Ritschl declares: "The kingdom of God is the divinely ordained highest good of the community founded through God's revelation in Christ; but it is the highest good only in the sense that it forms at the same time the ethical ideal for whose attainment the members of the community bind themselves to each other through a definite type of reciprocal action."[2] While Ritschl shied away from the notion that the kingdom of God is not simply brought about by human efforts, his emphasis is clearly on

1. I have tried to take account of them within the presentation of my own position. Since many of these approaches deserve more extensive attention, this chapter will be devoted to them.

2. Albrecht Ritschl, *Instruction in the Christian Religion,* §5, in Philip Hefner, *Albrecht Ritschl: Three Essays* (Philadelphia: Fortress, 1972), 222.

human solidarity and humanity's effort to shape itself according to the ethical ideal of the kingdom.[3]

Even Adolf von Harnack (1851-1930), the dominant Protestant theologian in Germany at the turn of the twentieth century, still claimed that though the kingdom of God and its coming was at the center of Jesus' proclamation, it does not come with outward gestures but is already present as "a still and mighty power in the hearts of men."[4] An actual rediscovery of the eschatological perspective occurred with the works of Johannes Weiss and Albert Schweitzer.

1. The Rediscovery of the Eschatological Perspective

a. The Kingdom of God as an Eschatological Concept

Johannes Weiss (1863-1914), a former student of Ritschl and his son-in-law, was professor of New Testament in Göttingen when he published *The Preaching of Jesus concerning the Kingdom of God* in 1892. In the first edition only some references to apocalyptic writings, with which he illustrated Jesus' preaching, showed a new turn in comprehending eschatology. But in the second edition of 1900, Weiss stated unmistakably "that Ritschl's idea of the kingdom of God and the idea with the same name in the proclamation of Jesus are two very different items."[5] The kingdom of God was not an ethical ideal and had nothing to do with Christian vocation, as Ritschl had emphasized. In clear opposition to Ritschl, Weiss wrote:

> The Kingdom of God, in Jesus' view, is never an ethical ideal, but is *nothing other than the highest religious Good*, a Good which God grants on certain conditions. This does not imply a Pharisaic conception of re-

3. For a more extensive discussion of Ritschl's understanding of the kingdom, cf. Hans Schwarz, "The Centrality and Bipolar Focus of the Kingdom: Ritschl's Theological Import for the Twentieth Century," in *Ritschl in Retrospect: History, Community, and Science,* ed. Darrell Jodock (Minneapolis: Fortress, 1995), esp. 104-11.

4. Adolf von Harnack, *What Is Christianity?* trans. Th. B. Saunders (New York: Harper, 1957), 54.

5. Johannes Weiss, *Die Predigt Jesu vom Reiche Gottes,* 2nd ed., in his preface, reprinted: 3rd ed., ed. Ferdinand Hahn (Göttingen: Vandenhoeck & Ruprecht, 1964), xi.

ward, but naturally only a person who is entirely detached from *aion houtos* can really possess and enjoy this Good in the Kingdom of God. Otherwise he lacks completely the proper spiritual disposition; hence, participation in this Kingdom corresponds only to that which is spiritually possible. This interpretation of the Kingdom of God as an inner-worldly ethical ideal is a vestige of the Kantian idea and does not hold up before a more precise historical examination.[6]

For Weiss the kingdom is totally otherworldly, and its realization is up to God alone and not reliant on human action. Humanity can only create the conditions for the kingdom demanded by God.

Weiss also denies that Jesus thought of a this-worldly development of the kingdom. When Jesus talked about the kingdom that has already commenced, he was expressing a prophetic, future-directed view. Generally, however, he thought of the realization of the kingdom as still outstanding. Therefore, Jesus showed no inclination to perceive in the newly shaped piety of his followers any preliminary realization of the kingdom.

According to Weiss, there can be no distinction between a preliminary inception and a final completion of the kingdom. "The disciples were to pray for the coming of the Kingdom, but men could do nothing to establish it."[7] Weiss therefore concludes that "[T]he dogmatic religious-ethical application of this idea in more recent theology, an application which has completely stripped away the original eschatological-apocalyptic meaning of the idea, is unjustified. Indeed, one proceeds in an only apparently biblical manner if one uses the term in a sense different from that of Jesus."[8]

Weiss does not want to preclude systematic theology from using the idea of the kingdom. To the contrary, he is convinced that it is a valid concept for awakening a vigorous religious life, but theologians should admit that they are using the concept differently from Jesus. We no longer share the eschatological sentiment of early Christianity, Weiss contends. We no longer pray that this world may pass away and God's grace

---

6. Johannes Weiss, *Jesus' Proclamation of the Kingdom of God* (1892), translated and edited with an introduction by Richard Hyde Hiers and David Larrimore Holland (London: SCM, 1971), 132-33.

7. Weiss, *Jesus' Proclamation*, 129.

8. Weiss, *Jesus' Proclamation*, 114.

may break in, but we live in joyful confidence that our own world is ever more becoming the arena of God's intended humanity. Though we are convinced that this world will continue, we hope that, as the community of Jesus Christ, we will someday be assembled in the heavenly kingdom.

Though Weiss chides Ritschl for omitting the eschatological fervor, his own view, too, fails to foster this fervor. Theologically he advocates, just like Ritschl, the belief in human amelioration, and historically he emphasizes Jesus' eschatological message of a completely otherworldly kingdom. While Weiss's approach gained considerable attention, it comes as no surprise that he was applauded neither by the conservatives nor by the liberals. The liberals preferred a spiritual kingdom of God in an inner-worldly or emotional manner, while, according to Weiss, Jesus proclaimed the imminent end of the world. This was too exclusively eschatological for their sentiments. Moreover, Jesus was seen as being too much in line with Judaism and not, as they preferred to see him, as the new religious figure that stood in contrast to that religion. Conservatives, too, while they applauded the emphasis on the parousia of Christ, preferred a kingdom that was already emerging in the present.

The actual problem was the ambivalence of Weiss's proposal. He affirmed on the one hand that "The important thing is that by virtue of his baptismal experience, Jesus reached the religious conviction that he had been chosen to be Judge and Ruler in the Kingdom of God. . . . The messianic consciousness of Jesus, as expressed in the name Son of man, also participates in the thoroughly transcendental and apocalyptic character of Jesus' idea of the Kingdom of God and cannot be dissociated from it."[9]

On the other hand he claimed: "The real difference between our modern Protestant world-view and that of primitive Christianity is, therefore, that we do not share the eschatological attitude, namely, that the shape of this world will pass away *(to schema tou cosmou toutou paragei)*."[10] He was still so much a child of the nineteenth century that he could affirm an actual eschatological transformation of this world and not only a being wafted away to a celestial sphere. In this way he was not that much different from Albert Schweitzer.

9. Weiss, *Jesus' Proclamation*, 128-29.
10. Weiss, *Jesus' Proclamation*, 135.

b. The Consistent or Consequent Eschatology

In 1901 **Albert Schweitzer** (1875-1965) published a small booklet with the title *The Mystery of the Kingdom of God: The Secret of Jesus' Messiahship and Passion.*[11] Here Schweitzer posed the alternative that Jesus was to be understood either in eschatological terms or in noneschatological terms, but not in both. Schweitzer himself opted for a consistent eschatological understanding.

While Schweitzer asserted that we do not know anything about Jesus' earlier development, he contended that "at his baptism the secret of his existence was disclosed to him, — namely, that he was the one whom God had destined to be the Messiah. With this revelation he was complete, and underwent no further development."[12] From that time on he was sure he had to work as the unknown and hidden Messiah until the messianic age appeared. He and his followers had to purify themselves in the final affliction. Thus the idea of suffering was present for him from the very beginning. His message was similar to that of John the Baptist: repent and attain righteousness, because the kingdom of God is close at hand. But, in contrast to John, Jesus performed miracles. These gave John the idea that Jesus could be the Messiah, and he sent disciples to him to inquire about him. Jesus' preaching did not yield much success, though he tried hard. This resulted in the first disappointment for Jesus. Then the coming of the kingdom was delayed, though all the necessary signs were present. As one of these significant signs of the coming kingdom, Jesus had discovered that John the Baptist was Elijah reincarnate. When John was beheaded and the kingdom still did not come, Jesus realized that he had to suffer death too. He turned with his disciples to Jerusalem and was determined to bring about the kingdom of God. Having entered the Holy City, he claimed to be the Messiah. The Jewish authorities, who had always been suspicious of him, accused him of blasphemy and put him to death. He died, but nothing happened.

11. Albert Schweitzer, *The Mystery of the Kingdom of God: The Secret of Jesus' Messiahship and Passion,* translated with an introduction by Walter Lowrie (New York: Macmillan, 1950). The extensive introduction by Lowrie provides good background on the immediate reaction this book received and also gives the translator's own evaluation of the book.

12. Schweitzer, *Mystery,* 160.

Schweitzer concludes his book with the hope that his critics will find no fault with his aim *"to depict the figure of Jesus in its overwhelming heroic greatness and to impress it upon the modern age and upon the modern theology."*[13] This was the first significant attempt to explain Jesus' mission as completely eschatological. But it saw that mission as founded on an idea that had proved to be wrong. This booklet contained enough dynamite to shatter the cherished thoughts of both conservatives and liberals. Yet in contrast to Weiss's book, it received hardly any attention.

A different reception greeted Schweitzer's next book in 1906. *The Quest of the Historical Jesus* opened with a study of the rationalistic skeptic Reimarus, who had been the first to grasp the eschatological worldview of Jesus. It concluded with William Wrede, one of Schweitzer's contemporaries, who had proved the noneschatological picture of Jesus to be untenable. Schweitzer again posed the alternative: "There is, on the one hand, the eschatological solution, which at one stroke raises the Marcan account as it stands, with all its disconnectedness and inconsistencies, into genuine history; and there is, on the other hand, the literary solution, which regards the incongruous dogmatic element as interpolated by the earlier Evangelist into the tradition and therefore strikes out the Messianic claim altogether from the historical Life of Jesus. *Tertium non datur.*"[14]

Again Schweitzer took a clear stand for a thoroughgoing eschatological interpretation of Jesus. He declared that Jesus' ethics were interim ethics which aimed at the preparation for the kingdom of God. Since the kingdom had not come when Jesus expected it, our ethics cannot be derived from Jesus' ethics. But his demand of world denial and perfection of personality is still valid for us, though it is in contrast to our ethics of reason.[15] We need more persons like Jesus. His enthusiasm and heroism are important for us, because they were derived from choosing the kingdom of God and from faith in this kingdom which was only strengthened by his encounter with obstacles. "In the knowledge that He is the coming Son of Man [Jesus] lays hold of the wheel of the world to set it moving on that last revolution which is to bring all ordi-

13. Schweitzer, *Mystery,* 174.

14. Albert Schweitzer, *The Quest of the Historical Jesus: A Critical Study of Its Progress from Reimarus to Wrede,* translated from the first German edition by W. Montgomery (New York: Macmillan, 1968), 337.

15. Cf. Schweitzer, *Quest,* 402-3, and *Mystery,* 174.

nary history to a close. It refuses to turn, and He throws Himself upon it. Then it does turn; and crushes Him. Instead of bringing in the eschatological conditions, He has destroyed them. The wheel rolls onward, and the mangled body of the one immeasurably great Man, who was strong enough to think of Himself as the spiritual ruler of mankind and to bend history to His purpose, is hanging upon it still. That is His victory and His reign."[16] It is relatively unimportant for Schweitzer that Jesus was actually deceived in his eschatological expectations. All-decisive is his attitude toward history and toward the obstacles he had to overcome in accomplishing his goal.

With his *Quest of the Historical Jesus* Schweitzer started an immense uproar. The liberals could tolerate Schweitzer's portrayal of Jesus as a kind of religious fanatic who was deceived by his own ideas. But they rebuked him because he had declared Jesus' ethics to be mere "interim ethics."[17] Regardless of how critical liberalism had been toward the Jesus of the New Testament, it cherished his ethical ideals. Now Schweitzer had declared quite rightly that it is impossible to separate Jesus' ethics from his eschatological proclamation. This meant that the attempt of liberal theology to eliminate the eschatological dimension of Jesus' proclamation and to confine itself to the "timeless" validity of his ethical teachings could no longer be founded in the historical Jesus.

Conservative scholars applied to Schweitzer's own position his claim that each scholar had projected his own image of Jesus back into

---

16. Schweitzer, *Quest*, 370-71.

17. Cf. Schweitzer, *Mystery*, 55, where he introduces the term "interim-ethics." Cf. also E. N. Mozley, *The Theology of Albert Schweitzer for Christian Inquirers*, epilogue by Albert Schweitzer (London: Black, 1950), 50-52; and Albert Schweitzer, *The Kingdom of God and Primitive Christianity*, edited with an introduction by Ulrich Neuenschwander, trans. L. A. Garrad (London: Black, 1968), in his section "Jesus' Ethic of Preparation for the Kingdom," 81-88. Cf. also Albert Schweitzer, *The Philosophy of Civilization*, trans. C. T. Campion (New York: Macmillan, 1955), 111, where he describes the worldview of Jesus as being fundamentally optimistic. "Biased by the expectation of the end of the world, however, it is indifferent to all attempts made to improve the temporal, natural world by a civilization which organizes itself on the lines of outward progress." Jesus' worldview concerns itself only with the inward ethical perfecting of individuals.

In pointing to the eschatological dimension, Schweitzer has certainly discovered the starting point and direction of Jesus' ethics. But it seems almost artificial to assert that the inward perfection Jesus advocated should have no implications for outward circumstances.

the New Testament in trying to write a life of Jesus. They concluded that the true historical Jesus could not be found by strictly historical investigation, but only through faith.[18] In England, however, Schweitzer's position found more approval. Francis C. Burkitt (1864-1935), a leading New Testament scholar, immediately translated the *Quest of the Historical Jesus* and wrote a preface to it. William Sanday (1843-1920), another prominent figure in British New Testament scholarship, initially praised Schweitzer's books, but after having actually read Schweitzer's first study, he realized the radical attitude behind it and quickly changed his mind.[19] Twenty years later Schweitzer published *The Mysticism of Paul the Apostle*[20] and received an entirely different response in Germany. He described the eschatological teaching of Paul as an eschatological mysticism that should lead to Christ. But the time was then ripe for an eschatological understanding of the New Testament, and Schweitzer's book was hailed as the work of a genius.[21]

The very few serious representatives of consistent or consequent eschatology are to be found mainly among Swiss liberal theologians. Martin Werner (1887-1964), for instance, tried to explain the whole development of the Christian dogma from the fact that the eschaton and the parousia did not come as expected.[22] The delay of the parousia was *the* problem in early Christianity and could only be bridged through the reinterpretation of the kerygma and the emergence of the church. Fritz Buri (1907-95) claimed that the Christian proclamation should be de-kerygmatized and de-eschatologized, because we no longer wait for the coming eschaton. Our eschatological possibility consists of being freed

18. Cf. Werner Georg Kümmel's instructive essay "Die 'konsequente Eschatologie' Albert Schweitzers im Urteil der Zeitgenossen," in *Heilsgeschehen und Geschichte: Gesammelte Aufsätze 1933-1964*, ed. E. Grässer et al. (Marburg: Elwert, 1965), 332.

19. Cf. Lowrie's introduction to Schweitzer, *Mystery*, 3. Cf. also Schweitzer's own assessment in *Geschichte der Leben-Jesu-Forschung*, 6th ed. (Tübingen: Mohr, 1951), 592.

20. Trans. W. Montgomery, prefatory note by F. C. Burkitt (New York: Macmillan, 1955).

21. Cf. Kümmel, "Die 'konsequente Eschatologie' Albert Schweitzers im Urteil der Zeitgenossen," 337.

22. Cf. Martin Werner, *The Formation of Christian Dogma: An Historical Study of Its Problem*, translated with an introduction by S. G. F. Brandon (New York: Harper, 1957), 47, 71-72, and other places. Werner attempts to describe the process of the formation of the Christian dogma as a process of de-eschatologizing the main apostolic doctrine caused by the crises that emerged when the parousia was more and more delayed.

from the anxiety of the world and being devoted to a reverence for life.[23]

Theologians following the path of consistent or consequent eschatology have never had many followers. One reason might be that their approach to eschatology is not close enough to the biblical witnesses to please a conservative, while for a liberal, secular philosophies prove more satisfying. Nevertheless, Schweitzer and his disciples made one point unmistakably clear: the New Testament provides in all its diversity a homogeneous outlook that is totally eschatological. But they failed to provide an adequate interpretation of this eschatological perspective. The interpretation they proposed seems to be inconsistent and unrealistic. They failed to show convincingly how Christianity could have survived and grown so rapidly if it originated and developed only through constant disappointments. And they could not explain what it was that gave the Christians of the first centuries the strength to maintain their faith in the face of persecution.

c. A Noneschatological Jesus

As if history would repeat itself at the close of the twentieth century, again a noneschatological Jesus is advocated. **Marcus J. Borg** (b. 1942),

---

23. Cf. Fritz Buri's response to Rudolf Bultmann, "Entmythologisierung oder Entkerygmatisierung der Theologie," in *Kerygma und Mythos*, vol. 2, ed. Hans Werner Bartsch (Hamburg-Volksdorf: Reich, 1952), 85-101; and Fritz Buri, *Christian Faith in Our Time*, trans. E. A. Kent (New York: Macmillan, 1966), 124-26, where, relying on Schweitzer and Karl Jaspers, he advocated the concept of awe or reverence for life as the guiding ethical principle in our attitudes toward ourselves and our environment. Cf. also John Macquarrie, *The Scope of Demythologizing: Bultmann and His Critics* (New York: Harper Torchbooks, 1966), 129-31.

Later Buri modified his approach gently, adopting more features of classical liberalism. In *How Can We Still Speak Responsibly of God*, trans. Ch. D. Hardwick (Philadelphia: Fortress, 1968), 40, he suggested that "love constitutes the fulfillment of human existence." And in his book *Theology of Existence*, trans. H. H. Oliver and G. Onder (Greenwood, S.C.: Attic, 1965), 110, he asserted that "the general resurrection of the dead, the Last Judgment and the New Heaven and the New Earth represent symbols for the communal context of existence as it shall be realized in the Church as Christian existence in community." Though he uses the term "universal *Heilsgeschichte*," he understands it as mythology that expresses this supra-individual character of existence.

professor of religion and culture at Oregon State University and a member of the Jesus Seminar led by Robert Funk (b. 1926), is, by his own admission, "a committed Christian deeply involved in the life of the church."[24] This means that he is, by his own estimate, by no means a liberal, nonattached to church life. Surveying contemporary scholarship, he claims that "the old consensus that Jesus was an eschatological prophet who proclaimed the imminent end of the world has disappeared."[25]

According to Borg, most North American New Testament scholars no longer accept the central thesis that the mission and message of Jesus were eschatological. Traditionally, Borg claims, the imminent coming of the Son of Man was understood to be connected to the coming of the kingdom of God, and both were used to account for the element of urgency and crisis: there is no time to waste because the end is near. The eschatological expectation of the early church was also thought to be a continuation of the eschatological message of Jesus. Yet, by the late 1960s "it became increasingly accepted that the coming Son of Man sayings were not authentic, but were created by Jesus' followers in the decades after Easter as 'second coming' texts, expressing the early church's conviction that the crucified and exalted one would return as vindicator and judge. But if these texts are seen as inauthentic, then the central reason for thinking that Jesus expected the imminent end of the world vanishes."

Moreover, a number of scholars suggested that Jesus' eschatology was not to be understood in a chronological temporal stance referring to an end of actual time. According to Borg, statements concerning the "kingdom of God" and "the coming Son of man" are not found in the same texts and therefore seem to represent two quite distinct traditions.[26]

Since for Borg the Son of Man sayings are later introductions, it is relatively simple for him to assert that the kingdom-of-God sayings by themselves do not have the element of imminence in them. Though they use the language of time to speak of the kingdom as near, present,

---

24. Marcus J. Borg, *Jesus in Contemporary Scholarship* (Valley Forge, Pa.: Trinity Press International, 1994), 161.

25. See Borg, 7-8, for this and the following quote.

26. Cf. for the following, including the next two quotes, Borg, 54.

or future, there is no clear link between the coming of the kingdom and the end of time which would tie both temporarily to the present generation. The only exception would be Mark 9:1: "Truly I tell you, there are some standing here who will not taste death until they see that the kingdom of God has come with power." But Borg feels that this verse is not without its problems. "It is not clear that the coming of the kingdom in power refers to the end of the world; the verse permits a number of interpretations and is sometimes viewed as inauthentic." Therefore, it would be ill-advised to base such a weighty decision on a shaky foundation. He concludes therefore: "The notion that the kingdom of God is the imminent eschatological kingdom is thus without foundation in the kingdom texts."

Borg does not want to conceive of the kingdom of God as a definite concept, but as a symbol pointing to the kingship of God, the divine power and sovereignty, compassion and justice. The understanding of the kingdom of God implying the end of the world is only one nuance among many. Jesus emphasized the present kingly power of God "and invited his hearers to 'enter' it and have their lives shaped by it."[27] The kingship of God refers to the past, the present, and the future. "Rather than supposing that the expectation of the imminent end of the world originated with Jesus, it is more plausible to affirm that it originated with the expectation of his return. . . . But the expectation of the early church does not need to be grounded in Jesus' own expectation."[28] More plausibly it is a post-Easter development deduced from the Easter event itself.

If we follow Borg's insistence that in the context of Judaism a "resurrection" as distinct from a "resuscitation" was an event expected at the end of time and therefore its occurrence was understood as an indicator that the general resurrection must be near, we are still confronted with the expectation of an imminent end, this time not with Jesus, but with the early Christian community. What shall we do with this expectation? Discard it as wrong or accept it? If we do accept it, what do we accept it as? Moreover, if Borg is correct in asserting that the expectation of an imminent future event as central to Jesus' own (eschatological) outlook "now seems to have become a minority posi-

27. Borg, 57.
28. Borg, 58.

tion in North American Jesus scholarship," we should not forget that more conservative scholars, regardless of their geographic origin, have never accepted the thesis that Jesus expected the imminent coming of the kingdom and was subsequently deceived.[29] They rejected both the deception theory and the imminence of the kingdom. Yet for many other scholars as well, the hypothesized disappointment over the delay of the parousia in the first Christian communities cannot be substantiated in the historical documents. Almost by necessity such disappointment should have happened if Borg were correct that the expectation of an imminent future event (meaning the general resurrection and the end of time) did indeed exist and that its realization was indefinitely delayed.

We cannot detect a disappointment either with Jesus or in the early Christian community in general over what Borg calls the expectation of an imminent future event. This leads us to conclude that both the Jesus of history and the early Christian community were rather close to each other in their expectation of the future and that expectation did not include the concept of imminence. Eschatology which also includes concepts such as the Son of Man and the kingdom of God allows for more than the one interpretation Borg suggests. It most clearly allows for an eschatological interpretation of Jesus. But Borg shies away from this since he prefers to suggest, as has been done most eloquently by John Dominic Crossan (b. 1934), that Jesus is *a teacher of subversive wisdom.*[30] With this assessment of Jesus we would nearly have returned full circle and would be back to nineteenth-century liberal scholarship, which understood Jesus mainly in the wisdom tradition, as one who would lead people to a morally superior life. Yet most eschatological proposals go in a different direction.

1. There is first the present-oriented approach to eschatology that emphasizes the existential character of Jesus' proclamation and, at the same time, attempts to consider the teachings of Jesus about the future eschaton as of lesser or no importance. Scholars such as C. H. Dodd, Rudolf Bultmann, and Amos N. Wilder have pursued this approach. Fu-

---

29. Borg, 74.

30. Borg, 9, and John Dominic Crossan, *The Historical Jesus: The Life of a Mediterranean Jewish Peasant* (San Francisco: Harper, 1991), 351, where he claims that Jesus taught "the wisdom of common sense" and thereby advocates "the radicality of obviousness."

ture eschatology was never an essential part of Jesus' message. In part, its emergence was due to the first Christians, who rephrased the original kerygma according to popular eschatological trends, such as Jewish apocalyptic. And in part it was also due to Jesus' own primitive first-century worldview.

2. Another approach tries to emphasize the future-directedness of eschatology. Conservative scholars such as Werner Georg Kümmel and Oscar Cullmann advocated this trend, as well as more evangelical scholars such as Anthony Hoekema. They assert that the expectation of an imminent breaking in of the eschaton played no role in the proclamation of Jesus, since he emphasized the all-decisive now and did not deal with categories of time. Therefore the imminent expectation of Jesus is not made obsolete by positing some kind of delay. The systematicians Jürgen Moltmann and Wolfhart Pannenberg also emphasized the future expectation of Jesus and claimed that the Judeo-Christian faith is essentially future-directed and part of the expectation of the end had already come to its fulfillment. Conservative and evangelical theologians also agree with this by emphasizing the tension between fulfillment and still-outstanding realization and rejecting the thesis of a delay of the parousia.

3. The liberating power of eschatology is emphasized by theologians who are often influenced by Jürgen Moltmann, such as Gustavo Gutiérrez. They claim that biblical eschatology is a world-transforming power that permeates all aspects of the Christian life. Since our eschatological existence is a present reality, society must be changed as well as our attitude toward nature. This is also reaffirmed by feminist theologians such as Rosemary Radford Ruether who opt for a transformation of society and of our approach toward the world.

4. Christian eschatology must also be seen in a universal context. Especially process theologians, such as John B. Cobb, emphasize that Christian eschatology must be understood in the context of other religious and secular hopes and is part of a universal hope for a new world. This is reiterated by theologians of religion, such as John Hick, who sees Christian eschatology in a universally religious context to which it must respond and of which it is part.

In the biblical foundation, we already attempted to make use of different interpretations without the possibility of an explicit dialogue with them. At this point we would like to deal with them at more length, yet the scope of this presentation often necessitates a more generalized fashion than we would have liked.

2. Present-Oriented Approach to Eschatology

In their own different ways, Johannes Weiss, Albert Schweitzer, and Marcus Borg have tried to diffuse one baffling issue: Jesus, or at least the early Christian community, expected the immediate coming of the kingdom or even already its presence. Yet since neither of these expectations materialized, one tried in different ways to circumvent this stumbling block. Those who opted for a present-oriented approach left the stumbling block stand as it was and emphasized the present as the decisive point in history. One attempt to accomplish this was to consider the present of the individual as the decisive moment in which one is encountered by the eschaton. This approach finds expression in the existential interpretation of New Testament eschatology and is mainly pursued by Rudolf Bultmann and his followers. Another variation of the present-oriented approach assumes that the decisive event has already happened. The kingdom has already come with Jesus of Nazareth, and thus it is unnecessary to wait for any future eschatology. C. H. Dodd (1884-1973) is the main representative of this trend, and he has coined the phrase "realized eschatology" for this approach.

a. Existential and Ethical Approaches

Characteristic of **Rudolf Bultmann** and his followers is a critical skepticism about the historical reliability of the New Testament documents. The criterion of Ernst Troeltsch (1865-1923), that all phenomena in the history of religions have to be subjected to the principles of analogy and correlation,[31] is generally accepted by the Bultmann school. Therefore it is ultimately quite difficult to ascertain what Jesus actually said and did, since the oldest traceable literary remains stem from the Palestinian Christian community and not from Jesus himself. But contrary to

31. For Troeltsch, cf. Wilhelm Pauck, *Harnack and Troeltsch: Two Historical Theologians* (New York: Oxford University Press, 1968), 66-67.

liberal theology, Bultmann is not much interested in the historical Jesus. He asserts: "How things looked in the heart of Jesus I do not know and I do not want to know."[32] Bultmann is therefore skeptical concerning Jesus' messianic self-understanding.

Though Jesus is presented in the New Testament as the Messiah and the Son of Man, both terms have very different backgrounds and are used differently. The term "Messiah" is always used by others in speaking about Jesus — never by Jesus himself — whereas Jesus often used the term "Son of Man."

Jesus uses the term "Son of Man" in three different ways in the New Testament.[33] The first class is scriptural references that describe the coming of the Son of Man as in apocalyptic expectation. The Son of Man comes from heaven as judge and Savior; he will come unexpectedly like a flash of lightning (cf. Mark 8:38; 13:26). These Son of Man sayings are the oldest, since they occur primarily in Mark and in Q.

However, all of these sayings talk about the Son of Man in the third person ("he will . . ."), and nothing is mentioned in them about his identity with Jesus, though the first Christian community took this identity for granted.[34] Bultmann, Günther Bornkamm (1905-90), Heinz Eduard Tödt (1918-91), and others contend that some of these references to the Son of Man were used by Jesus.[35] In using them he did not refer to him-

32. Rudolf Bultmann, "On the Question of Christology," in *Faith and Understanding,* edited with an introduction by Robert W. Funk, trans. Louise Pettibone Smith (New York: Harper, 1969), 1:132.

33. For the following cf. Rudolf Bultmann, *Theology of the New Testament,* trans. Kendrik Grobel (New York: Scribner, 1951), 1:30-31, and *Jesus and the Word,* trans. Louise Pettibone Smith and Erminie Huntress Lantero (New York: Scribner, 1969), 9, where he says: "Considering that it was really no trifle to believe oneself Messiah, that, further, whoever so believed must have regulated his whole life in accordance with this belief, we must admit that if this point is obscure we can, strictly speaking, know nothing of the personality of Jesus. I am personally of the opinion that Jesus did not believe himself to be the Messiah, but I do not imagine that this opinion gives me a clearer picture of his personality."

34. So Günther Bornkamm, *Jesus of Nazareth,* trans. J. McLuskey and F. McLuskey (Minneapolis: Fortress, 1995), 228. A former student of Martin Dibelius, Bornkamm agrees with Bultmann in saying that in this first group of sayings nothing is mentioned about the identity of Jesus with the Son of Man, "although the believing community was certain of it."

35. Cf. Bultmann, *Theology,* 1:30; Bornkamm, 228; and Heinz Eduard Tödt, *The Son of Man in the Synoptic Tradition,* trans. D. M. Barton (London: SCM, 1965), 224-25, where he gives a good summary of his careful exegesis.

self, but to someone else. However, to introduce such a distinction between Jesus and the Son of Man seems to pose more problems than it solves.[36] Therefore other scholars are more critical and suggest that none of these sayings are authentic.[37] They were all introduced by the first Christians and attributed to Jesus, and therefore they do not tell us anything about Jesus' self-understanding.

The next group of sayings talks about the suffering, death, and resurrection of the Son of Man. While Schweitzer was convinced that Jesus knew about his suffering and death and the subsequent coming of the eschaton, such a knowledge is commonly doubted by Bultmann and his followers. Jesus may have known that he would die a violent death. The sayings of the suffering, death, and resurrection of the Son of Man, however, presuppose the passion and Easter stories in detail. Furthermore, these sayings are mainly found in the tradition of Mark and have no connection to the sayings of the Son of Man who will come in power. Bultmann therefore suggests that these sayings are "probably later products of the Hellenistic Church."[38] This means that none of these sayings go back to the historical Jesus.

The third group of sayings refers to the present activity of the Son of Man. He has the power to forgive sins (Mark 2:10); and he is the Lord of the Sabbath (Mark 2:28). While Bultmann, in following an early thesis of Hans Lietzmann (1875-1942), assumed that the Son of Man reference in these sayings most likely results from a mistranslation and meant originally "man" or "I,"[39] most scholars today admit that it is an

---

36. Cf. the objections to Bultmann's position by Oscar Cullmann, *The Christology of the New Testament*, trans. S. C. Guthrie and Ch. A. M. Hall, rev. ed. (Philadelphia: Westminster, 1963), 156; and August Strobel, *Kerygma und Apokalyptik: Ein religionsgeschichtlicher und theologischer Beitrag zur Christusfrage* (Göttingen: Vandenhoeck & Ruprecht, 1967), 56-57.

37. So Philipp Vielhauer, "Gottesreich und Menschensohn in der Verkündigung Jesu," in *Aufsätze zum Neuen Testament* (Munich: Chr. Kaiser, 1965), 80; cf. also, in the same volume, his essay "Jesus und der Menschensohn: Zur Diskussion mit Heinz Eduard Tödt und Eduard Schweizer," 92-140, where he rejects the approach of Tödt. For a more contemporary assessment which goes in the same direction, see Borg, 84-86.

38. Bultmann, *Theology*, 1:30.

39. Bultmann, *Theology*, 1:30. Cf. Hans Lietzmann, *Der Menschensohn: Ein Beitrag zur neutestamentlichen Theologie* (Berlin, 1896). So still today Klaus Berger, *Wer war Jesus wirklich?* (Stuttgart: Quell, 1995), 128, who writes: "'Son of man' is a mysterious word. It says nothing else but 'man.'"

actual title. But again its authenticity is disallowed.[40] This group of sayings was used by the first Christians to endow the historical Jesus with the authority of the exalted one. Endowed with this authority, Jesus is shown as having the power to forgive sins and to free his disciples from keeping the Sabbath. Following his death and resurrection, the first Christians exercised the same authority.[41]

Günther Bornkamm asks why Jesus would have used such an ambiguous title like Son of Man, since it could designate either the Messiah or just mean "man." He argues that the Palestinian Christians used this title first and conferred it on Jesus. It expressed the essence of their faith and had an eschatological connotation.[42] Philipp Vielhauer (1914-77) brings this argument to its logical conclusion in contending that neither the Son of Man title nor the title Messiah was fitting for Jesus.[43] None of the Son of Man sayings mention the kingdom of God.[44] The kingdom of God and the Son of Man title are of different origin and have nothing in common. The Son of Man title is not an essential part of the hope for the eschatological kingdom of God. But Jesus' message had the eschatological kingdom of God as its center. Thus Jesus could not have thought of himself as the Son of Man. Vielhauer's argument seems to be logically conclusive and convincing. But is it impossible to assume that Jesus combined two concepts that, according to Vielhauer, were not previously connected, though they seem to point in a similar direction? If the first Christians did not hesitate to do it, why was it impossible for Jesus?

It should be mentioned here, at least parenthetically, that many scholars outside the Bultmann school are much more reluctant to abandon the idea that Jesus called himself the Son of Man.[45] Most arguments

---

40. Vielhauer, 61.

41. Cf. Bornkamm, 229; and Strobel, 60, who allows for the possibility that some of these sayings date back to Jesus of Nazareth.

42. Bornkamm, 230-31.

43. Vielhauer, 88.

44. So Vielhauer, 80, and today again Borg, 54. Ferdinand Hahn, *The Titles of Jesus in Christology: Their History in Early Christianity*, trans. H. Knight and G. Ogg (London: Lutterworth, 1969), 28, however, objects that the origin of some of the words concerning the eschatological working of the Son of Man on the lips of Jesus cannot be disputed. "Neither the relative lack of connection with sayings about the Kingdom of God nor the peculiar features of the teaching of Jesus furnish essential arguments against authenticity."

45. Cf., for example, Ben Witherington III, *The Christology of Jesus* (Minneapolis:

for the authenticity of the Son of Man sayings presuppose a messianic consciousness of Jesus. Knowing about himself as the Son of Man, Jesus must have realized from the common messianic expectations that after his suffering and death he was to be exalted.[46] It has also been argued that, as a faithful Jew, Jesus must have known that his actions would bring upon him persecution and death through the Jewish authorities.[47] A man who deliberately breaks the law and incites others to do the same will be summoned to death.

We have noticed that Bultmann and his followers are extremely hesitant to concede the authenticity of any Son of Man titles. Yet it soon became obvious that this did not eliminate the importance of the historical Jesus. Biblical eschatology, after all, is grounded in Jesus. Bultmann had already claimed that "Jesus' call to decision implies a christology."[48] This means that the proclamation of Jesus, which is essentially eschatological, expresses a certain self-understanding of Jesus. Ernst Fuchs (1903-83) developed Bultmann's idea further in also considering Jesus' actions. We remember that Fuchs asserted that Jesus' conduct was the actual framework of his proclamation and both word and conduct (action) point in the same direction.[49] The remaining question, however, is how we are to understand the eschatological vision of Jesus that originated out of a certain self-understanding on his part and was transformed in the Gospels through the impact of his life, death, and resurrection.

Fortress, 1990), 250-62, who also provides a good survey of scholars who support a stand similar to his own.

46. Cf. Strobel, 83-84; and C. F. D. Moule, *The Birth of the New Testament* (New York: Harper & Row, 1962), 63, who attempts to explain Jesus' use of the term "Son of Man" as the use of a symbol from Dan. 7, "which is both historical and eschatological." He also quotes other literature important to the highly technical discussion on the origin of the Son of Man terminology.

47. So Ethelbert Stauffer, *Jesus and His Story,* trans. R. Winston and C. Winston (New York: Knopf, 1960), 170-72. James H. Charlesworth, "The Dead Sea Scrolls and the Historical Jesus," in *Jesus and the Dead Sea Scrolls,* ed. James H. Charlesworth (New York: Doubleday, 1992), 33, correctly claims: "Some of his premonitions about facing martyrdom appear to be authentic and not created later by his followers."

48. Bultmann, *Theology,* 1:43. Hans Conzelmann, "Zur Methode der Leben-Jesu-Forschung," *Zeitschrift für Theologie und Kirche* 56, sup. 1 (1959): 6, calls this statement "perhaps the most important sentence in Bultmann's *Theology of the New Testament.*"

49. Ernst Fuchs, "The Quest of the Historical Jesus" (1956), in *Studies of the Historical Jesus,* trans. A. Scobie (Naperville, Ill.: Allenson, 1964), 21-22.

At first glance, the answer seems simple for Bultmann. "*The mythical eschatology* is untenable for the simple reason that the parousia of Christ never took place as the New Testament expected. History did not come to an end, and, as every schoolboy knows, it will continue to run its course."[50] Bultmann is convinced that we cannot reiterate the New Testament eschatology, because it is expressed in a mythical framework and is part of a past mythical worldview. This does not mean that we can simply discard it. Bultmann insists that the mythical worldview of a future eschaton does not even lend itself to a strictly cosmological interpretation, as one might assume, but to an anthropological or existential one.[51] Instead of taking the apocalyptic imagery literally, we have to ask about its existential meaning.

Bultmann is convinced that Jesus and the New Testament writers believed in a future eschaton.[52] They thought that the end of history had come and that the end of the world was close at hand. Since the announced parousia did not occur, the Christians eventually doubted the immediate coming of the end of the world. The early church still kept the hope for a future eschaton, though it increasingly expected the end of the world in a distant and unknown future. But Christians did not abandon the belief in a future eschaton altogether, because they thought God determined the course of the world. The end of the world coincided for them with the end and the goal of history that God had provided.

For Bultmann it is not necessary to understand the expected end as the goal of history. He finds that two important New Testament writers, Paul and John, distinguish between the expected end and the goal of history. While in Jewish apocalyptic, history is interpreted from the standpoint of eschatology, for Paul "history is swallowed up in eschatology. Thereby eschatology has wholly lost its sense as the goal of history

50. Rudolf Bultmann in his programmatic essay "New Testament and Mythology," in *Kerygma and Myth: A Theological Debate*, ed. Hans Werner Bartsch, trans. R. H. Fuller (London: SPCK, 1953), 1:5. Kurt Erlemann, *Endzeiterwartungen im frühen Christentum* (Tübingen: A. Francke, 1996), 17-18, states today, just like Bultmann had done some fifty years earlier: "Nobody will seriously claim that the biblical imminent expectation of the end is still viable."

51. Bultmann, "New Testament and Mythology," 15-16.

52. Bultmann, "History and Eschatology in the New Testament," *New Testament Studies* 1 (1954-55): 9.

and is in fact understood as the goal of the individual human being."[53] World history is no longer decisive, having been replaced in importance by the history of the individual. The encounter with Christ is the most important event for this history, because confrontation with this eschatological event enables the individual to exist truly historically. The individual encounters the eschaton in the here and now, and history becomes dissolved into eschatology. This permits the believer to exist truly eschatologically in radical openness for the future without being tied to the past.

Bultmann relies here on Paul, for whom the turn of the aeons has already come. In Christ the appearance of the future has become a present possibility. Judgment and resurrection are happening now. We die and rise with Christ in our baptism, and salvation is present for the believer who is in Christ. Our existence is not tied to the past. The future is open to us in the present as a dialectic existence of indicative and imperative, an existence according to flesh or to spirit. Bultmann admits that Paul still described the eschatological judgment in apocalyptic terms as some future event. He even points out that throughout his lifetime Paul expected the great drama of the eschatological events. Yet he feels that this is an unimportant sideline in Paul's actual eschatological outlook. It is only the "now" of one's own existence which bears eschatological significance.[54]

The Gospel of John and the Johannine letters are interpreted by Bultmann as substantiating this emphasis on the existential impact of eschatology. For both Paul and John the eschatological events start with the coming of Jesus and continue into the present. While Paul is indebted to Jewish apocalyptic terminology, John uses gnostic terms. In gnosticism the dualism between light and darkness, truth and falsehood, above and below, and freedom and bondage is usually understood in cosmological terms in referring to certain "places" in the gnostic worldview. Bultmann, however, affirms that John changed this cosmological dualism into *a dualism of decision.*"[55] Being confronted

---

53. Bultmann, "History and Eschatology," 13.

54. Thus Bultmann can say that the process of demythologizing began partially already with Paul (cf. Bultmann, *Jesus Christ and Mythology* [New York: Scribner, 1958], 32). Very fittingly he entitles his Gifford Lectures, in which he addresses himself to the problem of history, *History and Eschatology: The Presence of Eternity* (New York: Harper, 1957).

55. Bultmann, *Theology*, 2:21.

with Jesus, one has to decide for or against God. This decision is inevitable because Jesus is the revelation of God. Thus the coming of the revealer is the judgment, and the reaction to revelation is decisive. Salvation becomes a radical present act, and all who accept Jesus as the revelation of God already have eternal life; they have passed through judgment.

Bultmann understands the Gospel of John as a protest against the traditional, dramatic, popular, national, and primitive eschatology. Of course, he also recognizes passages in John that point to a future eschaton (John 6:44, 54). But he concludes that a later editor introduced these passages, which also indicate a cultic sacramental piety.[56] Although the existence of such a later editor is not unquestioned by other scholars, one might wonder whether it is not an implicit admission that in the long run Christian theology cannot exist without a future goal of history. If the original writer of the Gospel of John seemingly omitted the announcement of a future eschaton, a later generation found it necessary to reintroduce the future dimension of history into John's original interpretation of Jesus' proclamation.[57]

Far from being a student of Bultmann, **Amos N. Wilder** (1895-1993) also emphasizes the present impact of eschatology. He agrees with Bultmann that one can no longer take the future-directed mythological imagery of the New Testament literally. "Eschatology is that form of myth which represents the unknown future."[58] But he questions the "individualistic character" of Bultmann's interpretation,[59] since non-

---

56. Bultmann, *The Gospel of John: A Commentary*, trans. G. R. Beasley-Murray et al. (Philadelphia: Westminster, 1971), 220, 234-36, 472, and other places. Cf. also Bultmann, "Johannesevangelium," in *Religion in Geschichte und Gegenwart,* 3rd ed. (Tübingen: J. C. B. Mohr [Paul Siebeck], 1957-65), 3:841.

57. This convincing argument is advanced by Wolfhart Pannenberg, "Redemptive Event and History" (1959), in *Basic Questions in Theology: Collected Essays,* trans. G. H. Kehm (Philadelphia: Fortress, 1970), 1:25.

58. Amos N. Wilder, *Eschatology and Ethics in the Teaching of Jesus,* rev. ed. (New York: Harper, 1959), 21.

59. Wilder, *Eschatology and Ethics,* 65. He also mentions that Bultmann's reinterpretation verges on gnosticism and psychologism. In his essay "Kerygma, Eschatology, and Social Ethics," in *The Background of the New Testament and Its Eschatology,* ed. W. D. Davies and D. Daube (Cambridge: Cambridge University Press, 1956), 519, Wilder indicates that Bultmann's "theology of the Word of God has a strange resemblance to an older individual pietism," and he assumes that his individualistic interpretation of the kerygma

historical individualistic interpretations reflect the mood of pessimism induced by our present situation. They refuse to take into account a realistic modern view of the social process and of social progress as measured by the whole human story.[60] "Jesus anticipated a new and revolutionary this-worldly order. . . . Jesus felt himself the prophet and instrument of the coming of this new order and conducted himself with a fully realistic understanding of the circumstances involved."[61]

Of course, Wilder rejects Schweitzer's insistence that Jesus' ethics are purely for an interim.[62] Wilder observes that Jewish ethics were still ethics for an interim, primarily designed to prepare for the coming of salvation. But the character of ethics changed radically with the coming of Jesus. There was no longer an interim, since, through God's redemptive action, Jesus signified the presence of the time of salvation and the days of the new covenant. The transition from the old era to the new accounts for the urgency of Jesus' ethics, which commonly assumes the form of a summons by Jesus and confession of him. This urgency, however, cannot be expressed by an "anachronistic and literal Second Coming or forensic Judgment viewed as impending in our day."[63] The dynamic vision of God in his historical activity is the compelling force that continually redirects and animates us along the line of his purpose. Still, Wilder does not want to abandon the rich symbolic expression of New Testament mythological eschatology, because he is convinced that only by retaining it can the fullness and wholeness of the message be conveyed and safeguarded.[64]

Evaluating Bultmann's and Wilder's approach, we must note that

---

is presumably connected with Bultmann's "Lutheran background." Yet Luther never advocated an individualistic piety. Even associating Bultmann with an allegedly individualistic pietistic background would leave many questions unanswered.

Though Wilder is basically right in seeing Lutheran and pietistic influences in Bultmann's approach, we hope to show in this book that a Lutheran understanding of New Testament eschatology, i.e., an eschatology founded on Luther's basic insights in the New Testament proclamation, is neither exclusively individualistic nor exclusively otherworldly in orientation. Only in continuous tension between concern for the individual and the community, and between concern for this world and the world to come, can we live truly eschatologically.

60. Wilder, *Eschatology and Ethics*, 62.
61. Wilder, *Eschatology and Ethics*, 59.
62. For the following, cf. Wilder, *Eschatology and Ethics*, 176-77.
63. Wilder, *Eschatology and Ethics*, 193.
64. Wilder, *Eschatology and Ethics*, 69-70.

they emphasize rightly the present-oriented aspect of eschatology. Eschatology is not just something that has to do with the so-called last things out there, but it is also essentially connected with the here and now. Yet, both theologians seem to neglect the fact that eschatology determines the present because it has determined the future.[65] The future element in the New Testament, which in its ultimate sense speaks of the end of our particularistic and corporate history here on earth, cannot be fully expressed in strictly nonhistorical and existential categories or by taking it as a symbolic expression. Wilder modifies the highly individualistic approach of Bultmann by relating it to the ethical and social issues of our time.[66] In so doing he opens up the future dimension of eschatology. But his symbolic interpretation does not give a strong enough incentive to wrestle successfully with our present social and ethical issues. Jesus' call for a decision cannot be replaced by symbols or a mystical kingdom of God.

However, both Bultmann and Wilder pose a more serious question to which we too must give careful attention (cf. chap. 4): How can we, in the twenty-first century, still accept a future eschaton in the sense of the coming of a new world or of a total transformation of this present world? Our secular world in which we extend our dominion over more and more facets of life does not seem to allow for any God-provided novelty. It seems to run its own course according to its own scientifically predictable laws.

b. Transcendentalistic Approaches

Charles H. Dodd (1884-1973) is another influential theologian who emphasizes the existential impact of eschatology. But it is not the di-

---

65. Cf. Erlemann, 177, who in his critique of Bultmann claims that with the existential interpretation of eschatology, the bipolarity of the Christian hope is lost.

66. When Wilder talks about "mythopoetic images" (cf. his *Otherworldliness and the New Testament* [New York: Harper, 1954], 9), he does not talk about mythology in the same sense that Bultmann does. But do these images provide more than an incentive for immanent hope? While in his existential interpretation of the New Testament message Bultmann attempts to merge the dichotomy between immanent and transcendent, Wilder seems to leave the transcendent "up there" as a power to solve our problems here on earth (cf. 117-19).

chotomy between the worldviews of antiquity and modern science that leads him to a nonhistorical interpretation of the future-oriented eschatological imagery of the New Testament. Dodd starts with the unsolved question of the consistent eschatology of Albert Schweitzer: How is it possible that the false hope for an early return of Christ in glory could not touch the substance of the Christian hope?[67]

The first Christians expected the last judgment and the coming of Christ almost any day. "During the first century events occurred from time to time which raised hopes that it was at hand; but they were always disappointed, as similar hopes have been disappointed many times since."[68] Though their hopes for an early return of Jesus Christ proved to be an illusion, the center of their hope did not change. Gradually they realized that the decisive event had already happened: Christ had come. All these years when they were hoping for a second coming, they derived the strength to continue their hope in the face of disappointment from the fact that he had come and not, as they had thought, from the "prospect of his second coming." God had confronted the Jewish people in his kingdom, power, and glory. This world had become the scene of the divine drama, in which the eternal issues were laid bare. It was the hour of decision. It was "realized eschatology,"[69] because in Jesus the eternal entered decisively into history. The eschaton was realized in the coming of the kingdom of God. This means that while Jesus used the traditional apocalyptic symbolism to indicate the "otherworldly" or absolute character of the kingdom of God, he used parables to enforce and illustrate the idea that the kingdom of God had come upon people then and there. The coming of the kingdom of God even implied a judgment because those who censured Jesus for his work and teaching pronounced judgment upon themselves. They excluded themselves from the kingdom. "The act of acceptance or of rejection determines the whole direction of a man's life, and so of his destiny."[70]

Finally, the first Christians realized that God's victory was won, that Christ had won it, and that they already shared in it. This discovery allowed them to make the necessary readjustments in their thinking with-

---

67. Cf. C. H. Dodd, *The Parables of the Kingdom* (New York: Scribner, 1961), vii.

68. C. H. Dodd, *The Coming of Christ — Four Broadcast Addresses for the Season of Advent* (Cambridge: Cambridge University Press, 1951), 7.

69. Cf. Dodd, *Parables of the Kingdom*, 159.

70. Dodd, *Parables of the Kingdom*, 162.

out a disastrous disappointment. They did not, however, discard the hope for another coming of Christ. They knew about the tensions between realization and expectation: God's victory was won, yet there were many difficulties to overcome. But how was the victory won? Dodd points here to the characteristic signs of the Day of the Lord. Jesus, as presented by the Gospel writers, had announced threatening catastrophes which were more than mere personal disasters. And he proclaimed a final triumph. He would rise from the dead, the kingdom of God would come with power, and the Son of Man would come with the clouds of heaven. All this points to the same thing: "Immediate victory out of apparent defeat."[71] He returned to life after his death, gathered his disturbed followers, empowered them with his Holy Spirit, and sent them out into the world.[72] So a new era started with the kingdom of Christ on earth. Christ's resurrection invested him with power and glory, and he became the invisible king of all people. This source of power kept the church alive throughout the centuries.

> The Church prays, "Thy Kingdom come"; "Come, Lord Jesus." As it prays, it remembers that the Lord did come, and with Him came the Kingdom of God. Uniting memory with aspiration, it discovers that He comes. He comes in His Cross and Passion; He comes in the glory of His Father with the holy angels. Each Communion is not a stage in the process by which His coming draws gradually nearer, or a milestone on the road by which we slowly approach the distant goal of the Kingdom of God on earth. It is a re-living of the decisive moment at which He came.
>
> The preaching of the Church is directed towards reconstituting in the experience of individuals the hour of decision which Jesus brought. . . . It assumes that history in the individual life is of the same stuff as history at large; that is, it is significant so far as it serves to bring men face to face with God in His Kingdom, power and glory.[73]

71. Cf. Dodd, *The Coming of Christ,* 12-14.

72. Cf. C. H. Dodd, *The Interpretation of the Fourth Gospel* (Cambridge: University Press, 1953), 405-7, where he emphasizes that already John (13:31–14:31) understood Christ's return "in a sense different from that of popular Christian eschatology." After the death of Jesus, and because of it, Jesus' followers will enter into union with him as their living Lord. Thus death marks his departure from this earth, while resurrection stands for his enthronement in power and his return.

73. Dodd, *Parables of the Kingdom,* 164-65. Cf. also his *The Founder of Christianity*

Dodd's magnificent interpretation of the existential impact of eschatology has to wrestle with another line of thought in the New Testament. Dodd realizes that some passages in the New Testament mention a breakdown of the physical universe before Christ's coming. Though he does not want to take the imagery of falling stars and darkening sun literally, he knows that the most elegant symbolic interpretation cannot do justice to the reality behind it. Thus he asserts that the final coming of Christ will not be a coming in history, because the coming of Christ in history has already been fulfilled in his resurrection, but "*beyond* history."[74] In hoping for it as an event in history, we might also be tempted to see it in close parallel to the restoration of the kingdom of David, which was the utopia of popular Jewish hopes in the time of Jesus. But Jesus expressly rejected such thought, and no alternative utopia is suggested. "There is no hint that the Kingdom of God is Utopia."[75]

The attempt to escape both from an antiquated cosmology and from seeking the coming of the kingdom in an earthly utopia leads Dodd to a transcendentalistic approach that asserts the eschaton in the future but beyond history. Yet Dodd does not absolutize this approach but tries to balance it with an equal emphasis on the existential now of the aspired eschaton. He concludes that when John emphasized in his Gospel that *now* the judgment of this world had come, he was not mistaken, and whenever people believed that the Lord was near and the judgment was to come, they were not mistaken, because Christ comes beyond space and time. Although the blessedness of God's kingdom may be enjoyed here and now, "it is never exhausted in any experience that falls within the bounds of space and time."[76] But when all history is taken up into the larger whole of God's eternal purpose, Christ will come the last time, everything will reach its fulfillment, and we will see our lives the way God sees them.

We must admit that Dodd presents an impressive interpretation of eschatology which does justice to its emphasis on the present. He also seems to provide a convincing and scriptural approach to the future-oriented as-

---

(New York: Macmillan, 1970), 172, where he again emphasizes the experience of a new corporate life, made possible because God himself had come to humanity in a way altogether new.

74. Cf. Dodd, *The Coming of Christ*, 17.

75. Dodd, *Parables of the Kingdom*, 166-67.

76. Dodd, *Parables of the Kingdom*, 169, and *The Coming of Christ*, 19-25.

pect of eschatology.[77] But we cannot fully agree with him when he asserts that Christ comes whenever we firmly believe in his coming, and that all history will eventually be taken up into God. A twofold outcome of history is so firmly embedded in the New Testament that it cannot be changed to a universal homecoming as Dodd suggests, which indeed does not even coincide with the end of all history. Of course, it is always tempting to envision the final goal of history as an earthly utopia. Dodd rightly warns us against this fallacy, but his alternative of a spiritualization of the future eschaton is too high a price to pay.

John A. T. Robinson (1919-83) presented a very fascinating thesis in his book *Jesus and His Coming: The Emergence of a Doctrine* that sounds much like Dodd's conviction: The oldest synoptic traditions know nothing of a second coming. The idea of a second coming emerged shortly before Paul as a result of uncertainty as to whether or not the earthly life of Jesus was already messianic. The primitive tradition believed the climax of Jesus' ministry was his being received up into "the presence and triumph of God, from which, already glorified, he shows himself to the disciples, and from which henceforth he pours out his Spirit on the Church and comes to his world in judgment and power."[78] The future belongs to Christ until the final consummation of this age. The catastrophic climax is seen and interpreted as an integral part of the coming of the Son of Man which has already started in the ministry of Jesus.

Robinson sees no evidence in the teaching of Jesus, or in the earliest preaching and creeds of the church, that there should be a second eschatological moment, a second advent of Christ after a certain time has elapsed. In the Gospels "the application of the teaching of Jesus to a Parousia after an interval is a purely editorial feature."[79] Of course, Je-

77. We are inclined to agree with Dodd when he says (*Fourth Gospel*, 447) that the formula "the hour is coming, and now is" (cf. John 5:25), with the emphasis on the "and now is," without excluding the element of futurity, "probably represents the authentic teaching of Jesus as veraciously as any formula could."

Without engaging in a discussion whether the priority belongs to the synoptics or to John, we must ask if such an *ipsissima vox* could substantiate Dodd's claim to give priority to present-oriented eschatology? Hardly, because we cannot proclaim like Jesus, but like Jesus of Nazareth *and* under the impression of the resurrected Jesus Christ. This shifts the emphasis from the present to a "progressive" balance between present and future.

78. John A. T. Robinson, *Jesus and His Coming: The Emergence of a Doctrine* (London: SCM, 1957), 136-37.

79. Robinson, *Jesus and His Coming*, 138.

sus talked about the coming of the Son of Man. However, with this he did not refer to his second coming but to the "visitation of God to his people focused in the challenge and climax of his own ministry."[80] Why, then, did the church reinterpret these sayings as applying to a second coming? Similar to Dodd, Robinson finds the reason in an unresolved crisis in the Christology of the primitive church caused by the doubt as to whether or not the messianic event had taken place and whether or not the Christ had come. The result was a compromise: "part of it had taken place and part of it had not, the Christ had come and yet would come."[81] Thus the messianic drama had two main parts, separated by an interval. The Gospel of John represents the original teaching of Jesus best, since it was not so much exposed to and distorted by apocalyptic thoughts as most other New Testament writings. We notice in John a gradual change from a primitive nonapocalyptic eschatology to a subsequent and more apocalyptic way of thinking.[82]

Robinson rightly reminds us that Christ's first coming at "Christmas" and his last coming in the final parousia form a unity and must be equally emphasized. But, contrary to Robinson's assumption, they are not one and the same parousia. The sameness of Christ in both events does not mean that they should be merged into one single event. They mark the starting point of God's redemptive action in Jesus Christ on the one hand and his final mission on the other, and are thus to be distinguished as two different events.

Like Dodd, Robinson does not conceive of the end of history as coinciding with Christ's final coming.[83] The encounter with God does not change the confines of space and time, because it occurs beyond them. Again we notice that the twofold outcome of history is dismissed in favor of a universalistic approach when Robinson says: "Christ, in Origen's old words, remains on the Cross so long as one sinner remains in hell. That is not speculation: it is a statement grounded in the very necessity of God's nature. In a universe of love there can be no heaven which tolerates a chamber of horrors, no hell for any which does not at the same time make it hell for God. He cannot endure that, for *that*

80. Robinson, *Jesus and His Coming*, 141.
81. Robinson, *Jesus and His Coming*, 142.
82. Cf. Robinson, *Jesus and His Coming*, 163-64.
83. Cf. John A. T. Robinson, *In the End God . . . A Study of the Christian Doctrine of the Last Things* (London: James Clarke, 1950), 68-69.

would be the final mockery of his nature. And he will not."[84] In other words, God's omnipotent love excludes the possibility of hell and will not allow for anyone to be condemned.

3. The Future-Directedness of Eschatology

While existentialist and transcendentalist approaches to eschatology emphasize the present as the decisive moment, and while the future-directed approach does not neglect the present either, the main emphasis in this latter approach is on the future, not in terms of an escapist approach, but in the sense that the turning point of history lies in the past. In realizing that we are approaching the future fulfillment provided by God, we can face the realities of the present. This path is pursued both by New Testament scholars and also by systematic theologians.

a. Exegetical Considerations

Pointing to the necessary tension between the fulfillment which has already occurred and the still-outstanding future, many exegetes have no problem emphasizing the future-directedness of eschatology. Kurt

84. Robinson, *In the End God*, 123. At least parenthetically we must mention at the end of our brief survey of transcendentalist approaches the position of T. W. Manson, who, like Robinson, is influenced by Dodd's concept of realized eschatology. In his book *The Teaching of Jesus: Studies of Its Form and Content* (Cambridge: Cambridge University Press, 1959), for instance, in advocating a corporate understanding of the Son of Man title, Manson suggests: "The 'Son of Man' in the present is a name for Jesus plus any who take up the cross and follow him: the 'Son of Man' coming in glory and power is the same, Jesus and all who have faithfully followed him, Christ plus those that are Christ's, who suffer with him and are glorified with him" (269). However, the final victory of good over evil will not be delayed indefinitely, and the final consummation will come sooner or later, suddenly or gradually, otherwise the kingdom of God would become an empty dream (284). Again a universalistic tinge seems to come up when Manson asserts that "every generation will be judged by its response to such manifestation of the sovereignty of God as was available in its day" (271). Norman Perrin, *Rediscovering the Teaching of Jesus* (London: SCM, 1967), 206, seems to move in a similar direction when he points to the "inadequacies of a linear concept of time" and asserts that time is something in the proclamation of Jesus "which God fills and *fulfils,* and it is something which man experiences, rather than something which moves from past to future."

Erlemann (b. 1958), for instance, correctly states: "The new reality of salvation which was begun with Christ has still not gained the upper hand on earth visibly and universally. Christian existence is carried both by the certainty that the new has already started and by the enduring desire for a universal disclosure of the new."[85]

Eschatology as Fulfillment and Promise

Oscar Cullmann (1902-99) recognizes that Jesus expected the coming of the eschaton in the near future, but then distinguishes between the future dimension in Jesus' expectation and the setting of a date. He admits that the end was first expected within the lifetime of the present generation, while later this assumption was corrected without affecting the future dimension of Jesus' expectation.[86] Consistent in this expectation, however, was the future dimension which remained unchanged even though the parousia did not occur as expected. Jesus, too, was aware of an interim period which was to elapse between his ministry and his final parousia. Of course, he reckoned with a very short time span before this parousia would occur. In principle, however, this is no different from Luke's concept of the interim period as the time of the church. According to Cullmann, the idea of an *immediately* coming eschaton resulted from the immediate confrontation with the tension between the salvation which has already occurred in Jesus Christ and the final realization of this salvific act which has not yet occurred. Since salvation is *already* actually present, it guarantees that the *not yet* of its final realization will soon be changed, and thus the hope for an immediately coming eschaton can emerge.

Notwithstanding the emergence of this hope, the already present salvation strengthens the conviction that the coming of the end cannot be postponed indefinitely. Later, when the unknown duration of the interim is more strongly emphasized, the idea that we live in the last time is nevertheless not abandoned. The death of Jesus, together with the resurrection which followed, was conceived as the decisive event. The historical work of Jesus is concluded, and the midpoint of time is

---

85. Erlemann, 177.
86. Cf. for the following, Oscar Cullmann, *Salvation in History*, trans. S. G. Sowers et al. (London: SCM, 1967), 179-80.

passed.[87] Though we cannot emphasize either the salvation which has *already* occurred or the final realization of salvation which has *not yet* occurred in an exclusive way, the two are not in opposition. "The *decisive turn of events* has already occurred in Christ, the mid-point, and that now the future expectation is founded in faith in the 'already,' shows that the 'already' outweighs the 'not yet.'"[88] Jesus proclaimed the coming of the kingdom of God as a future event and anticipated it in his person in a proleptic way. But this caused the tension between the already fulfilled eschaton and the not yet completed eschatological events.[89] The combination of the parallelism and mutual dependence of the already and the not yet is the actual essence of Jesus' eschatological outlook. The already and the not yet depend on each other and presuppose each other: the present assertions point toward the coming fulfillment, while the futurist assertions are grounded in the present anticipation and initiation.

Cullmann's approach seems to be close to the New Testament. He emphatically asserts both the present and future dimensions of eschatology. However, can one really refute so easily the advocates of consistent eschatology in saying that essentially it does not matter whether the coming of the eschaton was expected within the next two years or within the next two thousand years?[90] Was Bultmann right after all when he pointed out that the early expectation of the approaching end of the world was part of Jesus' outdated worldview?

Although following an approach similar to Cullmann's, the Marburg New Testament scholar and successor of Bultmann, **Werner Georg Kümmel** (1905-95), seems to find a better solution to this dilemma. He claims that the eschatological proclamation of Jesus "cannot be regarded simply as a particular form of Jewish apocalyptic" or as "a

---

87. Cf. Oscar Cullmann, *Christ and Time: The Primitive Christian Conception of Time and History*, trans. F. V. Filson (London: SCM, 1962), 84-85.

88. Cullmann, *Salvation in History*, 183.

89. Cullmann, *Salvation in History*, 202.

90. Cf. Oscar Cullmann, "Das wahre durch die ausgebliebene Parusie gestellte neutestamentliche Problem" (1947), in *Vorträge und Aufsätze: 1925-1962* (Tübingen: Mohr, 1966), 422-23. Cullmann's reference to the Hellenization of eschatology which was connected with the growth of the church does not solve the problem either (cf. also *Christ and Time*), because the question must be asked if the process of Hellenization was a necessity and whether it can ever be reversed. Thomas J. J. Altizer's attempt to reverse this process shows what results one might arrive at.

completely non-Jewish, non-apocalyptic eschatology concerned only with the present."[91]

Kümmel rejects the idea of a re-Judaization of eschatology after Jesus' death as well as the attempts of Robinson and Ethelbert Stauffer (1902-79) to play the priority of the Gospel of John against the synoptics.[92] Neither an exclusive orientation toward the present or the future nor an elimination of the expectation of an immediately coming eschaton does justice to Jesus and the New Testament tradition. After Easter, Jesus' disciples and followers did not change the present-oriented eschatological proclamation of Jesus into a future-directed eschatology in the fashion of Jewish apocalyptic. The opposite assumption, that the first Christians expected salvation in the near future and then under the impact of Easter realized gradually that the eschaton was already present, is equally unfounded.

From the very beginning Jesus and the first Christians expected the impending coming of God and his salvation and expected at the same time the appearance of his anointed one from heaven. The first Christians combined, as did Jesus, the expectation of salvation with the belief in the presence of salvation in Jesus and his actions. But already Jesus reckoned with an interval between his resurrection and the parousia. This interval gained importance in the thinking of the first Christians.[93] Kümmel does not regard the expectation of the soon-approaching eschaton merely as an emphasis on the certainty of the present beginning of the kingdom of God. Jesus talked in the imagery of his time about the nearness of the kingdom of God in order to actualize God's redemptive action directed toward the consummation.

This means that the expectation of the nearness of the eschaton need not be repeated nowadays. It is part of an outdated imagery. However, the expectation of the future completion is essential and cannot be detached from Jesus' proclamation without distorting it. With such an expectation we can talk about God's redemptive action as an action in history.[94] The

---

91. Cf. Werner Georg Kümmel, in his excellent study *Promise and Fulfillment: The Eschatological Message of Jesus,* trans. D. M. Barton (Naperville, Ill.: Allenson, 1957), 141.

92. Cf. for the following, Werner Georg Kümmel, "Futurische und präsentische Eschatologie im ältesten Christentum," in *Heilsgeschehen und Geschichte,* 356-58.

93. Kümmel, "Futurische und präsentische Eschatologie im ältesten Christentum," 360-62.

94. Kümmel, *Promise and Fulfillment,* 152-53.

future expectation must be seen in correlation with the fulfillment in Jesus Christ. The future promise and the past fulfillment "are therefore inseparably united for Jesus and depend on each other; for the promise is made sure by the fulfillment that has already taken place in Jesus, and the fulfillment, being provisional and concealed, loses its quality as a *skandalon* [scandal] only through the promise yet to come."[95]

Kümmel's approach seems to be well balanced and very close to the scriptural basis. We have only one reservation, and it is more in the form of a question: Did Jesus really at any time advocate an impending eschatology?

Delay of the Parousia

Conservative or even evangelical theologians have often addressed the issue of impending eschatology and the claim of a delay of the parousia head-on. The German New Testament scholar Gerhard Maier (b. 1937), for instance, stated: "That the community or even Jesus himself mistakenly expected the end of the world as imminently impending is contradicted by the New Testament."[96] Exemplary for these theologians' way of argumentation is **Anthony A. Hoekema** (b. 1913). He distinguishes in the synoptics three rows of arguments regarding the future of the kingdom of God:

1. There are three references that seem to mention an immediate return of Jesus.
2. There is another group of sayings that implies a delay of the parousia.
3. There is a group of sayings of the Lord and of parables that emphasizes the uncertainty regarding the date of the parousia.[97]

Among the first group is Mark 9:1: "Truly I tell you, there are some standing here who will not taste death until they see that the kingdom of God has come with power." The issue here is that this

95. Kümmel, *Promise and Fulfillment*, 155.

96. Gerhard Maier, "Eschatologie," in *Das grosse Bibellexikon* (Wuppertal: R. Brockhaus, 1987), 1:349.

97. Anthony A. Hoekema, *The Bible and the Future* (Grand Rapids: Eerdmans, 1979), 112.

statement mentions that some will see the kingdom of God coming in power during their own lifetime. Having investigated the different possibilities for interpreting this statement according to their plausibility, Hoekema concludes that in the understanding of the disciples the resurrection of Christ and the parousia had been connected with each other. Presumably they thought Christ's resurrection would occur at the last day (cf. Mark 9:9-11). According to Hoekema, Jesus, too, in typically prophetic overstatement, sees his resurrection together with his parousia. This means: "He predicted that many who are living as he utters these words will witness his resurrection, which in one sense is a coming of the kingdom of God with power."[98] Therefore we cannot find an error on Jesus' side, because the resurrection will guarantee the parousia.

The next reference investigated by Hoekema is the assertion in Mark 13:30: "Truly I tell you, this generation will not pass away until all these things have taken place." Again, he looks for the appropriateness of the possible interpretations. Hoekema differs from Cullmann and Kümmel in that both understood by "all these things" also the parousia of Jesus and by "this generation" the listeners at that time. This would mean that to some extent Jesus was mistaken. Though Hoekema admits that "all things" points to the eschatological events, including Christ's return on the clouds of heaven, he asserts, contrary to Cullmann and Kümmel, that "this generation" does not signify this present generation. In a metaphorical sense it stands for the rebellious and unfaithful Jewish nation as it showed itself in the past and lives in the present and will continue in the future.[99] This means this nation will continue to exist until Christ's return.

The last passage that allegedly points to an imminent expectation which was not met is Matthew 10:23: "When they persecute you in one town, flee to the next; for truly I tell you, you will not have gone through all the towns of Israel before the Son of Man comes." Hoekema's procedure is similar to what we have seen with the two previous passages. First, he claims, we must take into consideration that in prophetic overstatement Jesus often connected facts which related to the near future with events of the distant past when talking with his disci-

98. Hoekema, 114.
99. Hoekema, 117.

ples. What Jesus mentions concerning the immediate persecution could then also have relevance for the people of God in the more distant future. Therefore this passage tells us that the church of Jesus Christ should care for Israel and proclaim the gospel to these people until the parousia, even if many Jews continue to reject the gospel. Hoekema concludes this part of his investigation remarking that these three assertions in no way need to be interpreted to indicate a return of Christ during the lifetime of Christ's audience.

Now Hoekema focuses on a second group of sayings in the synoptics which can be understood to say that the parousia would still be outstanding for a long time. Matthew 24:14 may serve as one example: "And this good news of the kingdom will be proclaimed throughout the world, as a testimony to all the nations; and then the end will come." Sayings of that kind as well as references in the parables which talk about a long time (Matt. 25:5) are properly interpreted to mean that Jesus left open the possibility that his return would not occur so quickly.

A third group of sayings asserts that nobody knows the exact time of his return (Matt. 25:13). Hoekema therefore concludes that the parousia will occur at a time when no one would expect it. This phenomenon of surprise implies that we must always be ready.

Hoekema summarizes the results of his investigation by saying that Jesus did not set a date for his return. Consequently we cannot talk about a mistake or a lack of perspective on Jesus' part. Of course, he admits, it is possible that some of his disciples or followers mistakenly understood him as announcing a date for his parousia, and one must note that he asserted that he would come in royal power during the lifetime of his listeners (Matt. 16:28). But these assertions point to his resurrection, which is a prelude and a guarantee for his parousia.[100] Even Paul did not move from an original imminent expectation to a later delay of the parousia. Only in a letter of Peter do we read that outsiders jokingly talked about a delay of the parousia, a point which is decidedly refuted by this letter.[101] In his investigations Hoekema refers especially to the results of George Eldon Ladd (b. 1911), who mentions "the prophetic tension between history and eschatology" in Jesus which has its parallels

---

100. Cf. to this result Hoekema, 122.
101. Hoekema, 127.

in the Old Testament prophecy and which was largely lost in the period of apocalypticism.[102]

Theologians of this more conservative camp maintain a bipolar tension between present and future in the kingdom-of-God proclamation of Jesus while they refute the thesis that an actual delay of the parousia has happened. They assert that Jesus did not err concerning the fulfillment of the kingdom of God, nor did he talk about such a delay. One must certainly concur with them that Jesus did not intend an actual imminent expectation which then did not materialize. One should also, we may add, not cavalierly talk about Jesus being mistaken and assert that Jesus was human and a mistake like this could happen to anyone. Admittedly, some mistakes hardly matter, while others are crucial. "If I wear the wrong necktie, this mistake may be forgiven, whereas if I use somebody else's credit card, this comes under the verdict of fraud. If Jesus was wrong about the time of the parousia, he was not simply mistaken, but his whole message was a fraud. At that point we should take Albert Schweitzer more seriously."[103] At the same time we should not overlook the fact that at the time of Jesus many people — presumably even some members of the more narrow circle of his disciples — hoped for a prompt and final establishment of the kingdom of God with clearly this-worldly connotations. They indeed were mistaken and subsequently disappointed.

b. Systematic Proposals

The positions reviewed so far were presented mainly by New Testament scholars who convinced us of the centrality of eschatology for the Christian faith. Yet by their very specialization these scholars have hardly moved beyond the limitations of their own field of biblical and exegetical theology. The case is different for the last group of scholars we want to review. Though they do not take lightly the biblical basis

---

102. Cf. George Eldon Ladd, *The Presence of the Future: The Eschatology of Biblical Realism* (Grand Rapids: Eerdmans, 1974), 320. Similarly Stephen H. Travis, *Christian Hope and the Future* (Downers Grove, Ill.: InterVarsity, 1980), 22-23.

103. Hans Schwarz, "The Significance of Matthew's Eschatology for Systematic Theology," in *1996 Seminar Papers*, ed. Society of Biblical Literature (Atlanta: Scholars Press, 1996), 184.

from which they argue, their field of competence as systematic theologians necessarily forces them to relate the biblical insights to the spiritual, social, political, and economic issues of today. But their main impetus for connecting the biblical horizon to life today seems to come from extrabiblical stimuli. For instance, Jürgen Moltmann has been initially influenced by the neo-Marxist philosopher Ernst Bloch (1885-1977), Wolfhart Pannenberg has been enriched by the thought of Georg Wilhelm Friedrich Hegel (1770-1831), and Gustavo Gutiérrez (b. 1928), as we will see in the next section, has been shaped in his outlook by Marxist sources.

Prolepsis of Eschatology

Had it not been for his own experience as a "liberated" refugee from Stettin (formerly part of Pomerania, Germany, and now part of Poland), **Wolfhart Pannenberg** (b. 1928) might have become the leader of the liberating and revolutionary aspect of eschatology. Certainly his system of thought emphasizes very strongly that eschatology does not simply pertain to the future, but is already proleptically anticipated within the Christian community. Pannenberg's understanding of eschatology is intimately connected with his perception of Jesus of Nazareth and the God-disclosive history of Israel. Therefore he claims: "God's revelation in history also has the form of an anticipation of the definitive manifestation of his eternal and omnipotent deity in the event of the consummation of all time and history."[104] In God's self-disclosure we are allowed to see something of that toward which all history moves.

In his widely discussed "Dogmatic Theses on the Doctrine of Revelation" (1961), Pannenberg claims that God's self-disclosure, as reflected in the biblical documents, does not occur in a direct way as a theophany, but indirectly through God's acts in history. Furthermore, Pannenberg observes that "revelation is not comprehended completely in the beginning, but at the end of the revealing history."[105] History discloses its full meaning as God's history only at the end. This is due to

---

104. Wolfhart Pannenberg, *Systematic Theology*, trans. Geoffrey W. Bromiley, 3 vols. (Grand Rapids: Eerdmans, 1991-98), 3:531.
105. Wolfhart Pannenberg, *Revelation as History*, ed. Wolfhart Pannenberg, trans. D. Granskou (New York: Macmillan, 1968), 131 (thesis 2).

the fact that the individual historical acts are transparent for God not in themselves but only if perceived in the universal historical context. This can be seen especially well in the Old Testament when, in the course of history, the content of revelation ascribed to various historical events had to be revised and expanded according to the historical progression.

But Pannenberg rejects the historical relativism that might result from the simple progression of history and the necessary revisions of our perception of God's self-disclosure derived from history when he states: "The universal revelation of the deity of God is not yet realized in the history of Israel, but first in the destiny of Jesus of Nazareth, insofar as the end of all events is anticipated in his destiny."[106] The destiny of Jesus does not have a universal character just because the end of all history *was envisioned* in that destiny. The assertion taken by itself would only be a repetition of the claim of Albert Schweitzer that Jesus believed that with his life, or at least with his death, the end of the world would come, a belief that was never realized. But Pannenberg goes a decisive step further, claiming that in Jesus the end of the world has indeed occurred in proleptic anticipation. This means that what had been anticipated as the end and fulfillment of history, the resurrection of the dead, in fact *happened* in a proleptic way in and with Jesus. Since history comes to its conclusion in the destiny of Jesus, this destiny is the key to our understanding of God's self-disclosure. The Christ event has a truly eschatological character, since there is no self-disclosure of God necessary beyond this event. At the end of the world there will only occur on a cosmic scale what happened in and with Jesus on an individual scale.

One might question why Pannenberg attributes so much significance to the resurrection of Jesus, since up to now it has been an exceptional event without any precedent or consequence in other resurrections. But Pannenberg counters that one must perceive it in its proper context, the time of apocalyptic and the expectation of the resurrection of the dead prevalent during that time. If we consider Jesus' resurrection in the apocalyptic context in which Jesus lived, it becomes clear that the resurrection must bear the significance of foreshadowing the

---

106. Pannenberg, *Revelation as History*, 139 (thesis 4; translation mine). For the discussion of Pannenberg's concept of revelation in history, cf. also Wolfhart Pannenberg, "Insight and Faith," in *Basic Questions in Theology*, 2:28-45, in his discussion with Paul Althaus; and "Redemptive Event and History," in *Basic Questions in Theology*, 1:15-80.

eschaton. It is, on the one hand, the validation of the claim of Jesus made before Easter that he represents and carries the authority of God. But it also means that in his destiny the end has started and God is revealed in him. Jesus therefore becomes the focal point for our understanding of eschatology.

Jesus is the paradigm and the anticipation of our own future and at the same time the inspiration and possibility of living toward that future. In Jesus, God's love was announced to us before his kingdom had fully come. Thus the coming of the kingdom should not cause surprise or terror. Since Jesus announced it, we are able to open ourselves to God's future. We can find communion with him who decides the future of all things and can anticipate the final significance and essence of all things. Of course, the communion with God which is possible through Christ necessitates our active participation in his creative love which supports all creatures, grants them their limited duration, and brings them to fulfillment of life by relating them to one another. Immediately we notice the individual and social ethical implications of Pannenberg's approach to eschatology. Since we are able to participate proleptically in the promised future, we are encouraged to anticipate this future proleptically.

Yet Pannenberg cautions that Jesus was only the forerunner and herald of the still-imminent kingdom. Thus we should not destroy and disdain the values of past and present in the name of the future. Pannenberg reminds us: "The history of modern revolutions illustrates the fatal flaw in living so exclusively for the future that all cherishing and celebrating of the present are precluded."[107] Pannenberg cautions us not to pursue such unrealistic futurism, since the ultimate fulfillment of the coming kingdom is beyond our human power to effect. But he also reminds us that we are far from being relegated to inactivity. On the contrary, we are inspired to prepare the present for the future to come. Such preparation is the work of hope carried out by love and will make our present conditions more attuned to the promised future. Together with the world we live in, we must be open beyond ourselves to the future of God's kingdom.

Wolfhart Pannenberg was one of the first systematic theologians in

107. Wolfhart Pannenberg, *Theology and the Kingdom of God*, ed. Richard J. Neuhaus (Philadelphia: Westminster, 1969), 126.

the twentieth century to show that the eschatology of Jesus had significance beyond our existential now. He directed our attention again to the relationship of eschatology and time and to the necessity of integrating nature and existence. We know God's kingdom will find its fulfillment in the future, since it can be proleptically anticipated in the present, and we know that this proleptic anticipation has implications beyond our own existence. Once Pannenberg had succeeded in making eschatology acceptable again in the sense of a new historical creation of the kingdom of God, his suggestion was picked up by many other theologians.

Theology of Hope

Unlike Pannenberg, the main emphasis of **Jürgen Moltmann** (b. 1926) is on the implications of eschatology. In his seminal book *Theology of Hope: On the Ground and the Implications of a Christian Eschatology* (1967), Moltmann makes clear from the first page that he does not want to confine himself to a strictly theological treatise. He is much more interested in showing the practical consequences of a biblical eschatological perspective as they inform church life and the burning political issues, such as social justice, world peace, and personal freedom. Eschatology is, for Moltmann, the doctrine of Christian hope "which embraces both the object hoped for and also the hope inspired by it."[108] He no longer wants to confine eschatology to discourse about the so-called last things which will happen in the end, but to consider the whole cause which drives toward this end. Backed by the earlier thesis of Ernst Käsemann that "apocalyptic was the mother of all Christian theology,"[109] Moltmann claims that Christianity in its totality is eschatological, and nothing that pertains to it is exempt from this. With this he reiterates, of course, the famous dictum of Karl Barth in his commentary on Romans: "If Christianity be not altogether thoroughgoing eschatology, there remains in it no relationship whatever with Christ."[110]

---

108. Jürgen Moltmann, *Theology of Hope: On the Ground and the Implications of a Christian Eschatology,* trans. J. W. Leitch (New York: Harper & Row, 1967), 16.

109. Ernst Käsemann, "The Beginnings of Christian Theology" (1960), in Ernst Käsemann, *New Testament Questions of Today,* trans. W. J. Montague (Philadelphia: Fortress, 1969), 102.

110. Karl Barth, *The Epistle to the Romans,* translated from the 6th edition by Edwyn C. Hoskyns (London: Oxford University Press, 1963), 314.

Moltmann distinguishes between the Israelite religion of promise and the static epiphanic religions in the environment of Israel. After the Israelites' conquest of Palestine, Yahweh still appeared as the promising God who pointed to a new future. This meant that the Old Testament promises were never superseded by historic events, but were constantly modified and expanded. Of course, some were realized in history. These "fulfilled" promises to which Israel owed its existence (the Exodus, the Promised Land, David's kingship) proved, amid all the upheavals of history, to be a *continuum* in which Israel was able to recognize the faithfulness of its God. Yet, the promises were not completely resolved in any event, but there remained an overspill that pointed to the future. "The tension between promise and fulfillment was not left behind by the simple progression of Israel's history, but was much more strongly creative of Israel's historic progress."[111]

Moltmann sees the same feature in the New Testament, because the revelation in Christ is at the same time good news and promise. This revelation presupposes the law and promise of the Old Testament, since Yahweh (the God of Abraham, Isaac, and Jacob, the God of promise) resurrected Jesus, and Jesus was a Jew. This means that Jesus is not to be understood as a particular case of humanity in general, but rather from the perspective of the Old Testament history of promise and in conflict with it. Jesus is not a *theos aner* (divine man) who descended from heaven and whose life on earth is only a temporary episode. On the contrary, Jesus' life, work, death, and resurrection have utmost significance and are described in the categories of expectation appropriate to the God of promise.

The Old Testament history of promise does not simply find its fulfillment in the gospel, but it finds its future in the gospel. Because the gospel is promise, it is a guarantee of the promised future.[112] Here the centrality of Christ's resurrection for the Christian faith becomes evident. The resurrection of Christ is a "history-making event" from which all other history is enlightened, questioned, and transformed.[113] The stories of the resurrection stand in the line of prophetic and apocalyptic expectations, hopes, and questions about what is bound to come accord-

---

111. Moltmann, *Theology of Hope*, 112.
112. Moltmann, *Theology of Hope*, 148.
113. Moltmann, *Theology of Hope*, 180.

ing to the promises of God. Cross and resurrection point toward the future in promising the righteousness of God, the new life as a result of the resurrection from the dead, and the kingdom of God "in a new totality of being."[114]

Moltmann understands the Easter appearances as call appearances in which recognition of Christ coincides with recognition of his mission and his future. Again the forward thrust becomes noticeable. Moltmann concludes that for theology the reality of the world becomes historic in that its mission to the world is seen to be the field of the missionary charge and is examined in a search for real possibilities for the world-transforming missionary hope. "The call to obedient moulding of the world would have no object, if this world were immutable."[115] The world must be open toward the future for good or ill. Secularization has realized these Christian expectations in the field of world history and has outstripped the Christian hope in a chiliastic way. Thus we cannot reject the revolutionary progressiveness of the modern age; we must incorporate the open horizons of modern history into the true eschatological horizon of the resurrection and thereby "disclose to modern history its true historic character."[116] The church cannot confine itself to serving individuals and acting as a conservative force, as society might expect it to. The task and mission of the church is determined by its own peculiar horizon — the eschatological expectation of the coming kingdom of God, the coming righteousness and the coming peace, and the coming freedom and dignity of all humanity. This means "the realization of the eschatological *hope of justice,* the *humanizing* of man, the *socializing* of humanity, *peace* for all creation."[117]

Moltmann's impressive approach makes eschatology meaningful for present-day life. He goes beyond Albert Schweitzer in pointing out that not only the proclamation of Jesus but all of biblical religion is totally eschatological in outlook. He rightly accuses the church of the past of leaving the earthly-eschatological anticipation of the kingdom of God too readily in the hands of "the fanatics and the sects."[118] In reacting against this evident neglect, however, Moltmann draws the future-directedness

114. Moltmann, *Theology of Hope,* 203.
115. Moltmann, *Theology of Hope,* 288.
116. Moltmann, *Theology of Hope,* 303.
117. Moltmann, *Theology of Hope,* 329.
118. Moltmann, *Theology of Hope,* 329.

of eschatology so much into human reach that autonomous humanity will have trouble understanding that all its work is only of anticipatory character. That some accuse Moltmann of reintroducing a concept of the kingdom of God once advocated by liberal nineteenth-century German Protestantism is indicative of this evident danger.[119] This coincides with another observation. Moltmann moves so far away from a one-sided emphasis on the so-called last things to a total eschatological outlook that he almost forgets to mention these last things. When he mentions them, however, they are mostly described as earthly, humanly engendered goals, such as peace for all creation and socializing of humanity.

In later writings Moltmann pursues the same topic from other angles. For instance, in *The Crucified God* (1972) he states at the outset: "The cross is not and cannot be loved. Yet only the crucified Christ can bring the freedom which changes the world because it is no longer afraid of death."[120] After developing a theology of the cross, Moltmann then arrives at the conclusion that since the rejected Son of Man was raised up in the freedom of God, "faith in the resurrection becomes faith that raises up, wherever it transforms psychological and social systems, so that instead of being oriented on death they are oriented on life."[121] Even the theology of the cross therefore urges the psychological and political liberation of humanity.

Similarly, we read in his ecclesiology, *The Church in the Power of the Spirit* (1975): "Prayer for the Spirit makes people watchful and sensitive. It makes them vulnerable and stimulates all the powers of the imagination to perceive the coming of God in the liberation of man and to move into accord with it. This prayer therefore leads to political watchfulness, and political watchfulness leads to prayer."[122] Eschatology, for Molt-

---

119. Cf. Heinz Eduard Tödt, "Aus einem Brief an Jürgen Moltmann," in *Diskussion über die "Theologie der Hoffnung" von Jürgen Moltmann*, ed. Wolf-Dieter Marsch (Munich: Chr. Kaiser, 1967), 197. Yet Moltmann's own intentions are just the opposite. He wants to "restore the messianic character of hope of the Christian faith" to contradict and resist the tendency to turn the Christian faith into a civil religion. Cf. Jürgen Moltmann, *Politische Theologie — Politische Ethik* (Munich: Chr. Kaiser, 1984), 31.

120. Jürgen Moltmann, *The Crucified God: The Cross of Christ as the Foundation and Criticism of Christian Theology*, trans. R. A. Wilson and J. Bowden (New York: Harper, 1974), 1.

121. Moltmann, *The Crucified God*, 294.

122. Jürgen Moltmann, *The Church in the Power of the Spirit: A Contribution to Messianic Ecclesiology*, trans. M. Kohl (New York: Harper, 1977), 287.

mann, implies liberation in this world in terms of political and economic liberation, human solidarity, solidarity with nature, and the struggle for hope. Moltmann rightly reminds us that eschatology leads to action instead of otherworldly passivity or resignation. But his almost exclusively sociopolitical emphasis reminds us too much of the vain human endeavors to establish a theocracy or an earthly utopia, so that we dare not assent to it without expressing a strong eschatological proviso to all such human pursuits.

In one of his most recent major writings, *The Coming of God,* while picking up on his emphasis in his previous *Theology of Hope,* he alleviates some of our fears. He still insists that Christian eschatology is not about apocalyptic final solutions, because its subject is not the end at all. "On the contrary, what it is about is the new creation of all things."[123] Eschatology does not focus on some kind of cataclysm, but again on hope, hope for eternal life, for the kingdom of God, for a new heaven and a new earth, and for the glory of God and what this hope effects. He wants to draw together the different horizons of hope into a single focus, "the cosmic Shekinah of God."[124] This cosmic dwelling of God in his creation is the eschatological goal. Therefore Moltmann puts forward "Advent as eschatological category, and the category Novum as its historical reverse side."[125] This means that the emphasis is not on what is going to happen somewhere out in the future, but the decisive facet is God's coming and his arrival. God's coming future enables a new human becoming. The arriving kingdom of God makes possible the conversion to this future. We notice here, again, as in all of his writings, the summons to action, yet a summons contingent on God's initiative. This becomes most evident in his extensive treatment of millenarian hopes.

While Moltmann rejects the secular millenarianism of the present that betrays a naive faith in progress, he also rejects a naive biblical apocalyptic millenarianism of a triumphalistic type. Yet he claims: "The 'Thousand Years' reign of Christ, 'the kingdom of peace,' is hope's positive counterpart to the Antichrist's destruction of the world in a storm of fire, and is indispensable for every alternative form of life and action

---

123. Jürgen Moltmann, *The Coming of God: Christian Eschatology,* trans. Margaret Kohl (Minneapolis: Fortress, 1996), xi.
124. Moltmann, *The Coming of God,* xiii.
125. Moltmann, *The Coming of God,* 6.

which will withstand the ravages of the world here and now. Without millenarian hope, the Christian ethic of resistance and the consistent discipleship of Christ lose their most powerful motivation."[126] This means that without the hope that Christ will erect his kingdom and indeed does so in a visible way, we are in danger of losing our incentive to resist the forces of evil. Eschatology therefore provides, for Moltmann, the energizing power to form a contrast community to society. Similar to Barth's claim in his *Epistle to the Romans,* but this time carried through the different loci of the Christian faith, theology is thoroughly eschatological.

How far Moltmann distances himself from a traditional doctrine of the last things can be gleaned from his understanding of the last judgment. Judgment, he says, is the side of the eternal kingdom that is turned toward history. When he claims that in the last judgment all sins, every wickedness and every act of violence, the whole injustice of this murderous and suffering world, will be condemned and annihilated, one might still conclude that Moltmann espouses the twofold outcome in the traditional sense. Yet he means that only the negativity will be condemned and annihilated, and not those who committed acts of negativity. Therefore Moltmann states: "In the divine Judgment all sinners, the wicked and the violent, the murderers and the children of Satan, the Devil and the fallen angels will be liberated and saved from their deadly perdition through transformation into their true, created being, because God remains true to himself, and does not give up what he has once created and affirmed, or allow it to be lost."[127] There will be a universal homecoming, which will include even the devil and the fallen angels. God's final victory therefore does not include any condemnation of what he has once created, but the condemnation and elimination of the negativity into which the created fell. God's judgment puts things right, and "in the truth of Christ it is the most wonderful thing that can be proclaimed to men and women." Who could object to that kind of prospect? Whether that vision is not too optimistic remains to be seen. One thing, however, is certainly clear in Moltmann's view: the new creation will be universal and all-embracing. There are no dark spots left on the landscape.

126. Moltmann, *The Coming of God,* 201.
127. See Moltmann, *The Coming of God,* 255, for this and the following quote.

4. The Liberating Power of Eschatology

Liberation seems to be a favorite theological term in many quarters in the latter part of the twentieth century and the first part of the twenty-first. It is not just a significant topic for underprivileged minorities and for those living in the so-called Third World, but for virtually everyone who is sensitive to injustice and domination. For instance, when Pope John Paul II addressed the Third General Conference of the Latin American episcopate in Puebla, Mexico, in 1979, millions of people listened to his words. John Paul II stated that violence, whether committed by those on the left or on the right of the political spectrum, is unchristian and therefore must be condemned. He further emphasized that a theology of liberation which is not founded on the gospel but on the Marxist analysis of reality is a false theology. Yet he recognized that many liberation theologies are not ideologically twisted, but consider Christian values and therefore are true theology. This three-part analysis shows in a nutshell the problematic as well as the promise of liberation theology. It is a response to violence committed in word and deed and recognizes Christian values. It propagates and hopes for evangelically grounded liberation. Yet often those who are concerned about liberation are similar to many of the earliest followers of Jesus. They attempt to take the inauguration of the kingdom in their own hands.

a. Eschatology from the Underside

While we cannot survey the whole gamut of liberation theologies, we must at least pay attention to its eschatological fervor. Johann Baptist Metz (b. 1928) puts the eschatological perspective correctly when he writes: "The faith in a messianic God, a God of the resurrection of the dead and of judgment, a God before whom even the past is not safe, before whom the past sufferings do not disappear subjectless in the abyss of an anonymous and infinite dispassionate evolution, this faith is not an opiate in the histories of liberation of humanity. Rather it guarantees the non-negotiable standards in the unabating struggle for the dignity of all human beings as subjects in the struggle for a universal liberation."[128] Liber-

128. Johann Baptist Metz, "Thesen zum theologischen Ort der Befreiungs-

ation theology believes in the future of God, in God's promises and in a final righting of all wrongs — nay, even already anticipations of that righting. Especially this anticipatory aspect caused some uneasiness in the Roman Catholic hierarchy, since liberation theology is still primarily a Roman Catholic phenomenon, having originated and still having its center of gravity in Latin America.[129]

Problematic and Legitimation of Liberation Theology

The Sacred Congregation for the Doctrine of the Faith, located in the Vatican, has addressed several times the issue of a theology of liberation. In 1984, for instance, it acknowledged that the yearning for liberation agrees with a deep-seated theme of the Old and New Testaments. "In itself, the expression 'theology of liberation' is a thoroughly valid term: it designates a theological reflection centered on the biblical theme of liberation and freedom, and on the urgency of its practical realization."[130] At the same time, the congregation noted that some liberation theologians "are tempted to emphasize, unilaterally, the liberation from servitude of an earthly and temporal kind."[131] Furthermore, concepts that are "uncritically borrowed from marxist ideology and recourse to theses of a biblical hermeneutic marked by rationalism are at the basis of the new interpretation."[132] Where this occurs, the revolutionary praxis becomes the highest criterion of theological truth.

Since these summary accusations concerning some aspects of liberation theology caused much dismay, the congregation issued an instruction, *On Christian Freedom and Liberation,* on March 22, 1986.[133] There we

---

theologie," in *Die Theologie der Befreiung: Hoffnung oder Gefahr für die Kirche?* ed. Johann Baptist Metz (Düsseldorf: Patmos, 1986), 152.

129. For Asia, for instance, cf. the texts reprinted in Douglas J. Elwood, ed., *Asian Christian Theology: Emerging Themes* (Philadelphia: Westminster, 1980), pt. 6, and for India: Thaveedu Aruldoss, *The Relevance of the Social Teachings of Martin Luther for Dalit Liberation* (Madurai, India: J. & D. Publications, 1997).

130. Sacred Congregation for the Doctrine of the Faith, *Instruction on Certain Aspects of the "Theology of Liberation"* (August 6, 1984), III/4 (Boston: St. Paul, n.d.), 8.

131. Sacred Congregation for the Doctrine of the Faith, *Instruction on Certain Aspects of the "Theology of Liberation,"* introduction, 3.

132. Sacred Congregation for the Doctrine of the Faith, *Instruction on Certain Aspects of the "Theology of Liberation,"* VI/10, 16.

133. For a direct response to this first instruction, see Juan Luis Segundo, *Theology*

find a more discerning statement concerning liberation theology. The congregation states: "Human history, marked as it is by the experience of sin, would drive us to despair if God had abandoned his creation to itself. But the divine promises of liberation and their victorious fulfillment in Christ's death and resurrection are the basis of the 'joyful hope' from which the Christian community draws the strength to act resolutely and effectively in the service of love, justice and peace. The Gospel is a message of freedom and a liberating force."[134] It becomes clear that liberation must be understood first of all in a salvational way. Only then does it find its continuation in the concrete and liberating task which results from an ethical demand. But this order seems to have often been lost in liberation theology, so that the emphasis was not just placed on orthopraxis over against orthodoxy, but right doctrine was accorded only secondary significance. This kind of admonition may be justified against some representatives of liberation theology. Yet one is surprised that the deliberations by the congregation show little concern for the eschatological emphasis of liberation.[135]

The congregation does not want to have its criticism of liberation theology interpreted as "setting [it]self up as an obstacle on the path to liberation."[136] Its pronouncements are also not an indirect approval of those who contribute to the continuation of the misery of the nations who profit from it, who are accomplices in it, or who remain untouched by it. In many countries, any criticism against the prevailing practice of injustice is brutally suppressed and the rich are privileged at the expense of the poor. Such conditions call for liberation, a redistribution of the riches and a radical social and economic reorientation. The modern technological resources of the industrial nations were originally readily

---

and the Church: A Response to Cardinal Ratzinger and a Warning to the Whole Church, trans. John W. Dierchsmeier (New York: Winston, 1985).

134. Sacred Congregation for the Doctrine of the Faith, *Instruction on Christian Freedom and Liberation* (March 22, 1986), in *Origins: NC Documentary Service* (March 17, 1986), 15:719 (3/43).

135. Though much is said in it about salvation, the term "eschatological" appears only in a side reference. In this situation the opinion of Metz, 154, makes sense, when he claims that the defense of "a culturally monocentric church of the west" is more at stake here than the propagation of the "messianic church of its origin."

136. Sacred Congregation for the Doctrine of the Faith, *Instruction on Christian Freedom and Liberation*, 20, 15:717.

adopted by almost all countries, since they brought the industrialized countries widespread affluence. But now these resources are regarded more and more as dubious means, since at the same time they dehumanize the lives of people in these countries and suffocate eternal values. The insight is growing that an opulent lifestyle in one part of the world is made possible by people who live in another part of the world. These laborers create this affluence by working for little money and under conditions that are nearly unbearable. By following the biblical admonition to care for the poor and powerless, theologians become more and more responsive to the needs of the exploited, oppressed, and underprivileged. While the congregation is not blind to the plight of the people, it reminds liberation theology: "The salvific dimension of liberation cannot be reduced to the socio-ethical dimension, which is a consequence of it. By restoring man's true freedom, the radical liberation brought about by Christ assigns to him a task: Christian practice which is the putting into practice of the great commandment of love."[137] It is exactly this suspicion of the congregation, that liberation theology is reducing soteriology to social-ethical activism, which caused uneasiness on both sides.

In direct response to the 1984 *Instruction,* **Clodovis Boff** (b. 1939) points out that *"The fundamental question of liberation theology is not theology but liberation.* Theology does not occupy the center, but the poor."[138] This means that we are confronted here with a decidedly contextual theology. This theology wants to demonstrate that the kingdom has not just a personal dimension (the soul) or a transcendental dimension (heaven) but an historical dimension, the relationship between people and the structures of society. Liberation theology therefore wants to overcome the dichotomy between this world and the world to come. Boff claims that the transcendental dimension of faith has been treated sufficiently by classical theology and is accepted and presupposed by the theology of liberation. Yet liberation theology intends to "connect the mystery of God with the history of humanity."[139] It seeks to accomplish a living unity of the experience of salvation with the experience of

137. Sacred Congregation for the Doctrine of the Faith, *Instruction on Christian Freedom and Liberation,* 71, 15:723.

138. Clodovis Boff, *Die Befreiung der Armen: Reflexionen zum Grundanliegen der lateinamerikanischen Befreiungstheologie* (Freiburg, Switzerland: Edition Exodus, 1986), 16.

139. Clodovis Boff, 27.

liberation. As **Leonardo Boff** (b. 1938) stated: "The historical process anticipates and paves the way for definitive liberation in the kingdom. Thus human forms of liberation acquire a sacramental function: They have a weight of their own, but they also point toward, and embody in anticipation, what God has definitively prepared for human beings."[140]

Liberation theology is the opposite of a pessimistic religiosity that turns its back on the world. The biblical Christian faith in salvation is drawn into the historical reality and into the seemingly secular human existence. The term "liberation" wants to counteract the "dualistic split of a purely religious salvation and a merely politico-social liberation. . . . Jesus did not bring a purely internal and otherworldly salvation, but a salvation which makes humanity whole and this means at a beginning stage already here and now all the way to its bodily and social dimension."[141] Yet in trying to overcome this dualistic split, liberation theologians were concerned so much with the liberating praxis that "the distinction between the divine initiative and the human response has frequently become blurry."[142] Often the human role seems to dominate, and the divine initiative is placed second by insisting that the kingdom of God has a dynamic, even utopian significance for human history already in the present.

This shows a basic difference between traditional Western theology and the representatives of liberation theology. While the former "has strongly emphasized that the kingdom of God proclaimed by Jesus was the kingdom *of God* . . . liberation theology stresses, by contrast, that the kingdom of God is *a kingdom*."[143] This claim for approximation and anticipation of the kingdom hope already in the present, signaled for the congregation and many others that there was a new version of the Social Gospel emerging.[144] When we now look at the eschatology of two major

140. Leonardo Boff, *Liberating Grace,* trans. John Drury (Maryknoll, N.Y.: Orbis, 1979), 152.

141. Hans Kessler, *Reduzierte Erlösung? Zum Erlösungsverständnis der Befreiungstheologie* (Freiburg: Herder, 1987), 14-15.

142. Craig L. Nessan, *Orthopraxis or Heresy: The North American Theological Response to Latin American Liberation Theology* (Atlanta: Scholars Press, 1989), 371.

143. Nessan, 374.

144. Cf., for instance, Walter Rauschenbusch, *A Theology for the Social Gospel* (New York: Abingdon, 1945), 146, as one of the most eloquent proponents of the Social Gospel, who claimed: "The social gospel tries to see the progress of the Kingdom of God in the flow of history; not only in the doings of the Church, but in the clash of economic forces and social classes."

proponents of liberation theology, we can easily discern to what extent these cautions are justified.

Eschatology in the Context of Liberation

As we have seen, the main emphasis of liberation theology is strategy and action, not doctrine and reflection. This becomes also visible in the book titles published by representatives of this theological approach: for example, *Theology for a Nomad Church* (1976) by Hugo Assmann; *A New Moral Order: Studies in Development Ethics and Liberation Theology* (1974) by Dennis Goulet; *Gospel Radicalism: The Hard Sayings of Jesus* (1984) by Thaddeé Matura; and *Theology and Praxis: Epistemological* (1987) by Clodovis Boff.

As we mentioned, liberation theology has been picked up in many Christian quarters and is no longer limited to a special segment of the underprivileged and exploited. James H. Cone, in his book *God of the Oppressed* (1975), for instance, indicates that the eschatological emphasis of liberation theology is valid for blacks and Chicanos, for whites and Native Americans, for people of the Third World and people of the First World. Yet it first captured its audience with the classic *A Theology of Liberation* (1972, English trans. 1973), by one of its most eloquent advocates, **Gustavo Gutiérrez** (b. 1928), professor of theology and social sciences at the University of Lima, Peru.

For Gutiérrez the theology of liberation is a theology of salvation incarnated in the concrete historical and political conditions of today. That theology is seen here under the aspect of salvation is understandable in light of the situation to which liberation theology primarily speaks. The situation of the oppressed calls for a revolutionary transformation of the very basis of a dehumanizing society. Though liberation theologians have often employed Marxist terminology, there is no conceptual panacea that would safeguard such a revolutionary transformation. Christians involved in the process of liberation proceed by trial and error in their attempt to build a different social order and to establish a new way of being human. While hope is central to a theology of liberation, one does not pursue its goal in euphoria. The joy of the resurrection first requires death on the cross.

But in his comprehensive *Theology of Liberation: History, Politics, and Salvation*, Gutiérrez makes it clear that "it is important to keep in mind that beyond — or rather, through — the struggle against misery, injustice, and exploitation the goal is the *creation of a new humanity*."[145] Gutiérrez learns from the Old Testament that God is a history-making God and that salvation is there spoken of in terms of a re-creation of history. The God who creates the cosmos out of chaos is the same God who leads Israel from alienation to liberation. Similarly, in the New Testament we hear of a new creation. Creation and salvation therefore belong together. By means of our labor we participate in the all-embracing salvific process, thereby engaging ourselves in the work of creation. By transforming this world we become human and build a human community. In our struggle against misery and exploitation and in our attempt to build a just society, we become part of the saving action that is on its way toward complete fulfillment. Salvation is not a return to the days of old, but a striving forward toward something new and unprecedented. In talking about the new creation, Gutiérrez rightly emphasizes Christ as the center and goal of the new creation.

The vision of salvation and new creation would lose its driving force without the eschatological promises that permeate virtually the whole Bible. Gutiérrez appropriately distinguishes between the promises made by God throughout history and the "Promise" that unfolds and becomes richer and more definite in these individual promises. "The Promise is not exhausted by these promises nor by their fulfillment; it goes beyond them, explains them, and gives them their ultimate meaning. But at the same time, the Promise is announced and is partially and progressively fulfilled in them."[146] The promises replacing each other urge history on to new horizons and new possibilities. The Promise is gradually revealed in its fullness. Since it is already fulfilled in historical events, yet not completely, it incessantly projects itself into the future and creates a permanent historical mobility. Gutiérrez knows that both the present and the future aspects are indispensable for properly aligning the relationship between the Promise and history.

When one asks what this Promise might be, Gutiérrez points to the efficacious self-disclosure of God's love and God's consequent self-

---

145. Gustavo Gutiérrez, *A Theology of Liberation: History, Politics, and Salvation,* fifteenth anniversary edition with a new introduction by the author, trans. and ed. C. Inda and J. Eagleson (Maryknoll, N.Y.: Orbis, 1988), 81.

146. Gustavo Gutiérrez, 92.

communication. This Promise, which is both revelation and good news, is at the heart of the Bible, and enters into a decisive stage in the incarnation of the Son and the sending of the Spirit. Since the Promise is intimately connected with salvation and the time of fulfillment, it is clear for Gutiérrez that, in the Bible, eschatology is "the driving force of salvific history radically oriented toward the future. Eschatology is thus not just one more element of Christianity, but the very key to understanding the Christian faith."[147]

Gutiérrez is adamant in pointing out that the intrinsic eschatological structure of the Christian faith is not to be spiritualized. Neither its present nor its future aspects should be related merely to spiritual realities, since their origin and goal have definitely historical bearings. For instance, when the prophets announce the kingdom of peace, this presupposes the establishment of justice on earth. Similarly, the coming of the kingdom and the expectation of the parousia necessarily imply historical, temporal, earthly, social, and material realities. A spiritualization, however, would tend to forget the human consequences of the eschatological promises and the power to transform the unjust social structures which they imply. The elimination of misery and exploitation therefore can be understood as a sign of the coming kingdom.

Gutiérrez emphasizes that the eschatological promises are being fulfilled throughout history. And he cautions that they cannot be clearly and completely identified with a specific social reality. Yet we are somewhat bewildered when we hear him say: "The complete encounter with the Lord will mark an end to history, but it will take place in history."[148] Does this mean that we are evolving toward a state of eschatological fulfillment, a state that, because it is eschatological, will not be just another point on the map of history? If that is the case, Gutiérrez would burden us with the impossible task of demonstrating that we are evolving toward that state. Gutiérrez is right when he claims that the liberating action of Christ is not marginal to the real life of humanity but strikes at

147. Gustavo Gutiérrez, 93.

148. Gustavo Gutiérrez, 97. While we cannot agree with the claim of Juan Gutiérrez, *The New Libertarian Gospel: Pitfalls of the Theology of Liberation*, trans. P. Burns (Chicago: Franciscan Herald Press, 1977), 97, that Gustavo Gutiérrez has emptied theology of its content, we agree with Juan Gutiérrez that in liberation theology evangelization in terms of conversion as the specific mission of the church certainly loses significance at the expense of sociopolitical reforms.

its very heart. The struggle for a just society can in its own right also be considered a part of salvation history. But Gutiérrez seems to neglect the fact that the immense depravity of humanity not only causes the conditions that cry out for liberation but also prevents liberation from becoming an historical event. That is why salvation calls for a totally new creation which cannot be realized by us. Notwithstanding all good endeavors to which Gutiérrez summons us, we are always confronted with the dilemma of Romans 7:19 ("For I do not do the good I want, but the evil I do not want is what I do"). Yet this cannot serve as an excuse but must be seen as our limitation.

How liberation theology can treat classical topics in a new way is demonstrated by Leonardo Boff in his book *What Comes Afterwards? Life after Death* (*Was kommt nachher? Das Leben nach dem Tode*, 1982). This book provides a summary of the teachings concerning the traditional last things. Boff starts with the anthropological fact that humanity is not focused on one particular object, but always on the totality of beings. Humanity is not satisfied with things, but wants being, the foundation of all things, and strives always beyond the limits at hand. "The vision of humanity always wants more than it can reach in its concrete grasping."[149] Utopia is an essential ingredient in the history of humanity because, with its help, humanity projects its whole thrust and yearning as already fully realized future. This betrays a continuous yearning of humanity for renewal, commencement, and completion, which means a display of human desires.

One can either deny utopia as unrealistic or believe that the desires of humanity can become realized. This second option maintains that humanity has an absolute future in which converge all the motions which concern it externally or internally. Yet such a faith cannot solve our existential needs, as they meet us, for instance, in undeserved suffering or inexplicable misery. Faith in an absolute future is thematized by religions because "religion always concerns itself with the meaning of the whole of reality."[150] According to Boff, in the Christ event the absolute future was so intricately connected with the history of humanity that it became one history with it. In the resurrected Jesus Christ the ab-

---

149. Leonardo Boff, *Was kommt nachher? Das Leben nach dem Tode*, trans. H. Goldstein (Salzburg: Otto Müller Verlag, 1982), 18.
150. Leonardo Boff, *Was kommt nachher?* 21.

solute future was disclosed to us. "The future of Jesus Christ which became present in history through the resurrection, is the future of humanity."[151] In him the hope of humanity was realized toward something final and absolute, namely, toward a new creation.

According to Boff, a cheerful calmness entered the world through the resurrection. Among all the ambiguity of the present situation, which is both regressive and progressive, violent and peaceful, one has the privilege of remembering the triumph of life over death, the victory of the Yes over the No. Now we can see how the future permeates the present and can celebrate the anticipation of the future in the life of Jesus Christ. Life is still dramatic, but it is no longer tragic, as it was exemplified by the myth of Sisyphus, because we know of a way which opens up for us in the present darkness. Yet the kingdom of God as the goal of this way has often been domesticated either as something that was put above or beyond this world, so that the world lost its meaning, or conversely as part of this world, so that one became oblivious to the need to press on to that heavenly reality. But Boff states: "Eschatology, rightly understood, teaches us that we should neither overvalue heaven nor earth, because heaven commences on earth. The kingdom of God is not a completely different world, but a completely new one."[152]

There is a continuity between this temporal life and the eternal life, not in mode but in substance. One can already experience heaven on earth when one finds happiness, does good things, and experiences joy in day-to-day life. But heaven on earth is only present in a form which can be misunderstood and is insufficient, since everything in this world is ambiguous. As Christians, however, we know life in its fullness and with all its possibilities; therefore we also know about its ultimate goal. What for others is a dreamed-for utopia, has already been realized for us in Jesus Christ. We are already drawn into this new being in faith and know it as a reality for which humanity longs with every fiber of its being.

With his exposition of eschatology, Leonardo Boff wants to get hold of the concrete hope which can be realized on the basis of the Christ event, though it is still ambiguous in the present, and which at the same time points to the promised future with which it is connected. Boff does not primarily emphasize the ultimate goal that is reached by humanity

151. Leonardo Boff, *Was kommt nachher?* 22.
152. Leonardo Boff, *Was kommt nachher?* 28.

at the end of life, but the hope that is being realized in the present and leads to that goal. Boff depicts an eschatological attitude not in the sense of every day being the last one, but in the sense that our respective posture of faith corresponds with the hoped-for and believed-in goal and in an anticipatory way shows already now something of that goal. But in developing this approach, the goal itself should not be left out of sight, a danger that is latently present in Boff's exposition.

b. Feminist Perspectives

"*The* feminist theology does not exist!"[153] Its diversity is even more noticeable than with liberation theology. It ranges from those who have discarded the Judeo-Christian tradition as normative by relying on those religions that emphasize the life-giving power of goddesses to those who rely on solid theological exegesis of the biblical texts.[154] Even within the biblical texts, feminist exegesis can arrive at surprising conclusions. For instance, we are told: "It is unmistakably men who speak in the visions of the apocalypse of John."[155] Otherwise the martyrs could not be adorned with victory wreaths and assume the heritage of force. There are no visions in the book of Revelation that describe mutuality, community in relationships, and interdependence. This stands in stark contrast to the synoptic Gospels and the stories about Jesus. In Revelation the elect are related to God, but not to each other. Therefore

> the apocalypse is a book about power and violence written from the perspective of men who resist (at the risk of their lives) the inimical and anti-Godly power of Rome. All relationships mentioned in this

153. So correctly Lucia Scherzberg, *Grundkurs feministischer Theologie* (Mainz: Matthias Grünewald, 1995), 11.

154. Cf. Maria Kassel, "Tod und Auferstehung," in *Feministische Theologie: Perspektiven zur Orientierung*, ed. Maria Kassel (Stuttgart: Kreuz Verlag, 1988), 191-225, where she weds together "the pre-patriarchal" Sumerian myth of Inanna's descent into the netherworld with the Judeo-Christian tradition of death and resurrection whereby the former becomes normative for the latter.

155. Luise Schottroff, "Die befreite Eva: Schuld und Macht der Mächtigen und Ohnmächtigen nach dem Neuen Testament," in *Schuld und Macht: Studien zu einer feministischen Befreiungstheologie*, ed. Christine Schaumberger and Luise Schottroff (Munich: Chr. Kaiser, 1988), 93.

book are described as relationships of power, be it the power of the animal from the sea, the dragon, be it the power of the lamb that is victorious over these powers and who has started, with its suffering, the process by which God gains rule over the earth and through which it becomes a new earth. History is understood as a struggle for the liberation of the earth. These relationships of power are almost exclusively those of power or rule over . . . or granted power and of submission.[156]

Instead of toward those symbols of power, one should look to Jesus, who is portrayed in the Gospels as the eschatological gatherer of the dispersed, and to Paul, who in Romans 12:12 encourages the Christians in Rome to "Rejoice in hope, be patient in suffering, persevere in prayer." Such perseverance has nothing to do with passivity.[157] It is the attitude of the martyrs in the Jewish and then the Christian tradition who take the conflicts of society upon themselves because they are expecting the kingdom of God on this earth and draw the consequences for their lives from this hope. Perseverance betrays an eschatological orientation through which the hope engendered causes them to resist the praxis and goals of society. The expectation of God as an eschatological hope does not reconcile them with the atrocities in human history, but it gives the faithful the power not to surrender on account of this violence. They expect the kingdom of God and the resurrection of the dead. From this hope they receive power, the will to resist, and resurrection already now. "Perseverance *(hypomonae)* is the power of the resurrection in the midst of the death structures in which I am entangled as an accomplice."[158]

When we leave the New Testament, we encounter in early Christianity an "extreme ambiguity toward women" as far as the eschaton is concerned.[159] "Female sexuality and giving birth are seen as the antithesis of the escape from mortal life that reborn virginal Christians seek." But the Christian virgins and especially Mary are understood as spiritual beings who bear rich fruit on account of their virtues. At the same time, the feminine is the symbol and expression of the perishable body

---

156. Schottroff, 97-98.

157. For the following, cf. Schottroff, 102-4.

158. Schottroff, 108.

159. For this and the following quotes, see Rosemary R. Ruether, *Sexism and God-Talk: Toward a Feminist Theology* (Boston: Beacon Press, 1983), 245.

from whom we should flee so that the soul is purified for eternal life. All feminine processes of life, such as pregnancy, birth, and the feminine itself, are impure and carry with them the blemish of decay and death. Symptomatic for this is the gnostic *Gospel of Thomas,* where we read in the conclusion: "Simon Peter said to them, 'Let Mary leave us, for women are not worthy of Life.' Jesus said, 'I myself shall lead her in order to make her male, so that she too may become a living spirit resembling you males. For every woman who will make herself male will enter the Kingdom of Heaven.'"[160]

This line of reasoning was even continued by some of the church fathers. Jerome (ca. 347/48–420), for instance, writes in a side comment in his *Commentary on Ephesians,* on 5:28: "As long as a woman serves procreation and the children, there exists the same difference between her and a man as between body and soul. But when she serves Christ more than the world, she will stop being a woman and will be called a man, because we desire that all will be advanced to a perfect man."[161] Augustine also dealt with whether women can enter eternal life as women, since God made only man from the earth and then took the woman from man. But he arrived at very different results than did Jerome. He reasoned: "For my part, they seem to be wiser who make no doubt that both sexes shall rise. For there shall be no lust, which is now the cause of confusion. . . . And the sex of woman is not a vice, but nature. . . . The woman, therefore, is a creature of God even as the man; but by her creation from man unity is commended."[162] Attempts were still made to consider with Aristotle the woman as a second-rate man and to see in the woman primarily a temptress that needed to be shunned at all cost. But especially the prioresses and nuns of the Middle Ages developed something like a female self-consciousness that no longer accepted the demand to become like men but considered themselves equal with

160. *The Gospel of Thomas* 114, in James M. Robinson, *The Nag Hammadi Library* (San Francisco: Harper & Row, 1977), 130.

161. Jerome, *Commentariorum in Epistolam ad Ephesios,* in J. P. Migne, *PL,* 26:533; and cf. Elisabeth Gössmann and Haruko Okano, "Himmel ohne Frauen? Zur Eschatologie des weiblichen Menschseins in östlicher und westlicher Religion," in *Das Gold in Wachs: Festschrift für Thomas Immoos zum 70. Geburtstag,* ed. Elisabeth Gössmann and Günter Zobel (Munich: Indicium Verlag, 1988), 400, who comment on these thoughts of Jerome on Eph. 4:13.

162. Augustine, *The City of God* 22.17, in *NPNF* FS, 2:496.

men.[163] Perhaps the Augustinian dictum that being a woman is not a vice, but nature, proved to be too persuasive.

In delineating a feminist eschatology, **Rosemary Radford Ruether** (b. 1936) starts with the notion of conversion or *metanoia*.[164] According to Ruether, conversion implies that, though there was no utopian state of humanity somewhere far back in an original paradise, there exist certain foundational elements of a just and vital society. These elements have their roots in nature and include the acceptance of finitude and of balanced relationships between persons and between human and extrahuman beings. A clue for these elements which make up a life intended by God can be gleaned from the Jubilee tradition in Leviticus 25:8-12. Each family has its own land and cultivates its own vineyard and fig trees. Nobody is a slave to anybody else. The land is not exploited and the animals are not overburdened. But human sinfulness always causes us to drift away from this intended state of peace and justice. Therefore the revolutionary transformation of the Sabbath tradition cannot be accomplished once and for all. "It is left to the new generation to undertake the project of a just and viable life for its time. But it is the responsibility of the present generation to create and preserve the base of a livable world that makes such a project possible for its descendents." It is our main responsibility to give shape to a community on earth that is interconnected in love, so that it can also be handed on to our children.

But what happens to our own individual eschatology? Ruether claims that to accept death is to accept both the ending of our individualized center of being and also the identification with the larger matrix of the totality of our self which comprises all of us.[165] Personal immortality has been created in the attempt to absolutize as eternal the personal and individual ego over against the total community of our being. Just as we are willing to transcend this kind of egotism for the sake of the relationship with the community, can we accept death as the final dissipation of the individualized ego in the larger matrix of all being? "Our responsibility is to use our temporal life to create a just and good community for our generation and for our children." Survival of the self

---

163. Cf. Gössmann and Okano, 405-6.
164. Cf. for the following, Ruether, 254-55, quote on 255.
165. Cf. for the following, Ruether, 257, quote on 258.

or its re-creation for eternal life is labeled by Ruether as an attempt to juxtapose one's own ego over against the community. With this kind of stance she is close to representatives of process thought, to whom we will turn next. Yet she is also contrary to some other feminist theologians who very pointedly emphasize the necessity of personal interrelationships of equality and nondomination, not only in this life but especially in its fulfillment and completion in the life hereafter. Feminist eschatology is indeed not a monolithic theology, but an attempt of different and differing women theologians to express their contextual concerns and observations concerning eschatology.

5. Christian Eschatology in a Universal Context

Since we have become more and more aware that the Christian faith has to be asserted within the context of many competing worldviews and religions, that multicultural and multireligious context needs to be taken into account. Especially process theology has taken note of this new situation.

a. Process Theology

According to the Anglo-American philosopher Alfred North Whitehead (1861-1947), who gave process theology most of its conceptual tools, we should not think of God as the "aboriginal, eminently real, transcendent creator, at whose fiat the world came into being, and whose imposed will it obeys."[166] Such a God is no longer attractive, and "if the modern world is to find God," Whitehead claimed, "it must find him through love and not through fear."[167] God acts persuasively upon the world, and since this persuasive power is of infinite duration, it is the greatest power possible. "It is because God exercises power upon us, persuasive power, that a space is opened up for us within which we are

166. Alfred North Whitehead, *Process and Reality: An Essay in Cosmology*, corrected edition by David R. Griffin and Donald W. Sherburne (New York: Free Press, 1978), 342.

167. Alfred North Whitehead, *Religion in the Making: Lowell Lectures, 1926* (New York: Macmillan, 1926), 76.

free."[168] This means that the future is not closed to us but open for good and for bad.

In creative love God takes this risk, and consequently there is sin and suffering in the world. Yet God does not abandon the world, but in his primordial and subsequent nature nudges the world and its processes toward the future. Therefore "the relationships which must develop in the interrelated community of being are the arena of relative good and evil. But given this structure of interrelationships, no evil is ever final: the structure is ultimately redemptive."[169] This does not mean that the evil we encounter in this world is not real, but that it will be transformed. Evil will be overcome either before the end of time or in the eschaton. Through God's providence the power of evil is already broken. Hence evil stands under the influence of grace that extends itself into the whole world so that the world might be redeemed. As Marjorie Suchocki (b. 1933) claims: "God is the future of the world and in every fresh moment; as the future of the world he is surely grace." Ultimately grace will be victorious, and there is no final judgment resulting in a twofold outcome of history. According to process theologians, a twofold outcome of acceptance would contradict God's very essence, since the persuasiveness of God demands or at least suggests that God will draw everything and everyone into Godself.

A complete union with God as the final goal affects the final destiny of the self or the person. As Whitehead wrote: "The everlasting nature of God, which in a sense is non-temporal and in another sense is temporal, may establish with the soul a peculiarly intense relationship of mutual immanence. Thus in some important sense the existence of the soul may be freed from its complete dependence upon the bodily organiza-

---

168. John B. Cobb, Jr., and David R. Griffin, *Process Theology: An Introductory Exposition* (Philadelphia: Westminster, 1976), 119.

169. For this and the following quotation, see Marjorie Hewitt Suchocki, "The Correlation between Good and Evil" (Ph.D. diss., Claremont Graduate School, 1974), 250. In a revised version of her dissertation, *The End of Evil: Process Eschatology in Historical Context* (Albany: SUNY Press, 1988), esp. 154, she once again emphasizes that our finite existence reveals a fundamental ambiguity in which good and evil are intertwined with one another and that this ambiguity produces evil as well as redemption. Thus redemption as the triumph of good over evil is seen as an historical process. Evil as a destructive power, which is not only active in this process but also opposes it, is not, however, taken into account.

tion."[170] This intense relationship of mutual immanence, which White-head suggests, lets some process theologians, such as Charles Hart-shorne (b. 1897) and Schubert Ogden (b. 1928), forcefully argue "against any subjective immortality, holding that as objectively experienced by God our lives are wholly preserved and cherished forever."[171] This means that nothing that has ever occurred in a positive way is lost for-ever. It will be integrated into God or in God's memory. Since we will all end up with God, one can even claim: "Whether there be subjective immortality or not is peripheral to the Christian faith."[172]

John B. Cobb, Jr. (b. 1925), the most prominent representative of process theology, shows in his book *Christ in a Pluralistic Age* (1975) why subjective immortality, meaning the "survival" of the self or the person in the hereafter, should not be an issue. One-third of this Christology is devoted to "Christ as Hope," showing how important the future per-spective is for Cobb. According to Cobb, in the Christian tradition the logos, the cosmic principle of order, the ground of meaning, and the source of purpose, is identified with the incarnate form of the transcen-dent reality, the Christ. From this he concludes: "Christ is the incarnate Logos. As such Christ is present in all things."[173] Since the logos is the power of creative transformation and the one principle of all significant order, there is no hope without this logos, namely, without Christ.[174] Through this creative transformation, there is a fundamental reason for hope. "Apart from Christ there is no hope for a better future," since he transforms the world by persuading it toward relevant novelty.[175]

Christ does not stand alone, since there are images of a hopeful fu-ture toward which he leads and through which we may be led by him. Cobb sketches out four of these images of hope: (1) the heavenly city for which the visionary architect Paolo Soleri provides the context in which a hopeful future can be lived; (2) the perfect love as it unfolds through

170. Alfred North Whitehead, *Adventures of Ideas* (New York: Macmillan, 1933), 267.

171. Cf. the good summary of different process positions by Lewis S. Ford, *The Lure of God: A Biblical Background for Process Theism* (Philadelphia: Fortress, 1978), 114.

172. So Ford, 120.

173. John B. Cobb, Jr., *Christ in a Pluralistic Age* (Philadelphia: Westminster, 1975), 142.

174. Cf. Cobb, 76.

175. Cobb, 186.

the encounter of the Christian faith in Buddhism and by which Christian existence goes beyond its individualism and finds the community of perfect love; (3) Alfred North Whitehead's understanding of the kingdom of God which overcomes continuous loss through temporality and the ambiguities of history; and (4) in the thought of Wolfhart Pannenberg, where the resurrection image is correlated with our modern understanding of reality and presented as the answer to the problem of death. Cobb concludes that "none of these images is persuasive to the modern mind, which has learned to live with much more limited hopes or with no hope at all."[176] But Cobb does not give up here in despair.

Since the multiplicity of unresolved images tends to reduce their persuasiveness, Cobb attempts to reconcile them with each other. Ultimately he wants to show a universal hope, since the whole cosmos witnesses to temporality and perishableness. We, too, cannot exempt ourselves from the destiny of creation, since we are interwoven with the fate of the biosphere. If Christ, however, is our hope, this implies that Christ comes ever more fully to expression in us; he becomes one with our very selves and we, too, become one with Christ. "Insofar as through love that inclusiveness is attained, the tension between personal purposes and the claim of the Logos declines. As self and Logos draw together, the Logos becomes more fully incarnate."[177] The direction of this movement is toward the structure of existence already realized in Jesus. Therefore all the images of hope converge on this one point. The separating individuality is transcended by a more complete community with other fellow human beings and with all things. Cobb can then conclude his "Christ as Hope" chapter with this vision: "In this community the tensions between self and Christ decline, and in a final consummation they would disappear. This is the movement of incarnation. Christ is the name of our hope."[178]

Everything finds its unity in Christ and ultimately in God, so that God can become all in all. Though the goal of the universe may be advanced with great and skillful persuasion toward this final cosmic harmony, one must ask whether the actual essence of the Christian faith is still maintained. Cobb's proposal seems more akin to the Hellenistic

176. Cobb, 244.
177. Cobb, 257.
178. Cobb, 258.

striving for oneness as demonstrated by Platonic and Aristotelian onto-logically grounded philosophy. The Christian faith, however, is charac-terized by individuality in unity. A similar unifying hope is also often advanced by those who attempt to find their way through the plurality of religions.

b. Eschatology among the World's Religions

Like John Cobb, **John Hick** (b. 1922) has taught in Claremont, Califor-nia. In his book *Death and Eternal Life* (1976) he presents a truly encyclo-pedic and global religious eschatology. Similar to process thought, he opts for a universal salvation. While he notices the grave warnings by Je-sus that people were heading toward destruction, these warnings were uttered in an existential mode and do not necessarily conflict with Paul's more detached theological observation of "a final universal salva-tion."[179] Since God has made us with an inherent gravitation toward him, there is no final opposition between God's saving will and our hu-man nature acting in freedom. God has made us for fellowship with Godself, and so he works in his creative power to enable us to reach that fulfillment.

Yet Hick is not so optimistic as to claim that once we die we will reach our final destiny — being with God: "The persisting self-conscious ego will continue to exist after bodily death. We shall not however, in most cases, attain immediately to the final 'heavenly' state. Only those whom the religions call saints or buddhas or arhats or *jivan-muktas* have fulfilled the purpose of temporal existence, which is the gradual creation of perfected persons — their perfection consisting . . . in a self-transcending state beyond separate ego-existence. But those of us who die without having attained to our perfection, continue further in time as distinct egos."[180]

Since there is an increasing attenuation of memory combined with the increasing inner distance produced by a continuous personal change from an individual who lived, for instance, a million years ago, to claim any ego identity would in actuality amount to real discontinuity. There-

---

179. John Hick, *Death and Eternal Life* (New York: Harper & Row, 1976), 249.
180. Hick, 399.

fore the self-apprehension extending back into the past or being projected into the future is not unlimited, since "we are not the angelic beings who can be imagined as a-historical denizens of eternity."[181] If the human ego is immortal, or if it persists for a period which multiplies the length of an earthly life many times, then its postmortal existence occurs in successive sections rather than in one continuous unit. The problem of maintaining one's ego identity together with growth through purposive life, Hick concludes, seems "to be more easily accommodated by the theory of many lives in many worlds than by the idea of the immortal ego."[182] This could also include the possibility of repeated "re-becomings" in other spheres beyond this world. There could then be a vertical rather than a horizontal reincarnation in which we develop to ever more perfected selves. For some it would mean reaching their perfection within one more life, for others within a few more, and for the worst, one should think in terms of tens or hundreds of lives. But what is in store for us at the end?

Hick points first to the idea of the kingdom of God as a society of completed persons dwelling together in ideal harmony in the divine presence. The individual human personality retains its individuality in this image, but in a perfected form. Yet there also arose later in Christianity a mystical understanding of eternal life as the beatific vision of God. Here the soul is so absolutely centered on God that other human beings seem irrelevant. Hick discerns that "in christian mysticism there is something analogous to the widespread eastern conviction that our approach to Ultimate Reality involves the transcending of ego-hood. We are to become so transparent to the divine life that we no longer live as separate self-enclosed individuals."[183] In attempting to line out a "possible eschatology," Hick suggests that as the human individual becomes perfected, it becomes more and more a person and less and less an ego. With this he means that a human person is essentially looking outward for relationships with other persons, while the ego forms a boundary limiting true personal life. Hick sees the paradigm of this personal community without boundary-drawing egos in the triune conception of God as three persons in one and one in three. There the community is "so intimate and harmo-

---

181. Hick, 412.
182. Hick, 413.
183. Hick, 446.

nious as to constitute a single corporate person."[184] This sense of ultimate belonging together in total community is, according to Hick, the unselfish love which the New Testament calls agape.

Hick concludes: "What Christians call the Mystical Body of Christ within the life of God, and Hindus the universal Atman which we all are, and mahayana Buddhists the self-transcending unity in the Dharma Body of the Buddha, consists of the wholeness of ultimately perfected humanity beyond the existence of separate egos."[185] With this weaving together of different images of the major world religions, Hick has shown that his attempt of a global religious eschatology can indeed be achieved. He starts with the presupposition that the teachings of the "great religious traditions have arisen out of permanently significant experiences at the interface between the human and the divine," and therefore concludes "that their eschatologies offer convergent indications, each pointing beyond our present human experience and yet each pointing in the same direction."[186]

Hick has penetrated the often conflicting diversity of religious manifestations to uncover the ultimate yearning and aspiration of humanity. In that respect there is indeed a convergence, if not a basic agreement. Yet in the same way, as Hick concedes, "reincarnation is not, and has never been, an orthodox christian belief"; we should also note that there is a big difference between mysticism in the East and in the West, as Rudolf Otto (1869-1937) pointed out long ago.[187] While the mystic in the West focuses on Christ, the mystic in the East focuses on the self. While the goal may be the same, overcoming the existential separation from the source of life or the ground of being, a Christian mystic never developed an eightfold path as Buddha has done, since he or she knows that salvation does not depend on our activity but on God's, to whom we can at best respond. This means that Hick, by correctly pointing to convergent ideas and aspirations, has neglected the fundamental difference in the assessment of human possibilities.

184. Hick, 460.
185. Hick, 464.
186. Hick, 427.
187. Hick, 365, and cf. Rudolf Otto, *Mysticism East and West: A Comparative Analysis of the Nature of Mysticism*, trans. Bertha L. Bracey and Richenda C. Payne (New York: Macmillan, 1932), 165, where Otto shows the affinity yet distance between these two strands of a common human experience.

4. Confronting Secular Varieties of Hope

The Christian faith must live with the impact of the Enlightenment. This is both a boon and a liability. While the Christian faith still enjoys a preferred position in many regions due to the respective sociocultural histories, it is no longer protected against rivals and misuse. The Inquisition is a phenomenon of the past, and there are no longer bonfires into which non-Christian or anti-Christian literature is thrown. Because of the necessity to assert itself in a free market of faiths, beliefs, and opinions, the Christian faith has grown up without shelters and crutches. By the same token, when it asserts itself with regard to the future, it must be able to defend its tenets with arguments accessible to everyone amid a variety of rival options. At this point we want to focus on three such options that have emerged under the impact of science, philosophy, and general religiosity.

1. The Impact of Science

During the last two hundred years humanity has changed the face of this earth and its own self-understanding more drastically than in all the years prior to 1800. For instance, the average life expectancy in eighteenth-century Europe was about thirty-six years. Today it has doubled and is in the seventies. In 1870, a typical nineteenth-century year, the number of people who died in Britain before reaching the age of twenty was equal to approximately 32 percent of all children born in the country in that year.[1] In 1970 the equivalent figure was approximately 3.6 percent. This means the mortality of infants, children, and adolescents has decreased by nearly 90 percent. On the other side, we have extracted more raw materials from this earth in the last fifty years alone than in all the years previous. Moreover, there are more people with earned Ph.D.s alive today than have ever lived before. These astounding figures would be unthinkable without the immense acceleration of scientific knowledge in all areas of life. For good or for bad, we are able to understand and manipulate ourselves and our environment to a degree undreamed of barely two hundred years ago.

It comes as no surprise that this advancement in scientific knowledge has deeply changed the outlook of most people, Christian and non-Christian alike. Auguste Comte (1798-1857) captured this sentiment well in his three-volume *Course of Positive Philosophy* (1835), where he claimed that human intelligence unfolds itself according to a grand fundamental law in three different theoretical stages.[2] The first of these stages is the theological or fictitious phase, the second the metaphysical or abstract phase, and the third the scientific or positive one. Each one is opposed to the others, and the first two have more or less transitional character. While in the first stage the human spirit wants to know the inner nature of being and postulates the existence of supernatural powers, in the second it thinks of abstract powers which are independent entities. Yet the human spirit gradually attains the insight that it is impossible to obtain absolute knowledge, and in a third stage, the positive one, it no longer asks for the origin and purpose of the universe and the inner causes of appearances. At the end of the metaphysical phase of the development of the human spirit, the scientific understanding of nature has won the upper hand. Positive philosophy, which is developing as a truly universal system, can explain the phenomena of nature by realizing that all phenomena are subject to the laws of nature and that these laws have irrevocable character. With this insight gleaned by a positive philosophy, as Comte calls it, we have encountered the basic ground rules of scientific materialism.

1. Cf. for the following, including the statistics, John Hick, *Death and Eternal Life* (New York: Harper & Row, 1976), 82.
2. For the following cf. Frederick Copleston, *A History of Philosophy* (New York: Newman, 1975), 9:78-79.

a. The Option of Scientific Materialism

Scientific materialism convinced people that the ironclad laws of nature do not allow for heavenly interruption, whether by divine miracles or by a divinely decreed end of the world. This view was substantiated with the law of the conservation of energy, which was first introduced by J. Robert Mayer (1814-78) in 1842. He asserted that within an isolated energy-system the amount of energy remains constant, while its form is changeable. Energy that disappears reenters the scene in a different form. Electrical energy, for instance, can be transformed into light and heat. Or the kinetic energy of flowing water can be changed into electrical energy. Energy can also be released by incinerating materials which disintegrate into oxidized substance and thereby produce light and heat, or by nuclear fusion through which part of the mass is converted into energy according to the famous Einstein equation $E = mc^2$. The decisive question is whether our universe is such a closed system that it can neither lose energy nor gain it from the outside. Scientific investigation has shown that it is unlikely that our universe is subject to outside forces. This would mean that our universe will always remain the same; it has no beginning and no end, and the future is only a modification of the past.

This kind of materialism was further developed by the French physician and philosopher Julien Offray de la Mettrie (1709-51). In his book *Man as Machine (L'Homme machine)*, published in 1748, he presented a naturalistic view of humanity and explained the spiritual processes through physiological causes. According to de la Mettrie, the soul originates from the organization of the body and the higher development of the reasonable human soul is due to the more intricate development of the human brain. Already in his *History of the Soul (Histoire naturelle de l'âme)* of 1745, he rejected metaphysical dualism and explained the intellectual faculties through a motorlike power which resides in matter. The German baron Paul Heinrich Dietrich von Holbach (1723-89) offered a similar explanation in his book *System of Nature (Système de la nature)*, published in 1770. He described humanity as a product of nature which is subjected to the laws of the physical universe. Beyond that there are no further ultimate principles or powers. According to Holbach, it is an illusion to consider the soul a spiritual substance. The moral and intellectual attributes of humanity can best be explained in a mechanistic way through physical, biological, and social interactions. The only possibility of understanding what humanity is all about, is to conduct empirical and rational research into matter. Nature is the sum total of matter and of its movement. There is neither accident nor disorder in nature, because everything occurs out of necessity and in an order which is determined through the irreversible change of cause and effect. The world in which we live is therefore not only interpreted in a materialistic way, but von Holbach also believed it is subjected to a stringent causal determinism.

This mind-set, which was persuasive through much of the nineteenth century, also decidedly influenced the philosopher **Ludwig Feuerbach** (1804-72). In *The Essence of Christianity* (1841), he tried to "objectively" examine Christianity by employing "the method of *analytic* chemistry."[3] Feuerbach claimed that, initially, humanity's survival instinct is synonymous with the desire not to die. Whatever lives asserts itself and consequently does not want to die. Only through a person's life experience is this negative desire projected into something positive, the desire of a life, meaning a better life after death. But this desire wants to ascertain the content of its hope. Reason cannot fulfill this hope. Therefore "all proofs of immortality are insufficient," and even "unassisted reason is not capable of apprehending it, still less of proving it."[4] The resurrection of Christ originated out of this desire to ascertain the truthfulness of its hope. The resurrection "is therefore the satisfied desire of man for an immediate certainty of his *personal* existence after death, — personal immortality as a sensible, indubitable fact."[5]

As he shows in his small book on immortality, Feuerbach is not totally opposed to the "idea" of the resurrection. He chides Christianity for having made immortality the most certain part of its faith, even though in antiquity it was always doubtful and uncertain.[6] The reason he is so negative on immortality is based on his understanding that any existence needs a material base. Even in a spiritual existence a person

---

3. Ludwig Feuerbach, *Das Wesen des Christentums*, in *Gesammelte Werke*, ed. Werner Schuffenhauer (Berlin: Akademie-Verlag, 1973), 5:6, in the preface to the first edition.

4. Ludwig Feuerbach, *The Essence of Christianity*, trans. George Eliot (New York: Harper Torchbooks, 1957), 135.

5. Feuerbach, *The Essence of Christianity*, 135.

6. Ludwig Feuerbach, *Die Unsterblichkeitsfrage vom Standpunkt der Anthropologie*, in *Gesammelte Werke*, 10:214.

cannot be without a head. Yet a head also has a body, and with this also comes eating and drinking, so that "the true, innocent, and unbeguiled faith in an existence of humanity after death is the faith that humanity even after death *eats and drinks*."[7] There is no disembodied existence possible. Here he sees the truth of the Christian belief in immortality that turned the abstraction of immortality into something sensual, and in place of a partial immortality it placed the undivided immortality, "the immortality of the *body* and the soul, in place of the immortality of the spirit or the soul the immortality of the human being — the *resurrection*."[8]

According to Feuerbach, the problem comes with the Christian concept of the resurrected person in heaven, since heaven for the Christian is the denial of everything fleshly or bodily, sensual, and human, because "in heaven the Christian ceases to be a human being, he or she becomes an angel. Yet an angel is nothing but the personification of an abstracted Christian, dissociated from a human being and therefore the true and completed Christian, nothing but a Christian without flesh and blood, the Christian imagined as an independent being."[9] Since the material is the dominant category for Feuerbach, he cannot think of an existence apart from the material base. Yet the resurrected human being, according to Christian understanding, is not simply a material human being. For Feuerbach, however, it must be a fiction because it cannot contain any reality.

As Feuerbach claims in his *Principles of a Philosophy of the Future* (1846), "matter is an essential object for reason. If there were no matter, reason had no incentive and no material to think, no content. One cannot abandon matter without abandoning reason, one cannot recognize it without recognizing reason. Materialists are rationalists."[10] Whatever is reasonable is material and vice versa. Therefore Feuerbach hails Jakob Moleschott's book *Doctrine of Food: For the People* (*Lehre der Nahrungsmittel: Für das Volk*, 1850), saying that it proves the "universal, revolutionary significance of the natural sciences" since there we are told, with the results of modern chemistry, that "humanity is what it eats," because life is

---

7. Feuerbach, *Die Unsterblichkeitsfrage vom Standpunkt der Anthropologie*, 10:231.

8. Feuerbach, *Die Unsterblichkeitsfrage vom Standpunkt der Anthropologie*, 10:236.

9. Feuerbach, *Die Unsterblichkeitsfrage vom Standpunkt der Anthropologie*, 10:242.

10. Ludwig Feuerbach, *Grundsätze der Philosophie der Zukunft*, § 17, in *Gesammelte Werke*, 9:289.

metabolism.[11] If there is a spirit or anything beyond the material, it must be either a projection of the material base or synonymous with it. There is only this space-time configuration since, "with the disappearance of space and time, human existence also disappears."[12]

If human existence is finite, as Feuerbach very well recognizes, he concludes that we do not need a religious or theological hereafter, "a future life to perfect humanity," since such a life would only be justified if humanity were to stay the same, if there were "no improvement of humankind on earth."[13] Yet humanity and the whole kingdom of animals and plants have a history and show continuous improvement. Therefore it is silly to postulate a future of humanity in a beyond in heaven or on the other side of our graves. Even if we would say that the beyond is necessary on account of a retributive justice, then immortality would only be for the unfortunate but not for those who already have been happy on this earth and find fulfillment in this life. By setting the goal on the beyond in order to fulfill the unfulfillable desires of humanity, Christianity has neglected reachable desires. Christianity has cheated people because it asked them to trust in God's help instead of in their own powers, to believe in a better life in heaven instead of a better life on earth, and to realize such a better life.

Feuerbach imbibed not only nineteenth-century materialism, but also the self-assured faith in progress on this earth. Things will get better and better. We do not care for a hereafter, because we should make the present a better place to live. Many people will tacitly agree with Feuerbach, even if they do not abandon the God notion as he did. Perhaps even many people who cling to this life with utter tenacity do so out of the unadmitted fear that there might be no hereafter. So you better stick to what you have. But our present situation leaves room for only limited optimism.

Soon after J. Robert Mayer discovered the first law of thermodynamics, the law of the conservation of energy, the German physicist Rudolf Julius Emanuel Clausius (1822-88) in 1850 and the British sci-

---

11. Ludwig Feuerbach, "Die Naturwissenschaft und die Revolution" (1850), in *Gesammelte Werke*, 10:356 and 367.

12. So Peter Chang, "Mensch als Denkhorizont bei Ludwig Feuerbach" (Dr. phil. diss., Munich, Ludwig-Maximilian-Universität, 1971), 115.

13. Ludwig Feuerbach, *Vorlesungen über die Religion* (1846), in *Gesammelte Werke*, 6:314, including the following.

entist William Thomson (the later Lord Kelvin, 1824-1907) in 1851 discovered the second law of thermodynamics, or the law of entropy. This law states that in an isolated system the entropy or nonconvertibility of energy never decreases but either remains constant or increases. In contrast to the opinion of many materialists of the nineteenth century, our world is not a *perpetuum mobile,* an arrangement which continuously keeps running. Rather it resembles an automobile which at one point will run out of gas and then coast on a little until its forward movement comes to a halt. In a movie we can reverse any conceivable process. Yet the amused reaction of the observers tells us that such events do not occur in reality. Similar to a watch running only as long as there is some resilience in its spring or some energy contained in its battery, all processes within our universe move toward a point at which they will stop. Therefore some scientists talk about a "time-arrow" that bars events from being repeated.[14] Considering the size of our universe and the exact maintenance of the planetary orbits, it is difficult for us to understand that all movements of these sidereal parties are singular. Yet the interstellar gas in our universe will slow down all the heavenly bodies until their kinetic energy is fully used up. Similar to the spring of a huge clock which is totally unwound, our universe will become more and more homogeneous until, at the end of the world, it drifts lifelessly afar and no changes occur within it.[15]

At this point we might be tempted to follow the French Jesuit and paleontologist Pierre Teilhard de Chardin (1881-1955), who claimed that entropy is perhaps sufficient to determine the future of inanimate nature, but it cannot be transposed to life.[16] Life, he asserted, shows at every moment that it is progressing toward a greater complexity and diversity; by its very success it clearly counteracts physical entropy. There

14. Arthur S. Eddington, *The Nature of Physical World: The Gifford Lectures, 1927* (New York: Macmillan, 1929), 68-70, seems to have used the term "time's arrow" for the first time.

15. Even if we assume a contracting and again expanding universe, the overall contractions and expansions would be subject to entropy, unless we assume that at the point of a reversal from contraction to expansion a totally new set of laws would be inaugurated. Then, however, we could not make any predictions about the future course whatsoever.

16. Pierre Teilhard de Chardin, *The Vision of the Past,* trans. J. M. Cohen (New York: Harper, 1966), 168-70.

cannot be a total extinction of the animate world, because in all adversity the stream of life is irreversible. This is certainly a persuasive argument against the final and total equilibrium of all energy levels, but we must remember where the building blocks of life are derived from. Only through exploitation of the inanimate world can life be sustained. But what happens when all of the natural resources are exhausted and the sun stops giving its life-nourishing light? We cannot exempt life from its context within nature. It may be uncomfortable or even offensive for us to face, but there is no eternal force within our world.

Nevertheless, we have become aware that our world is billions of years old and has a diameter of billions of light-years. Can we still as scientifically knowledgeable Christians envision for this immensely old and immensely huge structure a new heaven and a new earth, as Christian eschatology would suggest? Karl Peters seems to speak for many others when he claims that the original Christian universal future eschatology has been invalidated by the view of the cosmos as presented in twentieth-century science. He writes:

> A universe in which the overcoming of evil by good, in which justice is finally served, is vastly different from the current scientific picture of an expanding universe with billions of galaxies each with billions of stars. It is so different that it is difficult to see how the details of biblical eschatology can be translated into the current scientific view of a future, universal eschatology. This applies . . . even to the notion of the creation of a new heaven and a new earth. If the expanding universe is indeed open, expanding forever, then how can one speak of God recreating the universe? If the universe is closed, then it is likely to end in a "big crunch" of mammoth black-hole proportions. Again, it is difficult to see how a new creation can take place.[17]

As a solution to this dilemma Peters suggests two possible options. "Two types of eschatology consistent with the scientific picture of creation are . . . 'realized interpersonal eschatology,' and 'local, future societal or planetary eschatologies.'"[18] Concerning the possibility of a local

---

17. Karl Peters, "Eschatology in Light of Contemporary Science" (paper presented to the Theology and Science Group of the American Academy of Religion, November 1988), 9-10.
18. Karl Peters, 13.

eschatology within a universe headed, as a whole, toward thermal equilibrium, Peters writes: "The potential energy of the universe is sufficient . . . , when coupled with fundamental laws and forces of nature, to create a series of increasingly complex structures in some local regions of the universe."[19] By "realized interpersonal eschatology" Peters means small communities which realize the overcoming of evil within themselves and serve as "the catalyst towards the future, societal and planetary eschatological communities . . . in which . . . the gradual emergence of a Teilhardian *omega point* is realized: The reduction of evil to a minimum, the gradual conquering by science of disease and hunger, the eclipsing of hatred and war."[20]

The difficulty with Peters's proposal, however, is that it leaves little room for genuine Christian eschatology. By his own admission, even localized eschatologies cannot hold out indefinitely against the march of entropy and are only temporary "islands of matter, life, and intelligence."[21] And Peters's realized eschatology sounds like a humanly initiated postmillennialism which takes place quite apart from the eschatological activity of God, a postmillennialism in which science and "humans taking responsibility" usher in the omega point. It is a subjective experience of the overcoming of evil in small communities and bears little if any resemblance to the truly universal and eschatological vision of the Bible. We notice that in this approach science sets the tone and theology has to find out where there is still a niche for it. Science writes the eschatological script, and then Peters attempts to redefine the term "eschatology" in a way that would not bring it into conflict with modern cosmology. Yet in the end, by Peters's own admission, entropy looms in the background. Even a realized interpersonal eschatology or a localized eschatology cannot extricate itself from the strictures of the running down of the universe in general.

Peters writes as a theologian who tries to adjust his own vision to the possibilities left by science. Some scientists, however, are less inhibited by science and look for a way out. They are convinced that if it took billions of years for humanity to emerge and to leave its indelible imprint on the face of this planet, it would make little sense if it were to disappear with-

19. Karl Peters, 11.
20. Karl Peters, 14.
21. Karl Peters, 11.

out a trace. In 1986 the physicist **Frank J. Tipler** (b. 1947), together with John D. Barrow (b. 1952), wrote *The Anthropic Cosmological Principle.* This principle deals with the noteworthy fact that, from the beginning, the universal constants within the universe have been so arranged that intelligent human life is a possibility. Even minimal deviations in the values of these constants would have ruled out the emergence of such life. Tipler believes that if the emergence of intelligent life is of the essence of the universe as a whole, then the disappearance of the same life from the universe could not be without consequence. In a more recent publication with the telling title *The Physics of Immortality: Modern Cosmology, God, and the Resurrection of the Dead,* Tipler deals extensively with the future of that life. In his preface Tipler tells us that in this book "theology is a branch of physics, that physicists can infer by calculation the existence of God and the likelihood of the resurrection of the dead to eternal life in exactly the same way as physicists calculate the properties of the electron."[22] He also assumes that all forms of life, including human life, are subject to the same physical laws as electrons and atoms. A human being is nothing "but a particular type of machine," the human brain only "an information processing device," and the human soul "a program run on a computer called the brain."[23] Tipler wants in this book to describe the omega point theory, which he calls a testable physical theory entailing that one day in the distant future an all-present, all-knowing, and all-powerful God will resurrect each of us to an eternal life which in all its essential features will correspond to the Judeo-Christian heaven.[24] This God will exist primarily at the end of time.

Tipler knows that the future course of the universe is such that life as an information process cannot continue forever in its present form, that is, as a carbon-based organism. If life as an information process that can sustain communication is to continue at all, it must continue to exist on some other basis. Tipler is convinced that in the not too distant future computers will possess the capability for autonomous information processing and communication, and finally will even be able to reproduce themselves. Since Tipler understands a person as an entity capa-

22. Frank J. Tipler, *The Physics of Immortality: Modern Cosmology, God, and the Resurrection of the Dead* (New York: Doubleday, 1994), ix.
23. Cf. Tipler, xi.
24. Tipler, 1.

ble of autonomous information processing and communication, and since computers will be able to assume these functions, he sees the only possibility of future "life" on the basis of computers.

On this premise the physical mechanism of the individual resurrection is the emulation of all persons who have long since died, including their worlds, in computers of the distant future. These computer emulations are identical with the persons who have actually lived.[25] Tipler is convinced that within thirty years we will be capable of building a machine which is at least as intelligent as we are. We will develop such intelligent machines because, without them, we are prone to end in extinction. In the long run life has no other choice but to move beyond this earth in order to survive. As Tipler shows, life can continue only by reproducing itself through artificial intelligence mechanisms.

Tipler tells us that the extinction of humanity is the logically necessary consequence of eternal progress.[26] Since we are finite beings, we have definite limits. Our brains can only contain a limited amount of information. Since the advance of life to the omega point is a fact, the furthest developed consciousness must one day be a nonhuman one. But everything that we as individual beings contribute to culture will survive our individual death. The next step of intelligent life will be information-processing machines. The closer we move to the omega point, the more computer capacity is available to store our present world and to simulate it exactly. Finally there will also be the possibility of simulating all possible visible universes, of simulating "virtual" universes. At the end, "not only are the dead being resurrected but so are people who have never lived."[27] All people and all histories which could have existed will then indeed exist.

The dead will be resurrected as soon as the capacity of all computers in the universe is so large that the capacity required for the storage of all possible human simulations is only an insignificant fraction of the total capacity. According to Tipler, the "resurrection will occur between $10^{-10^{10}}$ seconds and $10^{-10^{123}}$ seconds before the Omega Point is reached."[28] He claims: "The Omega Point-Theory is the first physical

25. Cf. Tipler, 14.
26. For the following, cf. Tipler, 218.
27. Tipler, 223.
28. Tipler, 225.

183

resurrection theory to be fully consistent which totally agrees with the Christian resurrection theory. It is also the first redemption theory justified by reason, not by faith."[29]

Wolfhart Pannenberg points out that "Tipler's exposition of a future resurrection of the dead is particularly worthy of note in a time when the Christian expectations concerning the future are most often judged to be irreconcilable with the modern scientific worldview."[30] Yet we should also listen to Donald G. York (b. 1944), professor of astrophysics and astronomy, who cautions:

> There is abundant material here for intellectual offense. Many readers will find it hard to accept the thesis that what we mean by *life* includes computer-based copies of ourselves. Some will think it absurd to believe that our biosphere will expand, through information technology, to include the entire universe and that intelligence will be able to continue to exist by organizing the gravitational energy freed by the collapse of the universe. Tipler's view that there is no life other than our own in the universe will seem offensively narrow-minded to some. Christians of various persuasions will find the resurrection of which Tipler speaks to have only an incomplete relationship to mainstream ideas of Resurrection and will be insulted at what seems like an assault on, not an explanation of, faith. Theologians and physicists alike will ponder deeply the prime conclusion of the book that theology is now a branch of physics.[31]

This strong caveat goes together with Hans-Dieter Mutschler's (b. 1946) charge that "Tipler commits himself to physical reductionism."[32] This physical reductionism reduces human beings to information-processing entities. Unlike Teilhard, Tipler no longer talks about alpha and omega, since God is not the enveloping higher dimension but the endpoint, the omega point of our processes. Since this physicalism is unaware of its own limitations, it can propound eternal progress, which means, accord-

29. Tipler, 247.

30. Wolfhart Pannenberg, "Breaking a Taboo: Frank Tipler's *The Physics of Immortality*," *Zygon* 30 (1995): 312.

31. Donald G. York, "Something to Offend Everyone: Tipler's Vision of Immortality," *Zygon* 30 (1995): 477-78.

32. Hans-Dieter Mutschler, "Frank Tipler's Physical Eschatology," *Zygon* 30 (1995): 483.

ing to Tipler, that "knowledge will grow without bound, per capita wealth will increase to infinity."[33] Small wonder that Tipler has no use for entropy.

Even Tipler is aware that the world he portrays must finally turn in on itself; it must collapse through its gravitational pull. One wonders whether the facts that Tipler extrapolates are more credible than the trust Jesus evokes through his message and destiny. If theology is subsumed under physics and eschatology under cosmology, what avenues are there to counterbalance what Swiss philosopher Karl Jaspers (1883-1969) called *Wissenschaftsaberglaube*, the superstitious use of science? Once the scientific theories of the future are no longer mindful of the finitude of space, time, and matter, they are prone to replace Christian eschatology in the same manner as the latter will lead to religious superstition if it is oblivious to the earthly conditions to which it adds its ultimate evaluations.

The project of Frank Tipler shows that even if Christian premises are discarded, modern humanity has a deep-seated urge to ascertain that there is a future in store for us. If it is not here or in the hereafter, maybe it is on other planets or in other life-forms. Part of this drive comes from the evolutionary perspective that found its ablest expression in the nineteenth century in the work of Charles Darwin (1809-82).

b. The Evolutionary Perspective

While the material base of our universe is ruled by fundamental laws which do not seem to allow much optimism, the outlook becomes quite different once we consider life itself. The graphic symbol of the tree of life indicates that there is an unfolding of life and a continuous reaching up to new heights. Yet the theory of evolution, forever connected with the name of **Charles Darwin** and expressive of the progressive spirit of the nineteenth century, is essentially focused on the present and attempts to delineate laws according to which the present emerged from the past. Developmental theories are past oriented, trying to discern the causal relationship of organisms in the present world. They do not make any assertions about the end and goal of this world or about the laws

33. Tipler, 104.

and conditions in a future aeon.[34] Therefore they do not contribute anything to our knowledge of the last things.

When we read Darwin's *Origin of Species*, however, we notice on the one hand his focus on the present, but then we detect that, in the conclusion at least, he could not refrain from pointing toward the future by writing: "And as natural selection works solely by and for the good of each being, all corporeal and mental endowments will tend to progress toward perfection." Two words are significant in this statement: "progress" and "perfection." Indeed, the discerning eye will notice some kind of development in nature whether one follows Darwin's theory or talks about successive new creations. Therefore Darwin concludes: "From the war of nature, from famine and death, the most exalted object which we are capable of conceiving, namely, the production of the higher animals, directly follows."[35] Of course, in the *Origin of Species* Darwin did not yet focus on humanity.

But the question is unavoidable whether the present state of evolution, including that of humanity, will ever be surpassed. Superman and superwoman are not only TV characters. Did not Adolf Hitler (1889-1945) dream of an Aryan master race, a dream for which he would sacrifice millions of "inferior" beings of Jewish and Slavic origin? Friedrich Nietzsche, too, in typical nineteenth-century exuberance, wrote about the superman in his dramatic poem *Thus Spake Zarathustra*.[36] He stated that humanity is something that should be overcome and that the superman is as far above humanity as humanity is above the apes. Nietzsche claims: "The Superman is the meaning of the earth."[37] Indeed, in principle one could not discount the possibility of a development of beings higher than humanity. Yet such process

---

34. So somewhat optimistically Rudolf Schmid, *Die Darwin'schen Theorien und ihre Stellung zur Philosophie, Religion und Moral* (Barmen: Hugo Klein, 1876), 364.

35. Charles Darwin, *The Origin of Species by Means of Natural Selection or the Preservation of Favoured Races in the Struggle for Life* (Chicago: Encyclopaedia Britannica, 1952), 243 (in the conclusion).

36. Friedrich Nietzsche, *Thus Spake Zarathustra* LXXIII/2, in *The Complete Works*, ed. Oscar Levy (New York: Macmillan, 1924), 11:351.

37. Nietzsche, prol. 3, 11:7, and cf. to this passage Ernst Benz, "Das Bild des Übermenschen in der europäischen Geistesgeschichte," in *Der Übermensch: Eine Diskussion*, ed. Ernst Benz (Zürich: Rhein-Verlag, 1961), 123-25, who extensively deals here with Nietzsche's idea of a superman.

could not continue forever, since even such beings would be part of this earth and of its finitude.[38]

While cosmologically speaking we can talk about the development of the cosmos, starting perhaps with a big bang and continuously expanding into all directions, we must be more modest concerning the development of life. If there were several life-carrying planetary bodies, then with regard to life they would be totally independent from each other.[39] The scenario may be likened to a meadow in bloom. While one blossom is just unfolding, another one has already reached its maturity and is beginning to wilt and a third one has not even opened up. Even assuming a coincidence of development, the sheer vastness of planetary space does not allow for meaningful communication or interaction of life. Already within our relatively small solar system, it takes relatively long just to reach the next planet. When we turn to the New Testament and read of a new cosmos, a new heaven and a new earth, these theological assertions are made from a geocentric perspective.[40] They do not say anything about the cosmos in general, though extrapolations of that kind are not a priori excluded.

Considering the future of this earth and staying within the possible developments within our solar system and of life within it, there is not much cause for optimism. Through nuclear fusion in our sun, hydrogen is continuously transformed into helium. Since helium is less permeable for heat than hydrogen, it encloses our sun like an isolating coat. The more helium that is produced, the more our sun is heating up internally, until the heat pressure counteracts the helium pressure at the surface of the sun. In this process the surface temperature of our sun will increase a hundredfold. We need little imagination to see that our earth will get warmer and warmer until all the water has evaporated and the earth's surface resembles that of the planet Venus. In this process the radius of the sun will increase by several times its present size, and the radius with its high temperatures will draw near to the earth. This would signal

38. Cf. Schmid, 366, who emphasizes the finitude of this earth and its implication for any further development.

39. Joseph Meurers, "Ende oder Vollendung des Kosmos in der Sicht moderner Naturwissenschaft," in *Evolution und Eschatologie*, ed. Helmut Gehrig (Karlsruhe: Badenia Verlag, 1970), 20-21, has pointed out this problem with regard to the development of life in the cosmos in different places or in the cosmos as a whole.

40. Cf. Meurers, 22, who reminds us of the geocentric perspective of Paul.

the end of life on earth and most likely also the end of earth, which may be swallowed up by the sun. Another possibility looming on the horizon, though relatively unlikely, is that our solar system will be disturbed by some other planetary bodies, which might cause a destruction of the planets. Regardless of which scenario we prefer, at the very end is the burning out of our sun when it has concluded its stellar development, as far as we know that today. This would then mean the end of life.

It is not surprising that Charles Darwin, in his autobiography, pondered: "Believing as I do that man in the distant future will be a far more perfect creature than he is now, it is an untolerable thought that he and all other sentient beings are doomed to complete annihilation after such long-continued slow progress. To those who fully admit the immortality of the human soul, the destruction of our world will not appear so dreadful."[41] Perhaps this is also the reason why the Roman Catholic Church, since the encyclical *Humani Generis* of 1950, insists that one can surely investigate evolution of the human body and of life in general, as long as one maintains that the soul "is immediately created by God."[42] Regardless of the insistence of progress and development, there is no ultimate future for life as long as we refer alone to its own potential and evolutionary possibilities.

In this rather sobering situation, **Pierre Teilhard de Chardin** pursued a more promising track. Teilhard is both a scientist and a theologian and priest. In his social understanding the latter gains the upper hand, because he endeavors to find a new synthesis of his theological, physical, paleontological, and paleoanthropological findings with regard to a Christian view of the universe and of humanity.[43] His theological starting point is the incarnation. God has entered this world and

41. Francis Darwin, ed., *The Life and Letters of Charles Darwin, Including an Autobiographical Chapter* (1888) (New York: Johnson Reprint, 1969), 312, in an excerpt of an undated letter.

42. Encyclical *Humani Generis* (DS 3896), as quoted by John Paul II in an address to a conference on evolution and Christian faith. See "Ansprache des Hl. Vaters, Papst Johannes Paul II," in *Evolutionismus und Christentum*, ed. Robert Spaemann, Reinhard Löw, and Peter Koslowski (Weinheim: Acta Humaniora, VCH, 1986), 146. It is strange that in the English translation of Heinrich Denzinger, *The Sources of Catholic Dogma* (St. Louis: B. Herder, 1957), 645-46, this clause is missing.

43. So very clearly Ernst Benz, *Evolution and Christian Hope: Man's Concept of the Future from the Early Fathers to Teilhard de Chardin*, trans. H. G. Frank (Garden City, N.Y.: Doubleday, Anchor, 1968), 212.

will finally unite the world with himself. The universal Christ found by Teilhard in the New Testament is "the organic center of the entire universe."[44] He is the Alpha and Omega, the beginning and end. If Christ is universal, Teilhard concludes, then redemption and the fall "must extend to the whole universe" and assume cosmic dimensions.[45]

Teilhard wants to overcome the old static dualism between spirit and matter. He thinks this can be accomplished by viewing spirit and matter together in a universe which is historically advanced through an inward-guided evolution. There are four stages of development: (1) the cosmosphere as the origin of the cosmos; (2) the biosphere as the advancement of life; (3) the noosphere as "the Earth's thinking envelope,"[46] which is intensified through a psychophysical convergence, an event Teilhard calls planetization; finally, (4) the Christosphere emerges when the whole cosmos is permeated by Christ and taken up in God. Important for this process is the omega point. It is, so to speak, the inner circle of the universe which describes the endpoint of the development. God incarnate is reflected in our noosphere. He is the reflection "of the ultimate nucleus of totalization and consolidation that is biopsychologically demanded by the evolution of a *reflective* living Mass."[47] As the divine converges with the material, the universe becomes personalized and the person (of Christ) becomes universalized by merging with all of humanity and all that is material.[48] The whole evolutionary activity is therewith centered in a process of union or communion with God.

There is no pessimism in Teilhard's view, nor any despair over the problems of today. Even if our planet is seemingly becoming too small for our ever growing population, Teilhard is convinced that the psychosocial pressure will unify humanity, its society, and its culture. It will lead not to chaos but toward personalization, increased differentiation, and a richer fulfillment of the individual. Evolution is always an ascent to increased consciousness. Yet for Teilhard evolution is not an infinite

44. Pierre Teilhard de Chardin, "Note on the Universal Christ," in *Science and Christ*, trans. René Hague (New York: Harper & Row, 1965), 14.

45. Teilhard, "Universal Christ," 16.

46. Cf. Pierre Teilhard de Chardin, *The Heart of Matter*, trans. René Hague (New York: Harcourt Brace Jovanovich, 1978), 31.

47. Teilhard, *The Heart of Matter*, 39.

48. Cf. Teilhard, *The Heart of Matter*, 44-45.

movement, but it has a definite goal in the paroxysm under the intense psychosocial pressure that will lead to Christification. Everything will be received and end in Christ. This excludes any final catastrophe as the end of our present world, since such a sidereal disaster could lead only to the extinction of part of the universe, rather than to the fulfilling of the universe as a whole. Teilhard would not agree that he portrays an almost naive and blind trust in the future. On the contrary, he assures us that "worldly faith . . . is not enough in itself to move the earth forward."[49]

If we wish to properly understand Teilhard's confidence in the future, we must note three items:

1. Teilhard identifies the center of humanity's present crisis as a real but unnecessary conflict between two major forces. One, operating on the horizontal plane, is the forward energy of faith in humanity, in the world, and in human progress, moving toward the "ultra-human." The other is the traditional Christian faith, aspiring on a vertical plane in a personal transcendence and adoration toward God. The purely human drive, however, "can neither justify nor sustain its momentum to the end," because it discounts a center at its consummation and therefore needs to be centered in the Christian faith.[50] On the other hand, the purely upward drive is not the full story of the Christian faith either, since it is rooted in the incarnation and "has always based a large part of its tenets on the tangible values of the World and of Matter."[51] Teilhard wants to rectify and reconcile these two faiths into a mutually complementary, supportive, and fortifying synthesis.[52] He sees in the parousia the perfect example of this synthesis, a single case "which sums up everything."

2. Teilhard sees humanity's complete evolution and Christ's second coming in analogy to the conditions of Christ's first appearance on earth: "The mystery of the first Christmas which (as everyone agrees) could only have happened between Heaven and an Earth which was *prepared*, socially, politically and psychologically, to receive Jesus."[53] Why,

49. Pierre Teilhard de Chardin, *The Future of Man*, trans. N. Denny (New York: Harper Torchbooks, 1969), 277.

50. Teilhard, *The Future of Man*, 277.

51. Teilhard, *The Future of Man*, 279.

52. Cf. Teilhard, *The Future of Man*, 282, where Teilhard explains his view with the help of a diagram.

53. Teilhard, *The Future of Man*, 280 n. 3.

Teilhard asks, should we not also assume "that the parousiac spark can, of physical and organic necessity, only be kindled between Heaven and a Mankind which has biologically reached a certain critical evolutionary point of collective maturity"?[54] In other words, just as Christ first came to us when the time was fulfilled, so he will come again when the conditions for the parousia are ripe.

3. While Teilhard stipulates that humanity must reach maximum maturation, this alone is not a sufficient condition for Christ's second coming. The evolutionary climax is a necessary precondition for Christ's return, and is indeed assisted by Christ's presence which is presently veiled in all things. But it *cannot* itself cause the parousia to take place. The "supernatural" always predominates and makes the event more than the natural course of human evolution. Yet Teilhard insists that the parousia will not be "an *arbitrary* event, unconnected with the human evolutionary progress."[55] Just as the incarnation took place in "the fullness of time," so too will Christ's return take place in the ultimate and complete fullness of time.

A Christian understands, Teilhard says, that the process of hominization is only a preparation for the final parousia. Yet Christogenesis, when everything will be received and end in Christ, is not a natural phenomenon or a product of evolution. There is an ascending anthropogenesis and a descending permeation of Christogenesis. The natural evolution up to humanity and the "supernatural" descent in the incarnation have merged to form a unity in salvation history. The unifying movement of the human family (upward-slanting and forward-moving) and the activity of Christ in salvation history (from above and permeating the whole reality of humanity) are fused in the Christogenesis. Thus hominization serves as a preparation for and a way toward the parousia.

The Christian community must remain faithful and keep alive the expectation of the return of Christ. Teilhard affirms that we cannot determine the hour or the mode of this event, but we *must* expect it. "Expectation — anxious, collective and operative expectation of an end of the world, that is to say of an issue for the world — that is perhaps the

54. Teilhard, *The Future of Man,* 280.
55. So also Robert L. Faricy, *Teilhard de Chardin's Theology of the Christian in the World* (New York: Sheed & Ward, 1967), 210-11.

supreme Christian function and the most distinctive characteristic of our religion."[56]

We are to recognize that, historically, expectation has been the illumination of our faith. It has been the light at the end of the tunnel that offers us hope. Starting with the messianic hope of the prophets and culminating in the return of Christ so impatiently expected by many in the first Christian community, Christians have as their heritage the charge of "keeping the flame of desire ever alive in the world. . . . It is an accumulation of desires that should cause the Pleroma to burst upon us."[57]

Teilhard tempers the full expectation of Christ's return with the caution and encouragement to persist in this vigil, even in the seeming slowness of its advent. He cautions us not to follow the early Christians in their "childish haste" to expect an immediate return, since such an attitude leads to pessimism, disillusionment, and suspicion. But we are to rekindle and renew in ourselves the hope and desire for Christ's return, even when we know neither the day nor the hour.

Once again we hear Teilhard's call to the reconciliation and the potential harmony between this world and our hope in Christ. "The expectation of heaven cannot remain alive unless it is incarnate."[58] The body of our hope lies in the progress of the world, not in contempt toward it. "The progress of the universe, and in particular of the human universe, does not take place in competition with God, nor does it squander energies that we rightly owe to Him. The greater man becomes, the more humanity becomes united, with consciousness of, and master of, its potentialities, the more beautiful creation will be, the more perfect adoration will become, and the more Christ will find, for mystical extensions, a body worthy of resurrection."[59]

While the genesis of humanity is constitutive for the genesis of Christ in the human family through his church, it is this descent of Christ that superanimates humanity. It is not the crowding upon each other of the human family that warms the human heart; the union through and in love brings individuals together. In Christianity, Teilhard claims, we have witnessed the birth of love. He sees it as central to

56. Pierre Teilhard de Chardin, *The Divine Milieu: An Essay on the Interior Life* (New York: Harper & Row, 1960), 151.
57. Teilhard, *The Divine Milieu*, 151.
58. Teilhard, *The Divine Milieu*, 153.
59. Teilhard, *The Divine Milieu*, 153-54.

the Christian faith that the human individual cannot achieve self-perfection or exist in fullness except through organic unification of all people in God.

The universal movement, which is moving forward toward the future and upward in an evolutionary and metaphysical sense, does not express a neglect of the personal. The personal and universal at the summit of evolution rather endows our individual and corporate existence with meaning and direction. Teilhard asserts that in Christianity alone the faith in a personal and personalizing center of the universe is alive and has a chance of surviving today. In Christianity the hope is kept alive, growing, and set to work that one day

> the tension gradually accumulating between humanity and God will touch the limits prescribed by the possibilities of the world. And then will come the end. Then the presence of Christ, which has been silently accruing in things, will suddenly be revealed — like a flash of light from pole to pole. Breaking through all the barriers within which the veil of matter and the water-tightness of souls have seemingly kept it confined, it will invade the face of the earth. And, under the finally-liberated action of the true affinities of being, the spiritual atoms of the world will be borne along by a force generated by the powers of cohesion proper to the universe itself and will occupy, whether within Christ or without Christ (but always under the influence of Christ), the place of happiness or pain designated for them by the living structure of the Pleroma.[60]

The whole evolutionary process is directed toward and finds its fulfillment in the parousia of Christ, in the creation of a new heaven and a new earth.

We could still question whether Teilhard views the evolutionary process as too unilinear when he judges, for instance, the notion of original sin to be primarily "an intellectual and emotional straightjacket."[61]

60. Teilhard, *The Divine Milieu*, 150-51.
61. So Pierre Teilhard de Chardin, *Christianity and Evolution*, trans. R. Hague (New York: Harcourt Brace Jovanovich, 1969), 80. For an evaluation of Teilhard, cf. also Hans Schwarz, *Our Cosmic Journey* (Minneapolis: Augsburg, 1977), 116-17. For a good introduction to Teilhard, cf. Philip Hefner, *The Promise of Teilhard: The Meaning of the Twentieth Century in Christian Perspective* (Philadelphia: Lippincott, 1970); and Henri de Lubac, *The Religion of Teilhard de Chardin*, trans. R. Hague (New York: Desclee, 1967).

We might also wonder whether he does not perceive the evolution of humanity and the kingdom of God or salvation in and through Christ too much as two sides of the same homogeneous process. Lastly, we might ask whether he does not grossly underestimate the strain our growing population and our technological civilization put on the environment and its diminishing resources. Though we dare not pass over these questions too lightly, we should not forget that in an impressively christocentric manner Teilhard reminds us that the eschatological goal is a gift provided by God's grace and not a human attainment resulting from that grace. But his interest in a personal future notwithstanding, Teilhard's basic concern, similar to that of process theology, is for humanity and not for the individual person, for the cosmos and not for our earth. The individual does not matter much in an evolutionary scheme. The emphasis of the New Testament, however, contradicts this: Christ did not open the future to the world in general, but to individuals — to you and to me.

c. Facing a Possible Ecological Holocaust

While the material side of our earth and our universe, as far as we are able to discern it, advances toward the most probable conditions and arrangements, the phenomenon of life, as Teilhard de Chardin has pointed out, is essentially characterized "by an evolution towards the *least probable.*"[62] This means that life and its unfolding remains an aberration, a strange countercurrent to the general way of things. Therefore Teilhard postulates that entropy is a sufficient theory for inanimate nature but not for life. Life progresses toward a greater complexity and diversity, and by its very success it clearly counteracts physical entropy.

Similar to Frank Tipler, Teilhard asserts that a total death of the animate world simply cannot be possible, because in all adversity the stream of life is irreversible. Yet could life not also be likened to cancer? Cancerous cells also seem to multiply and spread irresistibly. Yet at the end they not only kill the host on which they grow, but by killing the host they kill themselves. We must remember the source that sustains

62. Pierre Teilhard de Chardin, *The Vision of the Past,* trans. J. M. Cohen (New York: Harper, 1966), 168.

life in this world. Life is sustained only by exploiting the inanimate world. But what happens when the natural resources are exhausted and the human population is too large to be sustained on this earth? We cannot exempt life from its context in nature. It may be uncomfortable or even offensive for us to face, but we are inextricably connected with the inanimate world in which we live and which ultimately sustains us. It is exactly this context that is threatened as never before.

World Come of Age or an Aging World?

In discussing here the vast field of ecology, we will consider it strictly from within the context of eschatology. Most people are convinced that we must make drastic and immediate decisions concerning our own future and that of our environment in order to survive. With rapid technological expansion the possibilities for good and evil have increased to such a Promethean dimension that none of us can escape the implications of the decision-making process involved in technological progress.

On a global scale, the Greenpeace movement has picked up ecological concerns. In Germany a sizable party, the so-called Green Party, has evolved. Both of these point out presumable aberrations in technological progress, but they are at the same time convinced that by following their direction we could avoid possible self-destruction. Their sensitivity to glaring issues of the environment and its resources deserves our respect. Yet at the same time they perpetuate the myth that humanity has reached maturity and, with sufficient determination and insights, can solve its problems and steer a more promising course. Is humanity really so clever as to extricate itself from the swamp into which it has fallen by simply pulling up its bootstraps? We cannot avoid the impression that each time in history when we thought we had solved a problem, a new and bigger one emerged. Our solutions have largely been patchwork.

Langdon Gilkey (b. 1919) aptly reminds us that the myth "of man come of age through an increase in his knowledge is not merely an inaccurate myth theologically. Even more, it is a dangerous myth in applied science."[63] Where we have become our own ultimate measure in the decision-making process, the development and use of technology have not

---

63. Langdon Gilkey, in his stimulating study *Religion and the Scientific Future: Reflections on Myth, Science, and Theology* (New York: Harper & Row, 1970), 95.

emerged as our true servants but have contributed to our bondage. They are used to exert technocratic tyranny and to stimulate our sinful and greedy impulses (e.g., the profit motive, national pride, and national or class paranoia).[64]

The assumption that we are autonomous contributes more to the aging process of the world than it indicates that we have freed ourselves and become mature. As a consequence we face mutual exploitation, misuse of the environment, and depletion of our natural resources. Mistreatment of the ecosphere is not limited to one nation; it is global because it is a human phenomenon; it occurs in the East as well as in the West and the Third World. Coupled with our rapid and gigantic technological progress, it has taken on such huge dimensions that we cannot escape the thought that we might involuntarily bring the eschaton upon ourselves and our environment within the foreseeable future.

The eschatological dimension of ecology cannot be overstated. We must get used to the idea that our environmental exploitation has presently taken on apocalyptic dimensions. Let us illustrate this with three examples:[65]

Greenhouse Effect

Through our rapidly increasing consumption of carbon-based fuels (coal, oil, gas), we release such a great amount of carbon dioxide into the earth's atmosphere that nature will no longer be able to balance this by absorbing carbon dioxide into the oceans or by using it up in plants and releasing the corresponding amount of oxygen. The dilemma is compounded by our encroachment on the world's forests, partly for agricultural reasons and partly for use of firewood and lumber. In the 1980s, for instance, 70 percent of the destruction of forests was due to population pressure.[66] Moreover, each year 25 million acres (an area of the size of Indiana) of tropical forests are cut down without replacement.[67]

---

64. Gilkey, 94.

65. For the following, cf. Hans Schwarz, "The Eschatological Dimension of Ecology," *Zygon* 9 (1974): 326-28.

66. For the statistics see *Der Fischer Weltalmanach 1998*, ed. Mario von Baratta (Frankfurt am Main: Fischer, 1997), cols. 1195-98.

67. According to Calvin B. DeWitt, *The Environment and the Christian: What Can We Learn from the New Testament?* (Grand Rapids: Baker, 1991), 15.

Thus not only immense water storage areas but also a vast exchange basin for absorbing carbon dioxide and releasing oxygen are rapidly disappearing.

Carbon dioxide, being relatively heavy, could easily perform the same function in our atmosphere as glass roofs do in greenhouses. It lets the sun's rays permeate but prevents the resulting heat from escaping. Of all the carbon dioxide produced by combustion, a large percentage remains in the atmosphere. "The concentration of carbon dioxide in the atmosphere has now increased by about 25 percent over its pre-industrial value."[68] If this increase continues, together with other pollution, it would cause a considerable increase in temperature. The onslaught on the earth's atmosphere is compounded by the continuous increase of the concentration of methane. This is due to more cattle ranches and the decomposition of organic materials in garbage dumps and surface water. Similarly, more agricultural fertilization and modern traffic lead to higher concentrations of nitrogen oxides in the atmosphere. Both methane and nitrogen oxides contribute to heat up the atmosphere. "There has been a general upward trend in average annual global temperature, from about 14.5 degrees Celsius in 1866, when reliable records begin, to around 15.4 degrees in 1995 — the warmest year on record. . . . Future warming, according to the IPCC [Intergovernmental Panel on Climate Change] will probably be in the range of 1-3.5 degrees Celsius by the year 2100, depending on air pollution trends. That may not sound like much, but the last time temperatures substantially exceeded current levels, 125,000-114,000 years ago, hippopotamuses were living in what is now Great Britain."[69]

Since 1977, a striking change in the atmospheric ozone concentrations during the Southern Hemisphere's springtime has also been observed. The so-called ozone hole has increased virtually every year and is now larger than the size of the United States. Further ozone loss is usually stopped by mid-October, and strong air circulation from the southern temperate zone in mid-November causes the dissipation of the hole by dilution with air that has not been so depleted of ozone. In

68. S. Fred Singer, "Overview," in *Global Climate Change: Human and Natural Influences,* ed. S. Fred Singer (New York: Paragon, 1989), 2.

69. Chris Bright, "Tracking the Ecology of Climate Change," in *State of the World, 1997,* ed. Linda Starke (New York: Norton, 1997), 79.

March 1995, for the first time, a smaller ozone hole was also detected over the North Pole, extending as far south as Scandinavia. This Arctic ozone hole is especially worrisome, since the Northern Hemisphere is much more heavily populated than the extreme Southern Hemisphere. The main culprit for this ozone depletion seems to be the chlorofluoro-carbons (CFCs) that destroy the biosphere's stratospheric ozone shield, which "filters off" harmful ultraviolet rays from solar radiation. It is "unlikely that life, at least as we know it, would have developed on Earth without an ozone layer in the stratosphere."[70] Though CFCs are, for the most part, no longer manufactured, reason for caution still exists, since these CFCs take more than a decade from emission to reach the alti-tudes at which they do the most harm, around forty kilometers (twenty-five miles). This also indicates a basic problem with the environment. Once we realize what the causes are for a special problem, it may al-ready be too late to reverse it, due to the delay between causation and effect.

How pervasive the changes that even small variations in tempera-ture can bring about can be gleaned from the last glacial period, which existed roughly 17,000-18,000 years ago.[71] The average temperature then was just five degrees Celsius (nine degrees Fahrenheit) lower than today. This led to such an increase in glacial ice that the sea level de-creased by approximately 150 meters (500 feet) and land bridges were established between Alaska and Siberia, Sri Lanka and the Indian sub-continent, and Papua New Guinea and Australia, for instance. However, if the greenhouse effect leads to a global warming, we could expect the opposite effect: a large reduction of glacial ice on both poles and a cor-responding increase of the sea level.[72] The dangerous consequences are not difficult to visualize when we remember that most of the Nether-lands is already below sea level and preserved through dikes and many Pacific islands, such as Tonga, or the Seychelles in the Indian Ocean, are

70. F. Sherwood Rowland, "Chlorofluorocarbons, Stratospheric Ozone, and the Antarctic 'Ozone Hole,'" in *Global Climate Change*, 150.

71. Cf. for the statistics and the changes in the sea level, *Der Fischer Weltalmanach 1998*, col. 1178.

72. Another possible cause for the melting of polar ice could be large oil spills in connection with offshore drilling in the Arctic Ocean. Cf. Mihajlo Mesarovic and Eduard Prestel, eds., *Mankind at the Turning Point: The Second Report to the Club of Rome* (New York: Dutton, 1974), 149-50.

only a few meters above sea level. It is no accident that most of the dikes along the coast of the North Sea are already being moderately increased in height, since a slight increase in sea level of ten to twenty-five centimeters (four to ten inches) has been realized in this century.

Other experts, however, claim that, like a sunroof, urban and agricultural atmospheric pollutants such as dust, sulfates, nitrates, and hydrocarbons tend to lower the earth's temperature. Which pollution will win in the end? Will we drown or will we freeze? Or should we continue to obscure the sky in trying to establish a balance of one form of pollution with another?

Pleonexia

The next phenomenon is pleonexia, or the naturalistic attitude of accumulating an ever growing and ever changing amount of disposable material goods.[73] Apart from the ensuing identity problems, this creates an increasing strain on our natural resources. The steeply rising demand on energy supplies has not only led to temporary shortages of gas and electrical power but will lead in the foreseeable future to the depletion of our natural and global carbon-based fuel resources. With present extraction technologies, currently known resources of oil will last another forty-two years. Natural gas reserves in the United States will run out in less than a decade, but there are still sufficient reserves globally to ensure approximately sixty-three years' use, provided there is no increase in consumption. Only if new deposits are discovered or better rates of extraction are developed, and especially if we are more efficient in using the reserves or switch over to other renewable energies, can we extend the limit of these resources.[74] Our coal deposits will last considerably longer, but burning it contributes considerably to environmental pollution and coal is also no actual replacement for oil. We could also expand our energy supply

73. With reference to these problems, the term "pleonexia" seems to have been used first by V. A. Demant (*The Idea of a Natural Order: With an Essay on Modern Asceticism*, Facet Books [Philadelphia: Fortress, 1966], 39), who advocates a practical asceticism that witnesses to the truth of the maxim "Production is for humanity, not humanity for production." According to Demant, such asceticism would be a testimony to the old teaching "that the really satisfying life does not depend upon the number of commodities one can acquire, but upon the fruitful exercise of our inner powers."

74. For the statistics see *Der Fischer Weltalmanach 1998*, cols. 1122 and 1126.

through the rapid expansion of nuclear power plants which operate on uranium 235. Yet at present most people are hesitant to endorse the construction of new nuclear power plants, since they are afraid of the long-term obligation to care for nuclear waste and also of the potential failures of such power plants after the disaster at Chernobyl.

The deployment of a fast breeder type of reactor which also uses uranium 238 and thorium 232 and leads to a conversion of nuclear fuel sixty to seventy times more effective than in conventional reactors, is even more seriously questioned because of the highly toxic plutonium 239 which is used in the process. Moreover, nowhere are people willing to allow nuclear waste to be stored near them. In the more distant future, nuclear fusion under controlled conditions may be a possibility for extending our energy resources. Approximately forty years of intensive research in this field has brought steady progress, and it seems feasible that in another two or three decades we can simulate and also sustain, on a larger scale, reactions such as the fusion of hydrogen into helium, or rather, of deuterium and tritium into helium, that normally occur only in stars. Yet we should not forget that from a thermodynamic viewpoint, nuclear plants are even less efficient than conventional power plants since they must reject 60 to 67 percent of their energy as waste heat.[75] Thus nuclear reactors must be considered a considerable source of thermal pollution.

While in the near future we may face problems with energy supply, things look different with other natural resources. If we consider the apparent lifetime of nonrenewable resources of ten crucial mineral commodities, such as iron ore, copper, mercury, and bauxite (aluminum), at currently minable grades and existing rates of consumption, we notice that their life expectancy lies between 35 and more than 200 years. We are also assured: "In contrast to the pessimistic assumptions of the 70s claiming a soon exhaustion of many mineral deposits, since the middle of the 80s we have seen ever more clearly, that with most of the minable minerals globally seen there has not occurred any shortage. As a rule there exists a sufficient supply."[76] Of course, this does not take into consideration an increase in consumption or, on the other hand, new deposits that might

---

75. Manfred Grathwohl, *Energieversorgung: Resourcen — Technologien — Perspektiven*, 2nd ed. (Berlin and New York: Walter de Gruyter, 1983), 341.

76. *Der Fischer Weltalmanach 1998*, col. 1069.

be found or the introduction of more intensive recycling processes. Many ore deposits are being depleted, and the minable grades are gradually being lowered so that more ore must be processed in order to obtain the same amount of minerals. For instance, "four centuries ago, copper ores typically contained about 8 percent metal; the average grade of ore mined is now under 1 percent."[77] This also increases the burden on the environment in terms of metal-contaminated wastes.

Overpopulation

The last example we will mention is overpopulation.[78] Our emphasis on extending medical aid in order to prolong life and to enable procreation has disturbed the natural equilibrium between birth and death. Our earth can sustain only a limited number of living beings. Regardless of new agricultural methods or housing plans, our ecosphere is able to support at the most 6 to 8 billion people. Beyond this number, problems of pollution, nutrition, and depletion of natural resources increase so vastly that only catastrophes can result. The tragic fact is that, taking present age structures and life expectancies of our world population into account, we can be certain that within a couple years we will have reached this limit, regardless of how well family planning is accepted and practiced. From there on, zero population growth is the only way to survive. But it is shortsighted to blame only underdeveloped countries (where the population is truly exploding) for putting us in such a precarious situation. To estimate the impact of population growth on the environment, we must also consider relative living standards. For instance, "the industrialized countries use about three times more commercial energy than developing countries and about 10 times more energy on a per capita basis."[79] This shows that increased responsibility accompanies an increased standard of living.

77. John E. Young, "Mining the Earth," in *State of the World, 1992*, ed. Linda Starke (New York: Norton, 1992), 108.

78. Most alert people are convinced that overpopulation lies at the root of our whole present ecological crisis. Cf. Christopher Flavin, "The Legacy of Rio," in *State of the World, 1997*, 16, who writes: "Population increase is the driving force behind many environmental and societal problems."

79. According to *World Resources, 1992-93*, A Report of The World Resources Institute in cooperation with the United Nations Environment Programme and the United Nations Development Programme (New York: Oxford University Press, 1992), 143.

It is already impossible to bring the rest of the world up to American or western European standards. For instance, if the world's food supply were distributed at the present American dietary level, it would feed only about one-third of the human race. While approximately 2.5 billion of the world's population are seriously poor and experience food, water, and energy shortages, there are nearly 2 billion who are absolutely destitute. They are the miserable of the earth, and their short lives are filled with deprivation, disease, grief, and uncertainty. In stark contrast to these there exists an exclusive luxury club of nearly 600 million people, almost exclusively North Americans and Europeans, who enjoy a rich and steadily more abundant diet as well as an incomparably high standard of living.[80] Not the children of the poor but the children of the affluent are the worst polluters and make the highest demands on the earth's resources. The poor, if left alone, would control themselves through famine, disease, and other factors which shorten their life expectancy. Yet drastic cutbacks in foreign aid to underdeveloped countries would not only be inhuman but would not solve the problem because it is we, the rich nations, who are no longer self-supporting.

The rapid increase of so-called global players among industrial corporations indicates that the highly "developed" nations are no longer self-sufficient. They depend on cheap labor in low-wage countries such as Romania or India, on cattle ranches in Latin America, and on timber from the rain forests of Asia. The supply for other natural resources, such as natural gas, oil, and ores, can also no longer be met domestically. It must come from other lands and must be found along other shores. Almost like parasites, we are eating away at other nations' resources. Thus controlling the poor is not the problem, but controlling the rich. And in terms of the world's population most Americans and Europeans, even many of those who are on welfare, are among the rich. If our present rate of "progress" and procreation continues, the limit of what our ecosphere can endure will be reached in less than twenty-five years.

---

80. Cf. the data provided by Samuel Baum, "World Population Trends in the Second Half of the Twentieth Century," in *Fallout from the Population Explosion,* ed. Claude A. Villee, Jr. (New York: Paragon, 1985), 9-26.

The Eschatological Context of Ecology

These examples show that we live in an apocalyptic age in which many of us sense that the end is threateningly close at hand. Immediate and drastic steps must be taken to avoid a global catastrophe. Most alert people agree on this premise. But when it comes to guidelines, goals, and limitations of such measures, there is a great deal of disagreement. Some feel that we should leave everything up to the technocrats, because they know best what measures can be taken. Others protest, saying that the dominance of technocrats is already in part the cause of our present dilemma.[81] Some feel that the crisis is so acute that only a dictatorial regime could enforce the necessary measures within the time available, while others rightly observe that dictators usually do not look out for the benefit of the people. Finally, some say that individualism has always been the American way to solve problems. But others object that our present dilemma is too complex for individuals to really make a difference.

Looking for the direction in which steps must be taken, we again face several mutually exclusive possibilities. We could embark upon an aesthetic approach and try to look for beauty and dignity as the values to be preserved. Or we could pursue the utilitarian route and say that it only matters how we can best use the available resources even if the environment will suffer. Of course, the conservationists would object here, saying that it also matters to what degree we can preserve the naturalness and diversity of our environment. When we come to the means by which we reach our goal, again we face the dilemma of mutually exclusive choices: Do we want a community of robots who, according to strict laws, do exactly what is best? Or do we want, within certain limits, an approach of free enterprise with all its possibilities of failure and disobedience?

Confronted with these conflicting opinions of what to do in our precarious situation, it is well to remember that we live in an apocalyptic age. An apocalyptic age is a period in which we presume to be close enough to the end of history that we can discern which unalterable course it will take. Since we live, however, in a largely secularized age, the horizon of

81. The power of the technocrats and of big business was first eloquently exposed as the cause of our environmental crisis by Rachel Carson in *Silent Spring* (Boston: Houghton Mifflin, 1962).

hope is restricted to the possibilities of this world. Any hope beyond these limits can only be gained if we reorient this apocalyptic mood according to the Judeo-Christian tradition in which it first originated, and then anchor it in the more comprehensive context of eschatology. This would mean that, as we are confronted with our possible future doom and with a multitude of proposals on how to escape this doom, a reliable directive for action can only come from the Judeo-Christian tradition out of which this apocalyptic prospect originated. Given this context, we must first consider the anticipatory aspect of eschatology.

The Christian understanding of the anticipatory power of eschatology gives us both the incentive and the possibility for stopping the exploitation of our environment and for preventing our own self-destruction. The Christian gospel tells us that we already participate in a proleptic way in the new creation which was initiated in and with the resurrection of Jesus Christ. In this way the representatives of the Social Gospel movement, such as Walter Rauschenbusch (1861-1918) and Shailer Mathews (1863-1941), were right when they emphasized the this-worldly dimension of the kingdom of God. In the face of human depravity, this provided a positive evaluation of our abilities as caretakers of God's creation.

At this point we can agree only partially with the penetrating analysis of Lynn White, Jr. (b. 1907).[82] White convincingly argues that technology is a Western phenomenon. Even in our present post-Christian era, our lives are still dominated by faith in perpetual progress, a faith unknown to Greco-Roman antiquity and to the Orient. This faith "is rooted in, and is indefensible apart from, Judeo-Christian teleology."[83] The Marxist movement, too, could not have developed without its Christian presuppositions. But when White labels Christianity the most anthropocentric religion the world has seen, he fails to convince us. We agree with him that the cause of our ecological crisis is our present anthropocentric attitude (that nature has no reason for existence save to serve us). But we have shown in our introductory chapter that this anthropocentricity is *not* a Christian axiom, as White believes.

---

82. Lynn White, Jr., "The Historical Roots of Our Ecological Crisis," first published in *Science* 155 (1967): 1203-7, reprinted in David and Eileen Spring, eds., *Ecology and Religion in History* (New York: Harper Torchbooks, 1974), 15-31.
83. White, in *Ecology and Religion,* 23.

On the contrary, it is the result of a process through which the theocentric worldview of the Judeo-Christian faith was turned into the anthropocentric worldview of our present secular age. When humanity elevated itself into God's place, the source and direction of history became obscured, and "for the glory of God" was replaced by the glorification and deification of humanity. Since White finally proposes Saint Francis (1182-1226) as a patron saint for ecologists, a suggestion picked up by many others, we wonder if he is not advancing an integration of our secular view of nature and progress into the context of a mystic religiosity. Yet what is necessary in the time of crisis is a reintegration of nature and progress into the Judeo-Christian tradition which made the desacralization of nature and the pursuit of progress both possible and meaningful. A mystical religion tends to neglect the real and either leads to contemplation instead of action or unrealistically pursues the establishment of an ideal world.

Similar to White, Thomas Berry and others distinguish between an inclusivist and exclusivist view of humanity and assign each profound ethical implications. The exclusivist view sees the human and the natural as two separate communities, and consequently carries forth a basic exploitative attitude of humanity toward nature. In contrast to that, the inclusivist view sees humanity within the context of nature. The earth is primary and humans are derivative. "Henceforth, all human activities must be judged primarily by the extent to which they generate and foster a mutually enhancing human/earth relationship."[84] Indeed, pitting nature and humanity against each other must necessarily lead to exploitation and eventual destruction of both humanity and nature. But can we be fully included in the context of nature, so to speak, as an epiphenomenon of nature, except on strictly biological grounds? When paleoanthropology, for instance, distinguishes between humans and animals by the criterion that animals use tools whereas humans manufacture them *(homo faber)*, this indicates that we largely shape the world we live in, whereas animals are basically just inhabitants of a given environment. Consequently, we must also be distinguished from the rest of nature. Wolfhart Pannenberg argues convincingly that our "openness to the world presupposes a rela-

---

84. Thomas Berry, "The Primordial Imperative," in *Theology for Earth Community: A Field Guide*, ed. Dieter T. Hessel (Maryknoll, N.Y.: Orbis, 1996), 2.

tion to God."[85] In other words, it is precisely because we are not just part of nature that we can responsibly administer it (i.e., as God's administrators).

Since we are not just extensions of nature, we are able to come up with the tools and the knowledge of how to change the world toward the better. We are free to design and implement agricultural reform and social and economic legislation, or even to redirect our understanding of basic family structures. Even the necessary reorientation of human progress, from accumulating more and more material goods at ever shorter intervals to the understanding of progress which intends the increase of true humanness, lies within the possibilities of human reason. In their advocacy of social betterment, some theologians, especially those who identify with the concerns of liberation theology, fail to perceive that these "reasonable" pursuits, while certainly consonant with the proclamation of the Christian faith, are not synonymous with it.

When the church assumes service functions, such as instituting family-planning centers or schools and hospitals in developing countries, neither is this social involvement the prerogative of the Christian community nor should such activities be confined to Christian groups. Apart from being an expression of the corporate dimension of the Christian faith, these actions are primarily intended to incite other people to do the same and to remind secular authorities that they do not serve the *whole* world (as they should), but only *part* of the world (at the expense of other parts).

The promise of a new creation foreshadowed in the resurrection of Jesus Christ can serve as a powerful stimulus to remind us that in faith we are new people and can already proleptically anticipate in this world something of the future glory in which we believe. As God's administrators, our task is not to exploit and abuse God's creation but to cherish, protect, and work in it. To accomplish this goal God has endowed us with reason and has given us his self-disclosure in Jesus Christ to remind us of this task. But in our bewildering and confusing time, the Christian faith must elucidate the future-directedness of eschatology so persuasively that it engenders an active hope for the future.[86]

---

85. Wolfhart Pannenberg, *What Is Man? Contemporary Anthropology in Theological Perspective,* trans. D. A. Priebe (Philadelphia: Fortress, 1970), 12.

86. Cf. for the following, H. Paul Santmire, *The Travail of Nature: The Ambiguous Eco-*

Future-Directedness of Eschatology

The fulfillment of the eschatological promise presented and partially realized in the Judeo-Christian tradition shows us the goals and limits of all human endeavors, including our involvement in the ecological crisis. The very fact that eschatology is essentially directed toward a God-provided eschaton reminds us of the limits of our own possibilities. It shows us that, no matter what techniques we devise or how hard we try, our ecosphere has no eternal value in itself but is subjected to transitoriness. The resulting interim character of our present situation does not *necessitate* a deterioration of present conditions and a subsequent attitude of resignation. On the contrary, the new creation has already started in Jesus Christ, and we are invited to participate in it in a proleptic way. Therefore the transitoriness of our present condition *can* also mean a transition toward the better. The apocalyptic metaphors of doom are not binding for us and should not stifle our positive endeavors.

Nevertheless, since our present situation is clearly marked as interim, we cannot expect perfection from our attempts. But it is realistic and indicative of responsibility to envision a state approaching perfection. Any attempt to transcend this limitation would result in the utopian venture of replacing the God-provided eschaton with an eschaton of our own making. But any imagined eschaton resulting from our own actions or aspirations would, in the long run, only magnify the ecological problems, because the present ecological dilemma has resulted precisely from that basic denial of the Judeo-Christian eschatological context.

Besides showing us the limitations of our own possibilities, eschatology can also provide us with goals for our ecological concern. Eugen Rosenstock-Huessy (1888-1973) once said, very appropriately: "Christianity is the founder and trustee of the future, the very process of find-

---

logical Promise of Christian Theology (Philadelphia: Fortress, 1985), who talks with regard to the Old Testament of an "eschatological vision of cosmic renewal" (199) and with regard to Jesus, that he "can be thought of as an ecological figure as well as an eschatological figure" (201). Christian Link, in his *Schöpfung: Schöpfungstheologie angesichts der Herausforderungen des 20. Jahrhunderts* (Gütersloh: Gerd Mohn, 1991), 2:462, advocates too "a comprehensive, biblically grounded perspective that is sufficiently broad enough to look at creation together with its goal of future completion and thereby regain the threatened unity of nature and history."

ing and securing it, and without the Christian spirit there is no real future for man."[87] In building upon the Jewish tradition, and at the same time in a significant modification of it, the Christian faith knows about Jesus Christ, the first perfect human being, who made the transition from suffering and fragmentariness to fulfillment and completeness. Thus the Christian faith is compelled to proclaim this transition as a possibility for all of us.[88]

In delineating our appropriate attitude during this present transitional stage, we have to point to Jesus of Nazareth, who has completed it. By imitating his way of life we discover that we should live as God-responsive and God-responsible beings within the matrix of our environment. This would rule out an understanding of progress either as an accumulation of material goods or as an emphasis on the quantity of life. It would also rule out a technocratic relinquishing of human responsiveness and responsibility on the one hand, and a neglect of this responsiveness and responsibility through carefree day-by-day living on the other hand. Instead, it would require the semidetached, ascetic attitude toward civilization and an emphasis on the quality of life and on finding personal fulfillment in enjoying pleasure and providing it for others.[89]

Stimulated by the attempt to imitate Jesus, our goal would be to increase our responsiveness and responsibility to God within the environmental matrix. But, recognizing that the final realization of this goal can be attained only in the eschaton, ultimate and lasting hope can come only from the expectation of Jesus Christ and from the new creation that he initiated. The proper understanding of the interrelatedness of the imitation of Jesus and the expectation of Christ can lead us to an ap-

---

87. Eugen Rosenstock-Huessy, *The Christian Future; or, The Modern Mind Outrun* (New York: Harper Torchbooks, 1966), 61.

88. Cf. Rosenstock-Huessy, 66.

89. Frederick Elder, *Crisis in Eden* (Nashville: Abingdon, 1970), 145, has advocated this new asceticism very eloquently. However, he cautions that, unlike medieval asceticism, this would not involve a withdrawal from the world, but simply a new way of acting toward and with the world. The basic elements of this new asceticism are restraint, an emphasis on the quality of existence, and reverence for life. Unlike Albert Schweitzer, Elder does not understand this reverence for life as a mystical and religious dedication to life, but as "an appreciation for *any* expression of life, based on scientific, aesthetic, and religious considerations" (152).

propriate evaluation and a proper attitude toward our present ecological crisis. It shows us that we presently live in an apocalyptic age, and that there is reason for hope and not for despair. Ulrich Körtner (b. 1957) rightly therefore concludes: "Faith does not stare anxiously transfixed toward the end of the world, nor does it surrender to apocalyptic pleasure in demise and destruction but rather affirms both the life God himself affirmed as well as the world God has affirmed, and does so through active engagement for the sake of both."[90] Körtner does not exclude the possibility of fear and suffering, but they do not petrify the Christian resolve to act since, in looking up to Christ, suffering and fear are overcome.

2. The Impact of Philosophy

We have seen that our present situation is serious, perhaps more serious than any human situation before. While through the millennia civilizations have emerged and disappeared in almost continuous fashion, today no nation is isolated from the rest of the global community. Yet the existence of this global community is threatened by a possible ecological holocaust. In looking at the evolutionary stream of life and its material base, we do not have any more reason for hope except that possible doom looms farther in the distance. There are always some thinkers who want to break through the strictures that nature seems to impose on us. Yet their options do not seem very promising.

It would be shortsighted, however, to say that this means we now have scientific proof that the eschaton is surely upon us. Teilhard de Chardin rightly warned us against the attempt to equate any global or sidereal disaster with the coming of the eschaton. Such a disaster would only affect part of the world but not the total world, and it would lead only to destruction but not to fulfillment in a new beginning. All we could gather from what we have seen so far is that this world in and by itself does not contain any long-scale hope or the promise of an entirely new beginning. At the most, we can have variations of what we already

90. So Ulrich H. J. Körtner, in his comprehensive and thorough study, *The End of the World: A Theological Interpretation*, trans. Douglas W. Stott (Louisville: Westminster John Knox, 1995), 276.

had, and in the end looms death. When we now consider the impact of philosophy, secular existentialism at least seems to affirm this scientific analysis.

a. The Option of Secular Existentialism

For Søren Kierkegaard (1813-55), the founder of existentialism, life was a venture sustained by trust in a gracious God. Secular existentialism, however, having emancipated itself from the all-embracing assurance of God's grace, starts with the assumption that ultimate questions are beyond our grasp. Existence does not find its fulfillment in the eschaton but is basically defined as "being there" and "being in the world."

Life Bounded by Death

Martin Heidegger (1889-1976), one of the pioneers of modern secular existentialist thought, conceives of life as being in the world; it is a being-there and a being-towards-death. Temporality and death are constitutive factors of being-there. Since in our being-there we face death as the end of life, this final end of our possibilities causes anxiety as a basic phenomenon of life. Yet it would be foolish to flee from our being-towards-death or to cover up this characteristic feature of our being-there. In so doing we would live inauthentically and, turning anxiety into fear, would attempt to hide from ourselves. Heidegger instead opts for resoluteness and authentic existence. He claims that we must recognize anxiety "as a basic state-of-mind" and as "Dasein's [being-there's] essential state of Being-in-the-world."[91] Similarly, "*authentic* Being-towards-death can *not evade* its ownmost non-relational possibility, or *cover up* this possibility by thus fleeing from it, or *give a new explanation* for it to accord with the common sense of the 'they.'"[92] Since death is being-there's innermost possibility, "being towards this possibility discloses to Dasein [being-there] its *ownmost* potentiality-for-Being, in which its very Being is the issue."[93]

91. Martin Heidegger, *Being and Time*, trans. J. Macquarrie and E. Robinson (London: SCM, 1962), 234.
92. Heidegger, 304-5.
93. Heidegger, 307.

Heidegger describes existence as occurring strictly within this world. While he could substantiate his claim by a phenomenological survey that all being-there ultimately faces death, his secular premise notwithstanding, he goes beyond the verifiable and calls for authentic existence as the optimum and goal of human existence. Yet this goal can really no longer be grounded in the being-there, and therefore Heidegger leaves the impression that his appeal is arbitrary[94] and subject to revision.

Ernest Becker (1925-74), in his award-winning book *The Denial of Death,* has pointed out with convincing clarity "that the fear of death is a universal."[95] Largely following the psychology of Sigmund Freud and combining it with the existential portrayal of humanity provided by Kierkegaard, Becker points out that "we are hopelessly absorbed with ourselves."[96] We hope and believe that the things we create in society are of lasting worth and meaning, "that they outlive or outshine death and decay."[97] Thus the urge to heroism is natural. But there is no escape from death. We are "doomed to live in an overwhelmingly tragic and demonic world."[98] We can drown our senses, but as soon as we awake we realize anew that we do not understand the purpose of creation and therefore the direction of life's expansion. "We only feel life straining in ourselves and see it thrashing others about as they devour each other."[99]

According to Becker, fear of death is a fundamental human motif and the repression of death anxiety can make human beings more dangerous in the way they relate to their worldviews and use them against one another. Though Becker won the 1974 Pulitzer Prize for general nonfiction for *The Denial of Death,* academics generally dismissed his work at that time because they thought it was another wild speculation "based on psychological constructs of dubious validity derived from

---

94. Laszlo Versényi, *Heidegger, Being, and Truth* (New Haven: Yale University Press, 1965), 184, rightly objects that Heidegger provides neither "a practical process nor usable criteria for distinguishing between authentic and inauthentic possibilities of Being."

95. Ernest Becker, *The Denial of Death* (New York: Free Press, 1973), ix.

96. Becker, *The Denial of Death,* xi, and quote on 2.

97. Cf. Becker, *The Denial of Death,* 5.

98. Becker, *The Denial of Death,* 281.

99. Becker, *The Denial of Death,* 284.

psychoanalysis."[100] But some social psychologists thought differently and reasoned that the ideas contained in that book were profound and could have powerful implications for understanding and affecting human behavior. Greenberg, Pyszczynski, and Solomon then developed the terror management theory and "acquired a large body of experimental evidence in support of Becker's central claim that concerns about mortality play a pervasive role in human affairs." Empirical research indeed validated Becker's claims. Yet Becker did not want to stay with the empirical.

As he noted in *The Denial of Death*, a sober examination of the motivational underpinnings of human behavior leads beyond psychology and directly to religion — to find the "courage to face the anxiety of meaninglessness."[101] As Solomon, Greenberg, and Pyszczynski realized, psychological equanimity "requires a meaningful conception of reality and no such conception can ever be unambiguously confirmed, all such meanings are sustained by faith and are hence fundamentally religious."[102] But the road to the religious was quite difficult for Becker.

Initially, similar to Heidegger, Becker was not content with our yearning to overcome death through heroic deeds. In his last book, posthumously published, he argued that our "natural and inevitable urge to deny mortality and achieve a heroic self-image are the root causes of human evil."[103] He was not as optimistic as Heidegger, however, that we can introduce a system by which we could live without causing painfulness and sorrow for each other. Still, he also refused to give up in despair. He closed his book, hoping for "that minute measure of reason to balance destruction."[104] Such hope is certainly not grounded in empirical data. But since the whole religious realm was explained by Becker as a device to escape the reality of "death and the dread of it,"[105] he could no longer resort to metaphysical powers. Neither was he willing to give

100. Cf. for the following, including the quote, Sheldon Solomon, Jeff Greenberg, and Tom Pyszczynski, "Tales from the Crypt: On the Role of Death in Life," *Zygon* 33 (1998): 10. It is noteworthy that the main feature of this issue of *Zygon* is the work of Ernest Becker.
101. Becker, *The Denial of Death*, 279.
102. Solomon, Greenberg, and Pyszczynski, 39.
103. Ernest Becker, *Escape from Evil* (New York: Free Press, 1975), xvii.
104. Becker, *Escape from Evil*, 170.
105. Becker, *The Denial of Death*, 12.

up living and hoping. This hope without faith and against overwhelming odds is the trademark of modern secular existentialism.

Yet Becker's life story has one more twist to it. After finishing *The Denial of Death* and before receiving the Pulitzer Prize, Becker was diagnosed with terminal cancer. He faced his own death true to his own writings with a Stoic form of heroism yet, as he added, with "the qualification that I believe in God."[106] He had been an atheist for many years, and it was not the prospect of dying that made him more religious. Long before that, at the birth of his first child, it dawned on him that new life was created, so to speak, out of nothingness. According to Becker, this must have something to do with God. Confronting death, he read each morning one or two psalms, and one of them (Ps. 131) made him ask: "What can man do when he has seen his own pitiful smallness, his inability to do and to understand, except 'hope'?"[107] Becker discovered here not only the finitude of life but also his own creatureliness, and thereby realized that all he could do is throw himself at the mercy of his creator.[108]

Again the discovery of his own creatureliness did not result from facing terminal illness. Before that, in a letter of September 20, 1965, he wrote to Harvey Bates: "At least I have been fortunate to learn that we do not achieve anything; that anything [that] is achieved, [is achieved] by grace. This is an immense discovery to me that is slowly transforming my whole world." But then he added: "Your view of Christianity as a self-discipline which grows out of thanksgiving for what is already given, and not for what is to come, is perhaps the highest one could achieve. . . . It is gratitude for being born to serve. Evidently, the genuine Hebrew religiousness — and Buber's — is very similar: the belief that when man has done all he could, then God would do the rest, he would act."[109] Creatureliness did not mean for Becker simply to be relegated to inactivity, but being gracious for having been born to serve. He also re-

106. As quoted by Sam Keen, "A Conversation with Ernest Becker," *Psychology Today,* April 1974, 78.

107. As quoted by Harvey Bates, "Letters from Ernest," *Christian Century* 94 (1977): 218.

108. For the following, cf. Sally A. Kenel, "A Heroic Vision," *Zygon* 33 (1998): 64-66, who emphasizes that Becker's anthropology is marked by "the religious symbol of creatureliness."

109. As quoted by Bates, 219.

alized that any service a human being could do would be within the limits of creatureliness. God indeed would have to do the rest. Having emphasized the dark side of life and realizing that "there is evil in the world,"[110] Becker had basically three options: resign himself to fate, a stance he considered inadequate for a human being; resort to heroic measures to, so to speak, "save the world," something he was convinced would only contribute to misery; or finally serve and hope even in the face of overwhelming odds. This truly existential note, fortified by a religious conviction that was not worn on his sleeve, allowed him to courageously face his own finitude.

Humanity Thrown upon Itself

When we come to **Jean-Paul Sartre** (1905-80), the French existentialist who radicalized Heidegger's philosophy, we are candidly confronted with a humanity that has lost its metaphysical reference point. Humanity is conceived of as an agent basically free of its destiny. But, in contrast to Heidegger, Sartre can no longer understand human freedom as beneficial. Humanity is "condemned to freedom."[111] We have no God, no truth, and no values, in the traditional sense of these terms. This individualized and nondirected world encounters us as a basically antagonistic world. Others are encountered as evil, even as "hell," desiring to infringe upon our freedom.[112]

Sartre claims that existence precedes essence and that our essence is what has been — or, in short, our past. But there is no common essence according to which we can act.[113] Rather each of us makes his or her essence as we live our lives. Thus we must transcend the nonconscious level of being-in-itself and rise to the conscious level of being-for-itself. At this level we express lack of being, desire for being, and relation to being. Yet in opting for being-for-itself we bring nothingness

110. As quoted by Keen, 74.

111. Jean-Paul Sartre, *Being and Nothingness: An Essay on Phenomenological Ontology*, translated with an introduction by H. E. Barnes (New York: Philosophical Library, 1956), 485. Sartre's claim of support from Heidegger seems to be unwarranted at this point.

112. Jean-Paul Sartre, *No Exit*, in *"No Exit" and Three Other Plays*, trans. L. Abel (New York: Knopf, 1949), 47.

113. Sartre, *Being and Nothingness*, 555-56.

into the world, since we now stand out from being and can judge other being by knowing what it is not. Sartre emphasizes that we must be-for-ourselves if we want to escape from "bad faith."[114] This bad faith arises if we oscillate between relying on the past and projecting ourselves toward the future or, equally bad, if we attempt to synthesize both. It is our destiny to venture toward the future without relying on the past or on any preestablished norms.

It is a grim picture that Sartre has offered us. We exist toward the future, solely relying on ourselves and in continuous conflict with others who, in a similar way, want to exist for themselves. But what should our motivation be for existing in this kind of solipsistic activism? One would find neither comfort nor assurance in such a world and opt for traditional values rather than relying solely on oneself.

Sartre's compatriot **Albert Camus** (1913-60) attempted to move beyond an arbitrary existentialist position to a moralist one.[115] In his essay *The Myth of Sisyphus* (1942), he describes the situation in which he found himself after having discovered that none of the speculative systems of the past can provide positive guidance for human life or guarantee the validity of our values.[116] Unlike Sartre, he at least poses the question of whether it makes sense to go on living once the meaninglessness of human life has been fully recognized. Camus maintains that suicide cannot be regarded as an adequate response to the experience of absurdity which results from our discovery that we must live without the value-supporting "standards" and ideas of the past. Cutting through the tension-provoking polarity between being human and the world by committing suicide would only be an admission of our incapacity. Camus argues that we have too much self-pride to seek this easy way out. Only by living in the face of our own absurdity can we achieve our full stature.

Camus realizes that our revolt against metaphysically guaranteed directives for conduct does not really improve the human predicament. Like Sartre, he portrays in his literary works the persisting injustice and cruelty committed by one human being against another. In his philo-

114. Sartre, *Being and Nothingness*, 70.

115. For a good assessment of Camus over against Sartre's position and Camus's sober limitation to concrete experience, cf. Germaine Brée, *Camus*, rev. ed. (New Brunswick, N.J.: Rutgers University Press, 1972), esp. 210-11.

116. Albert Camus, *The Myth of Sisyphus and Other Essays*, trans. J. O'Brien (New York: Vintage, 1991).

sophical essay *The Rebel* (1951), he concludes that it is precisely the revolt against metaphysics, against human conditions as such, that has led to twentieth-century totalitarianism.[117] Camus now rejects the metaphysical revolt and opts instead for an ethical revolt. He recognizes that the metaphysical revolt, while attempting to impose upon humanity a new world order, has resulted in the nightmare of an unrestrained power struggle. Yet Camus still calls for nihilism as a cathartic device. While he now knows that it does not provide a principle for action, he is still convinced that it will clear the ground for new construction by disposing of any kind of mystification by which we might try to rid ourselves of our radical contingency and confer upon ourselves a cosmic status. But how should this clearance be filled with positive content? Even an essentially nonmetaphysical and strongly moralistic humanism must derive its directives from somewhere, otherwise it would fall prey to what Camus rightly called "metaphysical" revolution.

In his last major work, *The Fall* (1956), Camus seems to imply that directives for ordering our lives cannot come from ourselves.[118] In this utterly pessimistic work Camus abandons political and social revolt. Evil is no longer understood as originating from the unjust social institutions in which we are doomed to exist; evil stems from the human heart. Then where does the incentive for life and living come from? In his short story "The Growing Stone" (1957), Camus seems to give an answer to this all-decisive question.[119] When the French engineer D'Arrast substitutes for the exhausted "mulatto" ship cook and picks up the stone to fulfill the cook's vow, he does not carry that stone to the cathedral, the place where the cook had vowed he would deposit it. Instead D'Arrast carries the stone back to the little hut in which the man lives. In other words, Camus indicates that help for us can only come from human solidarity in taking upon ourselves each other's burdens. But for Camus such solidarity must serve a human purpose and not a metaphysical one.

We wonder, however, whether this alternative that Camus poses

---

117. Albert Camus, *The Rebel: An Essay on Man in Revolt*, trans. A. Bower (New York: Knopf, 1961). Yet already at the conclusion of this book, Camus mentions that "rebellion cannot exist without a strange form of love" (304), without, however, elaborating any further on the meaning of love.

118. Albert Camus, *The Fall*, trans. J. O'Brien (New York: Knopf, 1961).

119. Albert Camus, "The Growing Stone," in *Exile and the Kingdom*, trans. J. O'Brien (New York: Vintage, 1965), 159-213.

could and even should not be bridged by suggesting that one can serve the metaphysical purpose in fulfilling a human need. If we are strictly confined to ourselves and the world around us, how could we ever experience the "fresh beginning of life" that D'Arrast so vividly senses? Admitting human depravity, secular existentialists opt for a heroic stand amid an antagonistic world. But they are unable to explain what would give us the continuing courage to wage a losing battle, nor are they in a better position to elucidate how there could be a fresh beginning. In other words, secular existentialism provides us with an accurate assessment of the human situation, but it is unable to lead us to a new future or even provide hope for the future unless it reintegrates its secular stance into a religious sphere.

b. Utopia from the Left

The term "utopia" dates back to Sir Thomas More (1478-1535), who wrote in 1515-16 his two books entitled *Utopia* that describe a pagan and communist city-state in which institutions and policies were entirely governed by reason. The order and dignity of such a state stood in stark contrast to the unreasonable polity of Christian Europe, which was divided by self-interest and greed for power and riches. Though this utopia, a composite from the Greek *ou* and *topos,* meaning no place or nowhere, was meant by More as a satire, utopia in a positive sense is a dimension of human yearning, often associated with wishful dreams, or theologically is the dimension of the future eschaton. Especially Karl Marx (1818-83) and Friedrich Engels (1820-95) advocated their socialist realm of freedom as a concrete utopia.

A New World through Revolution

Karl Marx stated his goal very precisely when he wrote: "The philosophers have only *interpreted* the world, in various ways; the point is to *change* it."[120] **Karl Marx** and **Friedrich Engels**, the founders of the

---

120. Karl Marx, "Theses on Feuerbach" (1845), in *Karl Marx: The Essential Writings,* edited with an introduction by Frederic L. Bender (New York: Harper Torchbooks, 1972), 155, in thesis xi.

Marxist movement, were influenced by a variety of sources. Progressive industrialization and popularized Darwinism gave them their optimistic outlook; labor conditions in the early years of the industrial revolution showed them the plight of the working class; biblical criticism, especially of the Tübingen school, removed for them most of the supernaturalness of the Bible; and Bruno Bauer (1809-82), a left-wing Hegelian and onetime close friend of Marx, gave them the idea that as a world religion Christianity was the product of the Greco-Roman world.[121] Especially for Karl Marx, two further influences need to be mentioned: Both of his parents were of Jewish descent, though they had converted to Protestantism. While he may not have had much of a religious upbringing, his vision of a new and perfect society had implicit religious overtones.[122] We must also note the influence of Ludwig Feuerbach and his book *The Essence of Christianity*. Engels tells us that Marx "enthusiastically welcomed this new concept," since Feuerbach reestablished materialism as the prime concept.[123] Nature exists independently of all philosophy; it is the foundation on which we as human beings have grown up as products of nature. There exists nothing outside nature and humanity, and the higher beings which were created by religious fantasy are just fantastical reflections of our own being.

The idea that Christianity, or religion as Marx and Engels usually call it, is the product of its environment was decisive for their thinking. But Marx felt that Feuerbach had only accomplished half the task. It is not sufficient to label religion as the projection of our unfulfilled desires on the screen of the beyond; it is necessary to recognize that this projection is a "social product" which belongs to a particular form of society, modern capitalism. If capitalism falls, religion will also disappear, as will many other products of the bourgeoisie, such as division of labor and the structures of the state.

121. Cf. Friedrich Engels, "On the History of Early Christianity," in *On Religion* (New York: Schocken Books, 1964), 324.

122. For details of his religious background and his own early views of God, cf. Walther Bienert, *Der überholte Marx: Seine Religionskritik und Weltanschauung kritisch untersucht* (Stuttgart: Evangelisches Verlagswerk, 1974), 15-17.

123. Cf. for the following, including the quote, Friedrich Engels, "Ludwig Feuerbach und der Ausgang der klassischen deutschen Philosophie" (I), in *Texte zur materialistischen Geschichtsauffassung von Ludwig Feuerbach, Karl Marx, Friedrich Engels*, edited with an introduction by Helmut Reichelt (Frankfurt am Main: Ullstein, 1975), 549.

Though the founders of Marxism admitted that early Christianity had notable points of resemblance with the modern working-class movement, being originally a movement of oppressed people, they faulted Christianity for refusing to accomplish social transformation in this world. Instead Christians hoped for salvation from their plight in heaven, in eternal life after death, in the impending "millennium."[124] Thus Marx concluded contemptuously: "The social principles of Christianity preach cowardice, self-contempt, abasement, submission, dejection."[125] Since the proletariat needs courage, self-esteem, pride, and a sense of independence to attain its goal, it must do away with religion. "The criticism of religion ends with the teaching that *man is the highest essence for man,* hence with the *categoric imperative to overthrow all relations* in which man is a debased, enslaved, abandoned, despicable essence."[126]

Since the religious world is but the reflex of the real world, Marx demanded that we abandon the search "for a superman in the fantastic reality of heaven" where we can find nothing but the reflection of ourselves.[127] Marx therefore claimed that "the abolition of religion as the *illusory* happiness of the people is required for their *real* happiness."[128] As soon as religion as the general theory of this world is abolished — a theory which provides the justification for the exploitation of the working class and the consolation of a better future — we will abandon the fantastic heavenly reality and face our reality on earth.

When we remember the overwhelming otherworldliness of the Negro spirituals, which usually dared to claim only a better beyond and not a better earth, we can understand Marx's claim that "religion is the sigh of the oppressed creature." But we cannot agree with his conclusion that religion "is the *opium* of the people."[129] Religion has certainly been used for this purpose, but since the Judeo-Christian faith is by its very nature a forward-looking and world-transforming faith, this could have never been its main intention. There is undoubtedly also some truth in the

124. Engels, "On the History," 317.
125. Karl Marx, "The Communism of the Paper *Rheinischer Beobachter,*" in *On Religion,* 84.
126. Karl Marx, "Contribution to the Critique of Hegel's Philosophy of Right," in *On Religion,* 50.
127. Marx, "Contribution," 41.
128. Marx, "Contribution," 42.
129. Marx, "Contribution," 42.

claim that religion is a tool of the capitalists to exploit the working class
and to sanctify this exploitation with the comfort of a better hereafter.
But it is a gross oversimplification to assert that religion is simply an interpretation of present conditions. Religion is just as decisively an anticipation of the "beyond" in earthly form. Engels may have sensed some
of this when he conceded that "in the popular risings of the Christian
West . . . a new . . . economic order . . . arises and the world progresses,"
while in the context of other religions, even when the uprisings "are victorious, they allow the old economic conditions to persist untouched.
So the old situation remains unchanged and the collision recurs period-
ically."[130] But both Engels and Marx were influenced by Feuerbach so
much that they could not have had any confidence in the function of religion.

Marx opted for "a total revolution" in the antagonism between the
proletariat and the bourgeoisie.[131] Once the working class is emancipated, "we shall have an association in which the free development of
each is the condition for the free development of all."[132] It is not without
significance that "free" appears twice in the above sentence. Instead of
enslavement and force, Marx envisions "the true realm of freedom"
when socialized people as "associated producers regulate their inter-
change with nature rationally, bring it under their common control, instead of being ruled by it as by some blind power."[133] While the "savage"
must wrestle with nature to satisfy his wants and to be able to live, modern socialized humanity is "beyond the sphere of material production in
the strict meaning of the term." Humanity has passed the point "where
labor under the compulsion of necessity and of external utility is required." Then the realm of freedom emerges. This new economic structure of society and the new cultural development thereby determined is
eloquently praised by Marx:

> In a higher phase of communist society, after the enslaving subordina-
> tion of individuals under division of labor, and therewith also the an-

130. Engels, "On the History," 317-18, in a footnote.
131. Karl Marx, *The Poverty of Philosophy* (1847), in *Karl Marx*, 239.
132. Karl Marx and Friedrich Engels, *The Manifesto of the Communist Party* (1848), in
Karl Marx, 263.
133. For this and the following quotes, see Karl Marx, *Capital*, vol. 3, in *Karl Marx*,
429-30.

tithesis between mental and physical labor, has vanished, after labor has become not merely a means to live but has become itself the primary necessity of life, after the productive forces have also increased with the all-round development of the individual, and all the springs of the cooperative wealth flow more abundantly — only then can the narrow horizon of bourgeois right be fully left behind and society inscribe on its banners: From each according to his ability, to each according to his needs.[134]

What does it mean that "labor has become not merely a means to live but has become itself the primary necessity of life"? If necessity still rules supreme, where then is the realm of freedom? Of course, if matter is the base of life, we can only get from matter what we put into it. Though we are now agents of our own fate, fate indeed it is, because as soon as our energies cease just for one moment, whatever we have built will collapse.

To establish here and now the ideal world once envisioned in the beyond, reason is able, according to Marx, to control the material processes of life.[135] Nature is subjected to humanity to serve humanity's needs and desires. The question is not whether nature will yield what Marx envisions for humanity, but whether humanity can really exercise that reasonable supremacy. Already Marx's notion (that in a fully developed socialism we need no institutions and no legal order, since everyone cooperates freely) has been contradicted by communist reality. Furthermore, the division of labor and the overcoming of the distinction between mental and physical labor is a pipe dream, as Mao's permanent revolution indicated when university professors were sent into fields of agriculture and peasants were supposed to teach.

While Marx develops a vision of paradisiac dimensions, he has forgotten two essentials: When Feuerbach called religion a projection, he claimed that humanity projected on the screen of the beyond that which it could not attain. Humanity then accorded divine attributes to that kind of deification. Yet it was exactly that ideal vision that was merged with humanity in Marx's ideas. Therefore he overestimated humanity and — as the Marxist revolution showed — his utopian vision ended in

---

134. Karl Marx, "Critique of the Gotha Program" (1875), in *Karl Marx,* 281.

135. Cf. Guntram Knapp, *Der antimetaphysische Mensch: Darwin — Marx — Freud* (Stuttgart: Ernst Klett, 1973), 139-40.

a catastrophe of apocalyptic dimensions. Furthermore, by disclaiming any beyond, Marx never allowed humanity to relax, since there was no one who could provide for humanity except humanity itself. This means his vision of a realm of freedom turned into a realm of new enslavement.[136]

Concrete Utopia

The German neo-Marxist philosopher **Ernst Bloch** (1885-1977) betrays an optimism about the future similar to Marx's. Our journey moves irresistibly ahead toward "that secret symbol toward which our dark, seeking, difficult earth has moved since the beginning of time."[137] In his monumental work *Das Prinzip Hoffnung (The Principle of Hope)*, Bloch shows that the principle of hope is a universal characteristic of humanity. From the first cry of a helpless baby, who wants to draw attention to its desires, to a tired old person, who is waiting for eternal bliss, human existence is characterized by hope and a movement to the future. Bloch is convinced that Marxism will realize this future because its motivation and goal is nothing "but the promotion of humanity."[138] In its own way Marxism aims for the human goals of the revolutionary bourgeoisie and strives for the immanent realization of religious transcendence.

Bloch even calls Marxism the "quartermaster of the future," because it overcomes the antithesis of soberness and enthusiasm by letting both cooperate toward "exact anticipation" and "concrete utopia."[139] Unlike most abstract social utopias, the Marxist striving toward a better world is not initiated to forget the world at hand, but to transform it in a dialectical and economic way. Marxism is not mere futurism; it "takes the *fairytale* seriously" and "the *dream of a Golden age* practically."[140] Like Marx, Bloch contends that the comforting aspect of the Marxist worldview lies not in contemplation but in guidelines for action.

136. For a good critique of Marx's vision, cf. Bienert, 261-70.
137. Ernst Bloch, *Thomas Müntzer als Theologe der Revolution* (Frankfurt am Main: Suhrkamp, 1969), 229.
138. Ernst Bloch, *The Principle of Hope*, trans. Nevill Plaice et al., 3 vols. (Cambridge: MIT Press, 1986), 3:1358.
139. Bloch, *The Principle of Hope*, 3:1368.
140. Bloch, *The Principle of Hope*, 3:1370.

For Bloch humanizing humanity is a calculable and reachable goal, and the "unfinished world can be brought to its end."[141] Thus Bloch advocates a militant optimism and, unlike Kant, does not need a purgatory to assure the perfection of humanity. His confidence is not based on past experiences, since the essential is that which is not yet but which strives for self-realization in the core of being and expects its own genesis. Since real, objective hope provides its own foundation for Bloch, he seems to resort here to an Aristotelian first unmoved mover to endow the future with a direction and a hidden goal which is the same for all humanity. It is insignificant for Bloch whether one calls this goal eternal happiness, freedom, the golden age, a land of milk and honey, or union with Christ in the resurrection. All these symbols and pictures illuminate hope and lead it to the ultimate goal which no one has yet reached and which will be our actual "homeland." *"True genesis is not at the beginning but at the end."*[142]

Bloch goes beyond the primitive projection hypothesis of Feuerbach and claims that this projection (i.e., the future) is certainly our god.[143] God is the utopian hypostasis of unknown humanity. When identity between our true humanness and our present condition is reached, we will occupy the place of God and religion will cease to exist. Consequently, Bloch has no reason to be hostile toward religion, because it enlightens hope and gives it its direction. But the metaphysical dimension of religion is collapsed in the physical, since the future of the resurrected Christ and the future of God are the future of the hidden humanity and the hidden world. Bloch thus offers a metareligion, *"transcending without any heavenly transcendence"* and conceiving the metaphysical as our ultimate goal in the physical.[144] Eschatology under these presuppositions becomes a fiction,[145] and we end up with a new earthly kingdom without God.[146]

141. Bloch, *The Principle of Hope*, 3:1373.

142. Bloch, *The Principle of Hope*, 3:1375.

143. Cf. Jürgen Moltmann, "Hope and Confidence: A Conversation with Ernst Bloch," *Dialog* 7 (1968): 43.

144. Cf. Bloch, *The Principle of Hope*, 3:1288, in his discussion of Feuerbach.

145. So Gerhard Sauter, *Zukunft und Verheissung: Das Problem der Zukunft in der gegenwärtigen theologischen und philosophischen Diskussion* (Zürich: Zwingli Verlag, 1965), 354.

146. Cf. the striking title of Alfred Jäger's investigation into Bloch's eschatology: *Reich ohne Gott: Zur Eschatologie Ernst Blochs* (Zürich: EVZ-Verlag, 1969).

Bloch is certainly right and realistic when he points to the discrepancy between our actual existence and our selfhood, between the individual and the society, and between humanity and nature, which has to be overcome if we want to attain the ultimate identity we are striving for. But even if we concede to Bloch that achieving this identity is an attainable goal, we are still faced with the ultimate discrepancy between being and nothingness. Moltmann captures this deficiency very well when he states: "All utopias of the kingdom of God or of man, all hopeful pictures of the happy life, all revolutions of the future, remain hanging in the air and bear within them the germ of boredom and decay — and for that reason also adopt a militant and extortionate attitude to life — as long as there is no certainty in face of death and no hope which carries love beyond death."[147] It is one of the bizarre tragedies of history that Karl Marx and Ernst Bloch have emerged as the leading messianic prophets in modern history of truly Old Testament stature and yet, by denouncing the God-inspired hope that made such messianic figures possible, have denied their own origin and proclaimed a new world of their own desires.[148]

The Right to Be Lazy

At least parenthetically, we must mention here **Paul Lafargue** (1842-1911), the son-in-law of Karl Marx who married Marx's daughter Laura. He was a close friend of Friedrich Engels who financially supported both him and Marx.[149] Lafargue's grandfather on his mother's side was a Jew of French nationality who had lived in Haiti, and there was also some French blood on his mother's side. Marx initially called him "the creole," and later "the nigger." Engels was less racially discriminatory against him. Lafargue had studied medicine but never exercised his profession, since, like Marx, he became a professional revolutionary, being the cofounder of the Spanish Socialist Party and one of the leaders of the French workers' movement.

147. Moltmann, 49.
148. Cf. Karl Löwith, *Meaning in History: The Theological Implications of the Philosophy of History* (Chicago: University of Chicago Press, 1949), 44.
149. For the following, including details of Lafargue's life, cf. Ernst Benz, *Das Recht auf Faulheit oder Die friedliche Beendigung des Klassenkampes* (Stuttgart: Ernst Klett, 1972), 13-17.

In 1883, the year Marx died, Lafargue published a small pamphlet with the title *The Right to Be Lazy*, a refutation of the "right to work" demanded in 1848 in the *Communist Manifesto*. Initially this pamphlet was considered satire, but Lafargue wanted to refute with it the hyper-puritanical work ethos of the new communist movement. In *The Right to Be Lazy* he advocated the old mythical dream of a socialist paradise which could be established through the help of the new technological age and would contribute to the liberation of humanity. He first pointed to the plight of the working class during the industrial revolution. Children and women were trying to compete with manufacturing machines and worked up to sixteen hours a day, whereas even slaves and prisoners in the West Indies worked only ten hours or less. While the working class had been confined to an ascetic lifestyle, the bourgeoisie had the duty of overconsumption. The produced goods were exported all over the earth, yet there was still an industrial surplus. Yet the proletariat continued the trend of being obsessed with work and claimed: "Who doesn't work, shall also not eat"; in 1848 the worker demanded "the right to work"; and the federated workers of March 1871 considered their insurrection the "revolution of work."[150]

Lafargue suggested that on account of overproduction and the limited raw materials, one should simply distribute work more equally and force each worker to work five or six hours per day throughout the year instead of twelve hours daily for six months and then be laid off for another six months without remuneration.[151] Fewer hours of work per day, he claimed, would not slacken productivity but would perhaps even increase it. Lafargue used the USA as an example where one employed modern machinery in agriculture and, as a result, the workers could sit down in leisure and enjoy a pipe instead of straining their backs as French farmers do. Once the technological means are even more perfected, the working class would also have to increase its consumption of what it produces. While the proletariat wanted to be employed by the capitalists for ten hours a day in mines and factories, Lafargue claimed that "Work must not be imposed but prohibited."[152]

150. Paul Lafargue, *Das Recht auf Faulheit & Persönliche Erinnerungen an Karl Marx*, edited with an introduction by Iring Fetscher (Frankfurt: Europäische Verlagsanstalt, 1966), 38.

151. Cf. Lafargue, 41-42, for the following.

152. Lafargue, 44.

Lafargue was convinced that through modern industrial production there would be less and less need to work and therefore the lost paradise could be regained through social revolution. Yet Marxist theory, being developed in Great Britain, was much more infected by a puritanical spirit. Work was essential for Marx, as we can see from both the *Communist Manifesto* and the *Capital*. In later communism, work heroes were highly decorated and the young Lenin, who delivered a eulogy at the graveside of Lafargue, became the spiritual head of that form of communism that perfected the right to work, abolished Sunday as a day of rest, introduced the gliding workweek, and through massive pressure of the party apparatus, made workers "voluntarily" exceed the stated production goals.[153] It is no surprise, therefore, that Ernst Bloch, in his three-volume *Principle of Hope*, does not even mention Lafargue, and that the latter has become an unperson in official communist literature.

Lafargue himself seemed to have gradually realized that the social revolution could not regain paradise lost. Therefore, together with his wife, he committed suicide on November 25, 1911, in their home in Paris. As Ernst Benz wrote: "He wanted to bring the kingdom of heaven down to earth and realize it here through social revolution. Once it became clear that the programming of a perfect life on earth was unrealizeable, he programmed his death and thereby forcibly pushed open the gate to another world which he thought he could negate."[154] The failure of modern utopia results from a wrong understanding of human possibilities. It is wrongly assumed that humanity can be developed in any direction needed and, once developed, that it will also remain that way. Against this fallacy, Reinhold Niebuhr cautioned: "The utopian illusions and sentimental aberrations of modern liberal culture are really all derived from the basic error of negating the fact of original sin."[155]

153. For details cf. Benz, *Das Recht auf Faulheit*, 115.
154. Benz, *Das Recht auf Faulheit*, 119.
155. Reinhold Niebuhr, *The Nature and Destiny of Man*, vol. 1, *Human Nature* (New York: Scribner [1941], 1964), 273 n. 4.

3. The Impact of Religiosity

Most of the secular varieties of hope use the Judeo-Christian tradition as a negative foil against which they construct their own hope-filled futures. Yet Immanuel Kant had claimed in his famous essay "What Is Enlightenment?" that human reason should seek its own way without resorting to external guidance. This demand has become especially true in contemporary religiosity. While there one relies on the authority of human leaders in a way most Christian denominations would refuse to pledge allegiance to their religious superiors, contemporary religiosity is at the same time highly individualized. Especially with regard to religion, "a spontaneous consensus has sprung up around the evolutionary image of human potentiality."[156] The individual human being forges his or her own religion, freely borrowing from here or there and continuously looking for new insights and better solutions.[157] This vagabond guru religiosity is especially noticeable in what is generally called the New Age movement and its varieties of eschatology.

a. A Homespun Eschatology

There are many roots and antecedents to this new religious movement — for instance, the hippies, the flower children, the anti-Vietnam movement, the new left, and everything entailed in what Theodore Roszak (b. 1933) called the counterculture. It claims many significant figures as its forebears, such as Hildegard von Bingen (1098-1179), Pierre Teilhard de Chardin, and even Werner Heisenberg (1901-76). Two current authors, however, are representative of it, Fritjof Capra and Marilyn Ferguson.

Fritjof Capra (b. 1939) writes: "In the seventies, the change in paradigms in California was especially propagated by humanistic psychol-

156. So, very perceptively, Theodore Roszak, *Unfinished Animal: The Aquarian Frontier and the Evolution of Consciousness* (New York: Harper & Row, 1975), 4.

157. While this self-styled religion "is capable of enhancing the quality of lives of those participating," as Paul Heelas, *The New Age Movement: The Celebration of the Self and the Sacralization of Modernity* (Cambridge, Mass.: Blackwell, 1996), 213, perceptively notes, he also admits that this movement "does not score well when it comes down to *well-informed* practices."

ogy, the so-called Human Potential Movement and the Movement of Integral Health. Additionally there were different spiritual movements and a general strong interest in esoterics and the so-called extra-sensory or paranormal phenomena. The followers of these trends called themselves at that time the New Age Movement."[158] It is not without significance that this movement started in California, the state in the USA that enjoyed in the latter part of the twentieth century huge migrations, both from Asian countries and also from the eastern USA, and therefore was less settled in its ways. Only much later did this movement spill over to Europe, as the religious hold of the established churches on the general population began to wane. Capra himself claimed that with his first book, *The Tao of Physics,* he was in 1975 at the center of the New Age movement.[159] Yet he did not use the term "New Age" after 1980, except to denote those who stayed with the spiritual mentality of the seventies and did not participate in the widening of the social and political consciousness. This does not mean that Capra is no longer at the center of things.

In his 1996 book *The Web of Life,* he calls for a new paradigm, deep ecology, and attempts to demonstrate the complexity and interrelatedness of the universal ecosystem which gave rise to life. "The success of the whole community depends on the success of its individual members, while the success of each member depends on the success of the community as a whole."[160] This ecological web needs to be understood and utilized for life to thrive and survive.

Most revealing is his book *Uncommon Wisdom* (1988), an autobiography in which Capra shows how, as a physicist, he was part of the hippie movement of the late sixties and how deeply he also was influenced by Hindu spirituality.[161] But then his 1975 best-seller, *The Tao of Physics,* appeared. There he attempted to overcome the old mechanistic world-view which he thought was expressed in Newton's universe in which there were discrete fundamental properties which remained as fixed data. "In the new world-view, the universe is seen as a dynamic web of

158. Fritjof Capra, "Die neue Sicht der Dinge," in *New Age: Kritische Anfragen an eine verlockende Bewegung,* ed. Horst Bürkle (Düsseldorf: Patmos, 1988), 15.

159. Capra, "Die neue Sicht der Dinge," 16.

160. Fritjof Capra, *The Web of Life* (New York: Doubleday, Anchor, 1996), 298.

161. Cf. Fritjof Capra, *Uncommon Wisdom: Conversations with Remarkable People* (New York: Simon & Schuster, 1988), 4 and 27-31.

interrelated events. None of the properties of any part of this web is fundamental; they all follow from the properties of the other parts, and the overall consistency of their mutual interrelations determines the structure of the entire web."[162] Already here he emphasized the universal web of life and attempted to provide a holistic and interdependent worldview. Capra sees a close affinity to Eastern mysticism, in which the laws are embedded in nature but are not decreed by a divine lawgiver.[163] Therefore the title of the book, *The Tao of Physics.* Capra sees in science and mysticism two mutually complementary manifestations of the human spirit, the rational and the intuitive. The extreme specialization of rational comprehension is complemented by an extreme sharpening of intuitive awareness.

What does this have to do with eschatology? Capra's emphasis on a new paradigm, on a turning point and immediately threatening catastrophes, reminds us of an apocalyptic view of the end time.[164] Over against this, a new age is dawning.

Indeed, in his book *The Turning Point* (1982) Capra points to a crisis in perception since we live in a poisoned environment that perpetuates other ecological catastrophes, in an arising flood of violence and crime, in an energy crisis, in a crisis of health care, and so forth.[165] Therefore we need a new paradigm, a new view of reality and a fundamental change in perception and values. With reference to systems theory, theory of evolution, and anthropology, Capra sketches out a system that concentrates on a dynamic of self-transcendence which allows us to understand biological, societal, cultural, and cosmic evolution as stemming from the same model of systems dynamic even if the different kinds of evolution presuppose very different mechanisms.[166] The emergence of the spirit is seen in close connection to the properties of self-

162. Fritjof Capra, *The Tao of Physics: An Exploration of the Parallels between Modern Physics and Eastern Mysticism,* 2nd rev. ed. (New York: Bantam Books, 1988), 276.

163. Cf. Capra, *The Tao of Physics,* 279.

164. Cf. Christoph Bochinger in his comprehensive study, *"New Age" und moderne Religion: Religionswissenschaftliche Analysen* (Gütersloh: Chr. Kaiser/Gütersloher Verlagshaus, 1994), 453, who points out the analogy to apocalypticism.

165. Cf. Fritjof Capra, *The Turning Point: Science, Society, and the Rising Culture* (New York: Simon & Schuster, 1982), 15, where he lists various threatening phenomena and calls for a radically new way of perception and action.

166. Cf. Capra, *The Turning Point,* 265.

organizing systems, and the spirit is an essential property of living systems, but not something that stands over against the material.[167] Capra sees in Teilhard de Chardin a mystic who comes closest to this new idea of system biology, since for him, too, evolution ascends to increasing complexity and thereby to an increase in consciousness and human spirituality.[168]

Over against a surface ecology, Capra calls here for a deeper ecology that understands the transcending human spirit "as the mode of consciousness in which the individual feels connected to the cosmos as a whole, [in which] it becomes clear that ecological awareness is truly spiritual. Indeed, the idea of the individual being linked to the cosmos is expressed in the Latin root of the word religion, *religare* ('to bind strongly'), as well as in the Sanskrit *yoga*, which means union."[169] By obtaining this new understanding that we are connected to the whole universe and that the human spirit is not just the center but the pinnacle of an evolutionary movement, we are ascending to new heights and leave the trivia of the old world behind us.

Capra has moved from physics to religion and from research in physics to writing best-sellers. Now earning his living from the lecture circuit, he calls for a change of paradigms to save humanity from self-destruction and destroying the world in which we live. Capra is not the only voice. There are many other interpreters who have secular qualifications but mediate religious content to an audience that no longer seems to listen to professional theologians and church dignitaries. It prefers those who come from a very different field and still find religion significant. "The best qualification for the credibility of a 'religious mediator' in the free religious scene, is therefore his or her descent from a sector . . . that is as remote from 'religion' as possible: If a physicist deals with 'religion,' then there 'must be something to it.'"[170]

Another important interpreter is **Marilyn Ferguson** (b. 1938), for whose book *The Aquarian Conspiracy* (1980) Capra wrote the preface. In a 1973 book, *The Brain Revolution,* one could already note that Ferguson was not entranced with technological possibilities such as cloning, organ

---

167. Cf. Capra, *The Turning Point*, 285-86.
168. Cf. Capra, *The Turning Point*, 303-4.
169. Capra, *The Turning Point*, 412.
170. So, very correctly, with significant details states Bochinger, 511.

transplants, and guaranteeing probable IQs. Instead she followed the lead of William James (1846-1910), Carl Jung (1875-1961), and Teilhard de Chardin in asserting that there is a good chance of "emerging from relative unconsciousness into the fuller awareness."[171] This could also result in psychic self-healing, whether through meditation, autogenic training, or relaxation-visualization techniques. Instead of engineering larger human brains, we should use what we already have, since the brain can take us wherever we might want. "The human brain, that 'perfect instrument,' that 'fabulous electronic dance,' can be our open sesame to an infinitely richer life than we have believed possible. The fluent, liberating, creative, healing attributes of the altered states can be incorporated into consciousness. We are just beginning to realize that we can truly open the doors of perception and creep out of the cavern."[172]

Ferguson is opting for human self-development, not in terms of using supertechnology but by self-evolving to new heights, new experience, and new wholeness. This was masterfully expressed in her "cult book" *The Aquarian Conspiracy*.[173]

In the preface Capra lauds Ferguson for being a leading figure in establishing networks among individual persons and groups.[174] Ferguson claims that though she is ignorant in astrology, she has been enthralled by the symbolic content of a pervasive dream in our culture, the thought that after a dark and violent era of the Pisces, an era of love and light is appearing according to the well-known song from the musical *Hair*:[175]

Harmony and understanding,
Sympathy and trust abounding,
No more falsehoods or derisions
Golden living dreams of visions,

171. Marilyn Ferguson, *The Brain Revolution: The Frontiers of Mind Research* (New York: Taplinger, 1973), 337.

172. Ferguson, *The Brain Revolution*, 344.

173. On the back cover of Marilyn Ferguson, *The Aquarian Conspiracy*, with a new afterword and an updated resource list (Los Angeles: Tarcher, 1987), it states: "*The Aquarian Conspiracy*, which *USA Today* called the handbook of the New Age."

174. Cf. Fritjof Capra, preface in Ferguson, *The Aquarian Conspiracy* (Los Angeles: Tarcher, 1980), 14.

175. Cf. Ferguson, *The Aquarian Conspiracy* (1987), 19, where she also refers to the theme song of the Aquarian age.

Mystic crystal revelation,
and the mind's true liberation
Aquarius Aquarius.

The age of the Pisces, which is connected with the names of René Descartes (1596-1650) and Isaac Newton (1642-1727), is the time of the big dualisms which ultimately led to all the crises of the present.

Inescapably the new age is dawning, whose trademark is a new consciousness through which the rescue of our world is made possible.[176] It consists in the knowledge of a universal unity and wholeness of God and the world, spirit and matter, humanity and nature, body and soul, I and You. Everything is interconnected and makes up a big web of being. This wholeness and interdisciplinary thinking, which has been successful in medicine, psychology, and biology, will be all-pervasive and will replace analytical thought. There is a powerful network operating which will bring radical change in the world. "This network is the Aquarian conspiracy."[177] Like a big earthquake, it irrevocably comes toward us and, according to Ferguson, is neither a new political, nor a religious, nor a philosophical system. There is a new spirit which allows us to break through the old limitations and opens up a richness of choice, freedom, and human interconnectedness. "You can be more productive, confident, comfortable with insecurity. Problems can be experienced as challenges, a chance for renewal, rather than stress. Habitual defensiveness and worry can fall away. *It all can be otherwise.*"

Ferguson refers to Thomas Kuhn (b. 1922) and his book *The Structure of Scientific Revolutions* (1962), in which he showed that scientific revolutions are brought about by changes in paradigms. Such a revolution is now coming because the paradigm of conspiracy in the sign of Aquarius regards humanity as embedded in nature. We are no longer victims limited by conditions, but heirs of evolutionary riches and capable of imagination, invention, and experience which up to now we have hardly visualized. "Human nature is neither good nor bad, but open for continuous transformation and transcendence. It has only to discover itself."[178]

---

176. For a good description of this new consciousness, cf. Medard Kehl, *New Age oder Neuer Bund?* (Mainz: Matthias Grünewald, 1988), 22.

177. For this and the following quote, see Ferguson, *The Aquarian Conspiracy* (1987), 23-24.

178. Ferguson, *The Aquarian Conspiracy* (1987), 29.

We are noting here a central tenet of the new kind of thinking, and it serves as a precondition for continuous transformation and transcendence toward the new and better. Human nature is indefinitely malleable, being neither tainted by original sin and sinful inclinations nor already good by itself.

It is not surprising that a theologian such as Ted Peters (b. 1941) cautions: "I have come to believe that the overall gnostic thrust of the new age is a big mistake. It leads to a naive and excessively innocent view of reality. It fails to acknowledge the strength of the powers of destruction and evil that are at work in the cosmos and in our own personalities."[179] Exactly this kind of innocence allows us to reach for new heights, and insights, and forms the basic presupposition for the dawning of the new age. In typical apocalyptic fashion we are told that we are at the eve of a new age, "the age of an open world, an age of renewal in which the fresh release of spiritual energy in the world culture may unleash new possibilities."[180] Referring again to Teilhard, Ferguson says wider consciousness will be kindled, humanity will regain the sublimation of the spiritual-sensual love as a new source of energy.[181] Omitted, however, is Teilhard's insight that the spirit of God, which in an incarnate form is already at work in the world, will warm the human heart, not the crowding together of humanity. Yet for Ferguson it is exactly the crowding together that makes the difference: "Rich as we are — together — we can do anything. We have it within our power to make peace within our torn selves and with each other, to heal our homeland, the Whole Earth."[182]

We do not live from the past but toward the future, as Ferguson states at the end of her comprehensive treatise. "Our past is not our potential. In any hour, with all the stubborn teachers and healers of history who called us to our best selves, we can liberate the future. One by one can we re-choose to awaken. To leave the prison of our conditioning, to love, to turn homeward. To conspire with each other and for each other."[183] We need teachers like Capra and Ferguson who can draw

---

179. Ted Peters, *The Cosmic Self: A Penetrating Look at Today's New Age Movements* (San Francisco: Harper, 1991), 91.

180. So Ferguson, *The Aquarian Conspiracy* (1987), 42, with reference to Lewis Mumford.

181. Cf. Ferguson, *The Aquarian Conspiracy* (1987), 403.

182. Ferguson, *The Aquarian Conspiracy* (1987), 406.

183. Ferguson, *The Aquarian Conspiracy* (1987), 417.

things together and who tell us that we have lived the wrong way and understood things the wrong way. Then they appeal to a new way of seeing things and teach us that history can come out all right. All our problems and anxieties can be overcome. We have the potential not only for a new chapter in world history, but for a totally new age. Against modern skepticism and frequent doomsday scenarios, the presently beginning age of Aquarius will provide rescue and salvation from the global crises, deliverance from personal crises and from everything which is threatening to us.[184] People like to hear this optimistic perspective of New Age literature. The world, including each individual being, can be changed toward the good and toward salvation. This kind of thinking can be understood as a replacement or even a perfection of Christian eschatology and other religious concepts of the future. It can be regarded as *the* comprehensive world religion that brings us to a new age and a new future.

A central aspect of New Age religion is the belief in "paranormal" realities which can be freely accessed by human beings. There are a variety of means by which we obtain insight into our own selves and into the essence of things, such as age regression, tarot, and Zen.[185] Important are teachers of wisdom and persuasive personalities in whom one has unconditional confidence and who promise to lead their followers to a new future. Many of these various techniques and insights can be subsumed under the term "esoterics," which is basically a primal knowledge toward completion. We learn here, for instance, that the spirit is of prime importance, matter is often regarded as secondary, and if we employ the right techniques and have the appropriate insights we can secure for ourselves and the world around us a new and promising future.

The access to new realities can be obtained through altered states of consciousness at which we arrive through certain spiritual techniques or which can also appear spontaneously. There is a "remarkable similarity between these 'worlds of the mind' or 'inner realms,' on the one hand, and the realities which the soul is believed to enter after physical death,

---

184. For the following cf., very perceptively, Kehl, 21-22.

185. Cf. for the following, Rüdiger Kerls, *Heilsame Glaubenskräfte: Kirche in Auseinandersetzung mit New Age* (Munich: Kösel, 1988), 87ff., who points to esoterics and shows that this is appearing in different gowns, e.g., Christian, Jewish, Buddhist, Hindu, etc.

on the other."[186] This means that heaven can already be experienced on this earth. Therefore the world we believe in as our destiny must have a reality, since it is already a present experience and not simply subjective fantasy. There is even a strong suggestion that present and future are one and the same. The next world is very much like the world to which we are accustomed, though it is much more beautiful. There is an unresolved tension, however, with regard to the structure of this new world. On the one hand there will be a unitive consciousness as the final goal of evolution, and on the other hand there exists unlimited creative unfolding, corresponding on the one hand to the return to unity and, on the other, more influenced by evolutionary thought, to an unlimited cosmic expansion.[187]

At the end of the journey, one usually assumes that there is reincarnation. While reincarnation is largely taken for granted as a universal element in New Age ideas, it is only part of a *"progressive spiritual evolution . . .* which started before birth and will continue beyond death."[188] This means it is a crucial part of a larger process which is claimed to be logical and rationally consistent with the prospect of life after death. In this kind of development it is seen as superior to the traditional Judeo-Christian belief in one final future reconstitution of dead bodies, meaning the resurrection. The spirit or the soul will survive bodily death and move forward to a new unfolding. Reincarnation also provides the foundation for a rational ethics, because the uneven distribution of earthly goods and talents, happiness or suffering is balanced out in another life. Particularly in combination with the belief in karma (i.e., the sum total of our present life), reincarnation is a mechanism which guarantees ultimate cosmic justice. Through reincarnation we do not just have one single life on earth which is then followed by eternal life in heaven or hell as Christians teach, but there are always new beginnings and new advancements.

Often it is unclear whether there is a continuation of one's ego in another life or whether only one's real individuality is to survive death

186. This is claimed by Wouter J. Hanegraaf, *New Age Religion and Western Culture: Esotericism in the Mirror of Secular Thought* (New York: SUNY Press, 1998), 259, in his comprehensive and insightful study.

187. Cf. Hanegraaf, 261, who calls these two strands "monistic pathos" and "evolutionary pathos."

188. So Hanegraaf, 262.

and provide the link of continuity between this life and former or future lives. There may also be just a succession of lives or realities of one's real individuality so that one's own spiritual evolution is furthered.[189] If there is so little emphasis on the ego and so much value accorded to interconnectedness and the web of life, the individual does not count much in the life hereafter. Only the true self is important, but even that must be seen in the context of the larger picture.

We encounter here some kind of gnostic spirituality. The gnostic salvation myth starts with the insight that we are entangled in the negativity of the present world.[190] Therefore an ambassador of the heavenly region must address us, reminding us that we are aliens in this world and lifting us out of our forgetfulness concerning our true higher origin and destiny. Recognizing our heavenly image and becoming one with it, we are led by our guide on the journey to a new and, at the same time, original future. At the end we return from estrangement to the place from which we originated. In order to arrive at our eternal destination, we cannot be bothered with insights from this world. We have our own guides who tell us with certainty what is true and right. Our consciousness is not just enlarged; it is intensified so that we regain the original archaic unity of humanity and the world and live in a continuous, undivided presence of the whole of the world and its origin. Living in the spirit is living in the present, not in the past or in the future, but it is a life outside of time according to life's real essence and its eternal principle.

These ideas show no sensitivity to human depravity, the need for God's undeserved grace, and a redeemer figure who demonstrates undivided solidarity with us. As Immanuel Kant claimed in his essay "What Is Enlightenment?" and as we have seen with other figures such as Lessing and even Karl Marx, who were imbued with the Enlightenment spirit, given the right insight we have enough potential to bring ourselves not just to new heights but to a new world. We can save ourselves. Indeed, the Enlightenment spirit has made possible immense progress.

189. Cf. Hanegraaf, 267, who points to the ambiguous assertions of what is actually continued beyond death.

190. Cf. Hans-Jürgen Ruppert, *Durchbruch zur Innenwelt: Spirituelle Impulse aus New Age und Esoterik in kritischer Beleuchtung* (Stuttgart: Quell, 1988), 105-6, who draws here the parallel between the gnostic Song of the Pearl and the esoteric understanding of salvation in the New Age movement.

But also the most abominable atrocities in the history of humanity have been committed during the last two hundred years. So we wonder whether humanity can really be its own savior. Perhaps we should heed Martin Luther's insight when he claimed that, as little as we are our own creator, we can also not be our own savior.

b. Ambivalence of Secular Humanism

While representatives of the New Age movement do not want to confine themselves to the material base of life, secular humanists accept a worldview of philosophy called naturalism, in which the physical laws of the universe are not superseded by nonmaterial or supernatural entities, such as demons, gods, or other "spiritual" beings outside the realm of the natural universe. They show a commitment to the use of critical reason, factual evidence, and scientific methods of inquiry rather than faith and mysticism. But like New Age representatives, their primary concern is with fulfillment, growth, and creativity for both the individual and humanity in general. They are also convinced that progress can be made in building a better world for ourselves and our children. Secular humanists describe themselves as atheist or agnostic and do not rely upon gods or other supernatural forces to solve their problems or to provide guidance for their conduct.

Faith in Human Reason (Humanist Manifesto I *and* II)

In 1933, the year Adolf Hitler came to power in Germany, a group of thirty-four liberal humanists in the United States defined and enunciated the philosophical and religious principles that seemed fundamental to them. They drafted *Humanist Manifesto I,* which for its time was a radical document and portrayed a thoroughgoing rationalistic approach to the world. Thesis 1 sets the tone: "Religious humanists regard the universe as self-existing and not created."[191] According to the *Manifesto,*

---

191. *Humanist Manifestos I and II,* ed. Paul Kurtz (Buffalo: Prometheus Books, 1973), 8. For a good introduction of the problematic nature of the secular humanistic approach to the future, cf. Ted Peters, *Futures — Human and Divine* (Atlanta: John Knox, 1978), 134-49, where he also examines the *Humanist Manifestos I and II* (137-38).

the nature of the universe depicted by modern science "makes unacceptable any supernatural or cosmic guarantees of human values."[192] Forty years later, *Humanist Manifesto II* became even more explicit when it stated that "humans are responsible for what we are or will become. No deity will save us; we must save ourselves."[193] Thus we are told in 1933 that "man will learn to face the crises of life in terms of his knowledge of their naturalness and probability. Reasonable and manly attitudes will be fostered by education and supported by custom."[194] This faith in education and reason was expressed at the same time Hitler was indoctrinating the Germans about the superiority of the Nordic race and the necessity of eliminating the Jews.

When *Humanist Manifesto I* was updated in 1973, the drafter, Paul Kurtz (b. 1925), one of the leaders of the humanist movement, admitted in the preface that events since 1933 "make that earlier statement seem far too optimistic. Nazism has shown the depths of brutality of which humanity is capable. Other totalitarian regimes have suppressed human rights without ending poverty. Science has sometimes brought evil as well as good. Recent decades have shown that inhuman wars can be made in the name of peace."[195] Yet we are still assured that we are reasonable beings and have no need of religion, since it would only divert people "with false hopes of heaven hereafter."[196] But the still-prevailing optimistic note is now coupled to caution when we are told that the future is filled with dangers and that "reason must be tempered by humility." Still, there is no doubt that "human life has meaning because we create and develop our futures."[197] Especially technology assumes salvific dimensions when we hear: "Using technology wisely, we can control our environment, conquer poverty, markedly reduce disease, extend our life-span, significantly

192. *Humanist Manifestos I and II*, 8.
193. *Humanist Manifestos I and II*, 16.
194. *Humanist Manifestos I and II*, 9.
195. *Humanist Manifestos I and II*, 13. Kurtz was editor of the *Humanist* from 1967 to 1977 and drafted *Humanist Manifesto II* in 1973 (reprinted in *In Defense of Secular Humanism* [Buffalo, N.Y.: Prometheus Book, 1983], 39-47); see Vern L. Bullough, foreword to *Toward a New Enlightenment: The Philosophy of Paul Kurtz* by Paul Kurtz, edited with an introduction by Vern L. Bullough and Timothy J. Madigan (New Brunswick, N.J.: Transaction Publishers, 1994), ix.
196. *Humanist Manifestos I and II*, 13.
197. *Humanist Manifestos I and II*, 17.

modify our behavior, alter the course of human evolution and cultural development, unlock vast new powers, and provide humankind with unparalleled opportunity for achieving an abundant and meaningful life."[198] It seems ironic that this faith in "achieving abundant life" was expressed on the eve of the first Arab oil embargo against the Western countries, an action that sent economic shock waves around the globe.

This document, however, was not quite as convinced of its own optimistic predictions concerning the future as it might sound. This becomes noticeable especially in the closing comments on "humanity as a whole," where it interchanges quite frequently indicative statements and imperative demands. So we are urged to use reason and compassion to produce the kind of world we want, a world in which peace, prosperity, freedom, and happiness are widely shared. "Let us not abandon that vision in despair or cowardice. We are responsible for what we are or will be. Let us work together for a humane world by means commensurate with humane ends. Destructive ideological differences among communism, capitalism, socialism, conservatism, liberalism, and radicalism should be overcome. Let us call for an end to terror and hatred. We will survive and prosper only in a world of shared humane values. We can initiate new directions for humankind."[199] While we certainly agree with the goals envisioned and may join secular humanists in pursuing them, we cannot but remain skeptical about their basis for attaining such goals and about their power to achieve them. Even if we disregarded our finitude, could we ever assume that there is a basis for hope if we trust in ourselves as the grantees of the future? While we cannot afford the luxury of despair, it is historically wrong to join with these manifestos in blaming traditional religion for the stifling of human initiative. As we have seen, our enterprising and progressive spirit is intimately connected with the Judeo-Christian tradition. Yet precisely when this spirit has been left to itself, when reason becomes the sole court of appeal, it turns against humanity itself. From the French Revolution (1789) to the Russian Revolution (1917), with many revolutions since, all too often the achievement of humanistic revolutionary ends has been replaced with permanent terror. Thus the big unresolved question remains: Who should educate or at least guide the educators

198. *Humanist Manifestos I and II*, 14.
199. *Humanist Manifestos I and II*, 23.

(or revolutionaries)? If there are no metaphysical values left, we are thrown back to our own predilections, which quite often means our own selfishness.

Yet the deep-seated optimism about our own potential cannot be so easily discarded. Until very recently, and despite ethnic and class revolts in many countries and occasional brief shortages of energy and material resources, the overall picture in the Western world remained one of optimism. For instance, in a memorandum, "The Triple Revolution," addressed in 1964 to President Lyndon B. Johnson (1908-73), the drafters (all advocates of socialist humanism) still declared: "The economy of abundance can sustain all citizens in comfort and economic security whether or not they engage in what is commonly reckoned as work."[200] Even if there was already doubt whether we were appropriately addressing the issues of the future, our resources were nevertheless seen as unlimited.

The German existentialist philosopher Karl Jaspers (1883-1969) summed up this sentiment well when he claimed that we are always capable of doing more and other things than anyone expected. Our future is never sealed. But he dampened this optimism considerably when he wrote, in the same essay, "Premises and Possibilities of a New Humanism": "Civilizations have perished before. What is new today is that all of mankind is threatened, that the menace is more acute and more conscious, and that it does not only affect our lives and property but our very humanity. If we consider the ephemeral nature of all undertakings, our way of living under a stay of execution, we feel as though anything we might do now would be senseless in the future."[201]

A Modest Assessment of the Future

Indicative of the more temperate mood in the present are **Paul Kurtz**, the founder of the Council of Secular Humanism, and those who follow his kind of reasoning. Since there is no evidence that life characterized by the processes of metabolism, growth, and reproduction can survive

---

200. "The Triple Revolution," in *Socialist Humanism: An International Symposium*, ed. Erich Fromm (London: Penguin, 1967), 420.

201. Karl Jaspers, *Existentialism and Humanism: Three Essays*, ed. Hanns E. Fischer, trans. E. B. Ashton (New York: Russell F. Moore, 1952), 83.

the death of the organism, it is questionable for Paul Kurtz whether consciousness, the "self," or the "body" can survive in some discarnate form and whether we can reify psychological functions. Even the so-called near-death experiences are of no help at this point.[202] Of course, a person's descendants, who carry his or her genetical endowment and his or her accomplishments, may have an influence on society or culture for a period of time. Yet it is clear for Kurtz that "The humanist considers the doctrine of immortality to be basically unrealistic and even morbid. It grows out of both fear of and fascination with death. . . . This mood of denial expresses a basic lack of courage to persist in the face of adversity. Immortality is a symbol of our agony before an unyielding universe and our hope for some future deliverance."[203] The key to humanist virtue is existential courage.

Contrary to secular existentialists, it is not enough to merely survive in the face of adversity. Secular humanists do not accept the status quo. They are summoned to remake their lives constantly in spite of all the forces in nature and society that seek to overwhelm them. "The humanist is not content with simply discovering and accepting the universe for what it is, in an act of piety; he seeks to *change* it. Nor is the task of life to discover what our nature is (whether God-given or not) and to realize it, but to *exceed* our nature." The task before them is twofold: analytical and transformative. Life again is seen as an opportunity which can be grasped and changed for the better.

Secular humanists are aware of their interrelatedness as individuals with each other. It is important that a human person continually unfolds his or her selfhood in the community and continually strives to become human.[204] This also means self-actualization of the person in the quest for the good life. Kurtz has called this approach "eupraxophy," meaning a good way of doing things.[205] "Self-actualizing people are gratified in

---

202. Paul Kurtz, "Near-Death Experiences: A Skeptical View," in *Toward a New Enlightenment*, 349.

203. See Paul Kurtz, *The Transcendental Temptation: A Critique of Religion and the Paranormal* (Buffalo: Prometheus Books, 1986), 415-16, for this quote and the following.

204. Cf. Khoren Arisian, "Ethics and Humanist Imagination," in *The Humanist Alternative: Some Definitions of Humanism*, ed. Paul Kurtz (Buffalo: Prometheus Books, 1973), 172.

205. Cf. Paul Kurtz, "In Defense of Eupraxophy," in *Toward a New Enlightenment*, 276.

all their basic needs embracing affection, respect, and self-esteem. They have a feeling of belongingness and rootedness. They are satisfied in their love needs, because they have friends, feel loved and love-worthy. They have status, place in life, and respect for other people, and they have a reasonable feeling of worth and self-respect."[206] Modern humanists hold that the shaping of human ends lies in our own hands. Our self-determination in connectedness with others can both enrich personal existence and provide a directive for association with others. Humans live in community, and human achievement depends on social culture. There is progress in freedom of choice, and this freedom is naturally connected with justice as equity of choice.[207]

In this development and progress, evil, sorrow, and death are not denied since they are the natural dark sides of our aspirations. Yet modern science has made it possible for the continued introduction of novel and unexpected dimensions of explanation and understanding in the world around us and also in our psychological behavior and our social and cultural institutions. Progress of science, however, has its pluses and minuses. We therefore face a crisis, unprecedented in human history because, having discovered the key to a rich and bountiful life, we find in the very process of our emancipation new forms of enslavement and destruction. But we cannot retreat to ignorance. We can only step ahead. Even Paul Tillich's courage-to-be is invoked, since "what is clear is that he [modern humanity] cannot afford the luxury of delay. For issues press in on him, and the terrible problems he faces will not wait for him to catch up to them. For the scientific humanist the option is clear. We should not retreat from scientific intelligence, but extend its range."[208] The reason for this optimism is also evident. For the first time the technological revolution allows us to develop a world community and to have a new global moral vision.

The vision of secular humanists is focused on this earth and not on a hereafter. In this respect they are quite optimistic: "Given dependence

206. A. H. Maslow, "The Good Life of the Self-Actualizing Person," in *Moral Problems in Contemporary Society: Essays in Humanistic Ethics,* ed. Paul Kurtz (Englewood Cliffs, N.J.: Prentice-Hall, 1969), 67.

207. Cf. J. P. van Praag, "The Humanist Outlook," in *A Catholic Humanist Dialogue: Humanists and Roman Catholics in a Common World,* ed. Paul Kurtz and Albert Dondeyne (Buffalo: Prometheus Books, 1972), 8.

208. Paul Kurtz, "Crisis Humanology," in *A Catholic Humanist Dialogue,* 52.

on intelligence and willingness to use our powers to solve our problems, human beings can still be saved in this life and we can discover and create a rich and meaningful existence. If we are to be saved, however, it is only by using our own resources, believing in *Man,* not depending upon overbelief, faith or mystery."[209] Of course, we should not overlook the "if" in this positive vision. Salvation is by no means assured. But if there is salvation, humanists claim, it can only come through us. Indeed, once God is excluded, who is left except for humanity? The reason for the iffiness of salvation also lies in the realization that we do not have everything under control. "Humanism does not mean that man is omnipotent."[210]

But secular humanists know that "men cannot live without hope. Men cannot live without faith. Hope has to do with the sense that something better is possible." Yet how can such hope be engendered and such faith be maintained if, at the same time, humanism "does not hold that man is perfect or perfectable"? It even concedes that no one who has ever lived has lived a perfect life, nor will such occur in the future. Therefore the sober admission: "Perhaps it is man's fate to strive even though he knows that he will never fulfill his dream of self and his dream of society."

What has been accomplished after so much effort, after so much pulling on one's own bootstraps? The dream of a good life may never become reality. It is a sober estimate that secular humanists provide without pretentiousness and usually without undue claims. At the same time there is very little actual hope. We are thrown in upon ourselves and the possibilities we have. Actual hope does not come from us or the world we live in. At the most, we can somewhat improve it. If there is hope, it must come from beyond, from outside ourselves and our environment, from the one who created and sustains us. Yet what can we, as Christians, actually offer in terms of the content of hope?

---

209. Kurtz, "Crisis Humanology," 58.

210. Cf. Algernon D. Black, "Our Quest for Faith: Is Humanism Enough?" in *The Humanist Alternative,* 75, 76, and 77, respectively, for this and the following two quotations.

Part III
What Can We Hope For?

Having briefly reviewed the bewildering array of views and issues in eschatology, and also the various attempts to circumvent death as the final point of our life, we will now follow the biblical admonition to give account of the hope that is in us (1 Pet. 3:15). It has become evident that, while we are able to survive some of the threatening thunderclouds that loom on the horizon of history, lasting hope cannot come from within us. Though we can always achieve temporary victories in pursuing our future, ultimately death will stare us in the face. When we give account of the hope that is in us, we can only do so because it has been placed in us from beyond our time-bound world. A tenable hope for the future cannot rest on us but must be warranted by the God who created the world, sustains it, and will redeem it. If the temporary hopes grounded in life's material basis are subject to many differing interpretations, we need not wonder that we face a similar divergence when we approach hope for the future grounded in God. As we approach the new world, we will first consider the transition between this life and the next. Then we must also deal with some problem areas in eschatology before we can pursue the prospect of a new creation, both in its present and future dimensions.

5. Approaching the New World

As we now attempt to outline the positive side of what we can hope for, we must guard against two frequent temptations: undue restraint and a travelogue eschatology. Undue restraint would be represented by a position which asserts that all we can say about life beyond death is that God, who was good to me in life, will also be good to me in death. Though this statement reflects part of the biblical message, it does not reflect biblical theology in its attempt to render the whole of the Christian hope. At key points the New Testament enunciates a hope which is enabled and characterized by terms such as "resurrection," "new creation," "heaven" and "hell," "parousia," and "judgment." Regardless of how we interpret these terms, we cannot pass over them in silence and at the same time claim to be scriptural.

Yet, in interpreting these terms we cannot succumb to the temptation of a travelogue eschatology. As far as we can reconstruct Jesus' proclamation, it was essentially a proclamation that enables us to reach the eschaton. But Jesus did not provide us with an eschatological timetable that would permit us to know exactly when the Son of Man will return, nor did he paint the eschaton in daring and vivid colors, as Muhammad, for instance, did in the Koran for his followers. With the exception of the book of Revelation, the New Testament shared this restraint with Jesus. This is in remarkable contrast to the exuberant speculation of the apocalyptic literature of the Old and New Testament period. The fact that the church did not accept a book of Enoch or an Apocalypse of Paul into the biblical canon, and that even someone like Luther had serious doubts about the right of Revelation to be in the canon, should caution us when we want to indulge in a travelogue eschatology.[1]

Nevertheless, we must explicate what we mean when we speak of the "eschaton." To talk here only about symbols[2] would endanger the depth of our assertions and would place them in the same category as such metaphors as "the symbols of Christmas" or "the symbols of peace." We are inclined rather to follow a suggestion of Rudolf Bultmann in his noteworthy essay "What Does It Mean to Speak of God?"[3] where he asserts that to talk *about* God is a sinful and blasphemous attempt, since it presupposes that we are on equal ground with him. We can only talk about something which is on the same level as we are, such as another person, or an animal, or a beautiful scene. In making assertions concerning God, we can only talk *from* God, that is, in repeating what God has spoken to us. This retelling of God's self-disclosure (in Jesus Christ), however, is not done in divine vocabulary (since we do not have any) but with our conceptual tools. Since God has come to us in the humanity of Jesus, we can talk from God as if he were one of us, though knowing that ultimately he is not. Bultmann concludes that even the attempt of talking *from God* is ultimately a (necessarily) sinful attempt.

Applying this to eschatology, neither the conceptual tools of the biblical witness nor our contemporary categories can adequately "describe" the eschaton. Our assertions, even if they are the most profound reflections on God's self-disclosure in Jesus Christ, are by necessity inadequate approximations of what the eschaton is all about. These limitations, however, do not release us from the necessity of searching for

1. Martin Luther could only justify the canonical value of the Revelation of John by interpreting it as a witness to the history of the church. Cf. Paul Althaus, *The Theology of Martin Luther,* trans. Robert C. Schultz (Philadelphia: Fortress, 1966), 84-85.

2. When Paul Tillich, *Systematic Theology* (Chicago: University of Chicago Press, 1957), 3:401, 411, 414, refers to the ultimate judgment, immortality, and the resurrection as symbols, we know, of course, that this means more than mere symbolism. Yet we wonder if the very term "symbol" does not endanger the reality for which these concepts stand.

3. Rudolf Bultmann, "What Does It Mean to Speak of God?" (1925), in *Faith and Understanding,* edited with an introduction by Robert W. Funk, trans. Louise Pettibone Smith (New York: Harper, 1969), 1:53-65. We cannot follow Bultmann, however, when he suggests that if we speak of God, we must evidently speak of ourselves (55). With this statement Bultmann seems to abandon his theocentric approach in favor of an anthropocentric one.

the most appropriate language in our time. If we do not continuously reconceptualize the biblical reflections on God's self-disclosure, we speak in ancient tongues and also misrepresent God's word, which is a word for our time and a pointer to our future.

1. Death

In starting with the understanding of death, however, we do not seem to encounter the dilemma of language. Death still pertains to this world, as the end of our life here on earth. The questions we face here more and more frequently are: "What is the actual moment of death?" and "What actually is death?" An answer to these questions is all the more necessary because the "life"-prolonging techniques of modern medicine sometimes make the length of a patient's life almost a matter of the relatives' or the patient's finances or of someone "pulling the plug."

a. The Ambiguity of Death

The verdict of clinical death is generally based on the criterion of an "irreversible loss of function of the organism as a whole."[4] The absence of peripheral pulse and heartbeat, the absence of respiration, the lack of eye reflex, and the presence of a bluish color that results from a lack of oxygen in the blood are some of the indications that this criterion is met. But with our constantly increasing medical skills, doctors can forestall the onset of these criteria even when the patient, on his or her own, cannot. Does this mean that in certain cases they are keeping dead corpses "alive"?[5] To reach an adequate definition of death, we have to get away from an exclusively biological definition of death and start rather with a definition of life itself. A human being is both a physical and a spiritual being. As Michael B. Sabom reminds us: "The practice of medicine needs more fully to understand and to integrate these two aspects of hu-

4. So Christopher A. Pallis in *The New Encyclopaedia Britannica,* 15th ed., s.v. "death," 16:984.

5. Leroy Augenstein, *Come, Let Us Play God* (New York: Harper & Row, 1969), 44, 48-50, illustrates this point very poignantly. Cf. also Harmon L. Smith, *Ethics and the New Medicine* (Nashville: Abingdon, 1970), 133-35.

man nature, if it is truly to be successful in meeting the needs of sick and dying patients."[6]

Life, as we experience it, is our active participation in the ongoing processes of our environment. According to our possibilities, this participation can vary considerably, and it is expressed in one way by a university professor in his best years and in a very different way by a youngster with multiple sclerosis and an IQ of 70. Dying as a process would mean a decline of this participation. It is not confined to terminal illness but accompanies the whole aging process of an individual.[7] Death as the final end is then the irreversible cessation of this active participation. Understanding death from the view of life as this active participation could free us from a strictly biological understanding of death as the irreversible end of certain processes, and at the same time, we could extend help to physicians who are daily confronted with the phenomenon of death. We could suggest to them that they might let the biological side of a person rest if they cannot restore that person to active participation in the environment through the most basic form of interaction such as eye reflexes or voluntary breathing.[8]

Since there is no clear line of demarcation between life and death, we cannot clearly determine at what point this irreversible loss of active participation occurs. Furthermore, one must more precisely determine what one means by active participation. For instance, the famous 1968 Harvard definition of an irreversible coma, a state of profound unconsciousness that cannot be reversed, centers on the functioning of the brain.[9] But the first problem is to determine the characteristics of a permanently nonfunctioning brain. Among the criteria listed are total unawareness and unresponsiveness to externally applied stimuli and inner

6. Michael B. Sabom, foreword in Bruce Greyson and Charles P. Flynn, eds., *The Near-Death Experience: Problems, Prospects, Perspectives* (Springfield, Ill.: Charles C. Thomas, 1984), viii.

7. Thornton Wilder's graveyard scene in *Our Town* is to some extent a good illustration of this definition.

8. We agree here fully with what Smith, 166-67, calls indirect or passive euthanasia.

9. As referred to in James L. Bernat et al., "Defining Death in Theory and Practice," in *Ethical Issues in Death and Dying*, ed. Robert F. Weir, 2nd ed. (New York: Columbia University Press, 1986), 101, who then advance their own definition of death, which focuses again on the brain but in the wider sense, namely, on "all functions of the entire brain, including the brainstem" (107).

need, no movement or breathing, no reflexes, and a flat electroencephalogram (EEG). If these criteria are met for a certain period of time, we may conclude that a person is clinically dead. This pronouncement then is an a posteriori conclusion, something we state after the fact. Since someone is already dead before we can pronounce him or her dead, we might have inflicted dehumanizing treatments on the patient prior to his or her "death" while we waited for the emergence of the appropriate criteria. Thus the issue of euthanasia, or "death with dignity," emerges as a consequence of both our increasing determination to pinpoint the exact endpoint of death and our medical advancements that allow us to interfere more and more with the process of dying and lengthen it virtually at will. Two cautions, however, are in order:

1. There is no good death, as the term "euthanasia" (meaning "good death" in Greek) intimates. Death is always ambiguous; it can be a release from suffering, but it is always the loss of this life.
2. The idea of a natural death that is presupposed in the claim of "death with dignity" is a fiction as far as its biological and physiological aspects are concerned.

All forms of biological death "do have a cause and that cause is potentially susceptible to description and control," or at least to modification.[10] It is painful to accept, but every death, along with the suffering that accompanies it, is the result of some human choice, even as we cannot ultimately escape it. As the philosopher Friedrich Nietzsche realized when he claimed "Die at the proper time"[11] — not too early and not too late — we can prolong or abbreviate the process of suffering and dying within certain limits, and we do indeed do so. This means that we cannot escape ultimate responsibility for this last phase of life.

While in the context of eschatology we cannot touch upon all the ethical issues involved in euthanasia, we must mention at least two extreme positions that are not acceptable for us: active euthanasia and maintaining life at all cost.

---

10. So rightly Robert M. Veatch, *Death, Dying, and the Biological Revolution: Our Last Quest for Responsibility* (New Haven: Yale University Press, 1976), 302.

11. Friedrich Nietzsche, *Thus Spoke Zarathustra* (I), trans. Marianne Cowan (Chicago: Henry Regnery, Gateway Edition, 1957), 70.

1. Since God is the giver of all life, we must treat life as a gift entrusted to our care. Therefore we cannot concede that it is proper to deliberately terminate life in cases of terminal illness, as is discussed today ever more loudly and even accepted in some parts of the world as the population ages and the (medical) care of older and extremely old people threatens to drain our economic and medical resources. Though we cannot brush aside these problems, active euthanasia implies a disrespect for God's gift of life and shows an appalling view of life where economic aspects are primary. As a gift entrusted to us, we should treasure life until it is taken away.

2. When we hang on to life and preserve it at all costs, we show a basic selfishness. There are not enough resources, financial and otherwise, that this extreme care could be given to everyone. Clinging to this life also illustrates the misunderstanding that this present life is all that is promised to us. Thus we cannot opt for preserving life at all costs.

But with every meal we eat to sustain ourselves and with every pill we take to alleviate pain, we prolong not only life but also the dying process. Life and death are too intricately connected to allow us an objectively correct answer as to the right point to let life go. Legislation concerning euthanasia and "death with dignity" can at the most establish legal boundaries within which we must assume responsibility for life and death. Even a living will which asks that no heroic measures be taken (i.e., measures that do not promise reasonable benefits and cannot be administered without excessive cost, pain, and considerable inconvenience) in case of terminal illness, is unable to remove the ambiguity in face of illness and the agony of making decisions about life and death. Yet our actions should always be guided by the knowledge that in all its forms life is a precious gift that we dare not corrupt either by the selfishness of unduly hanging on or by its willful and careful abolition. Rather, life should be enhanced by growth and maturation.[12] When life has become totally and irrevocably dependent on others for sustenance, when it can no longer, even in the foreseeable future, contribute to the sustenance of others (e.g., through

---

12. Elisabeth Kübler-Ross, *Death: The Final Stage of Growth* (Englewood Cliffs, N.J.: Prentice-Hall, 1975), 166, rightly talks about death and its acceptance as the final stage of growth in this life.

signs of joy or compassion), very likely life has run its course, and then we may allow the body to come to rest.

If we do not restrict death to the point of the cessation of life but see it as a process, we must also understand death as a necessary companion of life, and its actual presupposition. Processes in nature show us with convincing clarity that life can only be sustained if someone or something else dies. There is a great chain of being in which one form of life depends on another for growth and sustenance. For instance, humans come to stand at the end of the food chain and eat meat and vegetables; cattle eat grass; and grass dissolves chemicals to survive, live, and grow. But death is even more central to life; it starts already with conception. The sperm dies after the egg has been fertilized, and the egg cell, in turn, dies to permit the growth and division process of the cells. In each organism old cells are constantly being replaced by new ones, so that during the course of our life we are "renewed" several times and there is hardly anything original left in us once we die. The biological phenomena of aging and decay are shared by the whole of creation, and we are no exception. Yet the whole life stream gives the impression that it strives to escape death. Charles Darwin substantiated this observation with his concept of the struggle for existence, and the French philosopher Henri Bergson (1859-1941) even spoke of an *élan vital,* an original life force, that pervades all nature. Small wonder that Teilhard de Chardin claimed that life will evolve ever further, "rising upstream against the flow of entropy."[13] But as the manifold species of life that have died out show, this evolutionary struggle is not a sign of victory over death. It is a vain attempt to escape from the all-pervading power of death. Edouard Boné is correct when he writes: "Death clears ways and spaces, deceptively opens up the future for unforeseen forms of life, but also for which the final hour will come."[14]

Yet we are caught not just in the death-escaping, although death-determined, process of life. We are the only living beings on our earth who have an actual death-awareness.[15] Knowing about death, we live our lives; and knowing about death as the irrevocable, unconditioned,

13. Pierre Teilhard de Chardin, *The Phenomenon of Man,* trans. Bernard Wall (New York: Harper & Row, 1965), 289.

14. Edouard Boné, "Das Aussterben biologischer Gruppen: Tatsachen und Hypothesen," in *Tod — Preis des Lebens?* ed. Norbert A. Luyten (Freiburg: Karl Alber, 1980), 100.

15. This is very clearly expressed by Theodosius Dobzhansky, *The Biology of Ultimate Concern* (New York: New American Library, 1967), 68-70.

and ultimate end of our individual lives, we face death. Our reflections, feelings, and actions are accompanied by our knowledge of death, whether we suppress it or enhance it. Knowing about our finality and limitation need not lead to pessimism; we can live a fulfilled and satisfied life and die "in a good old age . . . and full of years" (Gen. 25:8). We can even long for an end of this struggle here on earth and be glad that this life need not be continued forever. Yet death can also strike in the middle of life, and an unfulfilled life can suddenly be terminated. Then we encounter death as bitterness, as an enemy we want to escape, even as we know that there is no ultimate escape.

The immense public attention that medical progress receives witnesses indirectly to our desire to be in charge of life and to escape death. A bizarre variation of this desire is the attempt of cryonics to deep-freeze people who have died of incurable diseases in the hope that someday medical progress will find a cure. The corpses would then be defrosted and brought back to life so that new medical advances may rejuvenate them.[16] We encounter death as a contradiction to our human nature, because it destroys everything that pertains to us. Thus we want to memorialize ourselves in our children, through charities, or through products of our mind. And when an idealistic philosopher exclaims that "It is impossible to conceive that Nature should annihilate a life which does not proceed from her; I do not exist for Nature, but Nature exists for me,"[17] he cannot convince us that he has found a remedy for death. He only helps us confirm that the biological naturalness and necessity of death is something extremely unnatural; it is an "ought not."

The Swiss-born psychiatrist Elisabeth Kübler-Ross (b. 1926) brings our death-denying attitude into focus when she proposes five discrete stages of death:[18]

1. *Denial and isolation:* Denial, Kübler-Ross claims, is used by almost all patients. It functions as a buffer after the unexpected shocking news

16. Cf. Robert C. W. Ettinger, *Aussicht auf Unsterblichkeit?* (Freiburg im Breisgau: Hyperion-Verlag, 1965), 148, who claims that "from a societal standpoint, initially it is not important how well the body is conserved as long as some hope is maintained."

17. Johann Gottlieb Fichte, *The Vocation of Man,* edited with an introduction by Roderick M. Chisholm (Indianapolis: Bobbs-Merrill, 1956), 153.

18. For the following distinction, cf. the extensive description by Elisabeth Kübler-Ross, *On Death and Dying* (New York: Macmillan, 1969), 38-137.

of terminal illness and allows patients to collect themselves and, in time, mobilize other, less radical defenses. "Since in our unconscious mind we are all immortal, it is almost inconceivable for us to acknowledge that we too have to face death."[19] Thus we deny the news of impending death and withdraw from the world. Yet sooner or later another method of defense sets in.

2. *Anger:* When "the first stage of denial cannot be maintained any longer, it is replaced by feelings of anger, rage, envy, and resentment."[20] Often the hospital personnel or the person's relatives are the targets of anger.

3. *Bargaining:* This stage is again an attempt to postpone the inevitable death. One bargains with God or with the doctors in a vain attempt to extend one's life.

4. *Depression:* Finally we come to the stage of depression. It sets in when we can no longer pretend that the symptoms of oncoming death will disappear, and when we become more and more incapacitated. Numbness and stoicism, anger and rage are now replaced with a sense of great loss. What has been so dear to us on earth — our shapely figure, our travel plans, or our financial security — is now taken away from us. We realize that our this-worldly dreams will not come true. We are in the process of losing everything and everyone we have. When we have passed through this stage, and through denial, grief, and anger, we finally reach what Kübler-Ross describes as the fifth stage.

5. *Acceptance:* Kübler-Ross cautions that this should not be construed as a happy stage. "It is almost void of feelings. It is as if the pain had gone, the struggle is over, and there comes a time for 'the final rest before the long journey' as one patient phrased it."[21] It is a gradual weaning away from life with longer and longer periods of sleep, similar to a newborn child but in reverse order.

Not all of these stages are always clearly discernible, and some may be more pronounced than others or may simply be skipped. Also, Kübler-Ross made her observations mainly on the basis of her work

19. Kübler-Ross, *On Death and Dying*, 42.
20. Kübler-Ross, *On Death and Dying*, 50.
21. Kübler-Ross, *On Death and Dying*, 113.

with terminally ill hospital patients, not with accident victims who die a sudden death or with people who simply die of "old age." But two items are particularly significant for us in Kübler-Ross's analysis:

1. When we look at her five stages, we notice that four of them deny our mortality. We seem to fight until the last moment. Kübler-Ross also notes how oblivious we are to death, and that when we have faced up to our finitude we live a different quality of life.[22]
2. Much more startling, however, is another insight. Kübler-Ross confesses: "Working with dying patients over many years has made me much more religious than I have ever been. . . . Before I started working with dying patients, I did not believe in a life after death. I now do believe in a life after death, beyond a shadow of a doubt."[23]

Kübler-Ross has observed many terminally ill people die and has attempted to describe the various stages these people go through. We should wonder why in research preoccupied with death she does not give up the notion of life after death, but instead discovers that it has immense validity. We could surmise that a defense mechanism against admitting her own mortality has been operative, inducing in her the strong notion of life after death. But could her newly found belief in life after death have not also resulted from the conclusion that this life, especially as it shows itself in its final stages, cannot be all that there is to one's existence? At least we should be open to this possibility.

Moving from the biological ambiguity of death to an understanding of death in the context of the Judeo-Christian tradition, at first glance we do not get a reassuring answer here either because death is conceived as the gate to the eschaton.

b. Death as the Gate to the Eschaton

According to the biblical witness, death is not just something unnatural. It is primarily and first of all a constructive factor of God's creation and

---

22. So rightly Elisabeth Kübler-Ross, *Questions and Answers on Death and Dying* (New York: Macmillan, 1974), 4.

23. Kübler-Ross, *Questions and Answers,* 166-67.

belongs to the fundamental order of our world.[24] This is nowhere better expressed than in Psalm 90, where the psalmist says:

> The days of our life are seventy years,
>   or perhaps eighty, if we are strong;
> even then their span is only toil and trouble;
>   they are soon gone, and we fly away.

(v. 10)

Death shows us our creatureliness, our distance from and dependence on God. He alone has immortality (1 Tim. 6:16), while everyone and everything else is subjected to death. There is an insurmountable chasm between us finite beings and God's infinity. Paul states this in a metaphorical way: "'The first man, Adam, became a living being'; the last Adam became a life-giving spirit" (1 Cor. 15:45).

At the very moment humanity emerged, it received its life from God and we became living beings. Only Christ, being true God, was not only a living — but a life-giving — being. In knowing about the finitude of our life and in knowing about death as our ultimate end, we recognize ourselves as human, as being created and not the creator. In realizing this decisive difference between the creator and the created, we become fearful before the creator, who can not only give and protect life but can also take it away. Even a king can plead with God that God should not take life away from him (Isa. 38:9-20).

Death gives each moment of our life its singularity; we cannot repeat one act of our life. Unceasingly and unresistingly we are on our way to the eschaton. Whether we want it or not, whether we realize it or not, we exist truly eschatologically, since the potential presence of the eschaton at any moment of our life gives our life its singularity. Even love has to be seen together with this aspect of death, since love is essentially giving away part of oneself to another person or persons. We irretrievably give away part of our life and die a little more whenever we extend our love. Thus love is sacrifice of our life. But it would be totally wrong to understand this kind of voluntary sacrifice as a heroic deed. Giving away life is possible only because we received it in the first place.

---

24. For the following, cf. Paul Althaus, *Die letzten Dinge: Lehrbuch der Eschatologie,* 7th ed. (Gütersloh: Bertelsmann, 1957), 83-85; and "Tod IV: Dogmatisch," in *Religion in Geschichte und Gegenwart,* 3rd ed. (Tübingen: J. C. B. Mohr [Paul Siebeck], 1957-65), 6:914-16.

Dying is primarily suffering; it is losing what we have received. Though naturally we would rather keep what we have received and not lose it, we know too that our life, because it is creaturely life, does not have a divine quality that could lead to union with God. It is a sign of the goodness of creation that we are able to die and thus cease being dimensionally separated from our creator. Jesus reminded us that we can gain real life only in the eschatological fulfillment beyond this present life: "For those who want to save their life will lose it, and those who lose their life for my sake, and for the sake of the gospel, will save it" (Mark 8:35).

Death does not just show us the dimensional difference between God and ourselves and our dependence on God's life-giving power. Death also discloses God's opposition to us sinful people. We encounter death not only as the inescapable end of our life but also as God's "no" to the way we conduct our life, to our continuous sinful alienation from God. The singularity of every moment of our life is finalized in death, and our total life with all its omissions, failures, and commissions becomes irreversible. In death we are immediately confronted with God, who holds us responsible for our actions and makes us accountable for our deeds.[25] Death also shows us that our life is not of eternal value. God regards the way we live our life here on earth as unworthy of preservation, and he rejects its antigodly character.

It would be shortsighted to conclude that biological death can be inferred from sin and the fall, as if there had been a time when death did not prevail. But Western theologians from Augustine onward have taught that humanity had once been in a whole and virtuous or original state, where it "was able not to sin" and consequently "not to die."[26] Death, sorrow, and pain came into the world through human sinfulness.[27] Only those outside

25. Gerhard Sauter, *Einführung in die Eschatologie* (Darmstadt: Wissenschaftliche Buchgesellschaft, 1995), 196, rightly reminds us that death is not only this final balancing, but it is also an enemy that we ourselves cannot overcome.

26. Augustine, *On Rebuke and Grace* 33, in *NPNF* FS, 5:485.

27. So W. Rohnert, *Die Dogmatik der evangelisch-lutherischen Kirche* (Braunschweig: Wollermann, 1902), 198. Francis Pieper, *Christian Dogmatics* (St. Louis: Concordia, 1950), 1:551-53, even ponders whether original sin caused immediate death or only started the process of dying which results in the complete separation of body and soul. Cf. also Chr. Ernst Luthardt, *Kompendium der Dogmatik,* new edition by Robert Jelke (Leipzig: Dörffling & Franke, 1937), 215.

the confines of orthodox faith dared to assert that the first human couple would have died whether they had sinned or not.[28] Fortunately, most contemporary theologians refrain from speculations about a premortal original state of humanity.[29] We can agree with the assertion in the Roman Catholic *Catechism* that "though man's nature is mortal, God had destined man not to die."[30] Humanity's very yearning to escape death shows this unresolved tension between our mortality and the attempt to go beyond it. Yet to say with the *Catechism* that death "entered the world as a consequence of sin," makes sense only if we concede that sin emerged with the emergence of humanity and therefore there was no sinless and consequently deathless state for humanity.

The idea of a premortal state for all creation would bring us into deep conflict with science, since paleontology shows that biological death already prevailed for millions of years before humanity emerged. That Paul does not intend to speak biologically of a person who lived long ago and whose sinful activity had cosmic consequences when he wrote that "the wages of sin is death" (Rom. 6:23), or that "sin came into the world through one man, and death came through sin, and so death spread to all because all have sinned" (Rom. 5:12), is decisive. The natural biological aspect of death is at most somewhere in the back of his mind, since he wanted to talk in an existential and theological way about the emergence of the age of death. "Adam and Christ stand there as the respective heads of the two eons. Adam is the head of the old eon, the age of *death;* Christ is the head of the new eon and the age of *life.*"[31] Unlike animals, we no longer experience death as a merely biological death. Knowing about our sinfulness, our alienation from God, and our shortcomings, we encounter death as the final irreversible termination in which these distortions of life can no longer be patched up or concealed. Fear of death becomes fear of judgment, the fear of this final inescapable confrontation with the God who is not only our creator but also our judge.

28. Marii Mercatoris, *Commonitorium de Coelestio* II, in Migne, *PL,* 48:83-85.

29. Althaus, *Die letzten Dinge,* 85.

30. *Catechism of the Catholic Church* (1008), 284-85. Karl Rahner, *On the Theology of Death* (New York: Herder & Herder, 1967), 35, presents a much more balanced view when he talks about death "as guilt and as a natural phenomenon."

31. Anders Nygren, *Commentary on Romans,* trans. C. C. Rasmussen (Philadelphia: Fortress, 1949), 210.

But judgment is not the final word. Luther, for instance, in following the biblical witnesses, talked about a threefold aspect of death.[32] First, there is the biological death, namely, the natural decay of the physical body, which is the same for all living beings. Then there is the spiritual or eternal death of those who are condemned. This death normally coincides with biological death and is for those who refuse to accept God's grace. Finally, there is a kind of "death" where we actually overcome this spiritual or eternal death. This "death" takes place whenever we accept God as a gracious God. Since grace is also the good news, we wish to call this third aspect "death in the light of the gospel."

We have already mentioned that death can be seen under the aspect of grace, since it shows us that we are not forced to live our life here on earth forever. The confrontation with God's grace shows us that our present life is inexorably connected with sin. Thus death as the end of this life means the end of the possibility of sinning, the end of our shortcomings and of our continuous estrangement from God. The gospel even indicates that this kind of death can already be anticipated proleptically before we encounter our biological death. Paul, for instance, emphasizes that in this life we should die to our sinful existence so that we can be resurrected with Christ. He even goes so far as to say that "we have been buried with him [Christ] by baptism into death, so that, just as Christ was raised from the dead by the glory of the Father, so we too might walk in newness of life" (Rom. 6:4). Though this "baptismal death" initiates the process of dying, it never comes to completion in this life. We always deviate from our eschaton-directed lifestyle. Thus Luther pointed out in his *Small Catechism* that our "old Adam" must die daily and be daily resurrected to the newness of life.[33]

Death in the light of the gospel is not just anticipation of the eschatological fulfillment, as this "daily resurrection" might indicate. Anticipation as prolepsis always reminds us that there is still something to come. Thus our daily dying points to a final fulfillment and perfection beyond all anticipation. It also promises us that even biological death is

32. For the following cf. Luther in his *Lectures on Romans* (1515/16) in his commentary on Rom. 6:3, in *LW,* 25:310. ("Hence we must note that death is of two kinds: natural, or better, temporal death and eternal death." "Eternal death is also twofold. The one kind is good, very good. It is the death of sin and the death of death.")

33. Cf. Martin Luther, *Small Catechism,* in *The Book of Concord,* ed. Theodore J. Tappert (Philadelphia: Fortress, 1959), 349.

not a departure into nothingness but the removal of the dimensional difference which separates us from the one who alone is immortal. We can even dare to say that death is the precondition and the reverse side of the resurrection. Death as judgment and condemnation is not God's final word, since God does not have "pleasure in the death of the wicked, but that the wicked turn from their ways and live" (Ezek. 33:11). God wants our death only insofar as it leads to our final fulfillment in the eschaton and to our real life.

Though not everybody admits that death is the reverse side of resurrection and the entrance to our fulfillment in the eschaton, most agree that death is not the entrance to nothingness. Even those people who do not claim to be religious usually affirm that death is not the ultimate end of life. While the concepts of existence beyond death vary, it is commonly accepted that we are not just mortal. Kübler-Ross, for instance, concludes from her observations and research that there are only "very few people who do not believe in some form of immortality."[34] There is or must be some sort of immortality. It is not without significance that in our rationally minded age there is "a profound shift . . . away from the exclusively material toward a more spiritual, integrated, and compassionate perspective."[35] We have noticed this shift with the New Age movement, which also has a tremendous interest in survival beyond death. It perceives life not as a onetime occurrence but as a continuum from one existence to the next. But is such a belief tenable, and is it not simply the result of our fear of complete annihilation once we die?

2. Immortality — Yes or No?

People express their desire for immortality in many ways: through cultural activities, through religious practices, and through the simple assertion that death cannot be the end, to name just a few. There are three phenomena, however, that seem to substantiate the idea of immortality: occultism and near-death experiences give the idea of immortality an

34. Kübler-Ross, *Questions and Answers,* 159.
35. So, in conclusion, David Lorimer, "Current Western Attitudes to Death and Survival," in *Death and Immortality in the Religions of the World,* ed. Paul Badham and Linda Badham (New York: Paragon, 1987), 229.

experiential basis; philosophy provides a theoretical reference system for immortality; and the biblical soul-body distinction endows the idea of immortality with theological sanctification.

a. Immortality and Occultism

The attempts of the late Episcopal bishop James A. Pike (1913-69) to communicate with his deceased son gave impetus to the idea of communication with the beyond in the late 1960s. A much older and classic example of this desire is the Protestant pastor John Frederic Oberlin (1740-1826) of Alsace, France, who also was a pioneer of church social ministry. He claimed that he communicated with his deceased wife for seventeen years until she informed him that she had to ascend to higher spheres. This kind of occultism is even found in the Bible. King Saul, in despair over his future, asked a medium at Endor to provide him with a chance to talk to Samuel, who had died a few years previously (1 Sam. 28). When Samuel appeared, Saul was able to recognize him immediately. But the message that Saul received provided little comfort. His kingdom would soon come to an end.

It is impossible to do away with the fact that human minds can extend themselves beyond the physical limitations of space, time, and matter.[36] Research in parapsychology has shown that, within certain limits, the existence of paranormal phenomena can no longer be doubted. But how should they be explained? When a medium is involved, one can apply an animistic explanation and understand occult phenomena as resulting from subconscious powers of the medium, or one can apply a spiritualistic explanation and understand them as being caused by the activity of the souls of deceased people. Even if we concede the spiritualistic explanation of communication from the beyond, what do we actually gain in our knowledge about immortality or the soul?[37] The "spirits" tell us minute and exact details about events of

36. Cf. J. B. Rhine, *The Reach of the Mind* (New York: William Sloane, 1971), esp. 51-85; and G. N. M. Tyrrell, *Science and Psychical Phenomena: Apparitions* (New Hyde Park, N.Y.: University Books, 1961).

37. After careful consideration of what we can say about survival beyond death and after claiming that we know details about the hereafter, Hornell Hart, *The Enigma of Survival: The Case for and against an After Life* (London: Rider, 1959), arrives at the conclusion

long ago, and they tell us about family ties we have long forgotten, but they are remarkably vague in their assertions concerning their own state. They hardly allow us to get a glimpse of the beginning of the new state of existence; on the contrary, they mostly dwell on irrelevant details of past events in this life.

The Bible concedes the possibility of establishing such communication with the beyond, but with the same breath it rejects these practices as antigodly (Deut. 18:10-14). It considers them attempts to bypass God, who is the Lord on both sides of death. According to New Testament testimony, our faith in the life beyond death is sustained not by our communication with the beyond, but by the one who was not consumed by death, Jesus Christ.

It is interesting that during the Enlightenment there was great interest in the appearances of spirits. Emanuel Swedenborg's (1688-1772) communications with the "spirits" caused considerable attention. The reason for this increased interest in spiritualism seems to be the fact that the Christian belief in life beyond death had become more and more uncertain in this rationally minded age.[38] One wanted to ascertain hope in a beyond through other sources. Perhaps the recent resurgence of spiritualism during this present second phase of the Enlightenment indicates a similar decline in the Christian belief in life beyond death.

b. Immortality and Near-Death Experiences

In recent decades the idea of life after death has gained new attention on account of reports of dying patients who continue to have a conscious awareness of their environment after being pronounced clinically dead. If they are resuscitated, totally against the expectations of medical personnel, they tell of experiences that are strikingly similar: "A floating out of their physical bodies, associated with a great sense of peace and wholeness. Most were aware of another person who helped them in their transition to another plane of existence. Most were greeted by loved ones who had died before them, or by a religious figure who was

---

that "human personality *does* survive bodily death" (263), and that the accounts of the astral world, though agreeing in many fundamentals, vary considerably (244).

38. Althaus, *Die letzten Dinge*, 96 n. 2, draws this convincing conclusion.

significant in their life and who coincided, naturally, with their own religious beliefs."[39]

The phenomena experienced in close encounters with death are not a current discovery. They are reported by Plato, especially in book 10 of *The Republic,* in the *Tibetan Book of the Dead,* by the Venerable Bede (673/74–735) in *A History of the English Church and People,* and by Sir Edward Burnett Tylor (1832-1917) in *Primitive Culture,* to name a more recent writer.[40] The American psychiatrist Raymond A. Moody (b. 1944), in his two seminal books, *Life after Life* (1976) and *Reflections on Life after Life* (1977), has systematically investigated reports on near-death experiences. He comes to the interesting conclusion that all these reports show a remarkable similarity, though none are precisely identical. People interviewed usually relate several of the following experiences:[41]

- Hearing their doctors or other spectators pronounce them dead;
- Extremely pleasant feelings and sensations during the early stages of their experiences;
- Unusual and often extremely unpleasant auditory sensations at or near death;
- The sensation of being pulled very rapidly through a dark space of some kind;

39. So Elisabeth Kübler-Ross in her foreword to Raymond A. Moody, *Life after Life: The Investigation of a Phenomenon — Survival of Bodily Death* (New York: Bantam Books, 1976), xi-xii. Moody also mentions that when Kübler-Ross was reviewing this book, she remarked that she had collected "hundreds of reports of this kind." So Raymond A. Moody, *Reflections on Life after Life* (Harrisburg, Pa.: Stackpole Books, 1977), 13. While Raymond Moody brought near-death experiences (NDEs) to the attention of the wider public and Kübler-Ross aroused public and professional awareness to NDEs, only later were these reports carefully recorded and examined. Cf. Kenneth Ring, "Near-Death Studies: An Overview," in *The Near-Death Experience: Problems, Prospects, Perspectives,* ed. Bruce Greyson and Charles P. Flynn (Springfield, Ill.: Charles C. Thomas, 1984), 5-16.

40. Cf. the extensive quotations in Moody, *Life after Life,* 115-28, and *Reflections,* 67-74. Cf. also Carol Zaleski, *Otherworld Journeys: Accounts of Near-Death Experience in Medieval and Modern Times* (New York: Oxford University Press, 1987), 206-9, where she provides a chronological table for medieval Christian otherworld journey literature. She also admits that in general, "academic circles have not seen much theological debate over the implications of near-death research" (186).

41. Cf. the numerous reports of each of these experiences in Moody, *Life after Life,* 26-84, and *Reflections,* 18-30.

- Looking upon one's own physical body from a point outside of it and floating in a weightless spiritual body;
- Awareness of the presence of other spiritual beings in the vicinity;
- Glimpses of other beings who seemed to be "trapped" in an apparently most unfortunate state of being (i.e., limited consciousness, unable to surrender their attachments to the physical world, and apparently kept in that state until their problems are solved);
- Encounter with a light that at first is dim and rapidly gets brighter until it reaches an unearthly brilliance, which is often identified with Jesus Christ or an angel;
- Rapid panoramic review of one's life presented to the dying person by the light(-being);
- A flash of universal knowledge and insight into the nature of things;
- A vision of a city of light of some sort;
- The approach to a border or limit of some kind; and
- The coming back into the physical body and to life and an initial regret about it.

Moody also relates that people report being saved from impending death by a voice or light manifesting itself and rescuing them "from the brink of death."[42] This means that these experiences are not just confined to instances in which persons have been somehow resuscitated after having been declared dead by a physician upon the failure of initial resuscitation measures. They are also reported by people who have simply been resuscitated once (e.g., after cardiac arrest), or who have found themselves in a situation in which they could very easily have been killed or have died, even though they have escaped without injury.[43]

It would, of course, be interesting to investigate whether those who were pronounced dead and subsequently regained consciousness had in fact been dead. Moody contends that, in many of these cases, the testimony of physicians and the clinical records show that death, defined as the absence of clinically detectable vital signs, had taken place.[44] Since

42. Moody, *Reflections,* 30.

43. Cf. Moody, *Reflections,* 113-14, where he lists five different types of near-death encounters.

44. For the following cf. Moody, *Life after Life,* 147-50. Moody, however, admits that the definition of "death" is by no means settled. That may be one of the reasons why, very appropriately, he uses the term "near-death experiences."

all cases of resuscitation involve a state of extreme clinical emergency, there was no time to set up an electroencephalograph (EEG) to measure brain wave activity. And even an EEG reading does not always give an incontestable answer to the issue of clinical death, since both overdoses of drugs which depress the central nervous system and abnormally low body temperature can also result in flat EEG readings. Thus Moody concludes that these people were clinically dead at least at the time when resuscitation was administered.

Since we have reports of near-death experiences from people who were not resuscitated, the decisive issue is not whether people have returned to life from death, but what kind of reality is reflected in their experiences. On a subjective level, Moody reports that although they were very reticent to tell others about what had happened to them, those who had the near-death experiences confessed that these phenomena had a profound impact on their lives. "They became more reflective and more concerned with ultimate philosophical issues."[45] They also acquired a different approach toward the physical life to which they returned. "Almost everyone has stressed the importance in this life of trying to cultivate love for others, a love of the unique and profound kind. . . . Many others have emphasized the importance of seeking knowledge."[46] But no one felt morally perfected or holier than others. Rather, their vision "left them with new goals, new moral principles, and a renewed determination to try to live in accordance with them, but with no feeling of instantaneous salvation or of moral infallibility."[47] There was a new reverence for life, and even those who had these experiences as the result of a suicide attempt mentioned that "they would never consider trying suicide again."[48]

In attempting to evaluate what is experienced in near-death phenomena, we must first note that Moody reports only on persons within the Judeo-Christian tradition.[49] This relatively homogeneous group of humanity may in part account for the similarity of the experiences (e.g.,

45. Moody, *Life after Life*, 89. David Lorimer, *Whole in One: The Near-Death Experience and the Ethic of Interconnectedness* (London: Penguin, 1990), 5, even wants to develop from these experiences an ethic of interconnectedness based on the Golden Rule.

46. Moody, *Life after Life*, 92-93.

47. Moody, *Life after Life*, 93.

48. Moody, *Reflections*, 48.

49. Cf. Moody, *Reflections*, 79.

identification of the bright light with Christ or an angel). We must also note that Moody is not trying to prove that there is life after death, and that he is even convinced that "*within the context of science alone,* there may never be a proof of life after death."[50] He is concerned that these "near-death experiences not be perverted by using them as an excuse for a new cult," and he rightly mentions that they "are also similar in many respects to mystical and religious visions described by great seers in the past" (cf. Acts 7:54-58).[51]

In assessing these experiences Moody leaves open the possibility of conceiving "near-death experiences either as intimations of immortality or merely as the result of terminal physiological events."[52] We might conclude that in cases of extreme shock or anxiety, whether induced by oneself or by external circumstances, some or all of the described phenomena can result. While this would explain these visions and experiences, it would not answer the queries of physicians who reportedly "just can't understand how their patients could have described the things they did about the resuscitation efforts unless they really were hovering just below the ceiling."[53]

The difficulty in coming to terms with these phenomena may lie in our conception of the mind or the psyche as being usually coextensive with the physical body. Psychic research, however, has amassed a plethora of data that seem to indicate that with certain people human knowledge can extend into the future in cases of precognition (the power of the mind to foretell certain events), into the past in cases of clairvoyance (the power of the mind to unearth events of the distant past), and into the distance in cases of telepathy (the power of the mind to tell what happens at distant places).[54] It has also been attested many times that, at the point of death, loved ones "have said goodbye" to close relatives or friends in geographically distant regions by stopping a clock at the time of their death or by appearing in some kind of vision to these people.[55]

---

50. Cf. Moody, *Life after Life,* 5, and *Reflections,* 128.

51. See Moody, *Reflections,* 103 and 90.

52. Moody, *Reflections,* 78.

53. Moody, *Reflections,* 101.

54. Cf. for details, Hans Schwarz, *Beyond the Gates of Death: A Biblical Examination of Evidence for Life after Death* (Minneapolis: Augsburg, 1981), 55-70.

55. Cf. Ian Stevenson, *Telepathic Impressions: A Review and Report of Thirty-five New Cases* (Charlottesville: University of Virginia Press, 1970), who presents many different

In some cases the mind or the psyche evidently can extend itself far beyond the physical boundaries of the body. This could also be the case in near-death experiences. In very unusual situations of extreme stress, the spirit or the psyche could temporarily go far beyond the body with which it is usually coextensive.

We might even shed more light on these near-death experiences by considering the broader question. Sir John Eccles (b. 1903), a Nobel laureate in medicine, has reminded us that the self-conscious mind effectively acts on the brain when we plan and carry out actions (voluntary movements) or when we try to recover a memory or solve a problem. He rightly claims: "There must be a partial independence of the self-conscious mind from the brain events with which it interacts."[56] Thus ultimately we are confronted with the issue of the origin and destiny of the self. Eccles ponders how "each of us as a self-conscious being comes to exist as a unique self associated with a brain. . . . What happens to the conscious self at brain death? . . . Is the self renewed in some other guise and existence? This is a problem beyond science, and scientists should refrain from giving definitive negative answers."[57]

Perhaps we should not rule out the conclusion that occasionally (not all near-death encounters result in conscious experiences) and in highly unusual situations we obtain a glimpse of a larger whole of which we are part, whether the experiences be induced by the self or by external circumstances. Since each moment in our life is unique and not open to repetition, each near-death experience included, such experience cannot lead to the conclusion that we have finally proven our immortality. At the point of our actual death we may not have such an experience again. Rather, it could make us appreciate more the transitory but precious and singular character of our present life, and it might also make us aware that our present existence is but a necessary prelude to a larger entity — life eternal. For some these near-death experiences may also give "assurances of continuing life"

---

and well-attested cases of precognition and visionary appearances. He also helped Moody with refining his methodology in obtaining and analyzing the reports.

56. John C. Eccles, in his noteworthy essay "The Brain-Mind Problem as a Frontier of Science," in *The Future of Science: 1975 Nobel Conference*, ed. Timothy C. L. Robinson (New York: Wiley, 1977), 87.

57. Eccles, 88.

after death without being able to provide us with scientific evidence for life after death.[58]

c. Immortality and Greek Philosophy[59]

A very different claim for immortality was brought forth by the founders of Western philosophy, Plato and Aristotle. Many eminent theologians, such as Augustine, Thomas Aquinas, and John Calvin, accepted their body-soul dichotomy and taught the immortality of the soul. According to Plato, the soul is invisible, immaterial, spiritual, and trans-earthly.[60] The Demiurge, the creator of the world, created each human soul. This means that a human soul, though it is of the same being as the universal soul of the world, is not an emanation or part of this soul.[61] Humanity is a combination of body and soul.

Plato leaves no doubt that the soul is of prime importance. For the soul the body is only accidental, a vehicle it uses. The soul is the actual human being, and the body is only a shell. Plato even conceives of the body as the prison of the soul, as an evil which never permits the soul to attain the full measure of its intentions, namely, to attain the truth.[62] But God will redeem the soul from its prison. Though Plato also talks about a soul of courage and a soul of desire, the soul in its actual sense is only the soul of reason or of spirit. Soul is not just spirit or consciousness; it is "the spring of motion in everything else that moves," and therefore the principle of life.[63] The whole world is animated by the soul because,

58. So Russell Noyes, "The Human Experience of Death or, What Can We Learn from Near-Death Experience?" in *The Near-Death Experience*, 275.

59. For the following cf. the illuminating remarks by Georg Scherer, *Das Problem des Todes in der Philosophie* (Darmstadt: Wissenschaftliche Buchgesellschaft, 1979), esp. 92-103 and 119-24.

60. Cf. Plato, *Phaedo* 79, in Plato, *The Complete Works*, edited with an introduction and notes by John M. Cooper (Indianapolis: Hackett, 1997), 69-70.

61. Plato, *Timaeus* 41-42, in *The Complete Works*, 1245-46.

62. Cf. Plato, *Phaedo* 67, in *The Complete Works*, 58, where Plato says: "We shall be closest to the knowledge if we refrain as much as possible from association with the body," and Plato, *Laws* 12.959, in *The Complete Works*, 1607, where he affirms that "the soul has an absolute superiority over the body" and that the body is "just the likeness of myself that I carry around with me."

63. Plato, *Phaedrus* 245, in *The Complete Works*, 524.

269

whether in humanity or animals or plants, wherever there is life, there is soul.

But why does Plato claim that the soul is immortal? According to Plato, one reason lies in its composition. Since the soul is invisible, immaterial, and indivisible, it cannot undergo change and be dissolved. It must be immortal. The other reason for its immortality lies in its content. The soul knows about the eternal ideas of truth, goodness, and beauty, and longs to attain them. Since these ideas do not occur at any place within our world, they must be recollections of perceptions that the soul had prior to its present state, that is, in its preexistent state. If the soul is preexistent, then the conclusion is unavoidable that it extends its existence also beyond death. Plato even assumes a continuing cycle of rebirth and purification until the soul attains union with the godly. Yet in his deliberations, even in *Phaedo*, Plato does not want to prove the immortality of the soul.[64] He knows as a philosopher that he can only show that the immortality of the soul is a distinct possibility. This way he could give hope by removing obstacles to that hope. Since hope cannot be founded on thought alone, it must have religious or "metaphysical" anchors.

Aristotle (384-322 B.C.) largely followed Plato in his understanding of the soul.[65] In his early dialogues Aristotle advocates a Platonic dualism. Body and soul are only formally connected and act like two separate and hostile substances. Later he regards them as still independent but cooperative entities. And when he writes his *Physics*, he conceives the soul as the energy of life that resides at a certain point in the body. Thus one can distinguish in all living beings between something that is moved (body) and something that causes the movements (soul). Finally, in his treatise *On the Soul* he abandons this distinction and regards a person primarily as a unity. Body and soul are merged into a unity of substance in which body and soul pertain to the whole person. But he still talks about a spiritual soul of the person.

In analogy to Plato, Aristotle also distinguishes between three souls:

64. Cf. the deliberations by Hans Michael Baumgartner, "Die Unzerstörbarkeit der Seele: Platons Argumente wider den endgültigen Tod des Menschen im Dialog 'Phaidon,'" in *Tod — Ende oder Vollendung?* ed. Norbert A. Luyten (Freiburg: Karl Alber, 1980), esp. 96-97.
65. For the following cf. Johannes Hirschberger, *Geschichte der Philosophie*, vol. 1, *Altertum und Mittelalter* (Basel: Herder, 1960), 211.

the soul which enables growth and procreation and emerges in the realm of plants; the soul which enables sense-perception, desire, and movement and emerges in the animal kingdom; and the soul of reason which is peculiar to humans and makes one into a rational animal.[66] In spite of his own delineation of different "souls," he polemicizes against Plato that he does not emphasize enough "the unity of the soul in a person."[67]

But Aristotle seems to be in a worse dilemma than Plato. While emphasizing the one human soul "by which primarily we live, perceive, and think,"[68] he asserts that the lower souls are passed on from father to child through procreation, while active reason "pre-exists" and enters from outside and alone is "divine."[69] This means that the actual soul, the soul of reason or spirit, is preexistent and not created. Unlike the lower soul, it does not cease to exist when the body dies but is immortal. Although Aristotle asserted the immortality of this soul of reason, he did not attempt to prove it.

In his *Critique of Pure Reason,* Immanuel Kant discredited the attempt to assert with certainty that there is something indivisible (e.g., a soul) in our world.[70] He also claimed that all our proofs can only pertain to the world we can conceive in the categories of space and time. Thus a strict proof of the existence of a soul is as impossible as a proof of the existence of God. Yet in his *Critique of Practical Reason* Kant claims "the immortality of the soul as a postulate of pure practical reason."[71] We know, he asserts, that the fulfillment of the moral law is the highest good. Though we strive to fulfill it, we never come to an end of our endeavors in this life. This evident disproportion between the direction of our existence (attaining the highest good) and the actual content of our existence (not completely attaining the highest good) demands a solution.

66. Cf. Frederick Copleston, *A History of Philosophy,* vol. 1, *Greece and Rome,* rev. ed. (Westminster, Md.: Newman, 1963), 328.

67. Aristotle, *On the Soul* 414a.21-24, in *The Complete Works of Aristotle,* edited with an introduction by Jonathan Barnes (Princeton: Princeton University Press, 1984), 1:659.

68. Aristotle, *On the Soul* 414a.14, in *Complete Works of Aristotle,* 1:659.

69. Aristotle, *Generation of Animals* 736b.20-30, in *Complete Works of Aristotle,* 1:1143.

70. Cf. Kant's second antinomy of pure reason and the conclusions he draws from these antinomies.

71. Cf. Immanuel Kant, *Critique of Practical Reason* 5.121, in Immanuel Kant, *Critique of Practical Reason and Other Writings in Moral Philosophy,* translated and edited with an introduction by Lewis W. Beck (Chicago: University of Chicago Press, 1949), 225-26, quote on 225.

The solution can only come from an infinite life beyond our present existence so that through infinite progress we may realize the fulfillment of the moral law as the highest good. Kant, of course, knows very well that an immortal soul can only be theoretically demanded and cannot be proved in reality.

If one cannot strictly prove the immortality of the soul, why have humanity's greatest philosophers pointed to the immortality of the person or the soul? Confronted with death throughout our life, we seem to feel that with death our existence cannot be completely over. There must be something beyond death. The idea of immortality shows the fundamental contradiction that we experience in our own existence and can rightly be regarded as an inborn idea of the human mind. But does Christian faith itself not hold the immortality of the human soul as one of its essential features?

d. Immortality and Christian Faith

Toward the end of the twelfth century the Arabic philosopher Averroes (1126-98) introduced Aristotle's philosophy to Christian theologians of the West. But the Western Church soon took steps to ban the resulting Averroistic movement in Christian theology, because Averroes had concluded from Aristotle's treatise *On the Soul* that the soul of reason, or of the spirit, is a single, universal, and active intellect in which all people participate during their lifetime. He believed that in death, however, this human participation ceases, so that only the one universal soul is left. According to Averroes, this means that the immortality of neither the person nor the soul can be proved philosophically.

Conservative theologians, such as Thomas Aquinas (*De unitate intellectus contra Averroistas,* 1270), protested immediately. At the Fifth Lateran Council in 1513, the church officially condemned the "pernicious errors . . . concerning the nature of the rational soul, namely, that it is mortal, or one in all men."[72] This decision reflects to this day the understanding of official Roman Catholic dogma, according to which each person is endowed with a unique immortal soul.

---

72. *The Human Soul (Against the Neo-Aristotelians),* 738, in Heinrich Denzinger, *The Sources of Catholic Dogma* (St. Louis: B. Herder, 1957), 237.

Once we assume that humanity gradually developed from prehuman forms, however, the claim of an immortal soul is very difficult to maintain. The Roman Catholic Church realized this too, and in 1950 Pope Pius XII tried to reconcile the theory of evolution with the doctrine of the immortality of the soul. He stated that "The *magisterium* of the church does not forbid that the teaching of 'evolution' be treated in accord with the present status of human disciplines and of theology, by investigations and disputations, by learned men in both fields; insofar, of course, as the inquiry is concerned with the origin of the human body arising from already existing and living matter; — the Catholic faith commands us to retain that the souls are created immediately by God."[73] The Roman Catholic Church thus attempted to solve the difficulties caused by the theory of evolution by claiming that the human body is procreated in a natural way, while its eternal soul is infused immediately by God. The *Catechism of the Catholic Church* still teaches "that every spiritual soul is created immediately by God — it is not 'produced' by the parents — and also that it is immortal: it does not perish when it separates from the body at death, and it will be reunited with the body at the final Resurrection."[74]

But the Roman Catholic Church is not alone in its emphasis on the immortality of the soul. Most Protestant hymns express the hope that after our life on earth our immortal soul will be united with God. Even many of the leading Protestant theologians of the past, such as Zwingli (1484-1531), Calvin, and to some extent Luther, advocated the immortality of the soul. But can this idea be maintained on biblical grounds?

When we consult a concordance of the Bible, we find many instances of the term "soul." But the creation accounts at the beginning of the Bible, where we would expect mention of the human soul, are remarkably quiet about a creation or infusion of the human soul through divine intervention. Genesis 1 simply states that "God created human-

73. Encyclical *Humani Generis* (1950), par 3896, in *Enchiridion Symbolorum*, 779, or Anne Fremantle, ed., *The Papal Encyclicals in Their Historical Context* (New York: New American Library, 1963), 297-98.
74. *Catechism of the Catholic Church* (366), 104. In the same vein E. J. Fortman, *Everlasting Life after Death* (New York: Alba House, 1976), 42, wrote, albeit in the seventies: "Traditional Christian doctrine has maintained, that every man is destined and capacitated for life after death by his very nature, in virtue of a naturally immortal soul that is an essential principle of every man." Small wonder then that an interim state and purgatory are real for him.

kind in his image" (1:27), and in Genesis 2 we hear in more picturesque language that "the LORD God formed man from the dust of the ground, and breathed into his nostrils the breath of life; and the man became a living being" (2:7).[75]

The distinction is made not between body and soul but between a lifeless and a living human being. In other words, God created the whole person according to the body (from dust) and then gave this body life through his life-giving breath. This can hardly substantiate the teaching that our "soul" is created immediately by God, while our body came into existence in a mediated way through evolution. It also runs contrary to the Platonic idea that the body is a prison of the soul. The divergence from Plato's conception becomes even more evident when we remember that in early Israelite thinking, after death a person leads a shadowy, bodiless existence in Sheol. One certainly cannot call this existence a genuine life, since it is not even possible to praise the Lord there. According to Plato, by contrast, it is precisely apart from the body that the soul attains full development of its life.

When we consult the New Testament, however, the distinction between body and soul is quite common. This is not surprising, since the New Testament writers use Greek terminology to express God's self-disclosure. But these writers do not conceive of the soul as good and the body as evil by nature. Both belong together and both are created by God. And together they can be influenced by flesh or by spirit. If we live according to the flesh, we live in a sinful existence in our totality of being as body and soul (Rom. 7:14). Paul can use the terms "flesh" and "sin" almost synonymously. Both denote demonic powers which enslave us.[76] If we live according to the spirit, we live our existence as children of God in our total being, in body and soul (Rom. 8:14). But neither the term "flesh" nor the term "spirit" *"is given with human existence as such."*[77] We must conclude that the analogy to Platonic ideas lies only in the terminology and not in their content.

75. Cf. Gerhard von Rad, *Genesis: A Commentary,* trans. John M. Marks, rev. ed. (Philadelphia: Westminster, 1972), 77, who calls this verse "a *locus classicus* of Old Testament anthropology."

76. Rudolf Bultmann, *Theology of the New Testament,* trans. Kendrik Grobel (New York: Scribner, 1951), 1:244-45.

77. Oscar Cullmann, *Immortality of the Soul or Resurrection of the Dead? The Witness of the New Testament* (New York: Macmillan, 1964), 33.

Besides Platonic philosophy, there is also gnosticism, which, in analogy to a soul-body dualism, asserts that we possess a divine spark which is contaminated in this life by the material body. Salvation is understood as redemption from the material and mortal body and entrance into the divine fullness of light. One might suspect that even Paul is influenced by gnostic ideas when he exclaims: "Wretched man that I am! Who will rescue me from this body of death?" (Rom. 7:24). But unlike gnosticism, Paul is not expecting redemption from his mortal body. Rather he is confident that Christ will give a totally new life to our mortal bodies through his Spirit who dwells in us (Rom. 8:11).

Paul, and with him the whole New Testament, is not longing for the liberation of the self from the bodily prison, but for the resurrection of the body.[78] He does not hope that from our mortal nature something worthwhile and immortal will survive (there is nothing to survive), but he hopes and is sure that through the resurrection of the body our mortal nature will be transformed into immortality (1 Cor. 15:35-57). So when the *Catechism of the Catholic Church* suggests that, in the resurrection, the soul is "reunited with the body," this reminds us more of a continuation of this life than a resurrection to a new form of life.

It is also interesting that, in this context, Raymond Moody in his analysis of near-death experiences distinguishes between the "physical body" that is temporarily abandoned and the "spiritual body" in which the person has his or her experiences.[79] Unlike gnostic thought or Platonism, the physical is not conceived as a prison or as being secondary. The image of a spiritual body implies that one is not faced with the experience of nothingness, but one encounters a continuation of one's existence on a different level. There is also no mention made that the continuation of existence is a (natural) result of the person having a spiritual body, a thought we might expect in the pursuit of a body-soul dualism. It is also clear that these near-death experiences do not yet reach the state of a resurrected existence, since they are temporary and are resolved in a continuation of life here on earth.

How incompatible the Greek idea of the immortality of the soul

---

78. Cf. Bultmann, *Theology,* 1:202, who shows convincingly that, according to Paul, Christians do not desire to be "unclothed," like the gnostics, but desire to be "further clothed" and "yearn for the heavenly garment."

79. Cf. Moody, *Life after Life,* 51.

and the Christian belief in the resurrection are, is demonstrated by
Paul's own missionary activity.[80] When Paul preached for the first time
in Athens, laughter erupted when he spoke of the resurrection (Acts
17:32). And in his letters to the congregation in Corinth, he had to devote a whole chapter (1 Cor. 15) to the Christian belief in the resurrection, since many (Christian) Corinthians claimed that there was no need
for this belief. Even around A.D. 150 Justin Martyr mentions people
"who say that there is no resurrection of the dead, and that their souls,
when they die, are taken to heaven."[81]

Even today the idea of immortality of the soul is "one of the greatest misunderstandings of Christianity."[82] Eberhard Jüngel (b. 1934) even
calls for a "de-Platonising of Christianity as a theological task."[83] Death
is the end of this life in its totality; nothing and nobody will survive.
Many Roman Catholic scholars fully agree with this insight. Karl Rahner (1904-84), for instance, says there is no rectilinear continuation of
our empirical reality beyond death. "In this regard death puts an end to
the *whole* man."[84] Though we sense our immortality, only God's word
reveals to us "the *actuality* of eternity."[85] When the Roman Catholic
Church proposes the doctrine of immortality of the soul, this is a "truth
of faith and not just a philosophical tenet."[86] According to Rahner, the
assertion of immortality is directed to both the *whole* reality and meaning of a person, as this individual depends on the creative and life-giving power of God, and what the philosopher as such may call soul in
contrast to body, with a destiny which one may try to trace after death.[87]

Consequently immortality can denote (1) immortality in the philo-

80. Cf. for the following, Cullmann, *Immortality of the Soul*, 59, where he quotes
Justin Martyr (cf. n. 81 below). We should also note that, according to Paul, death is not a
passage to new life or redemption from our earthly existence, but an enemy that has
been overcome by Christ. So Gerhardus van der Leeuw, *Unsterblichkeit oder Auferstehung*,
Theologische Existenz heute, 52 (Munich: Chr. Kaiser, 1956), 16.

81. Justin Martyr, *Dialogue with Trypho* 80, in *ANF*, 1:239.

82. Cullmann, *Immortality of the Soul*, 15.

83. Eberhard Jüngel, *Death: The Riddle and the Mystery*, trans. Iain Nicol and Ute
Nicol (Philadelphia: Westminster, 1974), 53.

84. Karl Rahner, "The Life of the Dead," in Karl Rahner, *Theological Investigations*,
vol. 4, *More Recent Writings*, trans. Kevin Smyth (Baltimore: Helicon, 1966), 347.

85. Rahner, "Life of the Dead," 351.

86. Rahner, "Life of the Dead," 352.

87. Cf. Rahner, "Life of the Dead," 352.

sophical sense and (2) a gift of God, which means that God continues his relationship with us beyond our biological death. One might even ask whether immortality can remain just a philosophical assertion or whether, as we see in Plato, it needs a religious context.[88] Especially in combating Averroism, Thomas Aquinas went beyond Plato in attempting to prove the immortality of the soul by its very composition. Since it was not composed, it could not undergo any change and decay. Therefore it must be immortal.[89]

Contemporary Roman Catholic authors seem to be divided on the issue of immortality. This is shown best in Joseph Ratzinger (b. 1927), when on the one hand he affirms that "the starting point of the Christian understanding of immortality is the concept of God, and from this it draws its dialogical character. Since God is the God of the living, and calls his creature, man, by name, this creature cannot be annihilated. In Jesus Christ, God's action in accepting humanity into his own eternal life has, so to speak, taken flesh: Christ is the tree of life whence we receive the food of immortality."[90] While here the gift character of immortality is clearly expressed, since we receive immortality through Christ, Ratzinger at the same time argues that since we are creatures, we cannot be dissolved. He even goes so far as to say that "like every other creature, man can only move within the ambit of creation. Just as he cannot bring forth being of himself, so neither can he hurl it back into sheer nothingness."[91] While we agree that wherever we fall, we fall into the hands of the living God, being kept within those hands does not imply immortality. If this were so, then everything would be endowed with a kind of immortality, everything created could never fall into nothingness.

The important point for Ratzinger, however, is not to advocate some

88. Joseph Ratzinger, *Eschatology: Death and Eternal Life*, trans. Michael Waldstein, ed. Aidan Nichols (Washington, D.C.: Catholic University of America Press, 1988), 141-42, points out that even for Plato the assertion of immortality comes to stand in a religious context which for him is the starting point of a philosophy of justice. It is also interesting how Ratzinger defends Plato against the accusation of a separation between body and soul, saying this issue is more or less irrelevant and certainly cannot stand for the Greek thought on body and soul.

89. Cf. Thomas Aquinas, *Summa Theologica* I.75.6 (London: Burns Oates & Washburne, n.d.), 4:16-19.

90. Ratzinger, *Eschatology*, 158.

91. Ratzinger, *Eschatology*, 156.

kind of panpsychism, meaning that everything is endowed with an immortal soul. His intention is to react against some kind of total-death theory which has been invoked by some Protestant theologians and, as he claims, has also become attractive for some Roman Catholics.[92] According to that theory, at death we completely die and cease to exist, and then we will be resurrected at some later "date." Ratzinger, however, wants to make sure that there is no void after death but a continuation, if only through an immortal soul. Of course, the notion of an immortal soul could easily lead to the idea that one is by nature immortal and does not need salvation, as idealistic philosophers have claimed. It also seems to betray a false understanding of death.

Death denotes a demarcation between this life and the hereafter, a demarcation so radical that it could hardly sustain the idea of a continuance, unless we talk about a "shadowy existence" in analogy to existence in Sheol. But the Old Testament writers never talked about continuity, for they realized that Sheol allowed for no life in the real sense. The notions of a new creation and a resurrection, so central to the New Testament, point to something so different from our life here that they contradict the idea of a continuity through and beyond death and a re-uniting of body and soul.

Since immortality as a gift of God is easily confused with an innate immortality of the soul, and thus with a nonbiblical soul-body dichotomy, most leading figures in contemporary Protestant theology reject the idea of immortality.[93] But a Lutheran theologian like Regin Prenter (1907-90) notes that the usual "polemics against the idea of the soul's immortality are often very superficial."[94] Contrary to its original, valid Christian meaning, immortality is often polemically construed as a denial of the Christian hope in the resurrection. Karl Barth (1886-1968), for instance, mentions the idea of the immortality of the soul only once in his *Church Dogmatics*, and calls it "a typical thought inspired by fear."[95]

92. Ratzinger, *Eschatology*, 105.

93. An excellent survey and evaluation from the Roman Catholic side is provided by Ansgar Ahlbrecht, *Tod und Unsterblichkeit in der evangelischen Theologie der Gegenwart* (Paderborn: Bonifacius-Druckerei, 1964).

94. Regin Prenter, *Creation and Redemption*, trans. Theodor I. Jensen (Philadelphia: Fortress, 1967), 576 n. 171.

95. Karl Barth, *Church Dogmatics* III/4, trans. A. T. Mackay et al. (Edinburgh: T. & T. Clark, 1961), 590. Cf. also Walter Künneth, *The Theology of the Resurrection*, trans. James W.

Emil Brunner (1889-1966) is more discerning when he rejects only the Platonist understanding of the immortality of the soul but accepts the genuinely "Christian Biblical and Christological concept of immortality" which we have "only in God's creative Word."[96] Paul Tillich seems to go one step further when he observes that of the two terms Christianity uses for the individual participation in eternal life, only "resurrection" is biblical, while "immortality" dates back to "the Platonic doctrine of the immortality of the soul."[97]

Tillich still concedes that, notwithstanding the inherent dualistic dangers, the term "immortality" can be used, not as an expression of a continuation of temporal life after death, but as denoting "a quality which transcends temporality." In this way even the term "immortality of the soul" can imply the power of universal essentialization. Though Tillich's symbolic understanding of immortality should be acceptable to Roman Catholic scholars, we wonder if they would also agree with his preference for Aristotle's ontological interpretation of Plato's teaching on immortality. Participation in a world-soul as life eternal not only seems relatively unattractive as the final goal of our individual lives but is also unbiblical.

Although the many misunderstandings caused by the term "immortality" necessitate that we treat it with extreme care, we do not want to discard its valid theological significance. "Theologically speaking immortality should not be understood in substantialistic terms as if the soul alone by its own power would be exempt from transitoriness."[98] Yet we do not advocate that death is the dissolution of the person or that we plunge into a state of blissful void once we die. If that were so, death would provide an escape from this life and its consequences, and one could simply commit suicide to escape them. However, nobody can

---

Leitch (London: SCM, 1965), 37, who understands the resurrection as the "antithesis to the idea of life and immortality." Cf. also Werner Elert, *Der christliche Glaube: Grundlinien der lutherischen Dogmatik* (Hamburg: Furche, 1956), 508, who claims that all ideas of immortality are shattered by the fact of bodily death.

96. Emil Brunner, *Dogmatics,* vol. 3, *The Christian Doctrine of the Church, Faith, and the Consummation,* trans. D. Cairns in collaboration with T. H. L. Parker (Philadelphia: Westminster, 1962), 383 and 390-91.

97. Tillich, 3:409-11.

98. So the Roman Catholic Anton Ziegenaus, *Die Zukunft der Schöpfung in Gott: Eschatologie* (Aachen: MM Verlag, 1996), 134.

withdraw from God and from his sustaining hand, because he is on both sides of death. Jürgen Moltmann therefore writes: "God's relationship to people is a dimension of their existence which they do not lose even in death."[99] God's relationship with us in this life is sustained and finalized in and through death. Thus death can result in eternal death as eternal damnation, or it can result in eternal life as eternal joy. This does not mean that death is already eternal damnation or eternal life, but it entails it. Death, in other words, is the reverse side of resurrection.

3. Resurrection

Since we are not endowed with divine qualities that could make us hope for a gradual purification of an immortal soul, our only hope for ultimate fulfillment is beyond death, in the resurrection from the dead. This hope of the resurrection from the dead is inseparably based on the certitude of Jesus Christ's resurrection.[100]

a. Decisive Character of Christ's Resurrection

The first Christian community was absolutely certain that Jesus was resurrected from the dead. Contemporary theology from the conservative wing to the extreme liberal wing is united on this basic insight. But as soon as we attempt to explain this observation and ask, for instance, what the statement means that "Jesus Christ was resurrected from the dead," there are many diverse opinions.

99. Jürgen Moltmann, *The Coming of God: Christian Eschatology*, trans. Margaret Kohl (Minneapolis: Fortress, 1996), 76.

100. John Macquarrie, *Jesus Christ in Modern Thought* (London: SCM, 1990), 412, states: "Suppose we omitted the 'joyful mysteries' that traditionally came after the cross? Would that destroy the whole fabric of faith in Christ? I do not think so, for the two great distinctive Christian affirmations would remain untouched — God is love, and God is revealed in Jesus Christ. These two affirmations would stand even if there were no mysteries beyond Calvary." However, he fails to convince. How could God be love if there is no "happy ending," as Macquarrie calls the ending with a resurrection? God's love would be rather pale, since he could never carry through the promises this love entails, because in the end death would stare us in the face.

We cannot agree with those who claim the statement has no meaning for us today.[101] It was precisely the resurrection of Jesus Christ which provided the focal point for the first Christian community and kept the Christian faith alive until today. But it is impossible for us simply to resort to the resurrection of Christ in order to remove the ambiguity of the cross. Rudolf Bultmann has made this point unmistakably clear. In contrast to the historical fact of the crucifixion, the resurrection of Christ does not lend itself to a strictly empirical proof. The resurrection is an inference drawn from other facts which can always be arranged to allow for differing interpretations.[102] Thus Albert Schweitzer could try to explain the resurrection as a psychological phenomenon that occurred within the disciples.[103] Though we have seen that such an immanent explanation has trouble sufficiently explaining how the Christian faith spread as rapidly and durably as it did, we notice that even Paul in his best attempt "to prove the fact" of the resurrection could at most refer to the faith of others and to the Scriptures (documents of faith). But it is an overstatement to claim that the "cross and resurrection form a single, indivisible cosmic event."[104] We agree with Bultmann that we cannot resort to the one event to prove the impor-

---

101. William Hamilton, *The New Essence of Christianity* (New York: Association, 1966), 116 n. 34, does not want to put the resurrection in one line with ascension and exaltation, assertions that, according to him, do not have any precise meaning today. However, he mentions the resurrection only as an afterthought, and then only in the context of humiliation and suffering, since the risen Lord still bears the marks of his suffering. This seems to run contrary to the New Testament affirmations, where the resurrection is conceived of as a part of Christ's kingly office, which is, according to Hamilton's evaluation, without precise meaning for us today.

102. Cf. George Eldon Ladd, *I Believe in the Resurrection of Jesus* (Grand Rapids: Eerdmans, 1975), 21. Ladd carefully marks out the limits of historical knowledge and comes to the conclusion that "Although it was an event in history, Jesus' resurrection had no antecedent historical cause — a sequence which the historian assumes" (125), and, we might add, attempts to establish, if necessary, even by hypothetical means.

103. Albert Schweitzer, *The Quest of the Historical Jesus: A Critical Study of Its Progress from Reimarus to Wrede,* translated from the first German edition by W. Montgomery (New York: Macmillan, 1968), 284-85, and 345-46; cf. also Richard R. Niebuhr, *Resurrection and Historical Reason: A Study of Theological Method* (New York: Scribner, 1957), 132-33.

104. Rudolf Bultmann, "New Testament and Mythology," in *Kerygma and Myth: A Theological Debate,* ed. Hans Werner Bartsch, trans. R. H. Fuller (London: SPCK, 1953), 39. Even Bultmann admits "that the resurrection of Jesus is often used in the New Testament as a miraculous proof."

tance of the other. There is, however, a decisive difference between the events of Good Friday and those of Easter Sunday. God acted very differently on these two occasions.

It is also questionable whether one can call the resurrection of Jesus Christ a means of interpreting the historical Jesus.[105] It is true that only in the light of the resurrection did the Christian community arrive at the interpretation of Jesus contained in the New Testament. The origin of the New Testament cannot be explained without the "happening" which the Christian community called the resurrection of Jesus Christ.[106] But the first Christians were not interested in ancestor worship. They did not just gather to remember that something unique had happened with Jesus. The resurrection is both the basis for the present and the provision for the future. This is especially expressed in the title *kyrios* (Lord) which was conferred on Jesus Christ by the post-Easter Christian community. The term *kyrios* was used, for example, to denote the emperor in the official Roman state cult. It was also used to refer to pagan gods, and it served in the Septuagint to render the Hebrew name Yahweh into Greek. In the hymn in Philippians 2:5-11, which describes the whole salvific mission of Jesus, the term *kyrios* indicates the end of Jesus' earthly career and implies equality with God: every knee shall bow and he shall be proclaimed *kyrios.* This new status does not threaten the sovereignty of God but rather is granted to glorify God.[107]

Of course, this new status is unthinkable without Jesus' resurrection. In one of the oldest creedal statements in the New Testament (Rom. 10:9), the confession of Jesus as Lord runs parallel to faith in his resurrection from the dead, and both have salvific character. This equal-

---

105. Cf. Willi Marxsen, *The Resurrection of Jesus of Nazareth,* trans. M. Kohl (Philadelphia: Fortress, 1970), 138-40, and Marxsen, "The Resurrection of Jesus as a Historical and Theological Problem," trans. D. M. Barton, in *The Significance of the Message of the Resurrection for Faith in Jesus Christ,* edited with an introduction by C. F. D. Moule (London: SCM, 1968), 48-50. Cf. also the valid criticism of Marxsen's position by Bas van Iersel, "The Resurrection of Jesus — Information or Interpretation?" in *Immortality and Resurrection,* ed. Pierre Benoit and Roland Murphy, vol. 60 of *Concilium* (New York: Herder & Herder, 1970), 65-67, who maintains that the resurrection is both interpretation and information.

106. Referring to Augustine's *Confessions,* Richard R. Niebuhr, 67, gives an excellent analogy to the influence of the resurrection on the formation of the New Testament. In his *Confessions* Augustine reflects on his entire life "in the light of his conversion."

107. For the following cf. Werner Foerster, "kyrios," in *TDNT,* 3:1089.

ity with God implies cosmic lordship as well as lordship over individual Christians. We remember, for instance, that it was decisive for Paul's call and missionary activity that Jesus Christ was Lord; this means he was designated Son of God *in power* through his resurrection (Rom. 1:4). But Jesus became more than just some superhuman mediator between God and us through his resurrection. He was declared God incarnate. At times Paul does not even distinguish between Jesus Christ and God. The term *kyrios* signifies the way in which God deals with the world; it expresses his rule over the world. All the powers and "lords" are derived and secondary, but Jesus Christ's lordship is unconditioned and all-pervading.

The fact that Jesus became Lord through his resurrection means also that he, the hidden Messiah, became the revealed Messiah. In other words, the term "Christ the Lord" expresses that the one who was Jesus of Nazareth was not just a human being, but God himself. Thus he is not a figure of the past. As Christ the Lord, he is the decisive agent who provides present and future.

b. Creative Newness of Christ's Resurrection

The quality of newness implied in the resurrection is already indicated in the affirmation that Jesus became Christ and Lord, and that as the hidden Messiah he was disclosed as the revealed Messiah. But the quality of newness becomes especially evident when we consider the resurrection of Christ in the context of God's creative activity. The Bible suggests in many places that God's salvific activity must be seen in analogy to God's creative activity in the beginning. For instance, Deutero-Isaiah, the book that proclaims that salvation is offered through the sacrifice of the Servant of Yahweh, intimately connects the creation in the beginning with salvation as the goal of history (cf. Isa. 42:5; 44:6; 45:8).[108] And in its opening sentences the Gospel of John sees the coming of Christ from the perspective of the creation in the beginning. Also Paul points out a clear correspondence between the appearance of the first Adam and the appearance of Christ as the last Adam (Rom. 5).

It would be erroneous to interpret this perspective of creation as if

---

108. Cf. also Werner Foerster, "ktizo," in *TDNT,* 3:1012-13.

the resurrection were to open the opportunity for us to return to an ideal state of the past. Such an interpretation would force us into the cyclical view of history represented by most religions and mythologies: after the cataclysmic end dawns a new beginning, the wheel of world history moves on to a new revolution. But a different course of history is indicated by Paul when he writes: "For in him all things in heaven and on earth were created, things visible and invisible, whether thrones or dominions or rulers or powers — all things have been created through him and for him" (Col. 1:16). This means that everything is created toward Christ. When Paul calls him the firstborn of all creation (Col. 1:15), he wants to emphasize that Christ, being equal to God, does not stand only at the beginning of creation. Through his resurrection Christ is also the goal toward which creation moves.[109] Clearly, such an understanding cannot condone a static view of creation that often sounds like the following: God created the world; through the fall this good and perfect creation was distorted; then came Christ and enabled its restoration; and in the final parousia the creation will be returned to its original beauty. Against this cyclical view we must assert that the "very good" which God pronounced over his creation in the beginning does not mean that it is unsurpassable. There lies the fallacy of understanding our world as the best possible one.[110]

Our present world, of course, is good, but as a fallen creation it is marred by sin and its consequences. To deny this is to belittle the facts of evil and death. To understand Christ as the goal toward which creation moves also requires a radical reorientation concerning the fall of humanity and our sinful state. The fall of humanity can no longer be viewed as a jump from a God-provided basis to some kind of lower level, namely, a state of constant sinfulness. The fall is the initial denial of the Christ line. Union with God is the intention for the whole of cre-

109. This has been pointed out especially clearly by Künneth, 164-66.

110. Cf. Gottfried Wilhelm Leibniz, "Vindication of God's Justice Reconciled with His Other Perfections and All Actions" (41 and 144), in *The Monadology and Other Philosophical Writings*, translated with an introduction and notes by Paul and Anne Martin Schrecker (Indianapolis: Bobbs-Merrill, 1965), 122 and 145, where he states "that among the infinite numbers of possible series God has selected the best, and consequently this best universe is that which actually exists." But then he continues to say: "But the most magnificent part of the world, the City of God, is a sight to which we shall at last be admitted some day." This means our present world is the best this side of heaven.

ation from its very beginning. Each sinful act is a reaffirmation of the initial denial, and thus a rejection of God's plan for us and of his redemptive act in Christ (cf. Heb. 2:1-4).

God is continually with his creation, even in its alienated or fallen state. Nothing is farther from the biblical understanding than a deistic God who dispassionately observes the predestined course of the universe. Even after the fall God does not angrily withdraw from the first humans, but, in an act of compassion, he provides them with necessary clothing (Gen. 3:21). And the church's attempt to detect in the words of the curse a primal gospel (Gen. 3:15), or the endeavor of a Gospel writer to trace the ancestry of Jesus back to Adam and finally to God himself, witnesses to the fact that God's acts in the beginning and in Jesus Christ are seen as a unity. Paul attests this too in pointing to Christ as the antitype of Adam. Through Christ in an antithetical manner, law is superseded by grace, sin by justification, and death by life.[111]

Death is not superseded by life to restore the original state. For the resurrected Christ, death is no longer even a possibility. In a similar way grace is not the opposite of law and justification, or the reverse of sinfulness. Jesus Christ's resurrection does not indicate the fulfillment of a restorative process that had started with the Old Testament covenant community. His resurrection is rather the first point of a *new* creation, a creation in perfection. Could it be just an accident that Paul in his letter to the Romans progresses from declaring Christ as the new Adam (Rom. 5), to our participation in the new creation through baptism (Rom. 6), to the tension within us as citizens of a new world yet still living in the old one (Rom. 7), to the implications for the whole creation of God's creative act in Christ's resurrection (Rom. 8)? God's creative act in Christ's resurrection goes beyond this present creation. It witnesses to the new creation which replaces this present creation at one specific point.[112] This inauguration of the new creation inspires in us the hope of being incorporated in it.

111. Cf. Otto Michel, *Der Brief an die Römer* (Göttingen: Vandenhoeck & Ruprecht, 1957), 121, in his explanation of Rom. 5:12-21.

112. This is where the question of the empty tomb becomes important, not as a proof for the historicity of the resurrection of Jesus Christ, but as an indication that this present creation has no permanence, that it will be replaced by and transformed into something new. Not even the first Christian community used the story of the empty tomb as proof of Christ's resurrection (cf. Matt. 27:62–28:15, esp. 28:15).

c. Christ's Resurrection and Our Resurrection

From the preceding, it should be clear that the Christian belief in the resurrection does not result from a gradual development of the idea of resurrection in the Judeo-Christian context. The Christian belief in the resurrection is basically Christ centered. The *idea* of the resurrection from the dead was well known to both Jesus and the first Christian community.[113] But the resurrection of Jesus does not just verify the validity of the apocalyptic idea of resurrection. For instance, Paul in 1 Corinthians 15 does not start with a common agreement between him and the Corinthians on the idea of a resurrection and then try to turn this idea into a fact. Rather he refers to and explains the Christian tradition concerning *Christ's* resurrection. This means, according to Paul, that "Christ is not merely the first to be raised," as could be expected according to apocalyptic thinking, "but is constitutive for our being raised."[114]

Paul drives this point home very clearly: "If Christ has not been raised, then our proclamation has been in vain and your faith has been in vain" (1 Cor. 15:14). The resurrection of Jesus Christ cannot be isolated from the rest of world history and treated as one event among others. It is the presupposition of the Christian existence as a community of people who participate proleptically in the newness of life, and it is the foundation of Christian hope in the final realization of this new life.

Nevertheless, the full implication of Christ's resurrection is only disclosed to us when we consider it in the context of apocalyptic hopes. Only in relation to the apocalyptic view of history, with its conviction of a resurrection at the end of time, can the resurrection of Jesus Christ be understood as an anticipation of this end.[115] Even the very fact that the disciples could recognize their once familiar leader in their post-Easter experiences, in something entirely different from the possibilities of this life, and that they called the reality behind these experiences resurrection, can only satisfactorily be explained in the context of apocalyptic

113. So Hans Conzelmann, *A Commentary on the First Epistle to the Corinthians*, trans. J. W. Leitch (Philadelphia: Fortress, 1975), 261, in his explanation of 1 Cor. 15:11.

114. Conzelmann, 249, in his explanation of 1 Cor. 15:1-11.

115. Cf. for the following, Wolfhart Pannenberg, *Revelation as History*, ed. Wolfhart Pannenberg, trans. D. Granskou (New York: Macmillan, 1968), 146; and his *Jesus — God and Man*, trans. L. L. Wilkins and D. A. Priebe (Philadelphia: Westminster, 1968), 81-82.

hopes. Otherwise it would have been interpreted as an encounter with a spirit or a phantom (cf. Luke 24:37).

In the context of apocalyptic hopes and expectations, the disciples realized that God had confirmed the authority that Jesus had claimed already in his earthly life. They also realized that in the destiny of Jesus as the Lord, the end had already occurred in proleptic anticipation, and God had already disclosed himself fully in Jesus as the Lord. In other words, through the resurrection of Jesus Christ the apocalyptic *idea* of a common resurrection is transformed to the Christian *hope* in the resurrection. Thus the New Testament proclaims Jesus not only as "the first to rise from the dead" (Acts 26:23), "the beginning, the firstborn from the dead" (Col. 1:18), but also as the one in whom we shall be united "in a resurrection like his," that we too "might walk in newness of life" (Rom. 6:4-5). And we trust in God who "raised the Lord and will also raise us by his power" (1 Cor. 6:14). Apocalyptic ideas provide the background material for a full understanding of the implications of Christ's resurrection; still our hope in a resurrection is not based on these ideas but depends solely on Christ's resurrection.

d. Resurrection of the Body

The hope for our resurrection is expressed in the Apostles' Creed with the phrase that we believe "in the resurrection of the body." Though the question already arises here as to what kind of body this will be, the issue gets more confusing when we notice that in the original Greek and Latin texts the word for body actually denotes flesh *(sarx* or *caro)*. Of course, in a biblicistic manner we could claim that the Apostles' Creed contradicts the Bible where Paul states: "flesh and blood cannot inherit the kingdom of God, nor does the perishable inherit the imperishable" (1 Cor. 15:50).

If we conceive of our resurrection in analogy to a strictly biological revivification, similar to what the biblical witnesses tell us about the young man in the village of Nain (Luke 7:15) and about Lazarus (John 11:44), we would encounter many additional problems.[116] First, there is

---

116. Pannenberg, *Jesus — God and Man*, 77, rightly asserts that these stories speak only of a *"temporary* return of a dead person" into *this* life.

the issue of the integrity of the body. The natural decay of the body means that after biological death our body becomes so much part of the whole web of life that our body can no longer be materially reconstituted without destroying other forms of life into which it has been integrated. Second, it would not be desirable to be resurrected with all the weaknesses and deformities that we might presently have on account of age or disease. To receive a body in analogy to our own present body would actually mean a continuation of the limitations and tensions to which we are now subjected. Third, our resurrection would not be analogous to Christ's resurrection, for he was resurrected as and into a new creation with different possibilities than those he possessed before. When the early church decided to include in the Apostles' Creed the belief in the resurrection of the "flesh," it did not intend to create these problems. Rather it was trying to protect itself against the idea that the resurrection is only a Docetic, spiritualistic resurrection in Greek or gnostic fashion. Not the soul or some other divine spark in us lives on in eternity, but we ourselves are resurrected. Such a resurrection is expressed as a bodily resurrection.

In colloquial Greek *sarx* did not just mean flesh, but it could also mean body. A bodily existence was thus conceived of as a real existence, "as distinct from one seen only in a dream" or as an image.[117] Here lies for us today the importance of the belief in the resurrection of the body. Resurrection is not a paranormal occurrence in analogy to occult phenomena or to hallucinations; it is a reality that involves our whole being. But what does "a reality that involves our whole being" mean? First of all, it means that death is not our final destiny. The resurrection which takes place at the parousia of the Lord includes everybody, with no exceptions. This is true for those who are accepted into the immediacy of God and for those who are banned from it.

It is simply too easy to say that the eternal judgment coincides with physical death and that those who are excluded from eternal joy will not be resurrected.[118] There is no escape from God because God, who is not confined to this life, is on both sides of death. Otherwise the last judgment

---

117. So Eduard Schweizer, "sarx," in *TDNT*, 7:100-101.

118. Joseph E. Kokjohn, "A Hell of a Question," *Commonweal* 93 (January 15, 1971): 370, seems to imply this when he suggests that the unjust person's moral catastrophe "is one of nonexistence, not only the isolation from other people and God, but the utter alienation from all forms of life."

would simply be God's acceptance of everybody (who is resurrected). Such a belief, of course, would run counter to the emphasis on the final judgment of humanity (cf. the parables of the kingdom, esp. Matt. 13). We must also affirm that this universal resurrection will be a resurrection in personal identity or one that "involves the whole being." If the one who is resurrected is not the one who died previously, redemption and damnation would be meaningless. It would involve our existence only as much as the news does that someone we do not know has just inherited a million dollars. But resurrection means that for me, as one who is bound to die, God will provide a future above and beyond death. Just as we cannot say that part of my ego will go in this direction and part in the other, we cannot say that only part of me will be resurrected.

The question of whether there will be different stages of resurrection seems almost speculative. The seriousness of the decision we have to make in being confronted with the gospel and the seriousness of the final judgment would suggest that all will be resurrected to an immortal state, since their future will be never ending. Apocalyptic ideas that the dead will first be resurrected in an unchanged way (so that they can be recognized), and that those who will be condemned and those who will be accepted will then be changed the way they deserve (cf. *2 Bar.* 50–51), seem to lie beyond the scope of the New Testament. When Paul, for instance, suggested that the dead will be raised imperishable, and we will be changed (1 Cor. 15:52b), he expected that he would still be alive when Christ returned, whereupon he together with other Christians would be transformed and participate in the new creation. Furthermore, even in mentioning the dead, he seemed to talk only about deceased Christians and not about the dead in general.[119] If we would suggest first a universal resurrection, then a final judgment, and then the respective transformation of the accepted and the rejected, we would be talking in terms of a sequential progression and introduce the concept of time, which is simply no longer applicable to anything beyond death.

Of much more importance is the question of what we can look forward to when we hope and believe in the resurrection of the body. To conclude from passages such as "in the resurrection they neither marry nor are given in marriage, but are like angels in heaven" (Matt. 22:30) that the state of the resurrection is an asexual state, is a gross miscon-

---

119. Cf. Conzelmann, 289-91, in his exegesis of 1 Cor. 15:50-58.

ception and indicates the desire for a travelogue eschatology. Such imagery indicates the same thing Paul points out when he says the mortal cannot inherit the immortal, nor the perishable the imperishable. Resurrection does not indicate a continuation of our present life, not even on a different level. Our whole life, including the antigodly desires to which it succumbs, must perish. This "otherness" of the resurrection makes it so difficult to talk about. Even Paul talks about the resurrection by negating our present conditions. Perishable and imperishable, dishonor and glory, physical and spiritual, weakness and power — these are some of the antitheses he uses (1 Cor. 15:42-54). These antitheses explain why resurrection is "a reality that involves the whole being." Nothing is exempt from this fundamental change.

If this change is so fundamental that we no longer live in dishonor, that we are no longer limited by the physical world and confronted with death, if we no longer age and are distinguished by certain sexual behavior patterns, is not the "I" who will be resurrected so different from the "I" who died that we shall face a tremendous identity crisis? Indeed, we would immensely underestimate the otherness of the resurrection if we held the idea that the resurrection does not imply a radical change in identity and personality. After all, we are looking forward to a *new* creation. Even now our personality undergoes steady changes when we advance from childhood to adolescence, maturity, and old age. Sometimes these changes cause considerable identity crises. But each time we remain the same person. So we need not be afraid that we would miss ourselves when we are received into God's new world.

e. "Between" Death and Resurrection

Realizing that death terminates our individual lives and that resurrection is our destination beyond death, the question emerges as to what happens "between" death and resurrection. We found the ideas of a purgatory and a continuance of life through an immortal soul to be highly dubious. We observe, however, that not everybody dies at the same time, and that death does not coincide with the universal resurrection we hope for. What is our destiny "between" our death and the common resurrection in which we will participate? Or does each person enjoy an individual resurrection?

Already Paul encountered this uncertainty when people asked about the destiny of those who had already died. Paul did not comfort them in their anxiety by elaborating on the ideas of immortality, reincarnation, or purgatory, ideas which were certainly known to them. He tried to point out to them that in relation to God there is no preferred state. It does not matter whether we are still alive once the Lord returns, or whether we have been dead a long time. Our destiny will find its completion in our encounter with the returning Lord (1 Thess. 4:15; 1 Cor. 15:25). Therefore it is neither necessary nor legitimate to speculate on an intermediate state between death and resurrection. This becomes especially evident when we consider that time is only a this-worldly entity.[120]

Time as a This-Worldly Entity

Already Augustine emphasized that time is an indication of transitoriness and is inextricably connected with this world. Time always needs something to pass by, because only through changes in objects can there be time. Thus it is pointless to talk in a literal way about "the time before the creation" of this world. "There would have been no time, if there had been no creation to bring in movement and change."[121] In a similar manner Martin Luther asserted that in the beginning there was nothing except God — no time, no objects, and no space.[122] And in his picturesque and drastic manner, quoting from Augustine, he tells those curious questioners who want to know what God did "before" he cre-

---

120. This has been elaborated very clearly by Pierre Benoit, "Resurrection: At the End of Time or Immediately after Death," in *Immortality and Resurrection,* esp. 112-14. He affirms that we are already here united in the Holy Spirit with the body of the risen Lord in a union that will not be interrupted by death. Thus there is no continuance through an immortal soul, but through the already initiated union with Christ. The "between" between death and consummation is relativized by the fact that our time is of a different nature than the time of the "future" or "new" or "higher" world.

121. Augustine, *The City of God* 11.6. Cf. also Augustine, *De Genesi; Contra Manichaeos libri duo* 2.3, in Migne, *PL,* 34:174-75, where he says: "God also made time: therefore before he made time, there was no time. And we cannot say that there was any time prior to God having made something."

122. Cf. Martin Luther, in *Genesin Declamationes* (1527), in WA, 24:24.8-9, in his comments on Gen. 1:1.

ated heaven and earth that God "was making hell ready for those who pry into these deep questions!"[123]

Concerning God, Luther asserts, one has to do away with time. Only for us is there time and hours, whereas for God everything occurs in the eternal now. This means that God is cotemporal to all possible and actual time constellations. God, who created the world and with it time and transitoriness, is not subject to change, but is equally present in each possible and actual change. In other words, past, present, and future are equally present before God. Time is an order of God for his creation (cf. Ps. 102:25-27 and Heb. 1:10-12). Thus we are always experiencing certain successions of time and cannot accomplish things properly unless it is the right time to do them. Since we are time-bound, we are not in command of time but subject to it.[124]

Immanuel Kant, in his *Critique of Pure Reason*, stresses the person-centeredness of time so much that he declared it to be an anthropological phenomenon. Like space, time is not an "empty box" into which our observation places certain objects, but time and space are, for us, necessary conceptual tools with which we perceive these objects. Kant recognized that time and space are not independent entities but exist only when relating certain objects to each other.

Finally, Albert Einstein (1879-1955), in his special theory of relativity (1905), came to the scientific conclusion that space and time are related not only to each other but also to matter. Each of these three entities necessitates the others, and all three depend on the observer. Einstein was unable to assert with Kant that time and space are just conceptual tools. Rather, more like Augustine, he affirmed that time does not make sense apart from something by which it can flow. But he also showed, much like Kant had suggested, that time, space, and matter are not independent entities. How space, time, and matter appear always depends on the correlating system, that is, on the standpoint of the observer.[125] Thus time can stand almost still or disappear rapidly, and mat-

123. Martin Luther, *Lectures on Genesis: Chapters 1–5*, in *LW*, 1:10, in his exegesis of Gen. 1:2, and Augustine, *Confessions* 11.12, in *FaCh*, 21:341.

124. Cf. Martin Luther, *Vorlesungen über den Prediger Salomo* (1526), in WA, 20:58.24-31, in his comments on Eccles. 3:1; cf. also the excellent treatment of Luther's idea of appointed *time (Stündelein)* by Gustav Wingren, *Luther — On Vocation*, trans. C. C. Rasmussen (Philadelphia: Muhlenberg, 1957), 213-34.

125. Cf. Werner Heisenberg, *Physics and Philosophy: The Revolution in Modern Science*

ter and space can shrink or increase accordingly. In affirming the inseparable unity of space, time, and matter, Einstein showed that time, as the indicator of our transitoriness, can only be conceptualized in the context of space and matter. This means that time is an inadequate category to describe anything beyond this material and space-bound world. When we talk about the state "between" death and resurrection and do not just talk about the biological decay of the physical body, then the category of time as denoting transitoriness is inadequate. Rather we must talk about the end or fulfillment of time or about eternity.

The Eternity of God as Fulfillment of Time

In talking about eternity we have to refrain from equating it with infinity, especially in its scientific sense. When used theologically, eternity denotes the dimension of God, and in talking about it we encounter the same difficulties as in talking about God. In the Bible, for instance, eternity is often anthropomorphically conceived as never-ending time.[126] Even for us sophisticated people of the twenty-first century, it is difficult to envision eternity as anything other than "endless time." Yet when the Bible talks about the eternity of God, it is also aware that this is not the same as time stretched out to such an extent that it does not have boundaries.[127]

In the Bible eternity is generally understood as belonging to God in contrast to the time of our world, which is limited by the creation in the beginning and by the end. In Greek philosophy, however, eternity is usually understood as timelessness, a state where there is no day, no month, no year. Plato, in his *Timaeus,* thinks of eternity as an ideal state,

---

(New York: Harper, 1958), 114-16, who gives a very good description of Einstein's theory and its implications.

126. Cf. Oscar Cullmann, *Christ and Time: The Primitive Christian Conception of Time and History,* trans. F. V. Filson (London: SCM, 1962), 63, who, however, claims that eternity can and must be expressed "in terms of endless time." We wonder if this is really the only way to talk adequately about eternity.

127. In the earlier writings of the Old Testament, however, the eternity of God is described with the metaphor "Everlasting God" (Gen. 21:33), which implies a conception of time "which extends forward and backward without end" (so von Rad, 237, in his exegesis of Gen. 21:33).

of which time is only a faint copy.[128] The Bible knows about the infinite qualitative difference between time and God's eternity too, since it knows that creation and its creator are fundamentally different. But it does not dissociate God's eternity from time. To envision the eternity of God as some kind of nirvana, where time is overcome and dissolved, would be impossible for biblical thinking. Not even the Greek position of a static relationship between time and eternity would be sufficient. Even the idea that each moment is equidistant from eternity is closer to a Platonic time-eternity dichotomy than to the biblical religion. The Bible proclaims not an eternal God up there but a living God who gives time its direction.

In Christian understanding, time is on its way from creation via redemption to perfection. Oscar Cullmann has rightly called Christ the midpoint of time, since he is God's visible sign pointing out the direction in which this time-bound world moves. To determine the direction of time is especially important in coming from a physical understanding of time. According to science, time is bound to matter; it is not directed by itself but receives its direction only from the correlating system of the observer. What happens, however, if we as observers have nothing absolute by which to orient ourselves, except the scientific doomsday version of an eventual rundown of our universe?[129] Here Christ provides us with a point of orientation beyond the confines of our physical world.

Dialectic theology, initiated by Kierkegaard's insistence on the qualitative difference between God and humanity and modified by Moltmann's christocentric future-directedness of history, has enabled us to rediscover the lost direction of our time-bound world. If time is on its way toward perfection, we can envision eternity neither as endless, infinite time nor as the end of time in the sense of continuous rest or quiescence. Eternity is rather the fulfillment of time in perfection. This means that all the life-impairing effects of time will be overcome. Tran-

128. Plato, *Timaeus* 37d, in Plato, *The Complete Works*, 1241; cf. also Cullmann, *Christ and Time*, 61-62; and Hermann Sasse, "aion," in *TDNT*, 1:197-98, who refers to Plato's *Timaeus*.

129. The relevance of such a christocentric worldview in an age dominated by science has been demonstrated very eloquently by Teilhard de Chardin. However, by taking the incarnation of Christ as the focal point, instead of the cross and resurrection, he arrives at an evolutionary type of eschatology.

sition, suffering, decay, and death are all inextricably connected with temporality and change.[130] God, who is Lord of life and death and who does not want the death of the wicked but rather that the wicked be saved and live, can give us hope for the perfection of time and for eternity.

Especially in the later parts of the Old Testament, the eternity of God is asserted to demonstrate his power to bring about salvation.

> The LORD is the everlasting God,
>   the Creator of the ends of the earth.
> He does not faint or grow weary;
>   his understanding is unsearchable. . . .
> . . . those who wait for the LORD
>   shall renew their strength.
>
> (Isa. 40:28, 31)[131]

The one who created the world provides its direction and completion since he is eternal. His eternal being extends beyond the time of the world. God is from eternity to eternity, and the psalmist confesses to him:

> The heavens are yours, the earth also is yours;
>   the world and all that is in it — you have founded them.
>
> (Ps. 89:11)

He was before the world was created, and when heaven and earth will have disappeared he still is.

> Long ago you laid the foundation of the earth,
>   and the heavens are the work of your hands.
> They will perish, but you endure. . . .
> . . . you are the same, and your years have no end. (Ps. 102:25-27)

It is not by chance that the writer of Hebrews quotes these verses and transfers them to Jesus (Heb. 1:10-12). Already John confesses that Jesus Christ was "before the foundation of the world" (John 17:24). Jesus

130. This has been pointed out especially well by Karl Heim in his book *The World — Its Creation and Consummation,* trans. R. Smith (Philadelphia: Muhlenberg, 1962).

131. Cf. Sasse, 1:201, to the Old Testament concept of time.

Christ is coeternal with God, he is before and after the aeons of the world. Only because he is coeternal with God can he give time its direction and signify through his first coming the turning point between this aeon and the coming aeon. In Jesus' coming and especially in his resurrection the future has already started. Christians therefore are no longer just waiting for the future, but they live in anticipation of the future, since in Christ the future has occurred already in proleptic anticipation.[132]

Eternity as the sphere of God (and of Christ) thus endows time with meaning and direction. In pointing to the fulfillment of time, eternity does not indicate a final monotony, but active, unrestrained, and unlimited participation in the new world in full harmony with the living God. But we have not yet addressed the question of when this fulfillment will be reached, whether at death or at some "time" after.

Death as Finality and Transition

The Bible does not seem to give us a clear answer to the question of when the fulfillment is reached. Death seems to be depicted, at times, as leading to a final state, and at other times, to a transitory state. In the New Testament the dead are referred to as those who are asleep or those who have fallen asleep (1 Cor. 15:18; Luke 8:52; 2 Pet. 3:4). They will sleep until Judgment Day, and then they will be resurrected. This would imply that they have not reached the final goal, heaven or hell, but are still waiting for it.

Other passages in the New Testament, however, indicate that with death some kind of finality is already reached. For instance, when Jesus tells the parable of the rich man and Lazarus, he mentions that both found their (preliminary) destinations, Abraham's bosom and Hades, immediately after they died (Luke 16:19-31). And Jesus also promised the one criminal on the cross: "Today you will be with me in Paradise" (Luke 23:43).

In the Gospel of John we can almost notice an attempt to bridge the obvious dichotomy between transition and finality. We hear Jesus say: "Very truly, I tell you, the hour is coming, and is now here, when the

---

132. Cf. Cullmann, *Christ and Time*, 81-83; cf. also the emphasis on the proleptic aspect of the Christ event by Pannenberg in *Revelation as History*, 139-41.

dead will hear the voice of the Son of God, and those who hear will live," and then, almost in the same breath, the comment is made: "for the hour is coming when all who are in their graves will hear his voice and will come out — those who have done good, to the resurrection of life, and those who have done evil, to the resurrection of condemnation" (John 5:25, 28-29).

The writers of the New Testament knew very well that the response to the confrontation with Jesus and his message determines the final outcome: acceptance or rejection by God. They also were realistic enough not to speculate that those who lived their lives in accordance with the incarnate word of God would at one point leave this life and immediately enter into a kind of visible heaven. They knew that at the end of this earthly life everyone had to die. Thus when they assumed that at death one fell into a sleep, we should not simply see this as an attempt to reconcile Jesus' decisive message of the immediacy of the eschaton with the idea of a sleep of the dead.[133] Rather they tried to maintain both finality and transition. They encountered in Jesus Christ God's final word and action, which allowed them to participate proleptically in the new creation, and they observed in death a cessation of this proleptic participation which pointed to something beyond death. Whether finality or transition, one thing was clear to them: there is no vacuum after death.

Martin Luther went along similar lines as the New Testament.[134] He was convinced that an intermediate state after death could not be a neutral state but would already presuppose our acceptance or rejection by God. Yet it would not be a final state, since this would preempt the fulfillment and perfection of the resurrection. Luther often "described" this state as a deep sleep without dreams, without any consciousness and feelings. He confessed that he often had tried to observe himself when he fell asleep, but he never succeeded. He remembered that he was awake, and then, suddenly, he woke up again. So it is with death: "In a similar way as one does not know how it happens that one falls asleep, and suddenly morning approaches when one awakes, so we will suddenly be resurrected

---

133. Cf. Rudolf Bultmann, *The Gospel of John: A Commentary*, trans. G. R. Beasley-Murray et al. (Philadelphia: Westminster, 1971), 257-58, in his exegesis of John 5:24-28, where he seems to imply this idea.

134. Cf. Althaus, *Die letzten Dinge*, 146-47.

at the Last Day, not knowing how we have come into death and through death."[135] And on another occasion he says: "We shall sleep until he comes and knocks at the tomb and says: 'Dr. Martin, get up!' Then in one moment, I will get up and I will rejoice with him in eternity."[136]

Actually, he confesses, we do not know much about this state between death and resurrection. Perhaps those who will be rejected will already suffer, and perhaps those who will be accepted will have a foretaste of the eternal joy they are waiting for and will listen to God's discourses with the angels. Endowed with a sound and natural curiosity, Luther would, of course, have liked to find out where and how we exist between death and resurrection. But he realized that in staying as close as possible to God's self-disclosure as reflected by the biblical witnesses, there is not much we can say about this state.

This restraint shows that Luther differed decisively from the tradition out of which he came. The church, for instance, had rejected the notion, once adopted in some sermons by Pope John XXII (1249-1334), that the human soul sleeps after death and does not enjoy the beatific vision until Judgment Day. In an edict of 1336, Benedict XII (the successor to John XXII) declared that the souls of the just already enjoy the beatific vision.[137] This face-to-face vision of the divine essence and the resulting enjoyment exist continuously "and will continue even up to the last judgment and from then even unto eternity." The souls of those, however, "who depart in actual mortal sin immediately after death descend to hell where they are tortured by infernal punishments, [but] nevertheless on the day of judgment all men with their bodies will make themselves ready to render an account of their own deeds before the tribunal of Christ."

It would surely be one-sided to absolutize a passage such as Revelation 6:9 and conclude that the souls of the deceased who were faithful will remain under the altar of God until Judgment Day and are not yet allowed to see God face-to-face. But does it not border on a travelogue eschatology to define our destiny between death and resurrection as beatific vision or infernal punishment? Moreover, this notion would make

135. Martin Luther, *Fastenpostille* (1525), in WA, 17/2:235.17-20, in a sermon on John 8:46-59.

136. Martin Luther, *Predigten des Jahres 1533*, in WA, 37:151.8-10, in a sermon on Luke 7:11ff. (September 28, 1533).

137. For the following, cf. "The Beatific Vision of God and the Last Days," pars. 530-31, in Denzinger, 197-98.

the final judgment into a reaffirmation of what had happened already in death, and thus no destinies will be changed. The New Testament is much more reluctant to settle for a definite either-or of what happens to us between death and resurrection. This ambivalence, or even disparity, within the New Testament itself reflects the difficulty we encounter when we attempt to conceptually "define" this state between death and resurrection.

Contemporary Roman Catholic theologians are more open at this point. They are aware that the dogmatic definitions of the church rightly wanted to safeguard the insight that death is the final end only of this life but not of human life altogether. Since the church refrained from defining how to talk about what results from death, various conceptualizations are available to us. Michael Schmaus (1897-1993), for instance, suggests two options:[138]

1. The more traditional option of the immortality of a spiritual soul which will continue to exist beyond death. He concedes that this option tends to devalue the significance of the resurrection. This option, however, has gained increased attention as a result of a publication of the Congregation for the Doctrine of the Faith: "Letter on Certain Questions in Eschatology" (May 17, 1979). This publication states: "The church maintains a continuation of the subsistence of a spiritual element after death which is endowed with conscience and will so that the 'I of the human being' continues to exist, though of course in the intermediate it lacks its full corporeality. To signify this element, the church uses the term 'soul' which is customarily used in Holy Scripture and in tradition."[139] Cardinal Ratzinger fully endorses this writing, since he sees in Roman Catholic theology a dissolution of the concept of the soul, and therefore also a threat to the concept of an intermediate state.[140]

138. Cf. Michael Schmaus, *Der Glaube der Kirche,* 2 vols. (Munich: Hueber, 1969-70), 2:744-46 and 773-75.
139. "Schreiben der Kongregation für die Glaubenslehre zu einigen Fragen der Eschatologie vom 17. Mai 1979," *Internationale katholische Zeitschrift "Communio"* 9 (1980): 224-25.
140. Cf. Joseph Ratzinger, "Zwischen Tod und Auferstehung: Eine Erklärung der Glaubenskongregation zu Fragen der Eschatologie," *Internationale katholische Zeitschrift "Communio"* 9 (1980): 212-13, and also reprinted in Ratzinger, *Eschatology,* 245.

2. The other option (that Schmaus favors) concludes that at death humanity enters into completion, and therefore in death occurs a change to a new life. Of course, he notes that this concept then faces the issue of reconciling many individual "resurrections" (at death) with the final universal resurrection. This second option seems to be on a collision course with the statement of the Congregation for the Doctrine of Faith. This statement, however, does not seem to be without problems, since the remark that the "I of the human being," which survives death, "in the intermediate time it lacks its full corporeality" was not contained in the original writing, but was added only a few months later.[141] This would indicate that perhaps it was initially proposed that the human person had found its completion in death and did not have for some "time" a diminished existence. Indeed, such fulfillment in death toward a resurrection is the preferred option of many Roman Catholic theologians.

But is it even necessary to assume a distinction or even tension between an individual resurrection and the final universal resurrection, as Schmaus surmises? First, we remember that our hope is not directed to a state between death and resurrection; we hope and believe in "the resurrection of the body and life everlasting."[142] Second, we realize that death is not only the border of this life but the border of time. Beyond death there is no diminishing, aging, or increasing; there is only God's eternal presence. Of course, we see people encountering their own individual death at different points in time and we know that the last judgment, which provides the end of all possible and actual time, does not coincide with these different points in time. Otherwise there would be an individualized last judgment, occurring at many different points, whenever someone departs from this life. "The concept of an intermediate state of the soul is the attempt to reconcile and harmonize the individual eschatological completion with the collective completion (of a still outstanding general resurrection in time)."[143]

141. For details, Gisbert Greshake, "Zum Römischen Lehrschreiben über die Eschatologie" (May 17, 1979), in Gisbert Greshake and Gerhard Lohfink, *Naherwartung — Auferstehung — Unsterblichkeit: Untersuchungen zur christlichen Eschatologie* (Freiburg: Herder, 1982), 190. This publication is representative of this second option.
142. For the following cf. Althaus, *Die letzten Dinge*, 158-59.
143. Hans Kessler, "Die Auferstehung Jesu Christi und unsere Auferstehung," in

As people cross the borderline of time at different points and leave our chronological time, it is legitimate to use New Testament imagery and say that the dead "sleep" until Judgment Day. But we also know that in God all the different points of time coincide. For God there is no sooner or later, not even a too late. In God's eternal presence there is no distinction between past, present, and future. This distinction exists only for us as time-bound creatures, not for the creator. In death we cross the borderline of time and encounter God's eternal presence. We are then coeternal not only with God but also with all human creatures. Regardless of when we cross this line, we will appear on the "other side" at the "same moment" as everyone else. Thus the confrontation with God in death will result in the eternal judgment. This is not to be understood as an individualized act, because together with everyone else we will encounter God's eternal presence.

As anything between death and resurrection is beyond space and time, we can only talk about the "transitory state" in approximations. When we call it a state of "bodiless sleep," this shows very drastically the limits of our conceptual tools. A "bodiless sleep" is an obvious contradiction, since we cannot conceive of sleep without thinking about a body. Yet in order to express that death and resurrection are not the same, and in order to attempt to relate our present experiences to the future we hope for, we have to resort to such inadequate, though necessary, concepts.

Excursus: Reincarnation and Transmigration of the Soul

Before we settle too quickly for the resurrection as *the* alternative to some kind of immortality, we dare not neglect reincarnation. According to recent surveys, at least one out of four North Americans and western Europeans believes in reincarnation of some kind. The amazing fact is that this is not simply a tenet of young unchurched people, but an even larger number of churchgoers hold this belief, and among them, people sixty-

---

Hoffnung über den Tod hinaus, ed. Josef Pfammatter and Eduard Christen (Zürich: Benziger, 1990), 81-82, who, however, observes that in so doing, conceptual logic systematizes and brings into temporal sequence that which, in the logic of content, should be related to each other as to their content only. This means the metaphors are turned into nonnegotiable concepts.

five years old and older.[144] The attraction of the idea seems to lie first in the increased religious emancipation of the people. It is no longer the denominational tradition or the one Christian faith that provides trustworthy guidance, but many people feel mature enough to explore "the full range of options." There reincarnation has the advantage of newness over against the more traditional belief in resurrection. There is also the rediscovery of meditation, of spirituality and interiorization that make use of Asian meditation practices and experiences and thereby encounter the supposedly Asian idea of reincarnation.[145] One should also not forget the increased interest in the occult and paranormal phenomena as additional stimuli to probe the notion of reincarnation.[146] Consequently the number of people who believe that they have already passed through an earlier life and who will have another life on earth (reincarnation), or who at least hope that their soul will enjoy further life cycles (migration of the soul), continues to increase.

The philosopher of religion John H. Hick proposes, in a fascinating way, reincarnation as a possible par-eschatology which leads to a final eschatological completion. Hick is convinced that "the persisting self-conscious ego will continue to exist after bodily death. We shall not however, in most cases, attain immediately to the final 'heavenly' state. Only those whom the religions call saints or buddhas or arhats or *jivanmuktas* have fulfilled the purpose of temporal existence, which is the gradual creation of perfected persons — their perfection consisting . . . in a self-transcending state beyond separate ego-existence. But those of us who die without having attained our perfection continue further in time as distinct egos."[147] The number of those reincarnations as distinct egos is limited for the individual. It can mean hundreds of new lives, or in the best case, only one additional life cycle.

---

144. Cf. Johannes Mischo, "Empirische Reinkarnationsforschung aus sozial-psychologischer und parapsychologischer Sicht," in *Reinkarnation oder Auferstehung: Konsequenzen für das Leben*, ed. Hermann Kochanek (Freiburg: Herder, 1992), 160, who refers to a Gallup survey between 1978 and 1982 (Gallup Poll: European Values [London, 1983]).

145. So Gisbert Greshake, *Gottes Heil — Glück des Menschen: Theologische Perspektiven* (Freiburg: Herder, 1983), 227.

146. To this whole issue, cf. Schwarz, *Beyond the Gates of Death*, where I deal extensively with the issue of the paranormal and reincarnation phenomena (esp. 55-110).

147. John Hick, *Death and Eternal Life* (New York: Harper, 1976), 399.

The goal of these embodiments is increasing growth in which the personal individuality is perfected by transcending it. "The distinction between the self as ego and the self as person suggests that as the human individual becomes perfected he becomes more and more person and less and less an ego."[148] Hick sees in the triune conception of God as three persons in one and one in three an important model for a community so intimate and harmonious as to constitute a single corporate person. The tensions and differences between the ego have disappeared, and perfect unity and harmony are attained. To attain this corporate person, Hick merges together different conceptualities of Eastern and Western religiosity, such as karma, nirvana, purgatory, and resurrection.

John B. Cobb seems to think along similar lines as Hick when he writes: "The encounter with Buddhism may prove an essential step for the West to free itself from its attachment to individualized personal existence as a final good."[149] He sees all our images of hope converging toward "a transcendence of separating individuality in a fuller community with other people and with all things. In this community the tensions between self and Christ decline, and in a final consummation they would disappear."[150] Indeed, while in the West there is an emphasis on differences even to the point of an ontological pluralism, Eastern religiosity prefers a connectedness and unity even to the point of monism.[151]

Before we quickly divide between an Eastern and Western way of thinking, we should note that the idea of further life cycles after death has never been restricted to one geographical area. It has been widespread and was tremendously influential. Plato and the pre-Socratics knew about it, and we encounter it in Roman religiosity, in Egypt of antiquity, and among the Canaanites neighboring Israel. Even the church fathers, such as Tertullian and Ambrose, have taken issue with this kind of thinking. Tertullian, in his usual eloquent manner, refuted the allegation that Jesus condoned reincarnation in his reference to the coming of Elijah (Mark 9:11-13). Tertullian's argument, brought forth nearly 1,800 years ago, is carefully worded and still persuasive today:

148. Hick, 459-60.
149. John B. Cobb, Jr., *Christ in a Pluralistic Age* (Philadelphia: Westminster, 1975), 220.
150. Cobb, 258.
151. Cf. Heinrich Beck, *Reinkarnation oder Auferstehung: Ein Widerspruch?* (Innsbruck: Resch, 1988), 23.

Heretics . . . seize with especial avidity the example of Elias, whom they assume to have been so reproduced in John (the Baptist) as to make our Lord's statement sponsor for their theory of transmigration, when He said, "Elias is come already, and they knew him not;" and again, in another passage, "And if ye will receive it, this is Elias, which was for to come." Well, then, was it really in a Pythagorean sense that the Jews approached John with the inquiry, "Art thou Elias?" and not rather in the sense of the divine prediction, "Behold, I will send you Elijah" the Tisbite? The fact, however, is, that their metempsychosis, or transmigration theory, signifies the recall of the soul which had died long before, and its return to some other body. But Elias is to come again, not after quitting life (in the way of dying), but after his translation (or removal without dying); not for the purpose of being restored to the body, from which he had not departed, but for the purpose of revisiting the world from which he was translated; not by way of resuming a life which he had laid aside, but of fulfilling prophecy, — really and truly the same man, both in respect of his name and designation, as well as of his unchanged humanity.[152]

Tertullian does not concede a reincarnation or an actual return of Elijah, but he affirms that John the Baptist continued Elijah's work by acting in his spirit and power. Important for him is that the Bible and Jesus do not advocate the idea of reincarnation. Most Christian theologians from the earliest time on were acquainted with the idea of reincarnation, since it was indeed a widespread notion, but they refuted it in favor of the belief in the resurrection.

Nevertheless, there are important commonalities between the Christian faith and the idea of reincarnation. Both emphasize that human existence does not come to an end with death. Furthermore, the Judeo-Christian faith knows about God's animating spirit, which is active in every living being, including humanity, and makes the difference between life and death. It is plausible that this divine "power of animation" does not simply disappear at death, but, in analogy to the idea of a migration of the soul, causes new life to emerge and to exist. But in the Judeo-Christian tradition this life-giving power is strictly dependent on God, while a soul which migrates from one life to another has a much more independent function and needs no externally active divine power.

152. Tertullian, *Treatise on the Soul* 35, in *ANF,* 3:216-17.

Karl Rahner and others have also pointed out that the Roman Catholic doctrine of purgatory has some commonalities with the idea of reincarnation, since both strive for a perfection of our present life beyond death, so that we become more like the one from whom we come and to whom we are going. The underlying conviction is that in our present life there are many things which should not have happened. We need some kind of purification which must be attained beyond this life. We could even say that the common ground for both purgatory and reincarnation is a deterministic karma concept: the difference between what we have done in this life and what we should have done is not simply annihilated in death, but stays with us. Yet according to Roman Catholic teaching, a human person is not pushed into a second life to make up for what he or she has missed in the first life: "even this purification is to be seen totally under the 'principle of grace.'"[153]

While the Christian faith does not belittle the idea that we are personally responsible for our own lives, salvation provided through Jesus Christ on the cross pertains to the whole of human existence and even, according to Roman Catholic teaching, to existence in purgatory. Paul therefore emphasizes that through Christ's death and resurrection in baptism, we have completely died to our old existence and are resurrected to new life. In its deliberations about the possibility of a second penance, the early church correctly realized that the efficacy of the baptismal cleansing does not only pertain to the former human being before baptism, but, through the proclamation of forgiveness which is received by faith, the baptismal cleansing continuously becomes a new reality for us.

With these remarks we have touched upon a basic difference between reincarnation and the Christian hope in the resurrection: though reincarnation can still mean that through the goodness of the godhead we are granted a new existence, the ultimate success of these cycles depends on us. If we conduct our lives appropriately, we can attain the ultimate goal, unity with the godhead or entering nirvana. If this does not occur, we must go through another cycle, attempting to do better this time. The actual efficacious power for salvation rests in the individual. This is certainly one of the reasons why Buddha taught his followers in so many ways how to live in peace and harmony with other people and

153. So Greshake, *Gottes Heil*, 241.

with the world. Essentially we work out our salvation. The universe is understood as some kind of school in which we must learn our lessons. Such a view, of course, is amenable to a society that is geared toward success. We can earn our salvation and do not need anything from anyone.[154] The underlying premise, however, is not work-righteousness but a comprehensive evolution toward perfection.

In the belief in resurrection, however, God is seen as the only really active component. The difference between our actual life and the promised goal can never be bridged by ourselves. If there is any possibility at all of reaching that goal, it can only be done by the help of God, who provides us with this new life in the resurrection. A Christian who realizes this totally undeserved hope will not conduct himself or herself in an ethically indifferent or irresponsible way. Being thankful for the undeserved acceptance through God, he or she will already attempt in this life to realize something of the goal promised for the future completion. When we remember the limited range of human possibilities, then the working out of our own salvation borders on self-deception. We can and should make this place a better place to live. For this we also should be thankful for the insights of Buddha and his followers. Yet all earthly hope stays within the limit that the psalmist soberingly enunciates when he said that our days "are soon gone" (Ps. 90:10).

We should also remind ourselves that the modern Western notion of reincarnation is based on the optimistic idea of progressive evolution. For many people the idea of reincarnation is a new chance to live a better life than the present messy condition in which they exist. Yet, according to Hinduism or Buddhism, every new migration of the soul toward final purification and completion is something to be dreaded. It is a curse, and one prays and does everything possible to come to the end of these cycles. Another life is not desired, but rather the release from all these lives is, since life also means embodiment and therefore being drawn into the material and ultimately inferior environment. For the Christian, however, the new life to come is the enjoyment of a new and uncorruptible body unhindered by the limitations of any earthly existence.

154. Jörg Wichmann, "Zur Veränderung des Reinkarnationsglaubens in der westlichen Kultur und Esoterik," in *Reinkarnation oder Auferstehung: Konsequenzen für das Leben,* ed. Hermann Kochanek (Freiburg i. Br.: Herder, 1992), 189, has pointed out the attractiveness of reincarnation for modern society.

Yet, is not reincarnation much more plausible than resurrection? Attempts have been made to scientifically prove the existence of several cycles of life through recall of earlier lives. This often results in surprising and provable knowledge of details from a distant past. In many cases these recollections of persons, items, and even languages of an "earlier life" could not have been learned later or acquired in some way or other. The Canadian-born psychiatrist Ian Stevenson (b. 1918) has extensively researched these phenomena. Though he personally tends more toward the idea of a survival of human personality after death, he admits that these phenomena do not provide us with a strict proof of reincarnation. They could be interpreted as "super-extrasensory perception."[155] This means that somebody has an extraordinary endowment for paranormal cognition and therefore can get in touch with details and even with languages that existed long ago. Taking all things in consideration, we must conclude that the idea of reincarnation is not in any way better proven empirically than the Christian faith in the resurrection.

155. Ian Stevenson, *Xenoglossy* (Charlottesville: University of Virginia Press, 1973), 87-88. Cf. also his more recent publication, *Unlearned Language: New Studies in Xenoglossy* (Charlottesville: University of Virginia Press, 1984), where he is more hesitant in his conclusions with regard to reincarnation and talks about the authentic cases of responsive xenoglossy providing "important evidence for the survival of human personality after physical death" (158).

6. Controversial Areas
of Eschatological Hopes

When we mention here four problem areas of eschatology — setting a date for the end, millennialism, universal homecoming, and purgatory — we notice at once that they often have been viewed as standing in conflict with God's eschatological promise. They are rejected by many Protestant denominations and, with the exception of the last one, also by the Roman Catholic Church. In spite of their "off limits" character, they have always proved attractive for those who did not feel bound to the teachings and confessional writings of mainline denominations.

1. Setting a Date for the End

The attempt to forecast the end of the world was already popular at the time of Jesus. In line with the apocalyptic tradition, some of Jesus' followers were convinced they could accurately predict the beginning of the eschaton and the parousia of the returning Christ. Jesus, however, rejected such attempts, saying: "About that day and hour no one knows, neither the angels of heaven, nor the Son, but only the Father" (Matt. 24:36), and "It is not for you to know the times or periods that the Father has set by his own authority" (Acts 1:7). The attempt to predict the coming of the eschaton denies our finitude, which prevents us from grasping the whole of history and of the world. Only God, who is beyond space and time and is also active in them, can have that kind of comprehensive knowledge. Knowing about the date of the end could also lead to security. We could then calculate when to start preparing for it. Moreover, such calculations would be demonic and antigodly. In denying our finitude we would try to put ourselves in the place of God.

Unlike our preparations for certain events within space and time, getting ready at a certain point for the eschaton would show a total lack of understanding of what the eschaton implies. It is the God-provided goal that will emerge at a certain God-provided point and toward which our own life should be directed. The classic illustration of this is Jesus' parable of the ten bridesmaids (Matt. 25:1-13). Those who had directed their whole life toward the preparation for the coming kingdom were able to enter into it when it came. The others, however, who thought they could start their preparation at a certain self-determined point, were excluded. The parable therefore concludes with the admonition: "Keep awake therefore, for you know neither the day nor the hour." Yet the idea of being able to calculate the date of the coming of the eschaton, in spite of its prohibition, has remained amazingly attractive.

a. A Fertile Tradition

Nostradamus (1503-66), a French astrologer of Jewish descent, had become a cult figure by the 1990s.[1] There are dozens of books about him; many people attempt to decipher his prophecies, even with computer programs; and an International Nostradamus Congress has been held in Hamburg, Germany. He began to prophesy around 1547, and in 1555 he published in Lyons a book of rhymed prophecies titled *Centuries*. They consisted of quatrains (verses of four lines) grouped in hundreds, each set of quatrains being called a century. Some of his prophecies have supposedly been fulfilled, such as the execution of Louis XVI and the life and death of Robespierre and Napoleon. But for the year 1999 he allegedly announced a cosmic catastrophe, a change of the movement of the earth, and a global eclipse. The Roman Catholic Church deemed his prophecies dangerous enough to put his *Centuries* on the *Index Librorum Prohibitorum* (Index of Prohibited Books) in 1781. Indeed, prophecies

---

1. Cf. for the following, Inge Schneider, *Countdown Apokalypse: Hintergründe der Sektendramen* (Berne: Jupiter-Verlag, 1995), 256.

can become self-fulfilling if people are more interested in the predictions than in preventing the catastrophes that are announced.

Martin Luther, who often emphasized the incalculability of the end, not infrequently indulged in speculations. In his world chronological table he remarked that he was convinced that the world will come to its end before its sixth millennium is completed (A.D. 2040).[2] And in one of his table talks in 1538, he calculates from the book of Daniel that it might take about another twenty years until the end will come. But then he concludes his speculations, saying: "Only God knows how he will do it. It is not up to us to soothsay at what time he will liberate his people, but to pray and to do penance."[3] In a sermon on Luke 21:25-36, an apocalyptic passage, he refers to many contemporary events in demonstrating that the end is near. "I do not want to force or compel anybody to believe me. Yet I also do not want anyone to dissuade me that I hold that judgment day is not far. These portents and words of Christ move me in this direction."[4] When he sees what is happening and how people conduct themselves, he becomes quite pessimistic and writes: "I am forced to firmly believe that Christ must soon return because their sins are so great that heaven can no longer tolerate them. They incite and resist judgment day so much that it must come upon them before too much time."[5]

While Luther's words express very much the sentiment of his own time, his assessment neither intensified his fears of the end nor resulted in doomsday speculation. To the contrary, he asked: "Why should believers be afraid and not rejoice to the utmost? Do they trust Christ and the judge who will come for the sake of their salvation and who is their portion?"[6] Then he lashes out at those "awful preachers of dreams" who attempt to scare people into piety by fire-and-brimstone preaching and demand that people make satisfaction for a sinful life through good works. According to Luther, nobody could survive if we were only presented with Christ as a stern judge. Since Christ, however, is the savior,

2. Martin Luther, *Supputatio annorum mundi* (1541-45), in WA, 53:171.

3. Martin Luther, in a table talk of April 10 and 11, 1538 (no. 3831), in WATR, 3:646.10-12.

4. Martin Luther, *Adventspostille* (1522), in WA, 10.1.2:95.17-19, in a sermon on Luke 21:21-36.

5. Luther, *Adventspostille,* in WA, 10.1.2:97.16-19.

6. Luther, *Adventspostille,* in WA, 10.1.2:110.31-33.

there can be hope and trust in the future. But neither his trust in a gracious judge nor the hope for a better hereafter made Luther escapist in his outlook on the future or indifferent to the present.

As the apocryphal story of the apple tree shows, the Christian also had a task in this world for which he was held accountable. According to this apocryphal story, Luther was asked one day what he would do if he knew that today would be the last day of this world. Without hesitating he responded: "I would plant an apple tree." When the surprised questioner asked Luther why he would do that, he responded: "I wanted to do this anyhow." Theologically significant for Luther was not the date of the end, but that there was an end. That made life both bearable and significant. We are not destined to stay here forever, and yet the present has its own value as our proving and testing ground. With this positive approach both to the end and to the present, Luther differed from most end-time prophets.

With the revivals in nineteenth-century North America, interest in the end again caught the attention of countless people. Among the most influential was William Miller (1782-1849), who up to his conversion at a local revival was simply a Deist. This experience made him an intense student of the Bible. He used a King James Version bearing Bishop Ussher's chronology in the margins. "Deeply concerned as to when Christ would come again, Miller pondered the Book of Daniel. Counting the days referred to in certain passages of this highly symbolic apocalypse (especially 9:24-27 and 8:14), making each 'day' a year, and accepting Ussher's date for these events as 457 B.C. (see Neh 2:1), he discovered that 'seventy weeks' added up to the date of Christ's death (A.D. 33, according to Ussher), while 'two thousand three hundred days' added up to A.D. 1843."[7] Initially, Miller was afraid to confront the world with this news. Yet he overcame his hesitation and won wide acceptance as a revival preacher in the northeastern United States.

Joshua V. Himes (1805-95), who had heard Miller in 1837 when Miller was already an ordained Baptist minister, became Miller's promoter. Between 1840 and 1843 meetings were organized all across the country with Miller lecturing over three hundred times during a six-month period alone. Though there were many warnings and condemna-

---

7. According to Sydney E. Ahlstrom, *A Religious History of the American People* (New Haven: Yale University Press, 1972), 479.

tions about this precise announcement of the Day of the Lord, hundreds of thousands began to prepare for the Lord's coming. Yet 1843 and 1844 passed and time still continued. While Miller was sick, discouraged, and cast out by his own Baptists, the hard core of true believers considered this great disappointment only to be a challenge. Finally, out of the Millerites the Seventh-Day Adventists emerged with their emphasis on Saturday as the day of rest and strong millennial leanings.

Charles Taze Russell (1852-1916), from Allegheny, Pennsylvania, is another example that not everyone will discredit the prophet when he miscalculates the end. Russell's independent Bible studies led him first to highly successful preaching and then to organizing his followers. His prophecies were focused on the end. The second advent of Christ had already occurred invisibly in 1874, and the end of all things was slated for 1914. The slogan of the early Russellites was: "Millions now living will never die." But when Russell died in 1916, the end still had not come. His successor, Joseph F. Rutherford (1869-1942), was no less specific with his predictions, and the years 1918 and 1925 were advocated as the new dates. Finally the year 1994 was determined for Jesus' visible appearance by the Jehovah's Witnesses, as the Russellites later called themselves.[8] Yet this date has also passed and nothing has happened. But the movement and the missionary activities of the Jehovah's Witnesses continue unabated.

Another prophet who is especially influential with apocalyptic movements is Edgar Cayce (1877-1945), who made his prophecies in a trance. He predicted that the San Andreas fault in California would cause an earthquake of unforeseen proportions and a drifting apart of two continents.[9] The poles were to change in 1998 when the Christ spirit set foot again on the earth, and toward the end of the millennium Japan would largely be immersed in the sea, the Midwest of the United States would be flooded, New York City would completely disappear from the map, and the European climate would become subtropical. Even Atlantis was to emerge again from the sea. We live in an age of heightened apocalyptic consciousness. We notice how dangerous these fears can become with the advent of suicide movements.

8. Cf. Schneider, *Countdown Apokalypse*, 35.
9. Cf. for the following, Schneider, *Countdown Apokalypse*, 259.

b. Bringing About the End by Force

Erika Bertschinger (b. 1929) comes from a Roman Catholic background in Switzerland, but has been influenced by Christian spiritualistic circles and, under her spiritual name, Uriella, has received direct revelations since 1975 through "her friend" Jesus Christ.[10] Her prophecies, directly mediated from Christ, sound like horror stories. She saw a worldwide economic collapse not only in Japan and Argentina but also in Europe. She predicted that all cities that are centers of sin would face natural catastrophes; that in the middle of 1998 there would be a third world war and that a small planet, on a collision course with the earth, would annihilate central Europe. She foresaw in 1999 another encounter with outer space; the American continent was to break apart and the West Coast was to disappear into the sea as Atlantis once did; then the poles would change. Yet before these catastrophes happened, millions of people were to be rescued from this earth through innumerable spiritual beings in UFOs. Uriella's group, Fiat Lux ("There shall be light"), has thousands of members in Switzerland, Germany, and Austria.

Whoever lives in the end time needs radical distance from the world. Therefore Uriella's followers have given up their earthly professions; dress themselves in white and lead a life of humility and simplicity by abstaining from meat, alcohol, nicotine, coffee, and TV; and prepare themselves for the advent of the Lord. Yet what happened when the date passed by without the end having arrived? Surely there was disappointment, and some may have left the Fiat Lux movement. Yet there are new revelations, and the delayed end will open up a new opportunity for members and others who are still "seeking the truth." For some groups, however, such a delay is no longer a choice. Already in 1978, Jim Jones and more than nine hundred of his followers committed mass suicide in Jonestown, Guyana, because he had promised to lead his family of followers from this sin-filled place to a new life beyond this earth.

---

10. Cf. for the following, Schneider, *Countdown Apokalypse*, 90-94, and "'Stellt bitte keine Bedingungen' — Uriellas Weltendprophezeihungen als Unterwerfungsstrategie?" in *Informationsblatt* (pub. Evangelische Informationsstelle: Kirchen–Sekten–Religionen) 35 (1998): 1.

Much more publicized through worldwide TV coverage was the end of the Branch Davidians.[11] From his youth Vernon Wayne Howell (1959-93) had studied the Bible and led a life of prayer, joining the Seventh-Day Adventists until they excluded him on account of his independent ideas. He joined the Disciples of David at Mount Carmel near Waco, Texas, finally taking over the group and calling them Branch Davidians. In 1990 Vernon Howell changed his name to David Koresh, and he called himself more and more often the "lamb of God." He accumulated all kinds of weapons and prepared his followers for the final battle between good and evil which would precede God's kingdom. It was only logical that Mount Carmel was renamed "Ranch Apocalypse."[12]

On February 28, 1993, agents of the Bureau of Alcohol, Tobacco and Firearms (BATF) wanted to enter the ranch to search for illegal weapons, but they were met with heavy gunfire. The Branch Davidians, however, claimed they encountered a burst of gunfire when they wanted to talk with the BATF agents.[13] The consequence of this attempted search was that four agents died and several more were wounded. Koresh and some of his followers were also wounded. Whether anybody had died on the ranch could not be investigated. After a fifty-one-day siege, federal agents stormed the ranch and the result was an inferno of flames. Within a few seconds the whole compound was on fire, since the members of the commune had presumably poured out petroleum and ignited it. The agents had wanted to free the children of the group since they had evidence that the children had been abused by Koresh. Yet the result was mass suicide, and some members who attempted to flee may also have been shot by more dedicated members of the group.[14] The fiery inferno of Waco was for the Davidians the battle of Armageddon (Rev. 16:16), and as the destructive angels of the divine judge of the world, the Davidians caused their own death and that of federal agents.

The suicide of the Heaven's Gate group in an affluent San Diego

11. For the following, cf. Clifford L. Linedecker, *Massacre at Waco, Texas: The Shocking True Story of Cult Leader David Koresh and the Branch Davidians* (New York: St. Martin's Paperbacks, 1993), 80-99.

12. Linedecker, *Massacre at Waco*, 105.

13. Cf. James D. Tabor and Eugene V. Gallagher, *Why Waco? Cults and the Battle for Religious Freedom in America* (Berkeley: University of California Press, 1995), 2.

14. Cf. Clifford L. Linedecker, *Sektenführer des Todes* (Munich: Heyne, 1994), 182.

suburb during Holy Week of 1997 was no less spectacular. This group was founded by Marshall Herff Applewhite (1931-97) and Bonney Lu Trusdale Nettles (1927-85). They also called themselves "Bo and Peep" or "Do and Ti," probably to document that names are unimportant. Again, they understood the present time as the time of the end; the world was coming to its fulfillment.[15] The goal of humanity, they believed, is to leave this earth and reach the next stage of development. Similar to a butterfly which obtains a totally new body but retains its identity with the previous caterpillar, so humanity is also destined to leave behind its human bodiliness and assume the bodies of UFO occupants. This transformation occurs on board a UFO, the advent of which was expected for 1975-76. Of course, not everybody will be well suited for this metamorphosis.

Bo and Peep targeted followers of the hippie culture in California with their message. Bo and Peep called themselves "The Two," in analogy to the two witnesses of Revelation 11. Since nothing significant happened in 1976, they changed their message. The future life on the next level is perceived as actual life. It is not a totally spiritual existence, but a real world, much more real than our present one. To overcome all humanness they developed a "Human Individual Metamorphosis cosmology."[16] Those who have overcome all humanness will receive a new receptacle on the next plane. A UFO will come and the old clothes, the human part, will be left behind and the new clothes, that of the UFOs, will be put on. Since the UFO did not come, the members of Heaven's Gate decided to return their present receptacles and to take their souls without receptacle on the journey to the next plane. They arranged everything meticulously, including the payment for the use of the present receptacle (putting some money into their pockets), and then committed suicide. Again, their outlook portrayed a terribly negative view of this earth. But in contrast to the Branch Davidians, they felt no need to fight it. Human civilization was a complete failure, and the vast majority of people were an inferior creation utterly incapable of enlightenment. "For the spiritually developed few, the only hope lay in removal from

15. For details of their teachings, cf. "Heaven's Gate," in *Informationsblatt* (pub. Evangelische Informationsstelle: Kirchen–Sekten–Religionen) 34 (1997): 15-24.

16. Brad Steiger and Hayden Hewes, *Inside Heaven's Gate: The UFO Cult Leaders Tell Their Story in Their Own Words* (New York: Penguin Signet Books, 1997), vii, in this informative but somewhat sensationalistic book.

the planet by extraterrestrials."[17] The two dozen members of the Heaven's Gate community thought they were the only ones eligible to reach the next plane.

A more secretive and international organization is the Solar Temple. Its founder, Luc Jouret (1947-94), was born in the Democratic Republic of the Congo (formerly named Zaire) and studied medicine in Brussels, Belgium. In southern France he had contact with a Rosicrucian society, but then founded his own lodge in 1984, the Solar Temple.[18] The center of the order was in Geneva, Switzerland, but Jouret was also active in Canada and France. He was convinced that it was the hour of the apocalypse as documented in the Revelation of John. He believed humanity has some prehension of a transcendent dimension, and it is important to overcome its alienation from nature and reach the highest degree of bliss. Through reorganization of the present chaos from the heap of ashes, the most beautiful rose will grow.

In the last will of the Solar Templers we read: "We have left the earth to find a dimension of truth and absoluteness in clarity and freedom without the hypocrisy and oppression of this world, and to lay the seed for a future world."[19] Jouret had realized that the hour of revelation had come, the hour of the apocalypse. Since he was convinced that life and death are only two sides of the same experience, there came the final climax in the night of October 4-5, 1994. Shortly after midnight the people of a small village in Switzerland noticed a fire on the horizon. When the firefighters arrived, they saw an estate in flames. The seventy-three-year-old owner was in bed, killed by a gunshot. In another part of the estate the police found a secret hall with candles and empty bottles of champagne. Beyond that was a secret door that opened to a hallway at the end of which was another room where police found more than twenty bodies neatly arranged in a circle, both men and women, old and young, all killed. With some kind of mechanism these people had set fire to the estate. In the same night fire was discovered in another village. The firefighters again found corpses in the two chalets. A house

17. So Gustav Niebuhr, "American Religion at the Millennium's End," *Word & World* 18 (1998): 8.

18. For details cf. Schneider, *Countdown Apokalypse*, 60-76. Rosicrucian societies exist in many countries. In their search for truth they use modern scientific methods as well as occult and mystic traditions.

19. As cited by Schneider, *Countdown Apokalypse*, 69.

was also set on fire in Canada. Altogether forty-eight people had died in Switzerland and five in Canada, including Luc Jouret, the founder of the Solar Temple. In December 1995, in the Swiss Alps, northwest of Grenoble, another fifteen corpses were found lying starlike around a fireplace.[20] There the Solar Templers left behind documents indicating that they had left this world to seek a new one. Together with the rising sun they wanted to journey at the winter solstice to the star Sirius.

What shall we make of these suicidal attempts to set a date for the end and to journey to a new world? As we have seen, there have always been apocalyptic movements. Many religions speak of a final doom beyond which there is a new creation. While we could question the sanity of these suicide gurus, we should see that they are never alone. They always have a following. Usually these are people who are looking for answers to today's problems and want to make sense of their lives.

There is widespread pessimism in today's global culture. The ecological crisis can no longer be ignored. Our natural resources are dwindling, the global population increases day by day, diseases are spreading, and countless people die every day of starvation in the so-called Third World. While the Cold War has come to an end and the danger of a global nuclear holocaust has receded, regional wars continue unabated. It is not surprising that people have become pessimistic. If the world were to go up in flames or collapse because of humanity's greed and sinfulness, as these gurus predict, these huge problems would no longer need to be solved. We can then tell ourselves that we are tied to these worldly conditions only for a short while. Though we still live in this world, we oppose it. We protest, but need not rebel. Soon we will leave this world to a better hereafter. Thus the message of the suicide gurus will sound comforting to some anxious souls. A fanatic world-denying prophet can easily take believers and seekers along to a self-determined exit. What should we do in this situation?

As the future — both of the world and of our personal lives — becomes more and more uncertain, the minds of many people in our secular society are increasingly deluded by fantasy and misguided by fear, rather than comforted by biblical hope. Ignorance about the Christian

---

20. Cf. Hans Rückerl, "Verängstigter Glaube: Apokalyptische Strömungen am Ende des zweiten Jahrtausends," in *Glaubensangst — Glaubenshoffnung: Anregungen für die Verkündigung*, ed. Wolfgang Beinert (Regensburg: Friedrich Pustet, 1997), 142-43.

message is paired with superstition, while responsibility and reasonable thought are often forsaken. In their attempt to counteract these tendencies, some popular theologians pour oil on the flames of apocalyptic fears with books that closely resemble the literature produced during the darkest years of the Middle Ages. Hal Lindsey (b. 1929) may be named as a representative for such theologians. His book *The Late Great Planet Earth* (1970) sold over ten million copies in ten years and has made an immense impact on countless people. It has even been made into a movie which was shown on cable TV throughout the United States. His books *The Liberation of Planet Earth* (1974) and the more recent *Planet Earth 2000 A.D.* were also quite successful.

Lindsey is also representative of those who attempt to give the prophetic word of the Bible new credibility. He is correct that, in an effort to satisfy the concern and curiosity about the future, modern-day "prophets" are enjoying the greatest revival since the ancient days of Babylon. It should also concern us that in the United States more people take to astrology or to esoteric cults than claim to belong to all the larger denominations taken together. The same can be said for many other countries. Given this context, we appreciate the biblical realism underlying Lindsey's endeavor to point to the immediacy of the coming eschaton.

Though Lindsey does not settle on a specific date but calls for continuous preparedness, he is convinced "that according to all the signs, we are in the general time of His coming."[21] The end will climax in World War III with four principal power blocs confronting each other. "The Arab-African Confederacy headed by Egypt (King of the South) launches an invasion of Israel. . . . Russia and her allies use this occasion to launch an invasion of the Middle East."[22] For a short while the Russian bloc will conquer the Middle East and set up "command headquarters on Mount Moriah or the Temple area in Jerusalem."[23] But then "the ten-nation Revived Roman Empire of Europe" (to which the United States may be aligned) will destroy Russia in Israel.[24] Thus "we have only two great spheres of power left to fight the final climactic battle of Armageddon: the combined forces of the Western civilization

21. Hal Lindsey with C. C. Carlson, *The Late Great Planet Earth* (Grand Rapids: Zondervan, 1970), 144.
22. Lindsey, 153-54.
23. Lindsey, 158 and 160.
24. Lindsey, 161.

united under the leadership of the Roman Dictator and the vast hordes of the Orient probably united under the Red Chinese war machine."[25] In the movie *The Late Great Planet Earth*, Lindsey is shown several times overlooking the plain of Jezreel, "which belts across the middle of the Holy Land, from the Mediterranean to the Jordan,"[26] pointing out that this is "Harmagedon" where the final battle will take place. "As the battle of Armageddon reaches its awful climax and it appears that all life will be destroyed on earth — in this very moment Jesus Christ will return and save man from self-extinction."[27]

Where does Lindsey get this information, complete with detailed maps and diagrams? He points to the Bible, predominately to the Old Testament prophets Isaiah, Jeremiah, Daniel, and Ezekiel, and also to the New Testament book of Revelation. He assures us that 70 percent of the biblical prophecies have come true and that the rest will find fulfillment in our lifetime. We certainly agree that ancient Israel received its courage to face the future from the fulfillment of certain Old Testament prophecies. The New Testament hope for the return of the Lord has also proved to be a powerful stimulus for the Christian church to transform the world and to spread the good news of salvation. Yet we wonder about the appropriateness of Lindsey's highly imaginative but entirely unhistorical approach to the Scriptures.

For two reasons it is unwarranted to take an Old Testament prediction or promise that has not yet been fulfilled and transpose it onto the contemporary scene with the claim that it will be fulfilled soon.

1. The Old Testament predictions and promises were continuously being revised and expanded in their own time to include new historical situations, as we see paradigmatically in the changes concerning the promise of the Messiah. The progress of history necessitated a continuous reappropriation, even in instances where a promise or prediction had come to fulfillment. Thus a specific pinpointing of their fulfillment would contradict the progress of history in which God's activity with Israel was understood in a continuously changing and expanding horizon.

25. Lindsey, 162.
26. Lindsey, 164.
27. Lindsey, 168.

2. It was the deep conviction of the New Testament writings and of Jesus himself that all the Old Testament promises had found their fulfillment, and not just their continuation, in the Christ event. In him God's full self-disclosure had occurred (Heb. 1:1-2) and the first fruit of the new creation was reaped (2 Cor. 5:17). All further events are contingent upon the Christ event. To go back with Lindsey to the Old Testament and look for signs and predictions that could be projected on the screen of the present or the future would not only turn the Bible into a jigsaw puzzle,[28] but would also relativize the Christ event as the culmination point of God's history with us. Christ would not be the answer to the Old Testament hopes and aspirations but a continuation of them. Thus the zeal for predicting the end instead of emphasizing preparedness leads to an undermining of our trust in God and a circumvention of Christ and his efficacious work.

Already in the New Testament the imminently expected end of the world is the stimulus for missionary activity. Therefore we do not stare at the end attempting to calculate the final eschatological drama, and we are not paralyzed by the prospect of the approaching end. On the contrary, each day before the end is understood as a gift, a gift that is to be used. As Lindsey's predictions have shown, and as many others have and will, even with the best imagination and the most diligent use of the Bible, we cannot predict the immediate future. One also wonders what the purpose of these predictions should be. The emerging Christian community was not about speculation but preparedness, not about outguessing the Lord but being faithful to the call. Augustine is correct when he writes in a letter: "It is not the one who asserts that He is near nor the one who asserts that He is not near who loves the coming of the Lord, but the one who waits for Him, whether He be near or far, with sincere faith, firm hope and ardent love."[29]

---

28. Cf. the book by T. Boersma, *Is the Bible a Jigsaw Puzzle . . . An Evaluation of Hal Lindsey's Writings*, trans. Elizabeth Vandenkooy Roberts (St. Catharines, Ont.: Paideia, 1978), 186, who rightly claims that Lindsey's views about the end times are "too speculative, too much directed to the future only."

29. Augustine, "Letter 199, chapter 15," in Saint Augustine, *Letters: Vol. IV (165-203)*, in *FaCh*, 30:367, and quoted in Franz Stuhlhofer, *"Das Ende naht!" Die Irrtümer der Endzeitpropeten* (Gießen: Brunnen, 1992), 217, who shows that end-time prophecies have always been marred by countless mistakes.

2. Hope for the Millennium

Millennial hopes are closely connected with the idea of the imminent return of Christ and gained renewed attention during the nineteenth-century revivals and especially in connection with the increasingly popular attention to doomsday prophecy. As the second Christian millennium gives way to the third, we may even see a further intensification of millennial hopes. Today millennial ideas are more widespread than ever in Christian conservative circles (i.e., among evangelicals, fundamentalists, and Pentecostals), even though they are largely ignored in mainline circles. Yet both Christian and secular utopias, from the hope of an inner-worldly realization of the kingdom of God to the attempt to build an egalitarian society, have received their main impetus from the Christian notion of the community of the faithful which is radically renewed historically and societally visible prior to Judgment Day. Millennialism, coming from the Latin "one thousand years," or chiliasm, meaning the same in Greek, stands for the expectation of a visible reign of Christ with the believers before the immediate coming of the end of the world. Though this idea is a distinctive Christian teaching, its roots are deeply embedded in foreign soil.

a. Origin and Growth of an Idea

In the New Testament the only explicit reference to the millennium is Revelation 20:1-15, where it says the martyrs will be resurrected at the first resurrection and Satan will be bound for a thousand years, so that the martyrs can reign with Christ during that period. But this vision of a thousand years must be seen against the background of Jewish apocalyptic traditions such as the *Sibylline Oracles* 3:652-53, where it says that "God will send a King from the sun who will stop the entire earth from evil war," or *2 Baruch* 40:1-3, where we read: "The last ruler who is left alive at that time will be bound, whereas the entire host will be destroyed. And they will carry him on Mount Zion, and my Anointed One will convict him of all his wicked deeds and will assemble and set before him all the works of his hosts. And after these things he will kill him and protect the rest of my people who will be found in the place that I have chosen. And his dominion will last forever until the world of corruption has ended and until the times which have been mentioned before have been fulfilled."

As we remember, there was an older national expectation according to which the Messiah should appear as the end-time king and reestablish the Davidic kingdom and give it its ancient splendor. But there was also the gradual development of a universal hope in a divine ambassador who would come from heaven, at which time the dead would be resurrected and all people would appear before his judgment seat. The national hope was then later connected with the universal one by signifying the rule of the messianic king prior to the end of the world and the beginning of the new aeon. "The earthly Messianic age will be for a limited time and it will be followed by a last assault of the powers of chaos prior to the commencement of the future world."[30] For Christians it was evident that Christ is both the messianic king and God's ambassador who will lead the faithful to the new world. While in apocalyptic thought the duration of the millennium varies (in 4 Ezra 7:28-29 the Messiah will rule for four hundred years), the seer of the book of Revelation clearly states it as a thousand years in analogy to the last thousand years of the great Sabbath of the world.

Prominent theologians of the early church, such as Justin Martyr, Tertullian, and Hippolytus of Rome, favored the idea of millennialism. Quite interesting is the position of Irenaeus, who connects the thousand years with his notion of recapitulation, meaning that Christ as the second Adam recapitulated what Adam had done, but this time without sinning. As there is a recapitulation of the days of Adam, there is also a recapitulation or development of humanity to the final fulfillment. This is now connected with the notion of a millennium, meaning as a preparation for the final salvation and as a chance to grow. Irenaeus writes:

> Inasmuch, therefore, as the opinions of certain [orthodox persons] are derived from heretical discourses, they are both ignorant of God's dispensations, and of the mystery of the resurrection of the just, and of the [earthly] kingdom which is the commencement of incorruption, by means of which kingdom those who shall be worthy are accustomed gradually to partake of the divine nature; and it is necessary to tell them respecting those things, that it behooves the righteous first to re-

---

30. Eduard Lohse, "chilias/chilioi," in *TDNT,* 9:470.

ceive the promise of the inheritance which God promised to the fathers, and to reign in it, when they rise again to behold God in this creation which is renovated, and that the judgment should take place afterwards.[31]

In the West, Lactantius, in *The Divine Institutes,* advocated millennialism using the *Sibylline Oracles* and a host of other sources to explain what this hope entails. He writes: "And as God laboured during those six days in creating such great works, so His religion and truth must labour during these six thousand years while wickedness prevails and bears rule. And again, since God, having finished His works, rested the seventh day and blessed it, at the end of the six thousandth year all wickedness must be abolished from the earth, and righteousness reign for a thousand years; and there must be tranquillity and rest from the labours which the world now has long endured."[32]

Once the Christian faith became an officially accepted religion in the Roman Empire, there was no need to hope for a future millennium in which the evil forces would be subdued. This can be seen most clearly from Eusebius's *Church History* when, in book 10, he expresses his joy over the freedom and imperial sanction that the Christians now received. Moreover, as Augustine explains, "the Church even now is the kingdom of Christ and the kingdom of heaven."[33] Additionally, some theologians such as Origen and Eusebius of Caesarea preferred a more allegorical and spiritual interpretation of the kingdom of Christ than the one to be set up "in material form on this very earth."[34] This means that the increasing acculturation of the church, with its implications for good and for bad, rendered the idea of millennialism more and more meaningless in the West, whereas the East, especially those influenced by Origen, had never been much fascinated by it. The material pleasures it promised could not sufficiently attract the ascetic-minded Greek theologians who longed for deification of humanity and not for a Christification of this earth.

The decline of millennial hopes did not mean that the belief in a fu-

---

31. Irenaeus, *Against Heresies* 5.32, in *ANF,* 1:561.

32. Lactantius, *The Divine Institutes* 7.14, in *ANF,* 7:211.

33. Augustine, *City of God* 20.9, ed. and trans. R. W. Dyson (Cambridge: Cambridge University Press, 1998), 988.

34. Eusebius of Caesarea, *Church History* 3.39, in *NPNF* SS, 1:172.

ture fulfillment of history had declined too. Augustine makes the point clear:

> Yet some have said that there may be as many as four hundred, five hundred, or even a thousand years to be completed between the Lord's ascension and His final coming. It would, however, take too long to demonstrate how each of these people supports his opinion. Nor is it necessary to do so; for they make use of human conjectures, and offer no firm evidence from the authority of canonical Scripture. Truly Christ commands all who make such calculations on this subject to relax their fingers and let them rest, when He says, "It is not for you to know the times or the seasons which the Father hath put in his own power."[35]

It took until after the turn of the first millennium for millennial ideas to be revived on a larger scale.

b. Joachim of Fiore and the Rise of Millennialism

As we have seen, millennialism has never been a central doctrine of the whole church. It was mostly promulgated by people outside the mainstream of theology and the church. This did not change with Joachim of Fiore (ca. 1135-1202), a Cistercian monk from Calabria, Italy, and the founder of a community of hermits.[36] After long studies and meditations in the wilderness of the Calabrian mountains, he had some kind of revelation at a Pentecost celebration between 1190 and 1195 wherein he discovered the meaning of the book of Revelation and the correspondence of the Old Testament with the New. In his exposition of the Apocalypse of John, he distinguished between those items which had already come to fulfillment and others where fulfillment was still outstanding. In a prophetic way he outlined the future stages of a providential development of history.

---

35. Augustine, *City of God* 18.53, 903.

36. Cf. for the following, Bernard McGinn, *Visions of the End: Apocalyptic Traditions in the Middle Ages* (New York: Columbia University Press, 1979), 126-41, who calls Joachim "not only one of the most important apocalyptic authors of the Middle Ages, but one of the most significant theorists of history in the Western tradition."

In analogy to the seven days of creation he saw the history of salvation as a sequence of seven ages, each lasting one millennium.[37] Using the forty-two generations (six ages times seven generations) leading up to Jesus (Matt. 1:1-17), he divided the old covenant into seven parts: six ages with seven generations which precede Christ, and then Christ signifies the seventh epoch. In analogy to that, the new covenant is also divided into seven parts: there are six ages, each with seven generations. Each generation lasts thirty years, corresponding to Jesus' age at his death. These calculations show that the new covenant will last 1,260 years. After that comes the seventh epoch, which is the time of the Spirit. While the old covenant is the time of the Father, characterized by law and fear, the new covenant of the Son lasts till A.D. 1260 and is characterized by grace and faith. The third and final epoch was inaugurated already by Saint Benedict (ca. 480–ca. 550) and is characterized by love and the Spirit. In many different ways and with many different pictures, Joachim presents these three different ages.

Joachim, who believed he belonged to the second epoch, "did not draw any revolutionary conclusions from the implications of his historico-eschatological visions."[38] While he saw his own time as a century of radical decay, he projected a messianic leader to bring about spiritual renewal for the sake of the kingdom of Christ and to disclose to all people what had hitherto been disguised in significant figures and in the sacraments. But his hope was not materialistic, antiecclesiastic, or anti-institutional, as with some of his successors. Even the thousand years of the new epoch he regarded to be only symbolic. Joachim opted more for a radical spiritualization of the world during the time of the spirit than for an earthly renewal.

Later followers of Joachim were less patient than he, and also more inclined to give his thoughts a material base. For instance, the Franciscan Spirituals in the thirteenth and fourteenth centuries attempted without compromise to fulfill the laws of the kingdom of God in the

---

37. For the following, cf. Medard Kehl, *Eschatologie* (Würzburg: Echter, 1986), 183-84.

38. So Karl Löwith, *Meaning in History: The Theological Implications of the Philosophy of History* (Chicago: University of Chicago Press, 1949), 151, and Bernhard Töpfer, *Das kommende Reich des Friedens: Zur Entwicklung chiliastischer Zukunftshoffnungen im Hochmittelalter* (Berlin: Akademie-Verlag, 1964), 48-103, esp. 102-3, who shows that Fiore's monastic idealism stayed within the boundaries of the church and did not exhibit any revolutionary impetus that was going to change the world.

present age. This brought them into tremendous conflicts with the Dominicans, who pursued similar ideas. It also led them into open confrontation with the imperial messianism of Emperor Frederick II and with the institutional Roman Catholic Church. While the Dominicans denounced them, and both church and state persecuted them, the idea of a total renewal and cleansing of this earth persisted.

Ernst Bloch asserts that Joachim drew up "the most momentous social utopia of the Middle Ages," because it abolishes both church and state.[39] Its third age is an age of "universalized monastic and consumer communism, an 'age of free spirit.'"[40] Bloch sees the fundamental principle of Joachimism in the "unconcluded revelation."[41] He appreciates the active fight of Joachimism against the social principles of a Christianity which had associated itself with the class-conscious society since the time of Paul and consequently had to compromise its message. This third period of history, as prophesied by Joachim, seems to emerge in the Soviet Union and, quite naturally, find its archenemy in the clerical domination of the second period. This clerical kingdom does not fully comprehend the third period, or if it does, it denounces it.[42] These extrapolations show how much Bloch is interested in the anticlerical and political-revolutionary implications of Joachim's thought.[43] In Marxist fashion Bloch also appreciates the "complete transfer of the kingdom of light *from the other world and the empty promises of the other world into history,* even though into a final state of history."[44] According to Bloch, the relegation of our hopes to a better beyond must then cease. Moreover, their attempt to date the projected kingdom of God made the sectarian revolutionaries employ their total energy, which for Bloch is a sign of the true sectarian.

---

39. Ernst Bloch, *The Principle of Hope,* trans. Nevill Plaice et al., 3 vols. (Cambridge: MIT Press, 1986), 2:510.

40. Bloch, 2:510.

41. Bloch, 2:514.

42. Cf. Bloch, 2:513.

43. Though Joachim's thought had an unmistakably revolutionary character (cf. Ernst Benz, *Evolution and Christian Hope: Man's Concept of the Future, from the Early Fathers to Teilhard de Chardin* [Garden City, N.Y.: Doubleday, Anchor Books, 1966], 42), Gerhard Sauter rightly cautions us against Bloch's interpretation of Joachim. The anticlerical and political-revolutionary impulses of Joachim were less direct than Bloch assumes. Cf. Sauter, *Zukunft und Verheissung: Das Problem der Zukunft in der gegenwärtigen theologischen und philosophischen Diskussion* (Stuttgart: Zwingli, 1965), 331.

44. Bloch, 2:510.

For centuries Joachim's writings were propagated, and pamphlets were written in his spirit and name. Even Thomas Müntzer (ca. 1490-1525), the apocalyptic utopian and "new Daniel" who wanted to rigorously enforce God's will in this eschatological end time, refers to Joachim.[45] In a letter attached to his discourse *On Contrived Faith* (1524), he mentions that his enemies call Joachim's teaching "with great mockery" the "Eternal Gospel." Müntzer holds Joachim in high esteem, though he claims that he does not derive his revolutionary ideas from Joachim, "but rather from the living speech of God."[46] Martin Luther and his followers, however, rejected categorically any utopian ideas in the Augsburg Confession of 1530: "Rejected, too, are certain Jewish opinions which are even now making an appearance and which teach that, before the resurrection of the dead, saints and godly men will possess a worldly kingdom and annihilate all the godless."[47]

Even with this rejection, the fire of utopian dreams was not extinguished. Gotthold Ephraim Lessing (1729-81), one of the spiritual leaders of the Enlightenment in Germany, shows a familiarity with a trinitarian periodization of history and refers to the third age as an age of "a new eternal gospel."[48] It is of much more far-reaching consequence that Engels, the coauthor of the *Communist Manifesto*, declared in 1842: "The self-consciousness of mankind, the new Grail, around whose throne the nations joyfully assemble . . . that is our profession, that we become the Templars of this Grail, to gird our swords around our loin, and joyfully

---

45. Cf. the extensive biography by Walter Elliger, *Thomas Müntzer: Leben und Werk*, 3rd ed. (Göttingen: Vandenhoeck & Ruprecht, 1976), 444-45.

46. As reprinted in Michael G. Baylor, ed. and trans., *Revelation and Revolution: Basic Writings of Thomas Müntzer* (Bethlehem, Pa.: Lehigh University Press, 1993), 84. Cf. also Bloch, 2:512. When Müntzer mentions here that he has read Joachim's *Commentary on Jeremiah*, this is based on a misunderstanding. The *Commentary on Jeremiah* was a pseudo-Joachimite document printed in Venice in 1516 (cf. Baylor, 213 n. 20). This shows us what popularity Joachim enjoyed in the sixteenth century.

47. Augsburg Confession 17, in *The Book of Concord*, ed. Theodore J. Tappert (Philadelphia: Fortress, 1959), 38-39.

48. Gotthold Ephraim Lessing, *The Education of the Human Race*, pars. 86-89, in *Lessing's Theological Writings*, selections in translation (London: Adam & Charles Black, 1956), 96-97. Though not mentioning Joachim explicitly, he refers to some of the enthusiasts of the thirteenth and fourteenth centuries, who, according to Lessing, have perhaps caught a glimpse of this "new eternal gospel," and only erred in predicting its arrival "so near to their own time."

risk our lives in the last holy war after which will be followed by the millennium of freedom."[49] In the context of these secularized versions of millennialism, we must also mention the idea of the kingdom of God in America, a country which is not called the New World just because it was discovered relatively late. Even Auguste Comte's idea of history as an ascent from the theological through the metaphysical up to the scientific phase is not unrelated to Joachim's notion of the three ages.[50]

Again the Marxian dialectic of the three stages of primitive communism, class society, and the final communism as the realm of freedom in which the state will have withered away, has its antecedents in Joachim's three ages. This is no less true of the phrase "the Third Reich," as a name for that "new order" which was to last a thousand years but fortunately only lasted from 1933 to 1945. The messianic self-consciousness of the Nazi ideology can be seen in the fact that Adolf Hitler was called *"der Führer"* (leader) of this Reich ("empire" or "kingdom") and was greeted by millions with *"Heil!"* (salvation).[51] As Norman Cohn perceptively writes: "Communists no less than Nazis have been obsessed by the vision of a prodigious 'final, decisive struggle' in which a 'chosen people' will destroy a world tyranny and thereby inaugurate a new epoch in world history. As in the Nazi apocalypse the 'Arian race' was to purify the earth by annihilating the 'Jewish race,' so in the Communist apocalypse the 'bourgeoisie' is to be exterminated by the 'proletariat.' And here, too, we are faced with the secularized version of a phantasy that is many centuries old."[52] While Joachim still was looking for a leader, both the communists and the Nazis thought well enough of themselves to provide this leadership. Yet as soon as finite humanity wants to bring about the conditions of the infinite, of eternal peace and equality, only terrorism results. Even after these dramatic failures, millennialism has not collapsed.

49. Karl Marx and Friedrich Engels, *Historisch-Kritische Gesamtausgabe* (Frankfurt am Main: Marx-Engels-Archiv, 1927), 1/2:225-26; quoted in Bloch, 2:515.

50. So Norman Cohn, *The Pursuit of the Millennium: Revolutionary Messianism in Medieval and Reformation Europe and Its Bearing on Modern Totalitarian Movements,* 2nd ed. (New York: Harper Torchbooks, 1961), 101.

51. Cf. Löwith, 159. It seems strange that in describing Joachim and his idea of the Third Reich, Bloch passes over Hitler and his utopian dreams with silence. Should this indicate that Hitler's program cannot be integrated into a "principle of hope"?

52. Cohn, 311.

c. Keeping the Fervor

The work of Daniel Witby (1688-1726) in England, Johann Albrecht
Bengel (1687-1752) in Germany, and Jonathan Edwards (1703-58) in the
American colonies fueled millennial ideas with new influence in the
nineteenth century.[53] These authors taught that the decline of the papacy would give way to a new outpouring of the Holy Spirit, the conversion and restitution of the Jewish nation, and the evangelization of
the world and then usher in a long period of peace and thriving for the
church on earth prior to the parousia. Edwards, a Congregational pastor
in Northampton, Massachusetts, paved the way for the Great Awakening (1734-44) in the American colonies with his powerful sermons. He
advocated a missionary eschatological activism in which evangelization
and the mission to the heathen were interpreted as signs of the approaching millennium. The emerging American nation was considered
by some a "savior nation" that furthered the salvation of the whole
world, and some even wondered whether the millennium was not already taking place there. Settlements with decidedly biblical names,
such as Bethel, Bethlehem, Palestine, and New Harmony, underscore
the biblical aspirations of many settlers. Also the French Revolution,
whether understood as something positive or negative, intensified apocalyptic aspirations.

The nineteenth century witnessed the emergence of larger millennial groups which are still quite attractive today. Foremost among these
are the Jehovah's Witnesses, who claim that the millennium is a time of
testing for those who have not yet found salvation in this life. The Mormons, or the Church of Jesus Christ of Latter-Day Saints, see the
United States at the center of their millennial hopes. In their creed,
point 10, we read: "We believe that Zion will be founded on the American continent, that Christ will personally rule the earth, that this earth
will be renewed and it will gain paradisiacal splendor."[54] Similarly, the
Seventh-Day Adventists expect a premillennial, personal, visible return
of Christ at a time unknown but close at hand.[55] After the millennium,

53. Cf. for the following, Richard Baukham, "Chiliasmus IV. Reformation und
Neuzeit," in *TRE*, 7:741-43.
54. Creed (10), as quoted by Åke V. Ström, "Mormonen," in *TRE*, 23:317.
55. Cf. Anthony A. Hoekema, *The Four Major Cults: Christian Science, Jehovah's Witnesses, Mormonism, Seventh-Day Adventism* (Grand Rapids: Eerdmans, 1963), 137.

from the ruins of the old earth, a new earth will be created as the final place for the immortal saints.

Often millennial expectations have been accompanied by withdrawal from the world. This can be seen best in utopian communities of this country such as the Shakers or the Oneida Community.[56] This leads us to the last group of occasional representatives of millennialism, namely, pietistic, fundamentalistic, and revivalistic groups. To demonstrate the necessity for conversion, they welcome chiliastic ideas.

Since such millennial ideas are becoming increasingly popular, and since their characteristics are quite often confusing, we would like to provide some systematization, tenuous as it may be.[57] Generally speaking, one can distinguish between the four main types of millennialism:

Historic Premillennialism

This notion is most closely patterned to Revelation 20:1-15 and holds that Christ will return to the earth prior to the last day in order to exercise rule over the nations for a thousand years in the last stage of human history. It is pessimistic concerning the role and prospects of the church in human history; therefore it posits a millennium between Christ's return and the last day. During this period Christ will rule in person over a theocratic kingdom to which all the nations of the world are subject. Periods of great personal and societal anxiety and despair have tended to intensify the hopes in a premillennial intervention of Christ so that the faithful have at least some respite amid the turmoil of this world.

---

56. The Shakers originated from a French Protestant sect and, under the leadership of Ann Lee (1736-84), came to this country via England toward the latter half of the eighteenth century. Their highpoint was during the 1840s when they had founded over a dozen villages in eight states. For more see Edward D. Andrews, *The People Called Shakers: A Search for the Perfect Society* (New York: Oxford University Press, 1953). The Oneida Community, based in Oneida, New York, was founded by John Humphrey Noyes (1811-86), who was converted to millennial beliefs at a protracted revival meeting in 1831.

57. A helpful and concise summary and critique of millennial ideas is given by Ted Peters, *Futures — Human and Divine* (Atlanta: John Knox, 1978), 28-36. An extensive and careful treatment of millennialism is also given by Anthony A. Hoekema, *The Bible and the Future* (Grand Rapids: Eerdmans, 1979), esp. 173-238.

Postmillennialism

This notion is more optimistic. Encouraged by the progressive spirit of nineteenth-century society, especially in the emerging American nation, it expects a future millennium or latter-day prosperity of the church prior to Christ's coming. It holds that the return of Christ introduces not a temporal kingdom but eternal peace and blessedness. It does, however, expect a period before the return of Christ and before the end of the age in which the church will have fulfilled its task in the world and proclaimed the gospel to all people.

The Reformed tradition especially has shown affinity to and support for the postmillennial perspective. This is due largely to the Reformed emphasis on the sovereignty of God, the belief that Christ is now Lord over all spheres of human life, and the conviction that the Christian community has been empowered by the Holy Spirit to call and work for the promulgation of the gospel and the transformation of culture and society to conform to the mind and will of Christ.

Amillennialism

This approach disregards the hope for a millennium. There will be no future golden age upon the earth for the church. Whatever rule Christ exercises within history is in the spiritual sphere, in the souls of individuals, or in the life of the church. It contains no vision of hope for its future prior to the last day when Christ returns to institute the new world and manifests his kingdom. Optimistic amillennialism concedes that the church will have *nearly* finished its task and that its Lord is near. Periods of spiritual awakening and missionary advance have generally reinforced postmillennial and optimistic amillennial expectations.

Dispensational Premillennialism

Dispensationalism provides a precise system for premillennial ideas. Human history is divided into a series of ages (dispensations) in which humanity is tested with respect to some revealed aspect of God's will. In each case humanity fails, is judged by God, and is then set on the course of history under new covenant conditions. The seven dispensations are labeled: innocence (in the garden), conscience (up to the flood), human government (since Babel), promise (since Abraham), law (since Moses), grace (since Christ), and kingdom (the coming millennium). The age of grace ends with the unseen coming of Christ for his church (the rapture), both the living and — by partial resurrection — the dead in Christ.

A period of seven years, marked by an international treaty of peace, including a protectorate of Israel, ensues on earth. These seven years are "the time of Jacob's troubles," a leftover of the seventy times 7 years, or 490 years, promised as judgment over Israel as the Babylonian captivity to Israel, but which lasted only 483 years.[58] Judgment ends with the expiating death of Christ. Midway in the final seven years the Antichrist reveals himself, claiming to be the Messiah, and institutes a controlled world economy and persecutes the Jews for their refusal to worship him. Christ appears with his church and the legions of angels to quell the Antichrist forces, bind Satan for a thousand years, and establish the millennial kingdom under the reestablished throne of David on earth and the church as the New Jerusalem hovering visibly in space above the earth. Following the millennium, sinful humanity rejects this era of enforced peace and plenty by following the then-released Satan in an effort to conquer the Holy City. The uprising is crushed. The general resurrection then occurs, the final judgment, the renewal of heaven and earth, and the dawn of eternity.

This elaborate futurology has strong appeal. It seems to accommodate affairs and events of the modern world to prophetic Scriptures, as other millennial theories have done in the past. It also places a benediction on the "world's mess" which only Christ can correct in visible power. It eliminates social responsibility other than the Christian's duty in citizenship. And it provides joy in every sign of approaching calamity, for calamity demands parousia. Finally it makes divine election absolute, and freedom of the human will is lost in the detailed chart of established future events.

Dispensational premillennialism, with its concept of a rapture of the Christians, seems to attract the curious or frightened minds of many people. The term "rapture" has been used since the nineteenth century

---

58. For the calculations see J. Barton Payne, *Encyclopedia of Biblical Prophecy: The Complete Guide to Scriptural Predictions and Their Fulfilment* (New York: Harper & Row, 1973), 384-85, where the different calculations are compared with each other.

to express the idea that living Christians will be caught up from the earth to meet Jesus Christ at his second coming. The term is derived from the Latin *rapere*, found in the expression "caught up" in the Latin translation of 1 Thessalonians 4:17. John F. Walvoord (b. 1910), former president of Dallas Theological Seminary and editor of *Bibliotheca Sacra*, writes in his book *The Rapture Question* that "if this is a literal, future event, it is a most important aspect of the hope of the church."[59] Since Christians will be spared the final tribulations, "at the time of the rapture the saints meet Christ in the air, while at the second coming Christ returns to the Mount of Olives to meet the saints on earth."[60]

Yet the concept of a rapture is not as old as some of its advocates would like to think. It gained prominence in Great Britain with John Nelson Darby (1800-1882), a founder of the Plymouth Brethren, when in the 1830s he advocated a "secret rapture" of the faithful.[61] In North America it became popular through the Scofield Reference Bible, first published in 1909, in which the Presbyterian minister Cyrus Ingerson Scofield (1843-1921) also advocated seven distinct periods of salvation, with the present time falling between the sixth and the seventh period and therefore close to the impending end. A certain intellectual and theological respectability was further given to it in Lewis Sperry Chafer's (1871-1952) seven-volume *Systematic Theology* (1948); Chafer was the founder and first president of Dallas Theological Seminary.[62] The tradition has been carried on under his successor, John F. Walvoord, in the seminary's theological quarterly, *Bibliotheca Sacra*. Dispensational theology is also taught at many Bible colleges and institutes and is promulgated by certain publishing houses. But it gained its greatest popularity with a graduate of Dallas Theological Seminary whose writings are saturated with dispensational theology, Hal Lindsey.[63]

There are at least four varieties of the idea of rapture:

59. John F. Walvoord, *The Rapture Question* (Grand Rapids: Dunham, 1964), 8.
60. Walvoord, 198.
61. Cf. the informed study by Larry V. Crutchfield, *The Origins of Dispensationalism: The Darby Factor* (Lanham, Md.: University Press of America, 1992), 172-74.
62. Cf. Lewis Sperry Chafer, *Systematic Theology*, vol. 4, *Ecclesiology-Eschatology* (Dallas: Dallas Seminary Press, 1948), 374-78.
63. Cf. C. Vanderwaal, *Hal Lindsey and Biblical Prophecy* (St. Catharines, Ont.: Paideia, 1981), 26-47, who gives a good introduction to the problematic nature of dispensationalism and Hal Lindsey's connection with this doctrine.

1. Pretribulationalism holds that the rapture takes place before the seventh week of Daniel (Dan. 9:27).
2. Midtribulationalism teaches that the rapture takes place in the middle of what Daniel calls the seventieth week.
3. Posttribulationalism postpones the rapture until the resurrection, since the first resurrection is not mentioned until Revelation 20:4-5.
4. Partial rapturism introduces the idea that there are both spiritual and carnal Christians and argues that only the spiritual are translated before the tribulation, while the carnal are left to be tested.

As the many and often conflicting ideas concerning rapture and millennialism indicate, these are highly controversial topics, even in "conservative" Christian circles where one or the other variety is advocated. We could simply discard these theories as "undue speculation over highly symbolic teachings."[64] Indeed, most of these speculations do not stand up to historically informed exegesis of the biblical texts, and, as we have seen with Lindsey, they often rest on dangerous theological presuppositions.[65] Even dispensationalists agree that they "must protect themselves and their churches from speculations and sensationalism which do not build up the body of Christ, but lead to delusion, resentment, and faithlessness when would-be prophecies under the guise of interpretation fail."[66]

Progressive dispensationalists question the validity of the historicist's approach that can provide us with a verifiable "countdown to Armageddon." Interpreters of the Bible who identify specific current events as the future tribulational fulfillment of the Day of the Lord or the mysterious visions of biblical apocalyptic are overstepping their boundaries. According to progressive dispensationalists, one should observe that in biblical history itself, prophetic fulfillment has always been identified and pro-

64. So rightly, Dale Moody, "Rapture," *Encyclopedia of Southern Baptists*, 2:1133, who also cites the above-mentioned four varieties of rapture.

65. Robert Jewett, *Jesus against the Rapture: Seven Unexpected Prophecies* (Philadelphia: Westminster, 1979), 139, shows that Paul wants to assure the Christians in Thessalonica that they will not be separated when Christ comes. Yet what was once "intended as a metaphor of togetherness" is now turned "into a theology of separation and escape."

66. Craig A. Blaising and Darrell L. Bock, *Progressive Dispensationalism: An Up-to-Date Handbook of Contemporary Dispensational Thought* (Wheaton, Ill.: BridgePoint, 1993), 294.

claimed by prophetic authority. Yet it is exactly this authority that is mistakenly claimed by modern doomsday prophets. Moreover, "the re-employment of literary descriptions in later prophecy and apocalyptic calls into question the assumption that this language gives *one concrete historical scenario* in partially codified form."[67] This means that we have to concede that we do not have a timetable eschatology outlining the millennium. We have only highly symbolic language.

Yet we notice that even Lutheran theologians such as Reinhold Frank (1827-94) and J. C. K. von Hofmann (1810-77) of the Erlangen school and Carl A. Auberlen (1824-64) of Basel, Switzerland, advocated millennial ideas.[68] Does this, however, change the shaky scriptural basis for these ideas? Many Christians are looking for a visible sign of the proleptic anticipation of the goal they hope for. It is also tempting for many to identify the results of their eschatological worldview with the fulfillment they are promised to reach in the eschaton. But can we really expect Christ, who during his life on earth rejected vehemently all nationalistic and political messianic aspirations, to establish a transitory kingdom of God on earth, as millennial thinking requires?

In conclusion we should note that the book of Revelation, the only New Testament writing that explicitly thematizes a millennium, does not occupy the center stage of the New Testament message but is on the periphery. From the very beginning, the interpretation of the vision in Revelation 20:1-15 has been controversial.[69] In the course of history, it has often been misused for political and religious purposes. Yet when we look at the book of Revelation as a whole, then in spite of all the difficulties and ambiguities of this passage, we can draw some important insights.

1. Confronted with a government which threatens the very existence of the church, the seer of Revelation announces the final rule of

---

67. Blaising and Bock, 294.

68. Cf. Paul Althaus, in his still unsurpassed treatment of eschatology: *Die letzten Dinge: Lehrbuch der Eschatologie,* 7th ed. (Gütersloh: Bertelsmann, 1957), 303-5.

69. Cf. for the following, Klemens Stock, S.J., *Das letzte Wort hat Gott: Apokalypse als Frohbotschaft* (Innsbruck: Tyrolia, 1985), 128-31. Cf. also Margaret Nutting Ralph, *The Bible and the End of the World: Should We Be Afraid?* (New York: Paulist, 1997), esp. 69-113, who shows that the book of Revelation belongs to apocalyptic literature written "to people suffering persecution. It is reminding them that God is always faithful to God's promises, so God can be depended upon to save them" (88).

Christ and of his kingdom. This means that those who have paid for their faithfulness to Christ with their own lives will not remain in death but will participate in Christ's rule. The details of this rule are not spelled out. The thousand years only express the fullness of its duration and do not stand for an exact timetable. Christ's rule is no fantasy land. This precludes that one could make this rule more impressive by citing Old Testament texts or using one's own imagination and desires. The rule is not brought about by humanity, nor can any of us calculate its inception. There are no hints in the text for such attempts. This is in line with the message of the book of Revelation, that the final victory and rule will certainly belong to Jesus and those who are faithful to him. Christ's rule is prior to the end-time completion. But it does not allow us to spell out in detail how both are related to each other.

2. All of the eschatological timetables that we could devise miss the intention of this vision that shows, in the face of seeming defeat, the victory of Christ and those who are faithful to him. Therefore the millennium is not to be understood in a triumphalistic manner, but as a pastoral comfort. It shows the conviction that God will ultimately make his kingdom triumph. Those who belong to God will not be abandoned, and their reward will be sure.

3. Universal Salvation *(Apokatastasis Panton)*

The idea that eventually everybody will be saved and enter into God's glory is often closely associated with some kind of purgatory. For instance, Immanuel Kant claimed that in order for our will to be fully appropriate to the moral law, we need "infinite progress" which can only be assured through a continued existence in another life.[70] While purgatory, however, seems to be reserved only for Christians, the vision in the idea of universal homecoming is expanded to include all people. As with all problem areas of eschatology, we have little biblical ground to go on for a universal homecoming or a restoration of all things to God.

70. Immanuel Kant, *Critique of Practical Reason* 5.121, in Immanuel Kant, *Critique of Practical Reason and Other Writings in Moral Philosophy,* translated and edited with an introduction by Lewis W. Beck (Chicago: University of Chicago Press, 1949), 225-26.

The Greek term for this idea *(apokatastasis panton)* occurs only once in the New Testament, in Acts 3:21, when Peter addresses the Jewish people, saying that Jesus "must remain in heaven until the time of universal restoration that God announced long ago through his holy prophets." Of course, it is evident that Peter refers here to the fulfillment of the Old Testament promises and not to a universal homecoming. Other passages in the New Testament, such as 1 Corinthians 15:22, where Paul says that, as in Adam all die, so "all will be made alive in Christ," and where the all-inclusiveness of Christ's redemptive act is emphasized, seem to provide a sounder basis for the idea of a universal salvation. In consulting some prominent representatives of this idea, we will soon notice, however, that they are not much interested in founding this idea on biblical grounds.

a. Origen and the Origins of the Apokatastasis Idea

The origin of the idea of a universal homecoming is obscure. In Parsism the dualism between the good god Ormuzd and the evil god Ahriman is resolved in a final monism. All people have the chance of eventual purification, and after the destruction of Ahriman and his demons, even hell will be purified. Plato, one of the founders of Western philosophy, holds that the human soul can return from Hades, the place of the "underworld," and be reincarnated. Then, after death, the migration starts again, because the human soul is like water. First it comes down from heaven, then it ascends into heaven, and again it must go down to earth in eternal change.[71] This cyclic view of history coincides with the astrology of antiquity, where the term *apokatastasis* stands for the return of the stellar bodies to their initial starting point. In Christian theology the Neoplatonist idea stands in the background for the doctrine of a universal homecoming where evil has no actual reality and, at the consummation of the world, will be exposed as such and lapse into nothingness.[72]

It is not surprising that Origen (ca. 185–ca. 254), one of the most

71. Cf. Plato, *Phaedrus* 247bff., in Plato, *The Complete Works,* edited with an introduction and notes by John M. Cooper (Indianapolis: Hackett, 1997), 525.

72. Cf. Kehl, 296, who points to Neoplatonism as one of the sources of the *apokatastasis* idea.

brilliant and provocative theologians of the early church and in all like-lihood a former student of the Neoplatonist philosopher Ammonius Saccas (†241/42), advocates both a cyclic view of history and an *apokata-stasis panton* when he states: "Such is the end, when 'all enemies shall have been subjected to Christ.' . . . For the end is always like the begin-ning; as therefore there is one end of all things, so we must understand that there is one beginning of all things, and as there is one end of many things, so from one beginning arise many differences and varieties, which in their turn are restored, through God's goodness, through their subjection to Christ and their unity with the Holy Spirit, to one end, which is like the beginning."[73]

Origen believes that, in his goodness, "God through Christ will re-store his entire creation; even his enemies being conquered and sub-dued."[74] By the instruction of angelic and higher powers and by the use of one's free will, everyone will be renewed and restored, having under-gone "various movements of progress."[75] In the end there will be a com-plete destruction of the body, "for wherever bodies are, corruption fol-lows immediately," and the end of all things will be incorporeal.[76]

> If then the end is renewed after the pattern of the origin and the issue
> of things made to resemble their beginning and that condition restored
> which rational nature once enjoyed when it had no need to eat of the
> tree of the knowledge of good and evil, so that all consciousness of evil
> has departed and given place to what is sincere and pure and he alone
> who is the one good God becomes all things to the soul and he himself
> is all things not in some few or in many things but in all things, when
> there is nowhere any death, nowhere any sting of death, nowhere any
> evil at all, then truly God will be all in all.[77]

Even the devil himself will not be excluded from the final spiritual unity with God. This return to the beginning is not, however, under-stood as a final goal or fulfillment, because it always includes the possi-

---

73. Origen, *On First Principles: Being Koetschau's Text of "De Principiis"* 1.6.2, trans. G. W. Butterworth, ed. Henri de Lubac (New York: Harper Torchbooks, 1966), 53.
74. Origen, *On First Principles* 1.6.1, 52.
75. Origen, *On First Principles* 1.6.3, 57.
76. Origen, *On First Principles* 3.6.1, 247.
77. Origen, *On First Principles* 3.6.3, 248.

bility of a new fall and new salvational cycles.[78] The constant scriptural references in Origen's discourse should not be overlooked (cf. Ps. 110:1; 1 Cor. 15:25, 27-28; John 17:22-23; and others). It must also be mentioned that Origen proposed his ideas only "for discussion" and not as dogmatic statements.[79] Nevertheless, he seems to miss the intention of the biblical references he quotes. He is more influenced by Platonic philosophy than by the eschatological outlook of the New Testament. Even so, his thoughts proved to be so stimulating for adventurous minds that the church found it necessary to condemn him twice, first at a local synod in 543, where some of his statements were considered heretical, and more summarily at the Fifth Ecumenical Council in Constantinople in 553.[80] Even the presbyter Rufinus (ca. 345-410), to whom we owe the Latin translation of Origen's book *On First Principles* from the Greek, made certain adjustments in his translation to make Origen's thoughts, especially on the topic of universal homecoming, more acceptable to the Western mind.

We should be careful, however, not to condemn Origen too quickly. While the notion of a final consummation or an *apokatastasis* is an important concept for him, the charge of universalism is quite tricky.[81] Origen emphasizes punishment in order to heal or to educate. He presents a picture of an evolutionary process toward an end and places more emphasis on the process than on the goal. Therefore the aspects of return and restoration but not consummation are of supreme importance.[82] Indeed, Origen does not even seem to rule out a twofold outcome when he writes: "The wicked, who in this life have loved the darkness of error and the night of ignorance, will after the resurrection be clothed with murky and black bodies, in order that this very gloom of ignorance, which in the present world has taken possession of the inner ports of their mind, may in the world to come be revealed through the

---

78. Origen, *On First Principles* 3.6.5, 250-52.

79. Origen, *On First Principles* 1.6.1, 52. This assertion might reflect more the opinion of the translator (Rufinus) than that of Origen.

80. Heinrich Denzinger, *The Sources of Catholic Dogma*, pars. 203-11 and 223 (St. Louis: B. Herder, 1957), 84-85 and 88.

81. Celia Ellen Rabinowitz, in her dissertation (Fordham, 1989), "*Apokatastasis and Sunteleia:* Eschatological and Soteriological Speculation in Origen," 182, rightly states that "the question of universalism . . . is one which will remain a paradox."

82. Rabinowitz, 161.

garment of their outward body."[83] We should not forget that for Origen, his Neoplatonic schooling notwithstanding, a universal homecoming is not a philosophical postulate. Ultimately, it rests on the christological conviction that through Christ God has redeemed the whole creation, a feat that does not tolerate any exception.[84]

Its problematic nature notwithstanding, the idea of a universal homecoming has always attracted speculative minds. During the Reformation, spiritualists such as Hans Denck (ca. 1495-1527) and certain Anabaptist groups advocated a universal homecoming. Therefore the Augsburg Confession found it necessary to take a stand against the idea that "there will be an end to the punishments of the condemned men and devils."[85] The Reformed *Confessio Helvetica Posterior* also condemned the idea of a universal homecoming. In more recent times it was especially the Enlightenment and then Pietism that proposed a universal salvation. In the so-called New World of the American colonies, theologians of various denominations, such as Anglicans, Presbyterians, Congregationalists, Baptists, Quakers, and Methodists, advocated universalist ideas. In 1790 the "Independent Church of Christ, commonly called Universalists," was explicitly founded to advocate the truth of a universal salvation.[86] Later on it was the influence of Schleiermacher that helped pave the way for more widespread acceptance of that idea.

b. The Apokatastasis Idea in More Recent Theological Reflection

Friedrich Schleiermacher's advocacy of a kind of purgatory is necessary within his theological system in order to allow for the universal homecoming of all humanity. For him world history was a developmental

---

83. Origen, *On First Principles* 2.10.3, 145. Cf. also Rabinowitz, 150 n. 32, who indicates the difficulty of clearly establishing whether Origen means here a twofold outcome as a preliminary or final event.

84. So also Werner van Laak, *Allversöhnung: Die Lehre von der Apokatastasis: Ihre Grundlegung durch Origenes und ihre Bewertung in der gegenwärtigen Theologie bei Karl Barth und Hans Urs von Balthasar* (Sinzig, Germany: Sankt Meinrad Verlag Christine Maria Esser, 1990), 90.

85. Augsburg Confession 17, in *The Book of Concord*, 38.

86. Cf. Ernst Staehelin, *Die Wiederbringung aller Dinge* (Basel: Helbing & Lichtenhahn, 1960), 27.

process made possible through God's foreordination and guidance to lead all of humanity to a comprehensive completion of highest spirituality. Already in 1819, in his treatise *On the Doctrine of Election,* he argued that eternal damnation was inconsistent with the eternal love of God. What one traditionally calls damnation is only a necessary developmental stage, and the difference between the faithful who die and those without faith who die is a difference only between earlier and later reception into the kingdom.

In his 1821/22 dogmatics, *The Christian Faith,* Schleiermacher again devotes considerable attention to God's divine foreordination. He concludes that God's grace is incessantly active, and that New Testament passages, such as Acts 2:41 and 13:48, certainly do not indicate that those who did not believe at one time could not possibly become believers at some later date. There are always some in whom the initiation of blessedness in Christ has not yet occurred. But those who, to us, appear to have been passed over by God's foreordination to blessedness are not outside all divine activity and divine decree. They are "objects of the same divine activity that gathered the Church together, and are embraced along with us all under the same divine fore-ordination."[87] As for Teilhard de Chardin, the church becomes the world and God's saving grace the spiritual development of humanity.

Schleiermacher asserts that, if there were a twofold outcome (blessedness and damnation) after the last judgment, the church would be incomplete. Furthermore, sympathy for the condemned would impair the happiness of the saved.[88] Thus divine foreordination will prevent the final victory of evil over even one part of the human race. Schleiermacher concludes:

> From whichever side we view it, then, there are great difficulties in thinking that the finite issue of redemption is such that some thereby obtain the highest bliss, while others (in the ordinary view, indeed, the majority of the human race) are lost in irrevocable misery. We ought not to retain such an idea without decisive testimony to the fact that it was to this that Christ Himself looked forward; and such testimony is wholly lacking. Hence we ought at least to admit the equal rights of the

87. Friedrich Schleiermacher, *The Christian Faith,* §119, ed. H. R. Mackintosh and J. S. Stewart (New York: Harper Torchbooks, 1963), 2:548.
88. Schleiermacher, §162, 2:716.

milder view, of which likewise there are traces in Scripture; the view, namely, that through the power of redemption there will one day be a universal restoration of all souls.[89]

In spite of his strong criticism of the Roman Catholic doctrine of purgatory, Paul Tillich sympathizes with the *apokatastasis* idea too, since it is a "powerful expression of belief in the unity of individual and universal destiny in Eternal Life."[90] Like Schleiermacher, he also rejects the idea of double predestination in which God has selected only a few for eternal bliss. God would thus become a demon, "contradicting the God who creates the world for the sake of fulfillment of all created potentialities."[91] According to Tillich, the idea of a twofold eternal destiny contradicts the idea of God's continuous creation of the finite as something "very good." "Everything as created is rooted in the eternal ground of being. In this respect non-being cannot prevail against it."[92] We find here a similar unity of God (the ground of being) and the world as we found in Schleiermacher. Similar to Schleiermacher, Tillich also feels that the condemnation of one person would impair the state of bliss of the other, because "his essence and that of the other cannot be absolutely separated."[93]

Tillich realizes very well that the fear that "the teaching of *apokatastasis* would destroy the seriousness of religious and ethical decisions" is not unfounded.[94] Still, he finds several reasons why a twofold outcome of life would be impossible. For instance, there are often distorted forms of human life where physical, biological, psychological, or sociological conditions make it impossible to reach a fulfillment of the essential goal of life even to a small degree, as in the case of premature death or mental illness. Furthermore, the total being, including both the conscious and unconscious sides, of every individual is largely determined by the social conditions which influence one upon entering existence.[95] There are uncounted millions who never had a chance to be exposed to the

89. Schleiermacher, §163, 2:722.
90. Paul Tillich, *Systematic Theology*, 3 vols. (Chicago: University of Chicago Press, 1951-63), 3:418.
   91. Tillich, 3:418.
   92. Tillich, 3:415.
   93. Tillich, 3:409.
   94. Tillich, 3:416.
   95. Tillich, 3:408.

proclamation of the salvific message of Christ. Finally, there is the ambiguity of life itself. Even a saint remains a sinner and needs forgiveness. And if a sinner rejects forgiveness, "his rejection of it remains ambiguous," because even if we are pushed into despair it is the divine spirit who works in us.[96]

Tillich proposes the term "essentialization" to describe a solution that maintains a seriousness of one's life decision and still secures a universal homecoming. Essentialization means "a creative synthesis of a being's essential nature with what it has made of it in its temporal existence."[97] Insofar as the negative has maintained possession of this existence, it is excluded from life eternal, but insofar as the essential has conquered the existential distortion, it will be lifted up into life eternal. The conceptual symbol of essentialization, according to Tillich, "emphasizes the despair of having wasted one's potentialities yet also assures the elevation of the positive within existence (even in the most unfulfilled life) into eternity."[98] This would mean that we are not accepted or rejected in our entirety. Part of us will participate in eternal life and part will be excluded from it. The decisive factor for participation is to what extent essentialization has taken place in our existence.

Karl Barth has made a very interesting proposal that does not plead for mercy on those who fall by the wayside, but starts with the triumph of grace. God gives humanity his grace and its universality. God's will for justice is expressed in the covenant God makes with humanity and through which humanity receives the sin-forgiving grace of God. According to Barth, sin is the human refusal to acknowledge God's justice and to insist, instead, on one's own justice. God's gracious election occurred in Jesus Christ, and according to Barth, this is a double predestination since Jesus Christ receives rejection and humanity receives election. As Barth writes: "In Jesus Christ thou, too, art not rejected — for He has borne thy rejection — but elected."[99] Barth even calls Jesus

---

96. Tillich, 3:408. Of course, we notice in Tillich's last example that his understanding of God as the all-embracing (monistic) power endangers the New Testament emphasis on the antigodly and not just nongodly reality of evil.

97. Tillich, 3:401.

98. Tillich, 3:407.

99. Karl Barth, *Church Dogmatics* II/2, ed. G. W. Bromiley and T. F. Torrance, 4 vols. (Edinburgh: T. & T. Clark, 1936-62), 322.

Christ "the only truly rejected man."[100] Each individual human being is predestined toward grace, and the only question that remains is how long one can resist this divine election which has been decided before all time and has already occurred in Jesus Christ and not at the end of time in some kind of *apokatastasis*. Therefore, Barth writes, "The church will then not preach an apokatastasis, nor will it preach a powerless grace of Jesus Christ or a wickedness of men which is too powerful for it. But without any weakening of the contrast, and also without any arbitrary dualism, it will preach the overwhelming power of grace and the weakness of human wickedness in face of it."[101]

This diminution of human sinfulness and wickedness by Barth goes together with him calling evil "nothingness" and not wanting to accord it any self-sufficient existence independent from God.[102] The gracious will of God is so strongly emphasized by Barth that what strives and works against God cannot approach a genuine existence. Ultimately, everything will be received into the salvific realm of God. Barth argues always from the grace of God, from God's covenant with humanity.

While Barth does not want to teach an *apokatastasis*, he still feels it is right to ponder whether that concept does not have some positive significance, though he feels it could lead to antinomianism and an inappropriate laissez-faire approach to God. But he claims he is sure "that we have no theological right to set up any sort of limit to the loving-kindness of God which has appeared in Jesus Christ."[103] Barth rejects the idea of an *apokatastasis*, since he regards it as a product of human fantasy, the result of human calculations which then would restrict God's freedom.[104] He sees in this idea the human claim that God eventually has to save all people. Yet such an idea is the result of human conceit.

For Barth, the universal hope is grounded in the cross and resurrec-

---

100. Barth, *Church Dogmatics* II/2, 319.

101. Barth, *Church Dogmatics* II/2, 477.

102. For Barth's understanding of nothingness, cf. Hans Schwarz, *Evil: A Historical and Theological Perspective* (Minneapolis: Fortress, 1995), 163-68.

103. Karl Barth, *The Humanity of God*, trans. Thomas Wieser (Richmond: John Knox, 1960), 62.

104. So correctly Rolf Rochusch in his 1974 dissertation "Untersuchung über die Stellung Karl Barths zur Lehre von der Apokatastasis in der 'Kirchlichen Dogmatik': Darstellung und Auseinandersetzung mit der Kritik" (Kirchliche Hochschule Berlin), 196-97 and 292.

tion of Jesus Christ when Christ has suffered in our place and was rejected instead of us. Yet one wonders whether, similar to Origen, evil is for Barth not simply an epiphenomenon that either goes away through God's power or can finally be integrated into the whole of salvation. While we agree with Barth that we should hope for the salvation of all, his hope is solidified into a doctrine, that of the election of all. All are elected and will be received into the fold. It is difficult to see how that differs from the *apokatastasis* that Barth rejects. Ultimately Barth does exactly what he does not want to do — limit God's freedom and sovereignty.

c. Apokatastasis or "Christ's Descent into Hell"?

When we look at the New Testament, we notice that the tenor is not one of universal homecoming but of a twofold outcome of human history, namely, acceptance and rejection. Jesus' parables, of which the ten bridesmaids (Matt. 25:1-13) and the rich man and Lazarus (Luke 16:19-31) are good examples, confront us with the prospect of a definite and irrevocable final judgment of rejection or acceptance. And a remark such as "if your hand causes you to stumble, cut it off; it is better for you to enter life maimed than to have two hands and to go to hell, to the unquenchable fire" (Mark 9:43) demands a decision which has ultimate consequences. Even Paul, when he emphasizes salvation as the universal intention for all people, does not tone down Jesus' call for a decision; he just expands it.

A universalistic message would contradict the New Testament's clear insistence that our response to the gospel determines our final destiny. God is not a puppeteer, and he takes us seriously as individual beings even if we deny him. The idea of a (double) predestination diminishes human freedom and likens God to a divine watchmaker who once determined the course of our individual histories and now dispassionately watches its fulfillment. But God is not aloof: he grants us the privilege of choosing our own destiny. A twofold outcome of the last judgment would not impair God's authority. God, who already rules over the saved and the condemned, will be revealed in the new world as the victor over hell and all antigodly powers. This is the deepest meaning of the statement that God is all in all. Consequently, we must conclude that God invites everybody to attain the final goal, but that there is also a "too late."

However, it should give us pause for thought that even for a conservative theologian like Walter Künneth (1900-1997), the idea of *apokatastasis* "represents an ultimate consequence of the doctrine of the aeons, and as such a theological necessity."[105] Similarly, Paul Althaus (1888-1966) states that until eternity commences, faith is always on the way from the fear of a possible twofold outcome to a prayerful hoping for a universal homecoming. Dogmatics, he says, can neither take a stand for or against *apokatastasis*, nor for or against a twofold outcome. Althaus concludes that only those who are prayerfully on the way from the fear of a twofold outcome for themselves and for others to the faithfulness of God can hope for a universal homecoming.[106]

We can receive guidance in this matter from the church's struggle with a similar issue, namely, whether those who had lived before Christ and therefore could not respond to him while he preached among the people of Israel would be eternally lost. This issue was even more bothersome because all the members of the first Christian community had loved ones who had not explicitly accepted Christ during their lifetime. In part, the results of their deliberations found their way into Scripture (cf. 1 Cor. 7:14 and 15:29),[107] and in a very significant way into the Apostles' Creed when it states that "he [Jesus Christ] descended into hell."[108]

The phrase "he descended into hell," or as it is now more adequately translated, "he went to the dead," is one of the last statements to be incorporated into the Apostles' Creed. Though the descent into the realm of the dead is nowhere explicitly mentioned in the New Testa-

---

105. Walter Künneth, *The Theology of the Resurrection*, trans. James W. Leitch (London: SCM, 1965), 291.

106. Cf. Paul Althaus, *Die christliche Wahrheit: Lehrbuch der Dogmatik*, 6th ed. (Gütersloh: Gerd Mohn, 1959), 671.

107. To the issues of sanctification of the unbelieving partner in a "mixed marriage" and "vicarious baptism," cf. Hans Conzelmann, *A Commentary on the First Epistle to the Corinthians*, trans. J. W. Leitch (Philadelphia: Fortress, 1975), 123-25 and 275-77, in his comments on the passages cited.

108. It is interesting that Jürgen Moltmann, *The Coming of God: Christian Eschatology*, trans. Margaret Kohl (Minneapolis: Fortress, 1996), 237-55, under the rubric "The Restoration of All Things," also concludes with Christ's descent.

ment, it is presupposed or at least implied in several passages.[109] For instance, Matthew 12:40 indicates a passive stay in that realm, whereas other passages point to Christ's actions in this realm. Passages such as Revelation 1:18 ("I was dead, and see, I am alive forever and ever; and I have the keys of Death and of Hades") show Jesus Christ as the one who has won victory over the powers of the realm of the dead. At other places, in the context of Christ's death and resurrection, the redemption of some or all of the dead is mentioned (Matt. 27:51-53). And finally, there are some places where this descent is understood as proclamation to some or all who are in the realm of the dead ("he went and made a proclamation to the spirits in prison," 1 Pet. 3:19).[110]

The neutral sojourn in the realm of the dead proved not very interesting for theological development.[111] Jesus' victorious entry into the realm of the dead, on the other hand, is vividly expressed by Luther. Following the tradition, Luther connected this entry with the liberation of the Old Testament patriarchs from the limbo of the fathers and with their transition to heaven.[112] That Jesus must have been active in the realm of the dead during the three days following his death on Good Friday is concluded from the idea that the divinity of Christ cannot just rest for three days and lie in the tomb.[113]

The church acted wisely when it never dogmatically decided that only some people could have benefited from Christ's descent, namely,

109. This is also admitted by Werner Bieder in his careful study, *Die Vorstellung von der Höllenfahrt Jesu Christi: Beitrag zur Entstehungsgeschichte der Vorstellung vom sog. Descensus ad inferos* (Zürich: Zwingli Verlag, 1949), 129, though he says that the way the descent into hell is referred to in the creed lacks scriptural foundation.

110. For the "descent of Christ," see more extensively Hans Schwarz, *Christology* (Grand Rapids: Eerdmans, 1998), 290-94.

111. Bieder, 202, mentions correctly that two factors contributed decisively to the development of the idea of Christ's descent: the postmortal concern for the destiny of those who had died in Israel prior to the Christ event, and the missionary concern of introducing a victorious Christ to the Gentiles.

112. Cf. Hans Schwarz, "Luther's Understanding of Heaven and Hell," in *Interpreting Luther's Legacy*, ed. Fred W. Meuser and Stanley D. Schneider (Minneapolis: Augsburg, 1969), 92-93.

113. The issue of whether Jesus had died according to his divinity and his humanity, or only according to his human form, was evidently not yet reflected on at that time. The development of the idea of Christ's descent was also furthered by influences from other religions and from Jewish apocalyptic literature (e.g., Enoch!). Cf. for the issue of outside influences, Bieder, 100-101, 203-5, and other places.

the Old Testament patriarchs.[114] Some church fathers (Melito [† ca. 190], Marcion [† ca. 160], and Ephraem [ca. 306-73]) even thought Christ redeemed all the dead except perhaps for some very bad persons. Others (the Alexandrian theologians and Origen) thought that those who had died before the great flood were saved too. It is interesting that the presbyter Rufinus of Aquileia, in northern Italy, who lived for a long time in the East and translated the works of Origen, mentions a creed being used in his hometown around 370 that already contained the phrase of Christ's descent which was subsequently introduced into the Apostles' Creed.[115]

But what does Christ's descent mean? Is it an illegitimate speculation based on uncertain New Testament passages which we should confine to their literal meaning (namely, that on Good Friday Christ went to the dead, as everyone else does when they die)? Theologians, whether in the early church or in more recent times, who have reflected on this phrase and on the biblical passages it interprets did not just speculate on the whereabouts of Christ's divinity during his death. They were much more concerned that those who were geographically or temporally disadvantaged and therefore unable to live their lives in conformity with Christ during their time on earth might be confronted with his offer of salvation in some other form. They found a possibility for such an offer beyond death in Christ's descent to the dead.

Christ's "proclamation to the spirits in prison" (1 Pet. 3:19) could not simply mean an indoctrination but rather a confrontation with the gospel. In some way or another this must imply human freedom and the possibility of reacting to that proclamation in a positive or a negative way.[116] When we hear of a proclamation to the flood generation at the

114. Cf. Ignatius, "Letter to the Magnesians" 9.2, in William R. Schoedel, *Ignatius of Antioch: A Commentary on the Letters of Ignatius of Antioch* (Philadelphia: Fortress, 1985), 123, who claims that the prophets were "disciples in the spirit" and were raised by Christ from the dead. Cf. also Melito of Sardis, "Homily on the Passion" 101-2, in Melito of Sardis, *On Pascha and Fragments,* texts and translation edited by Stuart George Hall (Oxford: Clarendon, 1979), 57.

115. Cf. J. N. D. Kelly, *Early Christian Creeds,* 3rd ed. (New York: David McKay, 1976), 378-83, who deals extensively with the probable origin of the descent in the creed.

116. Cf. for the following, Heinz-Jürgen Vogels, *Christi Abstieg ins Totenreich und das Läuterungsgericht an den Toten: Eine bibeltheologisch-dogmatische Untersuchung zum Glaubensartikel "descendit ad inferos"* (Freiburg: Herder, 1976), 136-37.

time of Noah, then this is not a limitation, since in the New Testament that generation serves as the prototype of disobedient humanity in general. Yet how is it with those who have died since Christ's own death and resurrection? Paul's statement that "all of us must appear before the judgment seat of Christ, so that each may receive recompense for what has been done in the body, whether good or evil" (2 Cor. 5:10), indicates that for us there is no automatism involved either. In his descent Christ has opened a way to salvation for those who died prior to his own death on the cross. After his resurrection and exaltation to the right hand of God, he is now opening a way for those who have died after his earthly sojourn and who will die in the future. Yet in saying this, do we not introduce some kind of purgatory where the dead are cleansed until they are acceptable to God?

According to Roman Catholic tradition, there is an intermediate state of the unjust souls which have not yet attained resurrection and which reside in a temporary prison: "Its existence was attested to for the first time in connection with Christ's descent to the dead, but it also exists thereafter. Those unjust dead will enjoy a resurrection only after their purification."[117] Even some Protestant theologians speculate that hardly anybody will have attained perfection in this life. Therefore "the salvational activity of Christ in humanity will be continued after their exit from the earthly life in a life beyond, with some as a purification, with others initially as a punishing judgment in the distance of God and in being guilty until, because of the proclamation of Christ among the 'spirits in prison,' they are led on the course of purification."[118]

This purgatorial topography with distinct phases of purification may sound persuasive. Yet at the same time we notice that some Roman Catholic theologians talk about a cleansing fire at the time of death and attempt to avoid any intermediate topography knowing that such could only result from human projection. It would be fitting for us to show a similar restraint and refrain from unnecessary speculation and fantasizing. We should rather adhere to the ancient and still amazingly modern confession of the church that asserts that we can be saved only by the compassion shown to us in Christ.

117. Vogels, 243.
118. So Staehelin, 44.

While the church maintained that the response to the existential encounter with Christ had ultimate significance, it did not feel that its task was to assert that everyone who did not have a similar chance during life on earth would have to suffer eternal consequences, the loss of eternal bliss. On the contrary, the church affirmed its hope that, without circumventing the salvific power of Christ, there was a possibility that those could also be saved who had not encountered Christ during their lifetime on earth. Yet the church never dared to declare that everyone will therefore eventually be saved, nor did it feel that its task was to define how someone could be saved through the descent.

Our reflection today must show similar restraint. While we fervently hope and pray that all of humanity will be saved, we cannot take for granted that it will indeed be so or outline a way in which God will reach this goal. But we know that a person will only be saved for Christ's sake. Contemplating the destiny of millions of people who have died since Christ's sojourn on earth without ever having known about him, or having known about him in such a distorted way that no appropriate response to him was possible, would it be unscriptural to conclude that these people might encounter a similar chance?

We agree with Prenter that the only criterion for the shape of our life beyond death is our relationship with Jesus Christ and the reconciliation with God which he offers.[119] We cannot quite agree with those who say that the principle of God's all-inclusive power and goodness necessitates or guarantees a universal homecoming, while the fear of a twofold outcome serves only as an ethical stimulus. We know that we are confronted with Christ's call for a decision. We know that the response to this call determines our life here and beyond. We know that we must confront as many as possible with this call. But with regard to the final destiny of those whom we cannot reach or who do not respond positively (as far as we can tell), we should not make their final destiny into a dogmatic issue[120] but should rest content with Luther's pastoral advice: "If you want to pray for your father's or your mother's soul, you may do so at home in your room, and that

---

119. Cf. Regin Prenter, *Creation and Redemption*, trans. Theodor I. Jensen (Philadelphia: Fortress, 1967), 574, where he argues for this over against an *apokatastasis* hope.

120. So also Wolfgang Trillhaas, *Dogmatik* (Berlin: Alfred Töpelmann, 1962), 460, who observes that the problems involved in the doctrine of *apokatastasis* cannot be solved theoretically.

once or twice, and afterwards let it be and say: 'Dear God, if the soul is in such a state that it can be helped, then dear God, have mercy on it and help it.'"[121]

4. Purgatory

The doctrine of purgatory presupposes an intermediate state between death and resurrection and is often viewed as a divisive issue between Roman Catholicism and the rest of Christendom. With the Council of Trent (1545-63) the final separation occurred between Roman Catholics and Protestants. One of the main arguments was the doctrine of purgatory, where the council fathers stated: "The Catholic Church, instructed by the Holy Spirit, in conformity with the sacred writings and the ancient tradition of the Fathers in sacred councils, and very recently in this ecumenical Synod has taught that there is a purgatory, and the souls detained there are assisted by the suffrages of the faithful, and especially by the acceptable sacrifice of the altar."[122]

The doctrine of purgatory has also been a point of controversy with the Orthodox Church. Only a few theologians of the Eastern Church admit a cleansing fire between death and final judgment. For instance, Basil the Great (ca. 329/30–379), in his *Commentary on Isaiah*, writes about a fire in another life and in another place which is reserved for the purification of the soul.[123] This position, however, is an exception. Nevertheless, Emperor Michael VIII Palaeologus of Constantinople (1224/25–82) had acknowledged the existence of a purgatory in order to achieve union with the West at the Council of Lyons (1274). Yet his own people never accepted this. Again, at the Council of Ferrara-Florence (1439), a council intended to reunite East and West, the first discussion point was purgatory. But the Greeks maintained their idea of a prisonlike receptacle of the souls after death and refuted any specula-

---

121. Martin Luther, *Predigten des Jahres 1522*, in WA, 10.3:409.9-13, in a sermon on November 2, 1522; and Paul Althaus, *Die christliche Wahrheit*, 673, who quotes this passage from Luther.

122. Denzinger, 298 (983).

123. Cf. Joachim Gnilka, *Ist I Kor 3,10-15 ein Schriftzeugnis für das Fegfeuer? Eine exegetisch-historische Untersuchung* (Düsseldorf: Michael Triltsch, 1955), 63, who extensively quotes Basil the Great.

tion of a postmortal cleansing, since that might imply advocating a universal homecoming.[124]

As Karl Lehmann admits: "The doctrine of purgatory has always had difficulties with excessive fantasy."[125] Pious people wanted to know exactly how one could be perfected, and the symbols and pictures of the hereafter were taken as objective realities. They also had a naive curiosity in the punishment and tortures of the soul. Purgatory became a torture chamber, an otherworldly concentration camp and a place of incessant agony. Small wonder that ideas abounded about the poor souls and the indulgences. Yet the concept of a cleansing fire does not even emerge prior to the eleventh century, and the official texts of the Roman Catholic Church never mention the term "fire." Even about a *place* of purgatory nothing is said by the Roman Catholic teaching office.[126] Indeed, the origins of the doctrine of purgatory have nothing to do with a torture chamber or indulgences. They arose from the universal concern of people for their loved ones who had died. But it may be an overstatement to assert that "in the Old and New Testament one cannot detect any references to a belief in purgatory."[127]

a. A Narrow Biblical Basis

The origin of purgatory lies somewhere in the intertestamental period. For instance, in 2 Maccabees 12:38-42 (dating from the first century B.C.) we read that under the tunics of Jewish resistance fighters who had been killed, one found "sacred tokens" of idols and therefore believed that because of that idolatry they had been killed. As a response one "turned to supplication, praying that the sin that had been committed might be wholly blotted out." Moreover, a collection was taken up and sent to Jerusalem "to provide for a sin offering. In doing this he [Judas] acted very well and honorably, taking account of the resurrection. For if he were not expecting that those who had fallen would rise again, it

124. For details cf. Ernst Koch, "Fegfeuer," in *TRE*, 11:73.

125. Karl Lehmann, "Was bleibt vom Fegfeuer?" *Internationale katholische Zeitschrift "Communio"* 9 (1980): 236.

126. Cf. for details, Lehmann, 237.

127. Erich Fleischhack, *Fegfeuer: Die christlichen Vorstellungen vom Geschick der Verstorbenen geschichtlich dargestellt* (Tübingen: Katzmann, 1969), 11.

would have been superfluous and foolish to pray for the dead. But if he was looking to the splendid reward that is laid up for those who fall asleep in godliness, it was a holy and pious thought. Therefore he made atonement for the dead, so that they might be delivered from their sin" (2 Macc. 12:43-45).

With these practices the Jews did not want to associate themselves too closely with pagan customs, on which they commented: "They slaughter their sacrifices to the dead, and to the demons they bow down. And they eat in tombs" (Jub. 22:17). Jews and Christians prayed *for* the dead and not *to* the dead. Augustine makes this clear when he writes: "Therefore, whatever offerings are brought by the pious to the places of the martyrs, these are only adornments of their memorials and not sacred or sacrificial objects given to the dead as though they were gods. Even those who bring food there — and in most countries this is not the custom — do this because they desire that it should be sanctified to them."[128] As Augustine well knew, Christians and Jews were walking a narrow line not only in terms of memorials of the dead, but also in their intercessions for the dead. For instance, Persitka Rabbati states in analogy to 2 Maccabees: "Perhaps you will say that once a man is plunged into Gehenna, there will be no coming up [resurrection] for him. When mercy is besought on his behalf, however, he is shot up from Gehenna as an arrow from the bow."[129] Many church fathers followed this custom of praying on behalf of the dead.

The first time purgatory is mentioned in Christian literature is in connection with the North African martyr Perpetua († ca. 202).[130] As she was thrown into prison and destined to be devoured by wild animals, she remembered her brother Dinocrates and realized that she was worthy to pray for that boy who had died of cancer at age seven. In a dream the following night, she saw him at a dark place where many people were gathered who were very sweaty and thirsty. There he was wearing dirty clothes and looking extremely pale. When she saw him suffering, she prayed for him day and night with sighs and tears. Then she saw him again in a dream all clean and well clothed and recovered and playing

128. Augustine, *City of God* 8.27, 357.

129. *Persitka Rabbati: Discourses for Feasts, Fasts, and Special Sabbaths,* trans. William G. Braude, 2 vols. (New Haven: Yale University Press, 1968), 1:401 (Piska 20.2).

130. *Acta SS. Perpetua et Felicitatis* 6-8, in *Bibliothek der Kirchenväter* (Munich: Kösel, 1913), 14:333-35, and cf. Fleischhack, 25.

like children play. Then she woke up and realized that his punishment had been revoked. At approximately the time of Perpetua's martyrdom, Tertullian writes in his treatise *On Monogamy*, while discussing a widow's rites: "She prays for his soul, and requests refreshments for him meanwhile, and fellowship (with him) in the first resurrection; and she offers (her sacrifice) on the anniversaries of his falling asleep."[131] Augustine, too, mentions in his *Confessions* that his mother Monica admonished him to remember her "at the altar of the Lord," that is, with intercessory prayers.[132] Yet he was still ambivalent concerning the existence of an actual cleansing fire.

In his *Enchiridion* Augustine writes: "It is a matter that may be inquired into, and either ascertained or left doubtful, whether some believers shall pass through a kind of purgatorial fire, and in proportion as they have loved with more or less devotion the goods that perish, be less or more quickly delivered from it. This cannot, however, be the case of any of those of whom it is said, that they 'shall not inherit the kingdom of God,' unless after suitable repentance their sins be forgiven them."[133] This cleansing fire is gathered from passages such as Deuteronomy 4:24 ("For the LORD your God is a devouring fire, a jealous God") or, in the New Testament, from the frequent association of Jesus with fire, for instance, that he will baptize with the Holy Spirit and fire (Luke 3:16). Often Paul's reference to the fire at the Day of the Lord is also adduced. He states in 1 Corinthians 3:13-15: "The work of each builder will become visible, for the Day will disclose it, because it will be revealed with fire, and the fire will test what sort of work each has done. If what has been built on the foundation survives, the builder will receive a reward. If the work is burned up, the builder will suffer loss; the builder will be saved, but only as through fire." This cleansing fire of purgatory is then equated with the eschatological fire, which means with God's own self, over against whom all things unfit for eternity will simply fall by the wayside.

Karl Lehmann writes: "When, in death, a human person is confronted with God's holiness and the splendor of his justice and love dawns on him, then his or her incompletion and sinfulness are fully dis-

---

131. Tertullian, *On Monogamy* 10, in *ANF*, 4:67.
132. Augustine, *Confessions* 9.11, in *FaCh*, 21:254.
133. Augustine, *Enchiridion* 69, in *NPNF* FS, 3:260.

closed. Everything which is not justice and love will be devoured by God's fire. Whoever wants to dwell in the eternal love of God must pass through that fire to emerge as tested and purified gold from the melting-pot of fire."[134] Of course, we notice that the biblical references can, at the most, be used metaphorically, as Lehmann himself admits. In the *Catechism of the Catholic Church,* however, we read: "The tradition of the Church, by reference to certain texts of Scripture, speaks of a cleansing fire."[135] The Scripture references given, 1 Corinthians 3:15 and 1 Peter 1:7, are not convincing. The extensive reference, however, is from Gregory the Great (ca. 540-604), who vigorously promoted the notion of a purgatory. Then the *Catechism* also states: "This teaching is also based on a practice of prayer for the dead, already mentioned in Sacred Scripture," here referring to 2 Maccabees 12:46. This means that the doctrine of purgatory is primarily founded on the tradition of the church and on the custom of praying for the dead which developed in late Judaism.

One cannot escape the feeling that there are other and more important issues at stake with the doctrine of purgatory. Otherwise the scriptural base or lack of it would receive more attention. Again, Karl Lehmann gives us a clue when he writes: "Here it becomes obvious that the doctrine of purgatory should not be totally separated from the understanding of justification and of sin."[136] In Roman Catholicism a distinction is made between mortal sins which exclude one from the kingdom of God and venial sins with which all of us are contaminated. Following Judaism, Christianity very early continued the practice of praying for the dead within and without official church services. This originally Jewish custom of commemorative and intercessory prayers for the dead served then as the actual starting point for the doctrine of purgatory.

b. The Human Component to Salvation

Referring to 2 Maccabees 12, Augustine named prayer, good works, giving of alms, and eucharistic sacrifice as means of intercession for the

---

134. Lehmann, 240.
135. For this and the following quotation, *Catechism of the Catholic Church,* 291 (1031 and 1032 respectively).
136. Lehmann, 238.

dead.[137] Augustine, however, makes it clear that "no one, then, need hope that after he is dead he shall obtain merit with God which he has neglected to secure here." Still Augustine talks about the profitability of such acts on behalf of the dead at least in some instances. Gregory the Great, who was pope on the eve of the Middle Ages, popularized Augustine's thoughts and understood the eucharistic sacrifice not as a remembrance of Christ's suffering, but as a real repetition of Christ's sacrifice. Since some of the more serious sins can be forgiven in purgatory, Pope Gregory stated that the eucharistic sacrifice was exceptionally efficacious for changing the lot of the souls of the dead, because it released them from purgatory.[138]

With the emergence of private penance at the expense of public penance, indulgences were introduced in the eleventh and twelfth centuries to change inconvenient church sanctions into more convenient ones, or to partially or even totally relinquish them. Soon the idea emerged that indulgences could also be applied to punishment in purgatory.[139] The church felt itself able to extend its power of absolution into purgatory. By their excess good deeds Christ and the saints had accumulated such a treasure of merits *(superabundantia meritorum Christi et Sanctorum)* as to easily make up for the deficiencies of those who suffered in purgatory. These merits were to be administered by the church. Thus we read in a 1518 decree of Pope Leo X: "The Roman Pope, as the successor of the keys of Peter and the representative of Christ on earth, can through the power of the keys . . . grant to those who are faithful Christians . . . in this life and in purgatory remission through the exceeding merits of Christ and the saints."[140] This can be done through actual remission or via intercession through indulgence. The possibility of indulgence is especially important for those who had not yet finished their preparation for death.

137. Cf. Augustine, *The Care to Be Taken for the Dead* 1.3, in *FaCh*, 27:353, and for the following quote Augustine, *Enchiridion* 110, in *NPNF* FS, 3:272.

138. Cf. Saint Gregory the Great, *Dialogues* 4.57-62, in *FaCh*, 39:266-75.

139. Cf. Gustav Adolf Benrath, "Ablaß," in *TRE*, 1:347-48. Cf. also the very instructive essay by Karl Rahner, "Remarks on the Theology of Indulgences," in *Theological Investigations* (Baltimore: Helicon, 1963), 2:175-201. After a good historical and dogmatic review, Rahner comes to the conclusion that indulgences should be found "not only in textbooks but also in the practical life" of the faithful (201).

140. *Lateran Council V (1512-1517)*, in Denzinger, 239 (740a; translation mine).

(The Church) says and teaches that those who after baptism slip into sin must not be rebaptized, but by true penance attain forgiveness of their sins. Because if they die truly repentant in charity before they have made satisfaction by worthy fruits of penance for (sins) committed and omitted, their souls are cleansed after death by purgatorial or purifying punishments.... And to relieve punishments of this kind, the offerings of the living faithful are of advantage to these, namely, the sacrifices of Masses, prayers, alms, and other duties of piety, which have customarily been performed by the faithful for the other faithful according to the regulations of the Church.[141]

The Synod of Florence (1439), the Council of Trent (1547-63), and the Roman Catechism of 1566 finalized the Roman Catholic understanding of purgatory.

When we remember that the Reformation started with a dispute over the practice of indulgences, it is not surprising that the Reformers and the Protestant churches rejected the idea of purgatory as a place or state where the living could still extend some influence and where the dead could make up for past deficiencies. John Calvin, describing the abuses and futility of indulgences and purgatory, calls the idea of purgatory a revelation "forged by Satan's craft" which can only be sustained through ignorant distortions of certain scriptural passages.[142]

In his Ninety-five Theses of 1517, Martin Luther reacted very strongly against the abuses of indulgences and declared in thesis 1 that, according to Christ's teachings, "the entire life of believers be one of repentance."[143] Still, being a faithful son of his church, he felt certain that "the Pope neither desires nor is able to remit any penalties except those imposed by his own authority or that of the canons." And the following year, in his explanation of the Ninety-five Theses, he still affirms: "I am positive that there is a purgatory."[144]

Due to the lack of a scriptural basis and the abuses connected with

141. *Council of Lyons 11 (1274)*, in Denzinger, 184 (464).
142. Cf. John Calvin, *Institutes of the Christian Religion* 3.5.6, ed. John T. McNeill, trans. F. L. Battles, The Library of Christian Classics (Philadelphia: Westminster, 1960), 2:676.
143. Martin Luther, *Ninety-five Theses* (1517), in *LW*, 31:25-26, in theses 1 and 5 for this and the following quotation.
144. Martin Luther, *Explanations of the Ninety-five Theses* (1518), in *LW*, 31:124.

purgatory, Luther became more and more skeptical about its reality and in 1530 wrote his *Rejection of Purgatory*.[145] In his *Smalcald Articles* of 1536, we finally read in his statements about the abuses of the Roman Catholic Mass: "Consequently purgatory and all the pomp, services, and business transactions associated with it are to be regarded as nothing else than illusions of the devil, for purgatory, too, is contrary to the fundamental article that Christ alone, and not the work of a man, can help souls. Besides, nothing has been commanded or enjoined upon us with reference to the dead."[146]

With these remarks Luther pointed out an important reason why the idea of purgatory had gained such momentum. The idea emerged from uncertainty whether God's justification of us sinners, as offered to those who accept Christ as their Lord, really covers all sins and makes us acceptable in the eyes of God. Once an uncertainty emerges, we want to make sure that we and our loved ones are safe from punishment. Thus the Roman Catholic Church distinguished between temporal punishment (in purgatory) and eternal punishment (after the last judgment). Only rare and deadly sins fall under the category of eternal punishment, while all others can be forgiven.

Another necessary ingredient for the idea of purgatory is the assumption that some or all people can influence our destiny beyond death. The popularized slogan of Johann Tetzel (ca. 1465-1519), indulgence peddler and contemporary of Martin Luther, "as soon as the coin in the coffer rings, the soul from purgatory springs,"[147] did not even present the official Roman Catholic doctrine of his own time. Especially today, indulgence and attribution of good deeds is thought possible only through intercession and not by such mechanical means.[148] But the idea

---

145. Martin Luther, *Widerruf vom Fegfeuer*, in WA, 30/2:360-90.

146. Martin Luther, *The Smalcald Articles*, in *The Book of Concord*, 295.

147. According to Roland H. Bainton, *Here I Stand* (New York: Abingdon, 1950), 78.

148. Rahner, "Remarks," 200-201, expresses this very clearly: "An indulgence is the sacramental of the remission of sin's temporal punishment before God, and this in conjunction with a jurisdictional remission of an (at least hypothetically) imposed ecclesiastical penance. Being a sacramental, it operates *ex opere operantis (orantis) Ecclesia*, and not *ex opere operato* . . . even although, for historical reasons, it is connected with a jurisdictional act of the Church which is concerned with the remission of an ecclesiastical penance and produces a sure effect in this regard." Rahner advances here a much more tenable position. He moves away from the jurisdictionally and mechanically misunderstood idea of relying on the treasury of the church (199), and refers to the prayers of the

of intercession for the deceased considers the afterlife as similar to this life,[149] a thought almost constantly rejected in the New Testament.

Looking at the New Testament, we can assume neither that justification is uncertain or partial nor that the afterlife is similar to life here on earth. We read in the Gospel of John: "Anyone who hears my word and believes him who sent me has eternal life, and does not come under judgment" (John 5:24), and Paul expresses the same conviction: "So if anyone is in Christ, there is a new creation: everything old has passed away: see, everything has become new!" (2 Cor. 5:17). The coming of the eschaton and the coming of death are not something one can prepare for from a certain point onward; they are factors that determine our entire worldview. In the same way the consequence is not open-ended or ambiguous, but definite. Any thought of extending our influence on the destiny of those beyond death would do away with the radicality of death and the difference between life here on earth and anything beyond this life. Jesus says that "in the resurrection they neither marry nor are given in marriage" (Matt. 22:30), and the parable of the rich man and Lazarus shows such an abyss between life here and the beyond that the rich man's plea for communication with his brothers on earth remains unheard (Luke 16:19-31). Both incidents illustrate the New Testament emphasis on the basic difference between our life here and our life beyond.

The New Testament writers are also very hesitant to make any assertions concerning the whereabouts of the dead. This is in striking contrast to popular piety and to medieval scholastic speculation that divided the hereafter into five receptacles: (1) heaven for the saints; (2) purgatory for the average Christian; (3) limbo of the fathers, where the Old Testament patriarchs rested until Christ descended to them and led them to heaven; (4) limbo of the infants, reserved for those children

---

church. Indulgence could then be understood as relying on God's gracious response to the intercessory prayer of the church and of individuals. Yet talking about indulgence as a sacramental raises additional questions.

149. This becomes obvious when Rahner, "The Life of the Dead," in *Theological Investigations*, 4:353, asserts that "the many dimensions of man do not all attain their perfection simultaneously and hence there is a full ripening of the whole man 'after' death, as this basic decision penetrates the whole extent of his reality." Though our basic determination does not change, our life comes to maturity. As we shall see, a similar idea of human growth after death has also been advanced by Schleiermacher.

who died unbaptized; and (5) hell for Satan and his followers. This elaborate topography runs counter to the eschatological restraint of the New Testament.

There have also been attempts on the Protestant side to assert a purgatory-like state after death. Friedrich Schleiermacher occasionally implied a future development of the individual human being beyond death. He wondered what happened when death intervened "in some individual case before fore-ordination has fulfilled itself."[150] He concluded that even if foreordination to blessedness has not been fulfilled during one's lifetime, one will still be "taken up into living fellowship with Christ." Our life on earth needs further development. Its brevity seems to indicate that it is only a "preparatory and introductory first stage."[151] We have noted that Immanuel Kant also postulated in his *Critique of Practical Reason* an infinite progress in a life beyond to allow us to fulfill the moral destiny of our nature and to show our due respect to the moral law.[152]

While popular piety has understood purgatory mainly as a torture chamber, contemporary Roman Catholic reflection comes closer to Kant and Schleiermacher. For instance, Cardinal Ratzinger writes that we should not understand purgatory as an otherworldly concentration camp where people suffer punishments which have been dictated more or less arbitrarily. "Rather it is the inwardly necessary process of transformation in which a human person becomes capable of Christ, capable of God and thus capable of unity with the whole communion of saints. Simply to look at people with any degree of realism at all is to grasp the necessity of such a process. It does not replace grace by works, but allows the former to achieve its full victory precisely as grace."[153]

Purgatory is considered to be a process of purification and growth. It is neither a place nor an intermediate state between heaven and hell, but part of the positive completion of a human being. As purification, it can be understood as the moment of acceptance into the completing love of God.[154] The message of purgatory can therefore

---

150. Schleiermacher, §119, 2:549.

151. Schleiermacher, §159, 2:703.

152. Kant, *Critique of Practical Reason* 5.121, 226.

153. Joseph Ratzinger, *Eschatology: Death and Eternal Life*, trans. Michael Waldstein, ed. Aidan Nichols (Washington, D.C.: Catholic University of America Press, 1988), 230-31.

154. So Kehl, 285-86.

even be called "good news," because God attains his goal: he purifies us. God cleanses us and attains his goal and thereby we attain our goal.[155] Purgatory therefore is not a halfway hell, and all the graphic images of popular piety with the poor souls suffering down there are completely mistaken.

If the tenor of purgatory is joy and God's grace attaining his goal, why does the *Catechism of the Catholic Church* state: "The Church also commends almsgiving, indulgences, and works of penance undertaken on behalf of the dead"?[156] Has popular piety again gained the upper hand at the expense of responsible theology? Perhaps there will always be this tension that may even be caused by a guilty conscience that we have neglected the deceased during their lifetimes, a tension between the good news of God's forgiving and accepting grace and our disbelieving attempts to do something just in case this grace is not sufficient. Therefore Ratzinger is correct when he states that the Reformers, on account of the expiatory all-sufficiency of Christ's death on the cross, could not give room to an expiation beyond this life.[157]

The concept of our spiritual growth beyond death expresses the right conviction that God's grace does not cease to work once we are dead. Unless we admit, however, that God manipulates our growth, similar to a puppeteer bringing about the movements of his puppets, such growth would require our response to God's activity. But how could we formulate a response if we existed only as bodiless souls? Apart from this obvious difficulty, the biblical witnesses do not conceive death as a mere transitional stage with a subsequent continuance similar to our life here on earth, but as a rupture and a dimensional boundary beyond which there is something entirely different from what we face here on earth.

Moreover, from the idea of a spiritual growth beyond death, it is only a small step to metempsychosis, the migration of the soul, and to reincarnation, ideas prevalent in many Far Eastern religions. Karl Rahner raises the interesting question of "whether in the Catholic no-

---

155. Cf. Gisbert Greshake, "Himmel — Hölle — Fegefeuer im Verständnis heutiger Theologie," in *Ungewisses Jenseits? Himmel — Hölle-Fegefeuer,* ed. Gisbert Greshake (Düsseldorf: Patmos, 1986), 93-94.

156. *Catechism of the Catholic Church* (1032), 291.

157. Cf. Ratzinger, 220.

tion of 'interval,' which seems so obsolete at first, there could not be a starting point for coming to terms in a better and more positive way with a doctrine of the 'transmutation of souls' or of 'reincarnation,' which is so widespread in eastern cultures and is regarded there as something to be taken for granted?"[158]

Indeed, the concepts of purgatory, transmutation of souls, and reincarnation can express the desire that human destiny will come to an ultimate fulfillment. Yet Rahner himself notes that "in Catholic theology the question is not yet settled with regard to the sense in which and the degree to which temporal categories can still be applied there." The Roman Catholic Church was indeed wise when it refrained from making dogmatic statements concerning temporal or spatial categories after death. It avoided patterning them too much according to the way we experience things in this life. The big question, however, is whether it is legitimate and helpful to speak with Rahner of an interval in a person's destiny between death and the corporate fulfillment of this person as a whole. If there is no "void" (purgatory) after death, but a final destiny in terms of acceptance or rejection, then neither the doctrine of purgatory nor the notion of a process of maturation "after" death for the whole person is warranted.

In this context Ladislaus Boros (b. 1927) advocates the fascinating hypothesis of a final decision at the moment of death, thus decisively modifying the traditional concepts of purgatory and death.[159] Boros agrees that the church has only gradually developed the doctrine of purgatory. Though the scriptural basis of purgatory may be obscure, the fact and the essential nature of purgatory are of such quality that it must be called a "truth of revelation."[160] With his hypothesis of a final decision, however, Boros seems to view purgatory as the "point" of intersection between life and death. It is no longer conceived of as a process of purification that can be measured similar to the days and years we live here on earth. According to Boros, "purgatory would be the passage,

158. For this and the following quotations see Karl Rahner, *Foundations of Christian Faith*, trans. William V. Dych (New York: Seabury, 1978), 442.

159. This notion has found such widespread acceptance in Roman Catholic theology that Joseph Cardinal Ratzinger found it necessary to take a stand against it. Cf. Ratzinger, 229.

160. Cf. Ladislaus Boros, *The Mystery of Death* (New York: Seabury Press, 1973), 129.

which we effect in our final decision, through the purifying fire of divine love. The encounter with Christ would be our purgatory."[161]

This hypothesis of a final decision would also do away with the idea of a limbo for children who died unbaptized, since in death they could make a decision for or against Christ and thus have the possibility of reaching the same status as all other believers.[162] Boros replaces an untenable concept of purgatory with the idea of a confrontation with Christ in death. Yet is it necessary to call this "purgatory"? It seems that Boros retains this not only as a concession to tradition but also because he views death as something positive and liberating. For instance, he calls death *"man's first completely personal act, and is, therefore, by reason of its very being, the place above all others for the awakening of consciousness, for freedom, for the encounter with God, for the final decision about eternal destiny."*[163]

It is certainly scripturally well founded to conceive of death as the point at which we will see God face-to-face and where the final decision about our eternal destiny will be made. Yet Boros would hardly find scriptural support for calling death *"a sacramental situation"*[164] and looking upon death "as a 'basic sacrament,' mysteriously present in the other sacraments and inwardly supporting them at the same time as it transcends them."[165] Though we agree with Boros that death can and must also be understood as implying God's grace, we cannot escape the notion that the Bible looks upon death primarily as something negative and as implying God's punishment. While sympathizing with many facets of Boros's approach, we cannot agree with his optimistic view of death. Since his optimistic view of death is so overpowering, we also wonder whether that does not finally lead him to opt for a universal homecoming.[166]

161. Boros, 139, and cf. his extensive footnote on the same page, n. 93.
162. Cf. Boros, 109-10.
163. Boros, 84.
164. Boros, 169.
165. Boros, 165.
166. Though Boros never explicitly advocates a universal homecoming, his "salvific" view of death points in this direction.

7. The New World to Come

For a long time the new world to come has been regarded as proper subject matter for eschatological inquiry. Yet at the same time "eschatology has often been regarded as the most questionable and speculative of all Christian doctrines since it deals with that which is completely inaccessible to man's observation and experience, namely, the future — not the immediate future about which some reasonable prognostications can be made, but the final future, beyond death, the end of history."[1]

We have seen that we are not alone in our belief in the new world to come. Most religions envision a final end of all history when our present world will come to a close and a new world will appear. Within Christendom these hopes have often been intensified, and sizable human communities have believed at one time or another that they lived in a time close to the end of the world. Mass conversions, fervent religious exercises, and exodus into remote areas to await the coming Lord were the immediately visible signs of such feverish expectations. But today, due to our secular education and our secular, rationalistic, analytical mass media, such attitudes are now restricted to some extremists. Many of us feel somewhat uncomfortable with the future, but even at the beginning of the new millennium there is no doomsday mood that captures the attention of the masses. To most of us it seems almost inconceivable that someone like Martin Luther could once interpret floods, wars, and comets as signs of the imminent end of this world.

In our technological age we are confronted with an ever increasing

---

1. Gordon D. Kaufman, *Systematic Theology: A Historicist Perspective* (New York: Scribner, 1968), 314.

number of people who have given up hope for God's new creation altogether. They have given up the idea of an intervention from "beyond," and they attempt to tailor the planet they inhabit according to their own ends.[2] Theologians are not exempt from abandoning future eschatology either. We have already noted that Rudolf Bultmann opted for an exclusively present-oriented eschatology. In Gordon D. Kaufman's systematic theology, *In Face of Mystery: A Constructive Theology,* the term "eschatology" does not even appear in the subject index. Under the rubric of salvation we are directed to the telling comment: "God as the *absolute Lord,* the tyrannical power who arbitrarily saves whomever 'he' chooses, and damns to everlasting hell whomever 'he' chooses . . . many of the readers of this book are unwilling to fall down in worship before such a God as that."[3] Kaufman (b. 1925) has given up on the notion of a Pantocrator. Yet, as he says, he still draws inspiration from the teachings of Jesus for participating in "actual ministries of healing and caring for the suffering and the estranged."[4]

Of course, one could say that the term "eschatology" is not biblical and did not even emerge until the seventeenth century. It was not until Johann Gerhard (1582-1637), one of the most influential teachers of Lutheran orthodoxy, and his *Loci theologici* (theological loci) (1610-21), that we find the first comprehensive teaching on *de novissimis* (literally: "the latest" or rather "the teachings about the end").[5] So we could simply forgo these teachings as being relatively new as far as the term "eschatology" is concerned. Yet at least four reasons militate against this:

1. There is the question of what occurs after we die. The answer that there is nothing after death has been rejected by virtually all religions, including the Christian faith. Therefore we are forced to deal with the issue of what comes after death.

2. Cf. Emanuel Hirsch, *Geschichte der neueren evangelischen Theologie,* 5 vols. (Gütersloh: Bertelsmann, 1949-54), 5:626. According to surveys, a sizable percentage of church members in Germany, for instance, do not believe in a hereafter.

3. Gordon D. Kaufman, *In Face of Mystery: A Constructive Theology* (Cambridge: Harvard University Press, 1993), 407.

4. Cf. Kaufman, *In Face of Mystery,* 409.

5. Cf. the comprehensive investigation by Sigurd Hjelde, *Das Eschaton und die Eschata: Eine Studie über Sprachgebrauch und Sprachverwirrung in protestantischer Theologie von der Orthodoxie bis zur Gegenwart* (Munich: Chr. Kaiser, 1987), 35-37.

2. We are aware of a continuous dying and rising throughout the world. Cosmology, for instance, tells us of the birth and death of stars, and biology tells us of the birth and death of all kinds of life-forms. We also realize that one generation passes away and another one will take its place. The question that emerges from this continuous process of dying and rising is whether there is any escape from it or whether it will continue forever. Moreover, what is the sense of life, if it simply grows, peaks, and then disappears?

3. We confront in this world evil and suffering on all levels: in nature when natural calamities such as floods or droughts strike; in human life when an incurable disease sets in; or when animals or humans maul and kill each other without being provoked to do it. The question arises whether this kind of cruelty will ever come to an end or whether evil will continue unabated. Of course, there have always been optimists who claim that finally evil will be overcome through our own efforts. Yet at the most, we have witnessed an increase of evil and suffering, not its gradual dissipation.

4. If we construct an eschatology on the basis of these three arguments, the charge could easily be made that eschatology is the result of wishful thinking. We cannot face reality as it is, and therefore we construct its sublimation in a Feuerbachian fashion.[6] To escape this charge we should start with Scripture. If we do not want to construct an eschatology of our needs and desires, there is no other way than to be guided by Scripture alone, the principle of the Reformation.[7] Of course, then we are immediately accused of resorting to naive biblicism. But have we not seen that the New Testament kerygma, the proclamation both of Jesus and the tradition he engen-

---

6. Carl Heinz Ratschow, "Eschatologie VIII: Systematisch-theologisch," in *TRE*, 10:349, brings forth these three reasons while adding a fourth one (soteriology). Yet he does not pose the issue of projection.

7. Friedrich Beißer, *Hoffnung und Vollendung* (Gütersloh: Gerd Mohn, 1993), 264, also states that a biblical foundation is the only really fruitful starting point to escape our own predilections and desires. Thomas N. Finger, *Christian Theology: An Eschatological Approach* (Scottdale, Pa.: Herald Press, 1985), 1:103, points out also that "the eschatological perspective was the one within which the kerygma was proclaimed, received, and lived out," and therefore he proposes it "as a starting point for theological reflection in the late twentieth century."

dered, is thoroughly eschatological? How else could we still be Christian and not eschatological in our outlook?

But do not many exegetes tell us that Jesus was wrong when he expected the near end of the world? As we have seen, however, there was no disappointment about the "delay of the parousia." The opposite was true: the first Christian community was unanimously convinced that Jesus was indeed the Christ, the anointed one, the hoped-for Messiah. The salvation-historical hopes and promises had found their fulfillment in the Christ event. While Christ was the answer to human hopes and anxieties, in various ways the New Testament authors pointed to the necessity of a completion at the last day, an eschatological fulfillment.[8] Because of Christ, because of his death and resurrection, Paul, for instance, could proclaim the future victory of death and propose eternal life in a new world and the ultimate victory over death and all antigodly powers.

Beyond Resignation and Futurist Activism

If we abandon the hope for an actual transformation of our world into God's kingdom, faith becomes empty and meaningless and is hardly bearable. Friedrich Nietzsche (1844-1900) was aware of these consequences when he proclaimed nihilism as the alternative to Christianity. Under the impact of our technological domination of the world and in response to the collapse of the earth-centered pre-Copernican worldview, Nietzsche's madman exclaims: "God is dead. God remains dead. And we have killed him. How shall we comfort ourselves, the murderers of all murderers?" And then he asks: "Whither are we moving? . . . Are we not plunging continually? Backward, sideward, forward, in all directions? . . . Are we not straying as through an infinite nothing? Do we not feel the breath of empty space? Has it not become colder?"[9] Like few before him, Nietzsche understood what it meant to live as an atheist in post-Christian fashion.

8. Cf. Friedrich Beißer, "Defizite und Aufgaben heutiger Eschatologie," in *Eschatologie in der Dogmatik der Gegenwart* (Erlangen: Martin-Luther-Verlag, 1988), 53, in his enlightening comments.

9. Friedrich Nietzsche, *The Gay Science*, 3.125, translated with commentary by Walter Kaufmann (New York: Random House, Vintage Books, 1974), 181.

While in other religious environments atheism does not amount to much, since there are always many other mysterious forces, it is different with Christianity. The Christian faith knows only of one divine force who is the creator, sustainer, and redeemer of everything. Everything else is profane and not divine or sacred. Even the "sanctuary" is only called that because people agree to worship together at this place, not because it is a divine place by its own quality. But once this one God is denied, nothing divine is left. This means that there is no point of orientation, and time is bereft of its origin and destination. Of course, one could claim that time is elapsing from a predictable future into a knowable past, but this simple process of growth and aging no longer endows life with meaning. Whether we adopt biological standards in saying that life always seeks self-expression, or anthropocentric standards in suggesting that everything must ultimately serve us, or any other standards, they are arbitrary and without firm foundation. Nobody knows what life is for.

Faced with a continuously onrushing future that allows no escape, we could simply tighten our belts and flex our muscles to make it on our own. Yet exactly this practical atheism, followed by many both within the Christian tradition and outside it, seems to be encountering increasingly larger obstacles. As soon as one problem is solved, at least two greater ones seem to emerge. Our faith in harnessing the future has become more and more uncertain. Even if we concentrate on survival instead of conquest and mastery, we ultimately have to face the question: Survival for what?

Confronted with our finite nature and our many compounding problems, we are apt to conclude that we come into life by accident, go through life in weakness, and vanish from life in resignation. But our present situation, with its threats of overpopulation, world hunger, scarcity of resources, and nuclear disaster, is so precarious that we cannot afford the luxury of despair. Yet any activism resulting from an assessment of our situation would only prolong our agony, since sooner or later we have to admit the finitude and futility of all our actions. If there is a meaningful future at all, it must come not by our own strength but by provision "from above." Thus we find it impossible to dispense with the eschatological expectations of the Christian faith and still maintain a meaningful hope in the future. "And yet one must also recognize that these are simply *hopes* not yet realized, hopes with a foundation outside themselves."[10] This means we have to avoid two extremes. We cannot, on the one hand, concentrate so much on the hereafter and the transitory character of earthly things that we undervalue the importance of this life; nor can we, on the other hand, ignore the terminal character of death so much that we canonize the goods of this world and distract believers from the pursuit of holiness.[11]

1. Proleptic Anticipation of the New World

Christians do not just sit around and hope. Taking their name from Jesus Christ, they recall God's visitation to his people and look forward to the final revelation of God's glory. Situated between memory and hope, they are allowed to anticipate proleptically the new world to come. In this context the church plays a vital role, as the symbol of the future in which eschatological hope is kept alive, as the semblance of the whole people of God, and as the anticipation of the heavenly city.

a. The Church as Reminder of God's Future

In our present world the church is an erratic entity, continuously in danger of becoming a stumbling block. The church does not fit into a world that assumes that the course of its history is predictable, being determined by humanity's own efforts and the resources available to it. As Martin Luther expressed in his hymn "A Mighty Fortress Is Our God," the church knows and confesses that "no strength of ours can match his [the devil's] might! We would be lost, rejected." In a secular and self-relying culture, the church gives witness to a future provided not by humanity but by God.

---

10. Kaufman, *Systematic Theology*, 325.

11. Cf. the refreshing booklet by Stephen Travis, *The Jesus Hope* (Downers Grove, Ill.: InterVarsity, 1976), and for laypeople the straightforward exposition by Val J. Sauer, Jr., *The Eschatology Handbook: The Bible Speaks to Us Today about End Times* (Atlanta: John Knox, 1981).

The Symbol of the Future

The involvement of the church in the affairs of the world, in the struggle for justice, human rights, and access to the necessities of life, serves a dual purpose. On the one hand the church does serve those who are in need. Yet, being aware that all of its efforts are at best patchwork, bandages on the wounds of a hurting world, the church also witnesses with its actions to a world that will be without anguish and suffering. Similar to the miracles of its Lord which were both a help for people in need and signs of a new creation, the church is the symbol of God's future. This eschatological symbol of the new creation becomes visible not just in social involvement, but in every activity of the church. Each time our sins are forgiven, we are reminded of the love of God that will one day find its completion. Each time we celebrate the Lord's Supper, we are reminded of the celestial banquet.

The twofold phrase in the words of the institution of the Lord's Supper, "Do this in remembrance of me," does not just imply that we should remember Christ's sacrifice. It also means that God should remember the sacrifice of his Son and speed up the coming and fulfillment of the kingdom. At every celebration of the Eucharist when "the community prays for the coming of the Lord," it proclaims the beginning of the time of salvation and "anticipates the blessed hour" of the parousia.[12] The community reminds itself and God that it will celebrate the Eucharist until Christ returns and the eschatological promises are fulfilled.

That the Christian community understands itself as the symbol of the future, a future that has already commenced, is again emphasized in the Lord's Prayer.[13] As a constituent part of the early church's communion liturgy, "the Lord's Prayer belonged to that part of the Service in which only those who were baptized were permitted to participate."[14]

12. So Joachim Jeremias, *The Eucharistic Words of Jesus,* trans. N. Perrin, 3rd ed. (Philadelphia: Fortress, 1977), 254.

13. Raymond E. Brown, "The Pater Noster as an Eschatological Prayer," in *New Testament Essays* (Garden City, N.Y.: Doubleday, Image Books, 1968), 319, rightly comments "how coherently the eschatological viewpoint binds together the petitions into one picture."

14. Cf. Joachim Jeremias, *The Lord's Prayer,* Facet Books, trans. J. Reumann (Philadelphia: Fortress, 1969), 2.

371

The petitions "hallowed be your name" and "your kingdom come" are in content closely related to the expectant cry, "Come, Lord Jesus!" (Rev. 22:20).[15] They yearn for the hour in which God's profaned and misused name will be glorified and the reign of his kingdom will be revealed. In a world enslaved by the rule of evil, a world of distress and conflict, they look forward to the revelation of God's glory.

These petitions are not wishful prayers but are filled with confidence. In the face of the world surrounding and encroaching upon the church, the Christian community takes God's promise seriously. It addresses him with utter confidence, saying, "Our Father." Remembering who taught this prayer, the Christian community is absolutely certain that God will redeem his promises as he spoke through the prophet Ezekiel: "I will sanctify my great name, which has been profaned among the nations, and which you have profaned among them; and the nations shall know that I am the LORD, says the Lord GOD, when through you I display my holiness before their eyes" (Ezek. 36:23).

Other phrases in the Lord's Prayer witness similarly to this yearning for and expectation of the eschaton. For instance, in the petitions for bread and for forgiveness the church asks that God might grant them today and in this place the bread of life and the blotting out of sins. Like a beacon of hope in the darkness of this world, the church prays amid failure, apostasy, and denial that God's kingly rule over the lives of his people might be realized. Though still symbols of the future, the bread of life and the endless mercy of God are already present now in the Lord's Supper, a symbol of God's almighty glory and the coming of his kingdom.

Considering baptism in this context, we recognize that the practice of infant baptism would be utterly ridiculous if we were to regard baptism simply as incorporation into the visible, institutional church. The notion of dying and rising with Christ or of being incorporated into his body envisions more than institutional membership. It even means more than being converted to Christ and becoming a confessing Christian. When Paul insists that as new creatures we should walk in the newness of life (Rom. 6:4), he makes two points:

1. We are still in a state of transition from this aeon to the future aeon. The world, though unable to hold us completely, still ensnares us.

15. So Jeremias, *The Lord's Prayer*, 22.

Luther was right when he called for a drowning of the old Adam "by daily sorrow and repentance" so that a new human person could emerge.[16]

2. Yet we must recognize that the Christian existence is dynamic and not static. Together with the whole creation, we are yearning and longing for the revelation of the children of God and for the manifestation of the kingdom (Rom. 8:19-21).

Dying and rising with Christ therefore can only instill hope if it implies a release from the natural cycle of birth and death from which this image is borrowed. It must point to a time when death will no longer score a victory and when we can walk forever in the newness of life. Similarly, becoming part of the body of Christ can only evoke hope when there is one point at which our separation from Christ is forever overcome. In other words, baptism remains an empty shell unless verified through the coming of the kingdom. At the same time, baptism today is still a sign and symbol of that future verification, and it is administered in trust and hope. The Eucharist too is intrinsically eschatological, foreshadowing and hoping for the final celestial banquet when we will be allowed to enjoy Christ's presence forever.

It has become clear that the church in its actions, in its liturgical celebrations, and in its prayer life is a symbol of the future, in part foreshadowing the things to come and in part patiently but intensely hoping and trusting for their ultimate verification. Yet the church would deny its own foundation if it were to attempt to bring about the realization of this future through its own actions. The power and the encouragement for both its anticipation and its expectation are derived from its experience of Christ. Through the presence of Christ and the power of the Spirit, the church realizes that the life and destiny of Jesus the Christ are the prime examples of its own life and destiny. Knowing about his death and resurrection, it acknowledges that ultimately all history will serve to make his kingdom triumph. We can be confident that God "will vindicate his people, / and have compassion on his servants" (Ps. 135:14), so that the hope he inspired in and through them will not be in vain.

16. Martin Luther, *The Small Catechism*, in *The Book of Concord*, ed. Theodore G. Tappert (Philadelphia: Fortress, 1959), 349.

The Whole People of God

Intrinsic to these hopes is the command to make disciples of all nations (Matt. 28:19). The hope for a common destiny of humanity includes the hope for the unity of the whole church, the unity of church and synagogue, and the unity of all people under the dominion of God. The church must be the vivid and living reminder that God wants all people to be saved. Its reason for being is to represent Christ in this world and to bring the gospel of Christ to the world. If the church wants to be the reminder of the future, it dare not leave humanity as it is, in its dispersion, antagonism, and self-destruction. Its faithful proclamation of the gospel must challenge every status quo, whether of Muslim or of Buddhist persuasion, whether socialist or capitalist. Yet the acknowledgment and proclamation of Christ as Lord of the whole world will not simply bring Christ to the world; the church must also ask how Christ is "present and operative in the faith of the individual non-Christian."[17]

Though we do hope that his Word will make a difference in this world, creating increasing solidarity among all people, we dare not assume prematurely that all people will eventually listen to him. Even our most sincere proclamation of the gospel in word and deed, through words of grace and acts of mercy, can never assume a universal homecoming of all people as a finished task. The realization of our common destiny as the whole people of God can only be a most daring eschatological hope and the content of fervent prayers. Still, sharing Christ even at the most remote places of the earth is a reminder that in one way or another, whether with everyone's consent or without, Christ will one day be acknowledged as Lord by all creation so that God may be everything to everyone (1 Cor. 15:28).

It would be totally irresponsible for the church to bring the gospel to non-Christians, calling for solidarity and mutual listening to the Lord of the world, without being utterly disturbed about its own divided house. The division into different churches and denominations is not just the fault of others. It is always also our own fault. While we realize more and more that the church must be Greek to the Greeks and Jewish to the Jews, the necessary cultural distinctiveness and diversity do not

17. So rightly Karl Rahner, *Foundations of Christian Faith*, trans. William V. Dych (New York: Seabury, 1978), 315, who, however, still seems to underestimate the necessity of proclaiming Christ to non-Christians.

justify our present divisions. Though immense progress has been made toward representing the whole people of God in the World Council of Churches (WCC), as well as various world federations of confessional families, national councils, and bilateral talks on all levels, institutional inertia and our sinful pride of being holier than others seem to be the greatest obstacles to actual unity.

Every day we discover anew how much we actually share in common. Thus in many cases division into different denominations and churches seems anachronistic and sinful. But the sentiment for institutional self-preservation looms high even in ecumenically minded circles. Nevertheless, in the last fifty years approximately sixty church unions have taken place, resulting in churches such as the Church of South India or the Evangelical Lutheran Church in America, and in about thirty countries negotiations toward union are being conducted. The Salamanca Consultation (1973) of the Faith and Order Commission of the WCC put our dilemma, our task, and our hope very succinctly: *"Jesus Christ founded one Church. Today we live in diverse churches divided from one another. Yet our vision of the future is that we shall once again live as brothers and sisters in one undivided Church."*[18]

A church which does not tolerate diversity within itself is an offense to its Lord and the gospel, and therefore an impediment to the proclamation of God's message of reconciliation and love. Divided Christendom is not only a reminder of our sinfulness and of the task still ahead. It is also a reminder of the eschatological future, when our human divisiveness will be overcome and no longer intrude on the manifestation of the whole people of God. Intermediate steps toward union are not necessarily designed to result in one superchurch. But involvement in joint mission projects, shared worship, public declaration of our common intention on all levels, united theological education, training of laity, Christian education and literary work, and joint evaluation of priorities and use of funds are all signs of repentance of a past that was often characterized by unholy crusades against other members of the body of Christ and by competing against each other in the name of our Lord. Our joint witness to the world is that the power of God's Spirit is at work in his people and that they are willing to anticipate something of

---

18. As reported in "Ecumenical Chronicle: Unity of the Church — Next Steps," *Ecumenical Review* 26 (April 1974): 293.

the great celestial banquet when all will share the same table and the same food.

The vision of the whole people of God would be incomplete without envisioning the union between church and synagogue, between Jew and Gentile (cf. Rom. 11:12-26). It should make us wonder why a people without a homeland for nearly two thousand years, a people who suffered the most cruel and systematic persecution ever inflicted, a people dispersed throughout the world — that such a people did not abandon their faith in God and in the promised Messiah. This people have now finally obtained a homeland, disputed and embattled though it may be. The Jewish people are both an enigma and a source of inspiration and hope. They remind us that God may lead his people through the valleys of shadow and death, but he will not abandon them forever. He sustains, calls, and nourishes them.

But the Jewish people are more than a symbol of survival. They are a symbol of insight. As the sculpture of the blindfolded synagogue on medieval churches shows, the Christians may have tolerated the Jewish people, but they never really accepted them as equals. Yet this did not prevent the Jewish people from perceiving all of humanity "as the descendants of one father and the creatures of one Creator," and similarly cherishing "the complementary vision of a reunited mankind under God at the end of time."[19] If, in light of its own history, Israel has not renounced the hope for a reunited humanity under God, how can the church ever dare to give up its hope for the visible union of the whole people of God? Moreover, the Christian community knows that the ethnic restrictions of the old covenant no longer hold and that the new covenant should include all people. The church will not want to take the Great Commission lightly, to go into all the world, proclaim the good news, and baptize those who follow Christ.

But the Jewish people remind us that it also is our task to keep ourselves holy and to sanctify God's name among all people. We would renounce our eschatological hope if we aim only at winning victories for our Lord. We must remind ourselves and others that the victory has already been won and that our Lord's compassion has been more powerful

---

19. So Moshe Greenberg, "Mankind, Israel and the Nations in the Hebraic Heritage," in *No Man Is Alien: Essays on the Unity of Mankind*, ed. J. Robert Nelson (Leiden: Brill, 1971), 35.

than our achievements. Thus Israel's hope for a reunited humanity can serve as a timely reminder that the wholeness of God's people does not depend on us. While it can be furthered by our own actions, it does not depend on them. We must trust that God's promises will not return empty.

The Anticipation of the Heavenly City

A theology of glory is not a proper topic in today's distressed world. Even the Roman Catholic Church, with which this notion has often been associated, is rediscovering the role of servanthood and suffering. But persecution and suffering are not the signs of the true church either.[20] God distributes suffering and pain indiscriminately among believers and unbelievers, among Christians and non-Christians. If the church is the living organism which connects the historical acts of God, through which he overcame our self-centered sinfulness, with the future acts of the establishment of the new Jerusalem, then it would be anachronistic to contemplate only suffering and pain. Festivity and celebration provide moments in a troubled world when we look forward to a time of eternal Sabbath, of continuous joy and rejoicing.

Remembering Christ as both crucified and resurrected, we celebrate our liberation and freedom as children of God, even while knowing that we are still entangled in this world. The church would betray its own source of strength and hope if it saw its function exhausted in rendering assistance to a world in need. The church also serves as a beacon of hope by demonstrating the Christ-won freedom in its own life and by manifesting its joy in that freedom.[21] A theology of glory need not be a betrayal of the gospel tradition if it means glorying in what God has done in and through the church, what God is doing, and what God will do. Anticipation of the heavenly glory both as a reminder of God's past acts and as a looking forward and hoping for the eschatological fulfill-

---

20. So rightly Paul Althaus, *Die christliche Wahrheit: Lehrbuch der Dogmatik*, 6th ed. (Gütersloh: Gerd Mohn, 1959), 503.

21. Cf. Jürgen Moltmann, *Theology of Play*, trans. R. Ulrich (New York: Harper, 1972), 71-72; and Jürgen Moltmann, *The Church in the Power of the Spirit: A Contribution to Messianic Ecclesiology*, trans. M. Kohl (New York: Harper, 1977), 300-301. Unfortunately Moltmann did not balance sufficiently the strong call for involvement with the need for rejoicing and festivity in his ecclesiology.

ment is as important for the church as remembering that it still lives in a valley of death and injustice.

When we focus here on the proleptic anticipation of the heavenly city, we must remember that the "ultimate hope in the lordship of Christ and the coming kingdom of God cannot be divorced from, or identified with, our historical hopes for freedom, justice, equality and peace."[22] The anticipation of the heavenly city cannot mean that we accomplish now what is promised to us as an eschatological, that is, a heavenly, reality. The church is an interim institution between Pentecost and parousia, waiting and hoping for replacement by the heavenly community of all the saints. Any utopian attempt to bring about in totality what the church lives by and toward would destroy the condition that makes its future-directed existence possible. For instance, it was one of the strange paradoxes of Marxism that it strived for the establishment of a classless society in anticipation of the heavenly community. But by refusing to admit that these attempts were only provisional, Marxism destroyed that which engendered and encouraged its hopes, the God-provided eschatological perfection. Moreover, since in a secular society perfection must be attained in this world, utopian systems by necessity behave intolerantly and dictatorially, diminishing the ideal vision they stand for.

The anticipation of the heavenly city is not a human accomplishment, but a divine gift. Community is not something we accomplish; we discover it as something given. We do not attempt to fulfill a dream or a utopian vision but live according to the presence of God through his Spirit. The theocentric structure of the Christian community reminds us of God, our ultimate allegiance and authority. All dreams and visions are destroyed by the cross of Christ, the vivid reminder that we still live under the realities of this world. Dietrich Bonhoeffer reminded us that

---

22. "A Common Account of Hope," statement on hope approved and adopted by the Commission on Faith and Order of the World Council of Churches at its meeting in Bangalore in August 1978, reprinted in the *Ecumenical Review* 31 (January 1979): 5-12; quotation on 7. Nevertheless, the statement focuses very much on the sociopolitical dimension of the this-worldly aspect of hope. The opposite is true of the "Votum des Theologischen Ausschusses der Evangelischen Kirche der Union," analogous to the UCC in the USA, under the title *Die Bedeutung der Reich-Gottes-Erwartung für das Zeugnis der christlichen Gemeinde* (Neukirchen-Vluyn: Neukirchener Verlag, 1986), which in sixteen catechetical statements shows a good balance between involvement and hope, 49-65.

"God hates visionary dreaming; it makes the dreamer proud and pretentious."[23] Living under the new life means living under God's word of forgiveness, the source of new life, which meets us through other Christians.

The anticipation of the heavenly city is not just a spiritual reality but something embodied in everyday life. Bonhoeffer rightly observed that "a purely spiritual relationship is not only dangerous but also an altogether abnormal thing."[24] The embodiment of the anticipation of the heavenly city has perhaps been captured best in the monastic ideal. Monastic groups are usually formed to strengthen the spiritual lives of their members. The monastic ideal, however, also informs their daily lives and transforms the surroundings in which they live and work through education, buildings and art, and community projects of charity. Similarly, their Protestant counterparts, such as the Oxford Group of the Lutheran pastor Frank Buchman (1878-1961) or the Moravians under Count Zinzendorf (1700-1760), had a profound impact on their own members and on the communities in which they lived and worked.

The same influence can emerge from the local worshiping community. The Christian faith is not a Sunday morning affair. It lays claim on the total lives of its members and has an impact on the community in which a congregation is located. As anticipation of the heavenly city on the local level, the church cannot but become a visible reality, a beacon of hope, a bastion of a new humanity in a fallen and hurting world. The vision of the church is always larger than the local church. As J. Robert Nelson (b. 1920) pointed out, "the primary task of the church in history is to be the bearer of that reconciling work in every generation."[25] Foreshadowing a heavenly city not torn by rivalry, strife, or injustice, the church not only manifests these signs on a global scale, but, by erecting them, it also serves as a powerful stimulus for sensitizing the whole of humanity. Without the presence of the church, the present would grow colder and more merciless.

It is unfortunate that the expectation of the heavenly future has rarely been sufficiently emphasized in the life of the church. Quite of-

23. Dietrich Bonhoeffer, *Life Together*, trans. J. W. Doberstein (New York: Harper, 1954), 27.

24. Bonhoeffer, 38.

25. J. Robert Nelson, "Signs of Mankind's Solidarity," in *No Man Is Alien*, 14.

ten it fell to sectarian groups to remind the church of the necessity and centrality of an eschatological gospel from which we derive our vision and power. In this century theology has recaptured the significance of an eschatological vision. Yet the rediscovery of the so-called last things still remains to be completed. Perhaps the church rightly feels threatened by the vision of the seer in the book of Revelation when he says: "I saw no temple in the city, for its temple is the Lord God the Almighty and the Lamb. And the city has no need of sun or moon to shine on it, for the glory of God is its light, and its lamp is the Lamb. The nations will walk by its light, and the kings of the earth will bring their glory into it. Its gates will never be shut by day — and there will be no night there" (Rev. 21:22-25).

In the midst of a cruel, unjust, and divided earth, such eschatological harmony among people and nations seems unreal. We also feel too solidly grounded in our own achievements on this earth to abandon them in favor of the complete dominion of God in a heavenly city. Some staunch church members and ecclesiastical administrators may also become uneasy with the vision of the city in which the presence of God will replace all temples. How dearly we love the church structures and ecclesiastical empires we erect and safeguard!

But the church does a disservice to its members and to the world when it neglects to remind us in time of trouble and turmoil of the eschatological future that God will establish in the midst of his people. Such a message, proclaimed with vigor and confident hope, will not induce a relinquishing of our responsibility and become a heavenly escape valve as Karl Marx predicted. On the contrary, it will encourage us to take the parable of the faithful steward seriously (cf. Matt. 25:14-30), because we know that our Lord and the Lord of all the world is coming. Only when we become oblivious to the coming of our Lord will we be tempted to shed our responsibility and set ourselves up as masters and oppressors (Luke 12:45), even in the name of freedom and liberation. When the church keeps the hope in God's future alive, it will instill hope, courage, and a sense of direction in a confused world. It will remain and become a beacon and a rallying point for the future, a stumbling block for some and a reminder for many others that the gates of hell will not prevail (cf. Matt. 16:18).

b. The Signs of the End

Quite often present and future are perceived as so radically disjunctive that neither one has any bearing on the other. Thus either otherworldly retreat or this-worldly activism results. But the very fact that we call ourselves Christians, followers of Jesus Christ, indicates that we embrace both the present by following Jesus and the future by expecting the return of Christ. The bridge between present and future is not only seen in Jesus Christ as our present Lord, but in individual Christians as well, as they mold themselves and are being molded through that presence. It is therefore no surprise that Bultmann, in his research on the Gospel of John, has pointed to the *now* as the decisive eschatological moment in which our decision between life and death is made.[26]

Anticipating the End

The last things are already anticipated in our present confrontation with the word of God. Through Jesus' whole life and destiny the decisive question was posed to the Jewish people, asking them whether they wanted to live in conformity with God or to reject him. We hear Jesus say: "Anyone who hears my word and believes him who sent me has eternal life, and does not come under judgment, but has passed from death to life" (John 5:24), or "those who do not believe are condemned already" (John 3:18). These would be difficult words to explain as a projection of human desires, as Feuerbach claimed. The present is the time of decision. It determines our future, not by way of complementing it, but as a consolidation and clarification of it.

This emphasis on the now as the anticipatory moment of the end is not restricted to John. Paul devotes almost a whole chapter (Rom. 6) to explaining that we are now dying and rising with Christ, and he declares that "now is the acceptable time; see, now is the day of salvation!" (2 Cor. 6:2). This is not an attempt to comfort us with the hope for a better "hereafter." And Jesus, referring to his actions, tells his inquirers: "But if it is by the finger of God that I cast out the demons,

---

26. Rudolf Bultmann, "The Eschatology of the Gospel of John" (1928), in *Faith and Understanding*, edited with an introduction by Robert W. Funk, trans. Louise Pettibone Smith (New York: Harper, 1969), 1:175.

then the kingdom of God has come to you" (Luke 11:20; cf. Matt. 12:28). This remark was directed to people who asked Jesus in whose name he performed his actions. In his answer Jesus points to the empirical concretization of the kingdom, while showing at the same time that the hoped-for and expected goal is not unambiguously demonstrable in its anticipation. Eternity in time is only possible in disguise. Even the evident results of the encounter of the divine with our earthly sphere are subject to contrary interpretations, as we notice with Jesus' miracles. Although this holds true for Jesus himself as well as for the life and actions of Christians, it does not exempt Christians from anticipating the end.

If Christians were to refrain from anticipation, that would modify not only their present but also their future existence. This means that decisions and attitudes in the present do not eliminate the final judgment but determine it. Thus the present is the decisive time for Christians, because the whole future is at stake. Of course, it would be a gross misunderstanding to conceive of the present activity of a Christian as works-righteousness and the final judgment as the big "awards day." Any anticipation of the end, whether in a positive or a negative way, is only possible because Christ has already anticipated the end in his resurrection — and we are invited to share in this anticipation. Our attitude can only be an attitude of response and not of initiative. Though Marxists were right in pointing out that, contrary to our own intentions, often we have not responded well enough to our eschatological situation, they went to the other extreme of exclusively emphasizing human initiative.

Christians are creative because they accept and anticipate the new world which will come by the provision of God.[27] No matter how much we emphasize the anticipatory character of eschatology, it is only proleptic anticipation and not the end itself. If it were otherwise, there would be no anticipation possible and we would understand our activities exclusively as the creative high point of evolution. But the anticipatory character of our activities is enabled by and points to the future fulfillment. Throughout the New Testament the now as the anticipated

---

27. Cf. Jürgen Moltmann, "Die Revolution der Freiheit," in *Perspektiven der Theologie: Gesammelte Aufsätze* (Munich: Chr. Kaiser, 1968), 210, in his discussion of Marxist anthropology.

end points to and enables the future fulfillment and vice versa.[28] This becomes especially evident in the so-called signs of the end.

The Birth Pangs of the New World

There are several major apocalyptic passages in the Gospels (Matt. 24; Mark 13; Luke 21) that describe the signs of the end: emergence of false prophets, climactic wars, catastrophes in nature, famines, persecution of the Christians, and the proclamation of the gospel to all people (Mark 13:10). The Gospel of John, which does not contain any long apocalyptic passages, is complemented by the book of Revelation, where the signs of the end are especially dealt with in chapters 6, 8, 13, and 16. Since many of these signs had already occurred when they were written down (cf. destruction of Jerusalem; Luke 21:20, 24), they are a theological evaluation of history in the light of the expected end and not a calendar according to which one can calculate when the end will come. Sentences such as "this generation will not pass away until all these things have taken place," with the following interpretation that "heaven and earth will pass away, but my words will not pass away" (Mark 13:30-31), show that the Evangelists did not want to enhance an apocalyptic fever in which people were convinced that they knew the course of world history, including its end.

The Evangelists returned to Jesus' own message, which culminated in the demand for immediate readiness. We hear Jesus say: "what I say to you I say to all: Keep awake" (Mark 13:37), and "for as the lightning comes from the east and flashes as far as the west, so will be the coming of the Son of Man" (Matt. 24:27), as well as the parable of the ten bridesmaids (Matt. 25:1-13). Even Paul asserts: "the day of the Lord will come like a thief in the night" (1 Thess. 5:2). These passages, and many more, convey the demand for immediate readiness. To interpret them as an indication of an immediate expectation of the end by Jesus or the first Christian community, an expectation which proved to be wrong, seems to miss the point.[29]

28. Cf. Gustav Stählin, "nun," in *TDNT*, 4:1118-20, where he mentions that the thought of a twofold fulfillment runs through the whole New Testament.

29. At this point it is difficult for us to agree with the otherwise excellent presentation of Paul Althaus, *Die letzten Dinge: Lehrbuch der Eschatologie*, 7th ed. (Gütersloh: Bertelsmann, 1957), 273-74, who states, on the one hand, that the expectation of the im-

Immediate readiness, similar to the decisive character of the now, does not necessarily express belief in the near return of the Lord, but it shows that our present attitude determines for us the outcome of the eschaton. Thus the watchword of the Middle Ages, *memento mori* ("be aware of your death"), was closer to the New Testament than the belief in the final end of history. *Memento mori* does not just mean that we never know when we will die, but that death will make our present life attitude irreversible. This is why we are called to respond to the demand for immediate readiness with an attitude of anticipation and not with a once-in-our-lifetime decision. That the demand for immediate readiness stands next to and is interspersed with indications of the end should also tell us that, no matter how carefully we interpret history, the coming of the end will be a total surprise. It will be absolutely unexpected. The consequence for Christians is that they will live their lives in active anticipation, as if each moment would be their last. Anthony A. Hoekema, in his extensive treatment of the signs of the end, rightly reminds us: "When they occur, we are not to become fearful, but are to accept them as the birthpangs of a better world."[30]

---

pending eschaton was not fulfilled and, on the other, that the end is in essence near and is at each point a threatening possibility. This spiritualist interpretation seems to neglect the progressiveness of history and comes close to a dualism of time and eternity.

It is certainly true that there were people in the first Christian community and at many other points in the history of the Christian church who expected the immediate return of the Lord. It is also true that Jesus unmistakably emphasized the nearness of the eschaton or, in other words, mentioned more than once that the end is close at hand. Yet he also consistently rejected any attempts to date the "point" at which the eschaton might come. This reservation would be inexplicable if he had expected the coming of the eschaton in connection with his death or with his resurrection, or after thirty or forty years (destruction of Jerusalem). Should Jesus not rather have meant: the hour of fulfillment has begun, the kingdom of God is manifesting itself already here and now, the final end will come soon; therefore, make use of the time as long as you can? But Jesus refused to limit God's sovereignty by imparting to us an eschatological timetable (cf. the excellent treatment of the issues involved by Joachim Jeremias, *New Testament Theology*, vol. 1, *The Proclamation of Jesus*, trans. J. Bowden [London: SCM, 1971], 131-41).

30. Anthony A. Hoekema, *The Bible and the Future* (Grand Rapids: Eerdmans, 1979), 129-63, quotation is on 163. He also reminds us that all of the signs of the end are present throughout the history of the church. While we agree with him as to their continuous presence, there is a building up of their intensity as the apocalyptic passages indicate.

The Antichrist

There is one sign of the end, however, which deserves special attention, the concept of the Antichrist.[31] The imagery which is incorporated in the concept of the Antichrist is partly of Jewish origin. For instance, in Daniel 9:27 we hear that someone, perhaps Antiochus IV Epiphanes, who ruled Syria from 175 to 164 B.C., will come who is "an abomination that desolates" the holy place (i.e., the temple). In the New Testament it is said that in the last days "false messiahs and false prophets will appear and produce signs and omens, to lead astray" (Mark 13:22). Paul warns of "the lawless one," who "opposes and exalts himself above every so-called god or object of worship, so that he takes his seat in the temple of God, declaring himself to be God" (2 Thess. 2:3-4). In the First Letter of John we hear that in the last hour the Antichrist is coming; therefore we know that it is the last hour (1 John 2:18), and a few verses further on we hear that the Antichrist denies the Father and the Son (2:22). In John's second letter we read of the many deceivers who have gone out into the world, "those who do not confess that Jesus Christ has come in the flesh; any such person is the deceiver and the anti-christ!" (2 John 7). Finally, in the book of Revelation the anti-Christian power is understood as being represented in the Roman state with its cult of the emperor (Rev. 13:1-10), and the Antichrist also signifies the false prophets who advocate this cult (13:11-18).

This diversity of the concept of the Antichrist shows us that the New Testament has no clear "doctrine" of the Antichrist. The Antichrist comes in disguise and in power and will mislead many. He looks like a lamb, but talks like a dragon. He wants to dethrone God and put himself in God's place. Sometimes there is just one Antichrist, at other times there are many. Sometimes the Antichrist comes from within the Christian community, for instance, when he denies the incarnation of God in Jesus Christ; sometimes he comes from outside.

The church accepted the idea of the Antichrist and used it widely. For the early church the Roman emperors, especially Nero (37-68) and Domitian (51-96), who persecuted the Christians, were called the Antichrist. In the Middle Ages, during the papal schism, usually the counterpope was declared the Antichrist, and he in turn called the orig-

---

31. For the concept of the Antichrist, cf. Sven S. Hartman et al., "Antichrist I-IV," in *TRE*, 3:20-43, where one finds an extensive discussion on this topic.

inal pope the Antichrist. The Franciscan Spirituals, who had followed the millennial ideas of Joachim of Fiore, were also quick to declare the pope the Antichrist, simply because he denied their claim for poverty. Later, John Hus (ca. 1372-1415) and John Wycliffe (ca. 1330-84), forerunners of the Reformation, sometimes extended the idea of the Antichrist to the whole Roman Catholic Church.

Luther was at first very reluctant to use the term "Antichrist."[32] However, under the impact of Laurentius Valla's (ca. 1406-57) discovery that the papacy had illegally usurped its supremacy over worldly authorities with the forgery of the Donation of Constantine, Luther came to the conclusion that the papacy, not an individual pope, must be the Antichrist because it puts its own authority above that of the word of God. With this conviction Luther regretted that the Augsburg Confession made no mention of the Antichrist. Though in contemporary history many dictators, such as Stalin or Hitler, have been labeled the Antichrist, the question for us is what to do with this concept. Shall we simply recognize its frequent and manifold use and then go on to more important business?

Without disregarding all the diversity in the use of this concept, three features seem to be consistent and noteworthy.

1. While in dualistic Parsism, which undoubtedly influenced the emergence of the concept of the Antichrist, there is a gradual disappearance of the antigodly powers, the Christian faith in contrast is aware of the threatening presence of the Antichrist up to the final consummation of the world. This shows the conviction that humanity does not gradually work itself up to the kingdom of God, with God sanctifying these human endeavors by recognizing the goal of their work as his kingdom. The alienation from God and the usurpation of antigodly sovereignty seem to increase instead of decrease.

2. The Antichrist is not a possibility of the future, but a reality of the present. The conviction that the Antichrist is already here emphasizes that we must constantly be on the alert. There is no neutral ground on which to stand and wait. Either we are engaged in active

---

32. Cf. for the following, Ulrich Asendorf, *Eschatologie bei Luther* (Göttingen: Vandenhoeck & Ruprecht, 1967), 173-76.

preparation for the eschaton, or we fall prey to the Antichrist, who will lead us to a different activism.

3. The activities of the Antichrist do not result in events whose theological significance has to be shown; they already *have* theological significance. The Antichrist, be it from within or from outside the Christian community, attempts to dethrone God and assume God's throne. Belief in technology and progress instead of faith in God, belief in essential human goodness instead of faith in the love of God, hope for the Christianization of all people instead of hope for the coming of the kingdom of God — these are only a few alternatives that show us the antigodly tendency of the Antichrist. Yet, realizing the seriousness of the *many* faces of the Antichrist, we know that this figure too is subject to temporality, and the last judgment will terminate all antigodly endeavors.

2. Entry to the New World

Evolutionary concepts imply a continuous expansion and perhaps even improvement of existing possibilities. Yet evolution allows for nothing genuinely new. We only encounter new arrangements of what we face now. The vision of a new world, however, goes beyond these possibilities and opts for something radically new. In such a vision our present world and its fundamental structures must give way to something new and unprecedented.

a. Consummation of the World

In relating the concepts of time and eternity with each other, we have noticed that the disclosure of eternity as God's immediate presence demands the consummation or at least transformation of the categories of time, space, and matter, or of the world as we know it. This is also the conviction of the New Testament.

> Immediately after the suffering of those days
>> the sun will be darkened,
>>> and the moon will not give its light;

> the stars will fall from heaven,
>> and the powers of the heaven will be shaken.

Then the sign of the Son of Man will appear in heaven, and then all the tribes of the earth will mourn, and they will see the "Son of Man coming on the clouds of heaven" with power and great glory. (Matt. 24:29-30)

And the Second Letter of Peter tells us in even greater detail: "But the day of the Lord will come like a thief, and then the heavens will pass away with a loud noise, and the elements will be dissolved with fire, and the earth and everything that is done on it will be disclosed" (2 Pet. 3:10).

Inquisitive spirits have always tried to investigate how such a consummation could be possible, and modern scientific insights have paved the road for much speculation. For instance, the possible collision of our earth with other planets or planetoids would certainly darken the sun and the moon for us and might perhaps lead to the extinction of life on earth. A cosmic nuclear reaction could also dissolve the elements with fire, and if militarists were to employ all our presently available "over-kill," they could even usher in the eschaton at their own wish. Also the looming prospect of a global pollution of life could lead to the end of life here on earth. But Teilhard de Chardin already observed that such a sidereal disaster would affect only part of the universe and not the total universe. Even the final heat death through an equilibrium of all energy levels, to which Karl Heim alluded, would not lead to the consummation of this world, but only to the end of life within it. At best, science can tell us that our universe does not contain any eternal life force. By its very nature science works within the categories of space, time, and matter, and this means with the universe in which we live.

The consummation of the world does not just affect existence in the universe; it affects the very existence of the universe. The only analogy we could draw from science regarding our future is of the cosmological model of an expanding and contracting universe. Once the universe has reached its maximum expansion, it could contract again so that it would end its existence in a "big crunch." Then another expansion could occur. However, no predictions could be made about such a new "life cycle" since it would be governed by an entirely new set of "laws." Moreover, at present everything seems to indicate that the expansion of the universe has not even slowed down — not to speak of reversal or contraction.

The New Testament witnesses envision a consummation of the world which is not primarily destruction. It is rather the universal incorporation into the creative and transforming act of Christ's resurrection. No one has expressed this more clearly than Paul in his Letter to the Romans, where he writes that "the creation waits with eager longing for the revealing of the children of God," that it will be "set free from its bondage to decay," and that we ourselves wait for adoption as God's children, "the redemption of our bodies." This is no vague or uncertain hope, because "he who raised Jesus Christ from the dead will give life to your mortal bodies also" (Rom 8:11, 19-23). The hope for a new world is grounded in the Christ event, in the cross and resurrection of Jesus Christ, where for the first time, out of death and decay, something entirely new had dawned.

Since Jesus is the exalted Christ, the Pantocrator, salvation in the eschaton pertains to our whole being, to the whole cosmos, and to the whole creation. It is a redemption from transitoriness.[33] Then our adoption as sons and daughters, which we have received in baptism, is made manifest, and we will, not merely in anticipation but in reality, be redeemed from transitoriness. The consummation of the world is perfection and completion. It is the completion of time[34] and the perfection of our limiting forms of space, time, and matter.

A foretaste of this new world, as far as it pertains to us, has already been given to us in the witnesses of those who encountered the resurrected Christ.[35] The biblical witnesses tell us that the risen Lord was no longer limited by time, space, and matter. The material and spatial bounds of a closed room or of hunger could no longer confine him. But, of course, he could appear in a room and he could eat. In a similar way, he was no longer bound to the transitoriness of time, yet he could appear sooner, or later, or now. Perfection of the forms of this world also means the elimina-

---

33. Otto Michel, *Der Brief an die Römer* (Göttingen: Vandenhoeck & Ruprecht, 1957), 171.

34. Walter Künneth, *The Theology of the Resurrection*, trans. James W. Leitch (London: SCM, 1965), 285-86. The term "consummation," which is used to translate the German *Vollendung*, does not render the full meaning of this term.

35. Cf. Karl Heim, *Jesus the World's Perfecter: The Atonement and the Renewal of the World*, trans. D. H. van Daalen (Philadelphia: Muhlenberg, 1961), 166.

tion of the antigodly distortion of this world, of sin, destruction, and death. Again this is shown in the resurrected Christ who is beyond the possibility of sinning and beyond the possibility of dying.

Whenever we talk about the new world to come, we must mention Christ and his resurrection because "all things have been created through him and for him" (Col. 1:16). There is no other goal of creation than Jesus, who as the Messiah enabled this creation to move toward this goal.[36] The consummation then is the disclosure of the new world which was enabled by and has started in the resurrection of Jesus Christ. Martin Luther, in his unique and picturesque language, has expressed the point of the consummation very well: "This world serves for God only as a preparation and a scaffolding for the other world. As a rich lord must have a lot of scaffolding for his house, but then tears the scaffolding down as soon as the house is finished . . . so God has made the whole world as a preparation for the other life, where finally everything will proceed according to the power and will of God."[37]

b. Final Judgment

The final judgment is a difficult subject to mention, because everybody wants to be saved but only a few are willing to accept judgment as salvation's prerequisite. H. Richard Niebuhr's famous phrase about nineteenth-century American liberalism, "a God without wrath brought men without sin into a kingdom without judgment through the ministrations of a Christ without a cross,"[38] is a vivid description of humanity in general. We desire heaven, but we do not want to accept that the only way to heaven is through judgment. But the New Testament in all its witnesses makes it unmistakably clear that the only road to the new world to come is through judgment, and that the consummation of the world does not mean final evolution but implies the parousia of the Lord and the final judgment.

---

36. So Eduard Lohse, *A Commentary on the Epistles to the Colossians and to Philemon,* trans. W. R. Poehlmann and R. J. Karris (Philadelphia: Fortress, 1975), 52, in his exegesis of Col. 1:16.

37. Martin Luther, WATR, 2:627.29–628.4 (no. 2741b), in a remark from 1532.

38. H. Richard Niebuhr, *The Kingdom of God in America* (New York: Harper Torchbooks, 1959), 193.

"For the Son of Man is to come with his angels in the glory of his Father, and then he will repay everyone for what has been done" (Matt. 16:27). "When the Son of Man comes in his glory, and all the angels with him, then he will sit on the throne of his glory. All the nations will be gathered before him, and he will separate people one from another as a shepherd separates the sheep from the goats" (Matt. 25:31-32). "For the Lord himself, with a cry of command, with the archangel's call and with the sound of God's trumpet, will descend from heaven" (1 Thess. 4:16). "For all of us must appear before the judgment seat of Christ, so that each may receive recompense for what has been done in the body, whether good or evil" (2 Cor. 5:10). "And I saw the dead, great and small, standing before the throne, and books were opened. Also another book was opened, the book of life. And the dead were judged according to their works, as recorded in the books" (Rev. 20:12). The imagery of these quotes from the New Testament, which could easily be multiplied, betrays Old Testament and Jewish apocalyptic influences. The language is that of a past age and need not necessarily be reiterated, but the tendency of these passages is crystal clear: there is a final judgment.

Often this final judgment has been conceived as the great awards day. This is especially the temptation of chiliastic hopes of a thousand-year rule of Christ with the faithful over, and at the expense of, others. Yet, the final judgment is not a judgment of our merits, but of our response to God's grace which he has extended to us in Jesus Christ. We are not awarded a certificate of loyalty simply because we happened to be on the right side at the right time. Such cheap grace would neglect our wrongdoings. The German poet Heinrich Heine (1797-1856) was not right when he said: "Of course [God] will forgive me; that's his business." Paul caught the seriousness of the final judgment much more appropriately when he cautioned: "For you reap whatever you sow" (Gal. 6:7). Our Lord will take into consideration each of our individual situations and judge to what extent we have attempted to respond to the promise he offers and to the exemplary life he has shown us.

The judgment is not an occasion when everybody will be measured by the same standards; it is rather a judgment according to one's possibilities. "Everyone to whom much has been given, much will be required; and from the one to whom much has been entrusted, even more will be demanded" (Luke 12:48). This does not mean that we should take it easy; we are called to measure up to the possibilities of our own response and not to some ambiguous standards we might adopt. Since this judgment will occur concurrently with the parousia of the Lord, it becomes evident that Christ will be the judge. In judging us in the name of God and as God, this judgment is irrevocable, final, and binding. There is no higher court of appeal.

Since Christ the Savior is also the judge, the judgment in all its seriousness has a comforting aspect. By confronting us with himself and his gospel, Christ has shown us the direction of our life, and through his dying and resurrection he has enabled us to pursue this direction of our life, to live in and toward conformity with God. The first Christian community, which preserved for us all the dreadful apocalyptic imagery of the final judgment, was not scared by the prospect of this judgment. It knew that it was the necessary "entrance gate" to the new world to come. Thus *marana tha* ("our Lord, come!") was a familiar word in the first Christian community (cf. 1 Cor. 16:22),[39] and the book of Revelation closes in a similar way with "Amen. Come, Lord Jesus!" (Rev. 22:20). Martin Luther recaptured this New Testament confidence in the face of the judgment when, contrary to the mood of the Middle Ages, he did not conceive of this day as a day of wrath, but as a day of the glory of God, a day to which he was looking forward when he said in many of his letters: "Come, dear, last day."[40]

But is not such an ultimate, universal judgment day as obsolete as the apocalyptic imagery in which its coming is expressed? Are we not finally indulging in a travelogue eschatology? Indeed, it should make us wonder when we read that as high as the place value of the aspect of a judgment according to works is "in the context of the New Testament and of the history of the church, it has a minor function in contemporary theological reflection and perhaps also in the life of the faith of the

39. Hans Conzelmann, *A Commentary on the First Epistle to the Corinthians,* trans. J. W. Leitch (Philadelphia: Fortress, 1975), 301, claims in his exegesis of 1 Cor. 16:22 that it must be left open whether this phrase invokes God's participation in the Eucharist or his parousia. Since the Eucharist must be regarded as an eschatological meal, the phrase in either way points to the coming eschaton.

40. Cf. Paul Althaus, *The Theology of Martin Luther,* trans. Robert C. Schultz (Philadelphia: Fortress, 1966), 420-21, in his excellent treatment of Luther's interpretation of eschatology, and cf. Bernhard Lohse, *Luthers Theologie in ihrer historischen Entwicklung und in ihrem systematischen Zusammenhang* (Göttingen: Vandenhoeck & Ruprecht, 1995), 349.

Christians."[41] Christ as judge reminds many people of the bygone age of absolutism when kings and princes ruled over their subjects, and for some it might bring up the aversion against imperialist patriarchy. Moreover, it would be completely contrary to Lutheran teachings, since Lutherans claim to obtain salvation by faith and by grace alone. "Whoever announces the absolute gift character of salvation cannot attribute decisive significance to judgment according to works."[42]

Before we too quickly discard as no longer tenable what we have said so far about the last judgment, we should remember that on the one hand Luther was almost driven to insanity when he realized that he could not face Christ as his ultimate judge and survive. On the other hand, we have just heard that because of his Reformation experience, he was no longer afraid of this day of wrath, but was looking forward to its coming: "Come, dear, last day." Especially a passage such as John 3:18 ("those who believe in him are not condemned") convinced Luther that those who believe in Christ have already passed judgment. Therefore he said, "if we could grasp this in our heart, what kind of joy would we experience in the Last Judgment that one would not fear it."[43] This means that a Christian need not be afraid of the final judgment because, by accepting the grace extended to him or her, he or she has already been accepted.

This does not mean that the final judgment is obsolete, since that judgment means the final public disclosure of our allegiance to Christ and the degree of our response to that allegiance. "Human destiny aims at participation in God's eternity."[44] If we were to realize this determination, then we would live at each moment in accordance with the eternity of God to which we are aiming. But we are self-centered, and instead of living each moment in the light of eternity, we live mainly in

---

41. So Eberhard Amelung, "Gericht Gottes V: Neuzeit und ethisch," in *TRE*, 12:492, who then turns to interpret historical occurrences under the aspect of God's judgment, concluding that such an evaluation is always arbitrary.

42. So Helmut Merkel, "Gericht Gottes IV: Alte Kirche bis Reformationszeit," in *TRE*, 12:492.

43. Martin Luther, *Auslegung des 3. und 4. Kapitels Johannes* (1538-40), in WA, 47:102.28-30, and Lohse, *Luthers Theologie*, 349, who refers to this passage.

44. For the following, cf. the profound thoughts of Wolfhart Pannenberg, *What Is Man? Contemporary Anthropology in Theological Perspective*, trans. D. A. Priebe (Philadelphia: Fortress, 1970), 76-81, quote on 76, and Wolfhart Pannenberg, *Systematic Theology*, trans. Geoffrey W. Bromiley, 3 vols. (Grand Rapids: Eerdmans, 1991-98), 3:608-20.

the light of ourselves or of transitoriness. When we die, we are unable to continue our self-centered life. Our temporal life ceases, and only the eternity of God is left, into which we are received. Thus death becomes the boundary line that we cross as we enter into the eternity of God.

Death also finalizes and completes our participation in the eternity of God. Our earthly life, which is only partially known to us as long as we live it, will become known in totality, not for itself but in confrontation with the "blueprint" of its eternal destination. Then its fragmentariness will become visible and irreversible, and the discrepancy between the possibility and the actuality of our earthly life will be what we experience as God's final judgment, a judgment which, in anticipation, we have already long ago pronounced upon ourselves in our earthly life. As Paul picturesquely writes: "For no one can lay any foundation other than the one that has been laid; that foundation is Jesus Christ. Now if anyone builds on the foundation . . . the work of each builder will become visible, for the Day will disclose it, because it will be revealed with fire, and the fire will test what sort of work each has done" (1 Cor. 3:11-13). Only those who are already in this life connected with eternity in time, with Jesus Christ, have the assurance that this discrepancy will be overcome, because Jesus Christ, though human, never allowed this discrepancy to develop in his life, in his death, and beyond death. Their self-centeredness will "go up in smoke," their virtues will "sparkle," and they will be received into the new world. Through their alignment with Christ, death will result in resurrection not only to judgment, but to eternal life.

c. Paradox between Justice and Love of God

The option for a universal homecoming becomes at no time more urgent than when we are confronted with the final judgment and realize that not everybody will be saved. But Jesus, and with him the New Testament witnesses, are convinced of a twofold outcome of this final judgment.[45] "The gate is wide and the road is easy that leads to destruction,

---

45. Jeremias, *New Testament Theology,* 1:131, in exegeting Matt. 22:14, mentions that the invitation is unlimited, but the number of those who follow it and are being saved is small.

and there are many who take it. For the gate is narrow and the road is hard that leads to life, and there are few who find it" (Matt. 7:13-14). And we read the same in the Gospel of John, only actualized in the now: "Whoever believes in the Son has eternal life; whoever disobeys the Son will not see life, but must endure God's wrath" (John 3:36). And the book of Revelation expresses in its typical apocalyptic fashion: "And the smoke of their torment goes up forever and ever. There is no rest day or night" (Rev. 14:11).

The answer to the question of a universal homecoming becomes even more difficult, because the New Testament also contains many assertions that God wants all people to be saved. Paul, for instance, in wrestling with the destiny of Israel, expresses the conviction that "God has imprisoned all in disobedience so that he may be merciful to all" (Rom. 11:32). The goal of the cosmos and of all saving history is universal salvation, a goal which embraces the destiny of all individuals, Jews and pagans alike.[46] In a similar way, to quote just one more reference, we hear that God our Savior "desires everyone to be saved and to come to the knowledge of the truth" (1 Tim. 2:4). All this boils down to a final paradox that states, on the one hand, that God's love wants all to be saved and declares, on the other, that God's justice requires all the disobedient to be punished.

Of course, we could attempt to solve the evident paradox by asserting that God's justice is only preliminary, and justice and love are related to each other like law and gospel. God threatens with his justice in order that we might flee to his love.[47] But this evidently anthropomorphic construct of a pedagogic God, who punishes only in order to save (cf. Schleiermacher!), does not take into account that the judgment is disclosure and finalization of one's life attitude and not a transition to the universal love of God. If one's life attitude runs counter to the love God extends, the result is a dichotomy that cannot be bridged through evolution or amelioration. Even the Roman Catholic notion of purgatory traditionally has not been construed to mean a gradual purification for everyone. It only opened the possibility of another chance.

Another attempt to solve the paradox between God's justice and

46. Cf. Michel, 253, in his exegesis of Rom. 11:32.

47. This misunderstanding seems to be implied in Emil Brunner's otherwise excellent book *Eternal Hope*, trans. H. Knight (London: Lutterworth, 1954), 182-84.

love, though only a halfhearted one, is to assert that the condemned will be annihilated and thus all (who are left) will be saved.[48] But how can there be an annihilation of anybody if there is no escape from God, since God is everywhere, even in death and beyond death? The solution must rather be sought in what we mean when we talk about the justice and love of God. Do we really mean that we *describe* God with these terms, or do they not rather *disclose* certain aspects of God *for us?* We must remember that God's self-disclosure to us can only be expressed in human language, and this means with necessarily anthropomorphic and inadequate conceptual tools.[49] Thus we can rightly conclude that God is beyond justice and love, just as he is beyond being a person when we call him a personal God.

We must remember too that we are confronted with God's decision-demanding word that says: repent and follow me. As we accept God's offer to direct our lives according to his eternal purpose, a universal homecoming will be meaningless for our salvation, since we will be saved according to the promise of his redemptive word. Ultimately, the idea of a universal homecoming can emerge only as (concerned and pastoral) speculation about the final destiny of others. Even in our most sincere concern for them, we have to acknowledge the ultimate hidden-

48. This idea is, for instance, implied by Maurice Carrez, "With What Body Do the Dead Rise Again?" in *Immortality and Resurrection,* ed. Pierre Benoit and Roland Murphy, vol. 60 of *Concilium* (New York: Herder & Herder, 1970), 101, when he suggests that resurrection implies the entering into the fullness of life with a transformed body. While all will appear before the Lord on the day of judgment, there is only one resurrection, namely, to eternal life.

But we must ask here, how can we meaningfully speak of a judgment of all if we do not speak of a resurrection for all? Of course, resurrection to a "newness of life" and a subsequent damnation (of this newness) seems to be an obvious contradiction. The question, however, is whether resurrection must be understood this way. Albrecht Oepke, "anhistémi," in *TDNT,* 1:371, claims rightly that "the predominant view" of the New Testament "is that of a double resurrection."

49. Karl Rahner, "The Hermeneutics of Eschatological Assertions," in Karl Rahner, *Theological Investigations,* vol. 4, *More Recent Writings,* trans. Kevin Smyth (Baltimore: Helicon, 1966), 344-45, points out very convincingly that each term conveys its own particular *imagery,* and that no new assertion "*adequately* renders the real content of the assertion" which it attempts to translate and interpret. This means that any new interpretation that replaces the old is not a better one, but it is a new and necessary attempt in our search for a more contemporary and adequate approximation in expressing God's relationship to us and to our final destiny.

396

ness of God, a God who is beyond justice and love. At this point we can only *hope* without *knowing* for sure that his never ending grace will ultimately prevail.

3. Disclosure of the New World

When we finally attempt to make assertions about the new world, it seems next to impossible to say something meaningful without indulging in speculation. To escape this temptation theology often emphasizes the this-worldliness of the Christian faith. Its value consists in creating a better world and providing better living conditions. Therefore the striving for peace, justice, and integrity of creation, to name just three areas, often replaces the proclamation of the hope in a new creation. While the Christian faith is by no means otherworldly, the correct attitude toward this world in thought and action is deeply informed by that which Christians are hoping for. Jesus and the New Testament invite us to put our trust in a discernible future, which we are summoned to anticipate already to some degree in the present. We can pursue this two-pronged approach, expecting the future completion and anticipating it proleptically in the present, since the goal of history and of humanity has already started with Jesus' coming. These two factors, the New Testament's own insistence on a "concrete" future and the anticipatory aspect of this future, provide room for positive assertions about the new world.

a. Disclosure of the Kingdom of God

When Jesus began his ministry, it was announced: "The time is fulfilled, and the kingdom of God has come near; repent, and believe in the good news" (Mark 1:15). The kingdom of God or the new world to come has already started with Christ's coming. But the kingdom also has a future, and admission into it demands a decision, because "not everyone who says to me, 'Lord, Lord,' will enter the kingdom of heaven" (Matt. 7:21).

All the parables of the kingdom seem to indicate that at one point it will become evident who has entered the kingdom of God and who has not, or in other words, good and evil will be separated (cf. Matt. 13:30,

397

49-52). Jesus even had to hold back enthusiastic disciples who demanded that, since the decision about entrance must be made now, the evidence of entrance or nonentrance must also be disclosed. But Jesus rejected any attempt to build a pure "Christian community" here on earth by pointing to the future dimension of such perfection: "Let both of them grow together until the harvest; and at harvest time I will tell the reapers, Collect the weeds first and bind them in bundles to be burned, but gather the wheat into my barn" (Matt. 13:30). This future dimension will find its fulfillment with the final judgment. The already existing invisible separation will then become visible and irreversible. The kingdom of God, or the new world, will be disclosed.

Millennial visions especially describe graphically the forces of evil and death which wage their continuous war in this world until the public disclosure of the kingdom. But then there will be an end to all uncertainty and anguish. The disclosure of the kingdom means the unrestricted assumption of power on God's part and the final banishment of everything ungodly and antigodly. The eternal laws of growth, maturation, and decay are eliminated, because death will be no more. The bridegroom will return (Matt. 25) and God will come into his own. Not only earthly power structures will disappear, but so will the church. This interim institution between Pentecost and the disclosure of the kingdom will have served as the vivid reminder of the end and of end-time living. Now the people of God will enter God's own kingdom and the great homecoming commences. Not only God and Christ will come to their own, but also God's people and with them the whole of creation. This disclosure of the new world is described with the term "heaven," while the term "hell" denotes exclusion from the new world.

b. Heaven and Hell

To talk about heaven or hell as the final stages of human destiny seems, at first glance, a remythologization of eschatology. We are not surprised that the prestigious *Theologische Realenzyklopädie*, the most comprehensive theological dictionary, has no subject entry under "heaven," but refers one to "worldview," and the subject entry on "hell" treats the topic only from the angle of the history of religion and church history, but not from the perspective of theology proper.[50] Yet the terms have not disappeared from public vocabulary. We encounter the term "hell" quite frequently in movies, rock and pop music, and also in curse words, while "heaven" enjoys increasing attention even in advertising.[51]

When we ask whether people really believe there will be heaven or hell, then, however, the results are quite different. According to an October 1985 survey among the Roman Catholic population in Romance language countries of Europe, only 38 percent believe in paradise and 26 percent in hell.[52] Americans fared somewhat better. According to a 1982 Gallup poll, 71 percent of the American public answered "yes" to the question: "Do you think there is a heaven where people who have led good lives are eternally rewarded?" while the same poll revealed a paucity of concrete ideas of what the afterlife was actually about.[53] This means there is widespread disbelief and ignorance concerning heaven and hell, and theology largely reflects this public trend.

While the religious acceptance of heaven is still larger than that of hell, we should not rejoice prematurely. Even conservative theologians who claim that heaven is still an active part of their belief system have precious little to say about eternal life. Often their attention is focused on what happens before the end. "The drama of the future is decidedly this-worldly; it occurs during the period before and during the millennium, not in a heavenly world."[54] Only in sectarian quarters is the hereafter more clearly enunciated, but then often at the expense of a travelogue eschatology.

The reticence with which theologians usually treat the subject of hell deserves more justification. For early Christianity, hell was not a central topic.[55] Christians portrayed an optimistic certainty concerning salvation

---

50. See *TRE*, 15:330 and 445.

51. Cf. the examples in Elke Jüngling, *Die Hölle — veralteter Glaubensartikel oder unverzichtbares Element im Gottesbild?* (Frankfurt am Main: Peter Lang, 1997), 21-38.

52. According to Albert Biesinger, "Kommt die religiöse Erziehung ohne die Vorstellungen von Himmel — Hölle — Fegefeuer aus?" in *Himmel — Hölle — Fegefeuer,* ed. Albert Biesinger and Michael Kessler (Tübingen: A. Francke, 1996), 17.

53. So Colleen McDannell and Bernhard Lang, *Heaven: A History* (New Haven: Yale University Press, 1988), 307.

54. McDannell and Lang, 352.

55. Cf. for the following, Tarald Rasmussen, "Hölle II. Kirchengeschichtlich," in *TRE*, 15:449-53.

and focused much more on heaven as a desirable state to reach. When the Christian faith had become the official religion of the empire under Emperor Constantine (ca. 280-337), the self-understanding of the eschatological community of the baptized as a community on its way to the heavenly reward was pushed to the background. Confronted with the challenges of a mass movement, theology and catechesis emphasized more than ever the final judgment and the possibility of damnation even for Christians who had led unchristian lives. Now the dreadful reality of hell and of eternal punishment gained in significance.

Throughout the Middle Ages hell was a significant topic. We should remember here Martin Luther, whose fear of hell and personal damnation was an important factor in his call for the reform of the church. The Reformation discovery of a gracious God, clearly enunciated in the New Testament, overcame this fear of hell and informed Luther's later assertions about hell. His discovery of a gracious God, however, did not let him discard the concept of hell. The respect for gracious but still awe-inspiring majesty of God left open the possibility that not everyone and everything must necessarily find its end in God. Only so much was certain: in the same way that Christians need not be afraid of judgment, they also need not be afraid of hell.

But what do we actually mean when we talk about heaven and hell? In most religions heaven is understood as the location of the gods, while hell is usually associated with the devil, with demons, and with other figments of a world of fantasy. When looking at the New Testament, however, we discover that the term "heaven" is used at least as frequently, and not just primarily in the Gospels, as the term "kingdom of God." At some places the terms are even merged to a "kingdom of heaven" (e.g., Matt. 3:2; 5:3). Here the Jewish respect for God's name seems to reverberate so that "God" and "heaven" are used as synonyms when one says "kingdom of heaven" instead of "kingdom of God."

Already Luther mocked the idea of depicting hell as "built of wood and stone," so that it would have "a gate and windows, locks, and bars as a house or castle does here on earth." And of course, Christ did not destroy hell with a flag of cloth in his hands.[56] For Luther, "hell means that

---

56. Martin Luther, *Predigten des Jahres 1533*, in WA, 37:65.30-33. Cf. for Luther's understanding of heaven and hell, Hans Schwarz, "Luther's Understanding of Heaven and

death is accompanied by the feeling that the punishment is, at once, unchangeable and eternal. Here the soul is captured and surrounded so that it cannot think anything else except that it is to be eternally damned."[57] In a similar way Luther mocked the *Schwärmer* (enthusiasts) who understood God's dwelling place in heaven in a cosmological way. Because the visible heaven or sky is constantly moving, Luther concluded that this would mean that God cannot sit still for one moment. It is, however, absurd to understand God's realm geographically so that one thinks of God as sitting on high, somewhat like a stork in its nest. But Luther was also aware that the Bible, in its pre-Copernican worldview, often uses the terms "hell" and "heaven" cosmologically.

Already in the Old Testament the term "heaven" is used not just in a cosmological topography, but also in a theological understanding in which heaven denotes the dimension of the source of salvation, namely, God and his power.[58] In rabbinical literature heaven can even become a paraphrase for God.[59] The differentiation between a cosmological and a theological understanding of heaven is intensified in the New Testament. Theologically speaking, heaven can be the dimension of God, the source of salvation, and the integrating focus for the present and future blessings of salvation in the new aeon.[60] That such a theological understanding of heaven demands a transcendence of the prevalent three-story worldview of the Bible is indicated in such passages as the exclamation of Solomon, "Even heaven and the highest heaven cannot contain you, much less this house that I have built!" (1 Kings 8:27), and the assertion of Paul, "He who descended is the same one who ascended far above all the heavens, so that he might fill all things" (Eph. 4:10).

Although in the earlier parts of the Old Testament Sheol, or "hell," is understood indiscriminately as the shadowy existence of all who have died (cf. Ps. 89:48), it is at the same time the dimension of alienation

Hell," in *Interpreting Luther's Legacy*, ed. Fred W. Meuser and Stanley D. Schneider (Minneapolis: Augsburg, 1969), 83-94.

57. Martin Luther, *Operationes in Psalmos* (1519-21), in WA, 5:497:16-19, in his exegesis of Ps. 18.

58. Cf. Gerhard von Rad, "ouranos, B. Old Testament," in *TDNT*, 5:507.

59. So Helmut Traub, "ouranos, C. The Septuagint and Judaism," in *TDNT*, 5:512. The term "kingdom of heaven," frequently used in the Gospel according to Matthew, reminds us of this usage.

60. Cf. Traub, "ouranos," in *TDNT*, 5:532.

from God in death. In postexilic times, perhaps through the influence of Parsism, Sheol is conceived as a temporary dwelling place and as different for the righteous than for the godless.[61] "Gehenna," the New Testament word for hell, already presupposes resurrection and final judgment.[62] The whole person with body and soul will be tormented in Gehenna, "where their worm never dies, and the fire is never quenched" (Mark 9:48). While hell does not just originate in the eschaton (Matt. 25:41), it is only after the resurrection and judgment that it will be disclosed as the realm of eternal torment. In apocalyptic thinking "gehenna" was still associated with the Hinnom valley near Jerusalem, where King Ahaz of Israel (741-725 B.C.) and King Manasseh of Judah (696-642 B.C.) had offered sacrifice to foreign gods. This kind of localization was abandoned in the New Testament. In contrast to apocalyptic literature, the New Testament usually did not paint the torments of hell in drastic colors, and when it did, it did so to awaken the conscience of the listeners (cf. Matt. 10:28).

When we now attempt to draw a final conclusion, we realize that hell and heaven receive their peculiarities neither from any cosmological localities nor from any images that are associated with them, but only from their respective relationship to God. Only in the world of fantasy is hell the domain of the devil. But according to the biblical witness, even the antigodly powers are under God's control.[63]

In talking about hell, we talk about something we do not know. The allusions of the New Testament, such as "deepest darkness" (2 Pet. 2:17), "the outer darkness," "weeping and gnashing of teeth" (Matt. 22:13), and "eternal fire" (Matt. 25:41), describe hell in terms of pain, despair, and loneliness. In so doing these words are taken from present negative experiences and attempt to transcend them. These negative experiences express the reaction to the disclosure and finalization of the discrepancy between one's eternal destiny and one's realization of this destiny. They express the anguish of knowing what one has missed without the possibility of ever reaching it. They witness to a state of extreme despair without the hope of reversing it. It becomes clear that

---

61. Cf. Joachim Jeremias, "hades," in *TDNT,* 1:147.

62. Cf. for the following, Joachim Jeremias, "geenna," in *TDNT,* 1:657-58.

63. A dramatic dualism occasionally introduced by biblical writers to emphasize the threatening power of evil cannot challenge their basic monotheistic outlook.

such anguish and despair will not just result from a spatial separation from God. It will be a dimensional separation from God and from the accepted. Yet God and the destiny of the accepted will be somehow present as a curse.

Since in the Apostles' Creed Christians do not confess faith in hell, but in the "resurrection of the body and life everlasting," hell is of no ultimate concern to them. It serves only as an admonition to reach our eternal destiny. In talking about life everlasting or about heaven, we have to agree with Luther's fitting remark: "As little as children know in their mother's womb about their birth, so little do we know about life everlasting."[64] When we read about our habitation in the new Jerusalem, a city of gold, similar to pure glass, with walls of precious stones and with twelve gates, each made of one pearl (Rev. 21), this apocalyptic imagery resembles so much a world of fantasy that it looks more like an attraction in Disneyland than the eternal goal of our lives. Even the much more restrained assertion that once we have reached our final goal we will see God "face to face" (1 Cor. 13:12) sounds unreal. And the promise that God will dwell with the elect, that

> they will be his peoples,
> and God himself will be with them;
> he will wipe away every tear from their eyes.
> Death will be no more;
> mourning and crying and pain will be no more,
> for the first things have passed away,
>
> (Rev. 21:3-4)

and that God will be "all in all" (1 Cor. 15:28), looks like wishful thinking.

Union with God, abolition of anguish and sorrow, and permanent beauty and perfection seem so unreal to our life of alienation, pain and suffering, transition and change that we are about to discard these hopes as utopian dreams. We would be right in so doing if Jesus Christ had not shown us through his death and resurrection that this fulfillment is attainable. Because of Jesus Christ and the promise contained for us in the Christ event, the hope for a final realization of such a destiny is a realistic hope. It shows us that our immanent and perpetual yearning for self-transcendence, for deification, for elimination of death, and for progress

---

64. Martin Luther, WATR, 3:276.26-27 (no. 3339), in a remark from 1533.

toward perfection is not a utopian dream but will find its fulfillment in life everlasting.

c. Completion

It would be an anthropocentric mistake and myopic to admit that only humans will enjoy life everlasting. Since *we* reflect on eschatology, it is understandable that *our destiny* will be given center stage. But we do not live in isolation. The new world comprises a new heaven and a new earth, meaning the completion of the universe. God as the creator of heaven and earth will conclude his creative activity. There will be no realm of reality that is not under his domain, that does not owe its existence to him, and that cannot count on his love. Therefore a partial new creation in one part of the universe, while other parts continue their evolutionary course, would severely compromise such creative completion. It would mean that though we enjoy the newness of life, in other parts of the created order business goes on as usual. As the prologue in the Gospel of Saint John indicates, however, there is an identity of savior and creator. He who has already created will also bring the creation to completion. The death and resurrection of Jesus Christ has universal significance, and God is the God of the whole universe.[65]

Through the mission of Jesus of Nazareth we have realized that in surprising and, compared with the magnitude of the universe, a totally undeserved way salvation has been brought first to humanity. From there it extends to the whole created order. Therefore the exploitation and injustice that humanity brought on nature, from the extinction of animal species to the pollution of the environment, and from animal farming to monocultures — this kind of exploitation will have an end. The whole created order will participate in the completion of creation. The subjection to futility (Rom. 8:20) will cease, and the eschatological peace within the animal kingdom and between animals and humans, of

65. "Universal significance," however, would still hold true if the new creation would only affect our solar system and perhaps its immediate environment, since we seem to be unable to interact with the whole of the universe. Therefore the destiny of that larger whole would leave us unaffected, provided an entirely new creation is indeed ushered in for our "habitation." This might even allow for additional *eschata* for other parts of the universe and its humanities, provided they do exist.

which Isaiah 11:6-9 foretells, will become reality. Even those powers higher than humanity will be freed from the constant battle against the destructive and antigodly forces because these forces will be permanently banished from the presence of the Lord. The whole creation will enjoy an eternal Sabbath, and we will finally be allowed and able to enjoy together with all other creatures in harmony and unity the immediate presence of God, which until then is impossible on this earth. God's plan for the universe will be completed, and all the different constituent parts of creation will be unrestrictedly and unreservedly centered on him to glorify him and to gain unending strength from this source of life.

Once we have realized the full implications of this eschatological completion, we must ask ourselves: Do we understand our attempt to fulfill our inborn yearning for a new tomorrow through pursuit of technological progress and peace for all people as ends in themselves, thus excluding ourselves from any true fulfillment that is not provided by us? Or do we understand our endeavors here on earth as proleptic anticipation of "what God has prepared for those who love him" (1 Cor. 2:9), and consequently hope for a God-provided true fulfillment? "Only one who is certain of the future can relax and turn to today's business."[66] It is necessary to check our life attitude and once again put our trust alone in Jesus, who is "the pioneer and perfecter of our faith" (Heb. 12:2).

We have concluded the survey of Christian eschatology. We have seen how the understanding of eschatology has developed, and what views and factors we must consider if we want to talk meaningfully about it. Confronted with life and its possibilities for the future, we have also noticed that we can choose among the three basic attitudes of despairing resignation, futurist activism, and proleptic anticipation.

Despairing resignation is perhaps the least viable option. Once we give up wrestling with the future, we no longer participate meaningfully in it and cannot offer any solutions for the course it should take. Since our future is not absolutely predetermined, it asks for our contribution. We cannot afford the luxury of despair. Yet so many do drop out of the future-directed stream of life and dull their minds with drugs, alcohol, and medications of all sorts. This should make us wonder whether we

66. Pannenberg, *What Is Man?* 44 (translation mine).

are still meaningfully pursuing the future or whether we have turned it into a dehumanizing monster from which many people, young and old, want to escape.

Considering *futurist activism* as the next possibility, we become aware that for a growing number futurist activism in the classical Western materialistic fashion seems no longer attractive. It has been tarnished by doubt in the possibilities of technological expansion and by the growing awareness of its undesirable side effects. Many voices are raised these days warning that we cannot live by the increase of the gross national product alone. We also need a vision by which to live. Here Marxist communism once claimed to have the solution. Though materialistically oriented, it dreamed of a new world. And, endowed with a deeper messianic consciousness than any other philosophy, it attempted to create a classless society through worldwide revolution. Though the fact should not be overlooked that Marxism enthralled the masses primarily in countries much less technologically advanced, its missionary influence was felt throughout the world. It has overcome the narrow Western materialistic understanding of progress as a goal to be pursued for its own sake. In Marxist communism progress was directed toward the betterment of the human community.

Two important factors were totally amiss: (1) Marxist communism showed a decisive lack in its understanding of humanity. Contrary to Marxist ideology, people are not just an extension of matter. Therefore they are not only interested in the future of society, but in the ultimate future of their personal existence and of the world in which they live. To reserve a semblance of hope in that ultimate future, they refused to dedicate themselves unreservedly to the Marxist movement. (2) Since the Marxist movement was messianic in its intent, but refused to accept the Messiah, Marxist leaders usurped messianic qualities. Since they were limited, as all human beings are, but refused to admit this, their human sinfulness in terms of greed, ruthlessness, and contempt of others led to the demise of the movement.

In technologically advanced countries the New Age movement has emerged. It is an attempt to counteract blatant materialism and pursue a vision of wholeness and personal freedom. In eclectic fashion it borrowed from the rich Christian heritage as well as from the religious traditions of the East and from many other sources. While both its protest and its vision are well taken, we should note that it shares with all other messianic movements the lack of the true Messiah. Lasting hope cannot come from us or from the plans we design. It can only come from above ourselves, from the source of power that has shown itself in its human embodiment, in Jesus Christ.

Here the Christian view of the future as *proleptic anticipation* seems to provide the most viable option. Knowing that the future has already begun in the resurrection of Jesus Christ, it dares to anticipate proleptically this future along the avenue which the Christ event provides. This process of active anticipation strives for a better humanity, a more just society, and a more worldly world to live in. But since it is only anticipation, Christian faith is realistic enough to take into account our intrinsic alienation from God, who is the source of all wisdom and all good things. Thus we must reject the illusion that we could ever create a good humanity, a just society, or a new world. Ultimate perfection and removal of death as the dimensional border between our world and the new world to come will be brought about by God's gracious action, undeserved by us.

Unfortunately, the right understanding and true expectation that the new world will be brought about through God's own activity has often been used as an excuse to take the Christian attitude of active anticipation less seriously. To indicate that such neglect can surely impede the credibility of the Christian message, I close this postscript with a little story. In a dialogue with people who were contemplating Christianity, they were asked what they looked for in Christians. They were well acquainted with all the different varieties of relevant Christians, born-again Christians, secular ones, and charismatics. But they said: "We wish the Christians would try to speak of and live with their own great teachings. We would like to see how different the world would look if incarnation, crucifixion, and resurrection were taken seriously." And what a difference it would make.

Index of Names

Abbahu, Rabbi, 74
Ahaz (King), 402
Ahlstrom, Sydney E., 312n.
Albright, William Foxwell, 7
Althaus, Paul, 144n., 248n., 257n., 263n., 297n., 300n., 336n., 347, 377n., 383n., 392n.,
Altizer, Thomas J. J., 137n.
Amelung, Eberhard, 393n.
Andrews, Edmond D., 331n.
Ansgar, Ahlbrecht, 278n.
Antiochus IV Epiphanes, 52n., 66, 385
Applewhite, Marshall Herff, 316
Aquinas, Thomas, 269, 272, 277n.
Arisian, Khoren, 241n.
Aristotle, 2, 9, 10, 164, 269-72, 279
Aruldoss, Thaveedu, 153n.
Asendorf, Ulrich, 386n.
Assman, Hugo, 157
Auberlen, Carl A., 336
Augenstein, Leroy, 249n.
Augustine, 13, 100, 163, 258, 269, 282n., 291-92, 321, 324-25, 354-57
Averroes, 272

Badham, Linda, 8n.
Badham, Paul, 8n.
Baillie, John, 15n.
Bainton, Roland H., 359
Barnabas, 99

Barnes, H. E., 214n.
Barnes, Jonathan, 271n.
Barth, Christoph, 39n.
Barth, Karl, 69n., 146, 151, 278, 344-46
Basil the Great, 352
Bates, Harvey, 213n.
Bauer, Bruno, 218
Bauckham, Richard, 330n.
Baum, Samuel, 202n.
Baumbach, G., 62n.
Baumgartner, Hans Michael, 270n.
Beck, Heinrich, 303
Beck, Lewis, 271n.
Becker, Ernest, 211-14
Bede, the Venerable, 264
Beilner, Wolfgang, 93n.
Beißer, Friedrich, 347n., 367n., 368n.
Bender, Frederick L., 217n.
Benedict XII (Pope), 298
Benedict, Saint, 326
Bengel, Johann Albrecht, 330
Benoit, Pierre, 291n.
Benrath, Gustav Adolf, 357n.
Benz, Ernst, 16n., 17n., 186n., 188n., 224n., 226, 327n.
Berg, Werner, 32n.
Berger, Klaus, 122n.
Bergson, Henri, 253
Bernat, James L., 250n.
Berry, Thomas, 205

Bertschinger, Erika ("Uriella"), 314
Bieder, Werner, 348n.
Bienert, Walther, 218n., 222n.
Biesinger, Albert, 399n.
Billerbeck, Paul, 74n.
Black, Algernon D., 243n.
Blaising, Craig A., 335n., 336n.
Bloch, Ernst, 95n., 143, 222-24, 226, 327-29
Bochinger, Christoph, 229n., 230n.
Bock, Darrell L., 335n., 336n.
Boersma, T., 321n.
Boff, Clodovis, 155, 157
Boff, Leonardo, 156, 160-62
Boné, Edouard, 253
Bonhoeffer, Dietrich, 1, 378-79
Borg, Marcus, 115-18, 120, 123n.
Bornkamm, Günther, 95n., 121, 123
Boros, Ladislaus, 363, 363-64
Brandon, S. G. F., 73n.
Brée, Germaine, 215n.
Bright, Chris, 197n.
Brown, Raymond E., 58n., 371n.
Brunner, Emil, 279, 395n.
Buchman, Frank, 379
Bullough, Vern L., 238n.
Bultmann, Rudolf, 68n., 69n., 70n., 72n., 75n., 79n., 89n., 90n., 91n., 94n., 108n., 115n., 118, 120-27, 128-29, 137, 247n., 248, 275n., 281, 297n., 366, 381
Buri, Fritz, 114, 115n.
Burkitt, Francis C., 112n., 114

Calvin, John, 269, 273, 358n.
Camus, Albert, 215-17
Capra, Fritjof, 227-31, 231n.233
Carlson, C. C., 319n.
Carrez, Maurice, 396n.
Carson, Rachel, 203n.
Cayce, Edgar, 313
Chafer, Lewis Sperry, 334
Chang, Peter, 178n.
Charlesworth, James, 124n.
Clausius, Rudolf Julius Emanuel, 178

Cobb, John B., Jr., 119, 167n., 168-70, 303
Cohn, Norman, 329
Collingwood, R. G., 13n.
Comte, Auguste, 174, 329
Cone, James, 157
Constantine (Emperor), 99, 400
Conzelmann, Hans, 69n., 81n., 83n., 84n., 86n., 87n., 89n., 90n., 91n., 94n., 95n., 124n., 286n., 289n., 347n., 392n.
Copleston, Frederick, 174, 271n.
Crossan, John Dominic, 118
Crutchfield, Larry V., 334n.
Cullmann, Oscar, 73n., 74n., 119, 122n., 136-37, 140, 274n., 276n., 293n., 294, 296n.
Cyrus (King), 48

Darby, John Nelson, 334
Darius the Mede, 59, 60n.
Darwin, Charles, 15, 185-88, 253
Darwin, Francis, 188
Demant, V. A., 199n.
Denck, Hans, 341
Denzinger, Heinrich, 188n., 272n., 298n., 340n., 352n., 357n., 358n.
Descartes, René, 14, 232
DeWitt, Calvin B., 196n.
Dibelius, Martin, 93n., 121n.
Dinocrates, 354
Dobzhansky, Theodosius, 253n.
Dodd, C. H., 89n., 90n., 92n., 118, 120, 128-34, 135n.
Domitian (Emperor), 385
Donahue, John, 77n.

Eccles, John C., 268
Eddington, Arthur S., 179n.
Edwards, Jonathan, 330
Eichrodt, Walther, 35n., 40n.
Einstein, Albert, 175, 292-93
Eisenhower, Dwight D., 1
Elder, Frederick, 208n.
Elert, Werner, 279n.

Elliger, Walter, 328n.
Elwood, Douglas J., 153n.
Engels, Friedrich, 217-22, 224, 328-29
Engnell, Ivan, 28n.
Ephraem (the Syrian), 349
Epiphanes (King). *See* Antiochus IV
Erlemann, Kurt, 125n., 129n., 135-36
Ernst, Josef, 87n.
Ettinger, Robert C. W., 254n.
Eusebius (of Caesarea), 98-100, 324

Faricy, Robert L., 191n.
Ferguson, Marilyn, 227, 230-33
Feuerbach, Ludwig, 176-78, 218, 220-
    21, 223, 367, 381
Fichte, Johann Gottlieb, 254n.
Fiedler, Peter, 80n., 84n., 86n., 87n., 88n.
Finger, Thomas N., 367
Fiore, Joachim of, 325-29
Flavin, Christopher, 201n.
Fleischhack, Erich, 353n., 354n.
Foerster, Werner, 282n., 283n.
Fohrer, Georg, 29n., 36n., 40n., 43n.,
    45n., 49n., 50n.
Ford, Lewis S., 168n.
Fortman, E. J., 273n.
Francis (of Assisi), 205
Frank, Reinhold, 336
Freud, Sigmund, 211
Fridrichsen, Anton, 92n.
Froitzheim, Franzjosef, 92n.
Fuchs, Ernst, 68n., 70n., 78, 124
Funk, Robert W., 68n., 116

Gallagher, Eugene V., 315n.
Geiger, Ruthild, 87n.
Gerhard, Johann, 366
Gilkey, Langdon, 195-96
Gnilka, Joachim, 352n.
Gössman, Elisabeth, 164n., 165n.
Goulet, Dennis, 157
Gowan, Donald E., 31n.
Graham, Billy, 2
Grässer, Erich, 83n.

Grathwohl, Manfred, 200n.
Greenberg, Jeff, 212
Greenberg, Moshe, 376n.
Gregory (the Great), 356-57
Gregory of Nyssa, 102-3
Greshake, Gisbert, 300n., 302n., 305n.,
    362n.
Gressman, Hugo, 48n.
Griffin, David R., 166n., 167n.
Gutiérrez, Gustavo, 119, 143, 157-60
Gutiérrez, Juan, 159n.

Haenchen, Ernst, 77n.
Hahn, Ferdinand, 73n., 74n., 108, 123n.,
Hamilton, William, 281n.
Hanegraaff, Wouter J., 235-36
Hanson, John S., 63n.
Harner, Philip B., 75n., 76n., 77
Hart, Hornell, 262n.
Hartman, Sven S., 385n.
Hartshorne, Charles, 168
Heelas, Paul, 227n.
Hefner, Philip, 107n., 195n.
Hegel, Georg Wilhelm Friedrich, 143
Heidegger, Martin, 210-12, 214
Heidel, Alexander, 34n.
Heiler, Friedrich, 56n., 57n.
Heim, Karl, 69n., 295n., 388, 389n.
Heine, Heinrich, 391
Heisenberg, Werner, 227, 292n.
Hermas, 101
Herod the Great (King), 63, 66
Herodotus, 9, 33
Herzog, Frederick, xii
Hewes, Hayden, 316n.
Hezekiah (King), 37-38
Hick, John H., 24n., 119, 170-72, 174n.,
    302-3
Hildegard von Bingen, 227
Himes, Joshua V., 312
Hippolytus (of Rome), 323
Hirsch, Emanuel, 366n.
Hirschberger, Johannes, 270n.

411

Hitler, Adolf, 186, 237-38, 329, 386
Hjelde, Sigurd, 366n.
Hoekema, Anthony A., 119, 139-42, 330n., 331n., 384
Hofmann, J. C. K. von, 336
Holbach, Heinrich Dietrich, von, 175-76
Homer, 9
Hooke, S. H., 28, 70n.
Horsley, Richard A., 63n., 64n.
Howell, Vernon Wayne, 315
Hus, Jan, 386

Iersel, Bas van, 282n.
Ignatius, 349n.
Irenaeus, 98, 102, 323-24

Jackson, A. V. Williams, 55n.
Jacob, Edmond, 46n.
Jäger, Alfred, 223n.
James, William, 231
Jaspers, Karl, 60, 115, 185, 240
Jeremias, Joachim, 70n., 78n., 79n., 371n., 372n., 384n., 394n., 402n.
Jerome, 164
Jewett, Robert, 335n.
John Paul II (Pope), 152, 188n.
John XXII (Pope), 298
Johnson, Lyndon B., 240
Jones, James H. (Jim), 314
Josephus, Flavius, 61-62, 64
Jouret, Luc, 317-18
Judas Maccabaeus, 74
Jung, Carl Gustav, 231
Jüngel, Eberhard, 276
Jüngling, Elke, 399n.
Justin (Martyr), 99, 101, 276, 323

Kant, Immanuel, 14-15, 223, 227, 236, 271-72, 292, 337, 361
Käsemann, Ernst, 67, 146
Kassel, Maria, 162n.
Kaufman, Gordon D., 365n., 366, 370n.
Kaufmann, Walter, 9n., 368n.

Keen, Sam, 213n., 214n.
Kehl, Medard, 232n., 234n., 326n., 338n., 361n., 362n.
Kelber, Werner H., 78n.
Kelly, J. N. D., 349
Kenel, Sally A., 213n.
Kerls, Rüdiger, 234n.
Kessler, Hans, 156n., 300n.
Kierkegaard, Søren, 210-11, 294
Klein, Günter, 89n., 93n.
Klimkeit, Hans-Joachim, 55, 58n., 96n.
Knapp, Guntram, 221n.
Koch, Ernst, 353n.
Koch, Klaus, 41n., 66n., 67n.
Köhler, Ludwig, 40n., 43n., 44n.
Kokjohn, John E., 282n., 288n., 396n.
Koresh, David, 315
Körtner, Ulrich H. J., 209
Kraus, Hans-Joachim, 29n., 39n.
Kübler-Ross, Elisabeth, 252n., 254-56, 261, 264
Kuhn, Thomas, 232
Kümmel, Werner Georg, 93n., 98n., 114n., 119, 137-40
Künneth, Walter, 278n., 284n., 347, 389n.
Kurtz, Paul, 237n., 238, 240-43

Laak, Werner van, 341n.
Lactantius, 42n., 324
Ladd, George Eldon, 141, 281n.
Lafargue, Paul, 224-26
Lanczkowski, Günter, 56n.
Lang, Bernhard, 80n., 399n.
Lee, Ann, 331n.
Lehmann, Karl, 353, 355-56
Leibniz, Gottfried Wilhelm, 284n.
Lessing, Gotthold Ephraim, 15, 19-20, 236, 328n.
Lietzmann, Hans, 122
Lindsey, Hal, 319-21, 334-35
Linedecker, Clifford, 315n.
Link, Christian, 207n.
Linnemann, Eta, 70n., 71n.

Lohfink, Gerhard, 300n.
Lohmeyer, Ernst, 77n.
Lohse, Bernhard, 392n., 393n.
Lohse, Eduard, 323n., 390n.
Loisy, Alfred, 97
Lorimer, David, 261n., 266n.
Löwith, Karl, 9, 17, 18n., 224n., 326n., 329n.
Luthardt, Chr. Ernst, 258n.
Luther, Katharina, 5n.
Luther, Martin, 5, 88, 127n., 247, 248n., 260, 273, 291-92, 297-98, 311-12, 328, 348, 352n., 358-59, 365, 370, 373, 386, 390, 392, 393, 400-401, 403

Macquarrie, John, 115n., 280n.
Madigan, Timothy J., 238n.
Maier, Gerhard, 139
Maier, Johann, 63n., 65n., 67n.
Maisch, Ingrid, 80n.
Manasseh (King), 402
Mandela, Nelson, 27
Manson, T. W., 135n.
Marcion, 349
Marx, Karl, 3, 4n., 217-22, 224-26, 236, 329n., 380
Marxsen, Willi, 282n.
Maslow, A. H., 242n.
Mathews, Shailer, 204
Matura, Thaddee, 157
Mayer, J. Robert, 175, 178
McDannell, Colleen, 80n., 399n.
McGinn, Bernard, 325n.
Melchizedeck, 11
Melito, 349
Mercatoris, Marii, 259n.
Merkel, Helmut, 393n.
Merklein, Helmut, 71n.
Mettrie, Julien Offray de la, 175
Metz, Johann Baptist, 152, 154n.
Meurers, Joseph, 187n.
Michel, Hans-Joachim, 87n.
Michel, Otto, 285n., 389n., 395n.
Miller, William, 312-13

Mischo, Johannes, 302n.
Moleschott, Jakob, 177
Moltmann, Jürgen, 43n., 54n., 119, 143, 146-51, 223n., 224n., 280, 294, 347n., 377n., 382n.
Moody, Dale, 335n.
Moody, Raymond, 264-67, 275
More, Sir Thomas, 217
Morenz, Siegfried, 32n., 33
Moule, C. F. D., 124n., 282n.
Mowinckel, Sigmund, 28-29
Mulder, M. J., 8n.
Müller, Hans-Peter, 48n.
Müller, Karlheinz, 54n., 64n.
Müntzer, Thomas, 328
Mußner, Franz, 97n.
Mutschler, Hans-Dieter, 184

Narr, Karl, 24
Nelson, J. Robert, 379
Nero (Emporer), 66, 385
Nessan, Craig, 156n.
Nettles, Bonney Lu Trusdale, 316
Neuner, Peter, 97n.
Newton, Isaac, 228, 232
Niebuhr, Gustav, 317n.
Niebuhr, H. Richard, 17, 390
Niebuhr, Reinhold, 226
Niebuhr, Richard R., 281n., 282n.
Nietzsche, Friedrich, xi, 9n., 186, 251, 368
Nostradamus, 310
Nötscher, Friedrich, 39n.
Noyes, John Humphrey, 331n.
Noyes, Russell, 269n.
Nützel, Johannes M., 84n.
Nygren, Anders, 259n.

Oberlin, John Frederic, 262
Oepke, Albrecht, 396
Ogden, Schubert, 168
Okano, Haruko, 164n., 165n.
Origen, 134, 139, 324, 338-41, 346, 349
Otto, Rudolf, 172

Ozols, Jakob, 24, 25

Palaeologus, Michael VIII, 352
Pallis, Christopher, 249n.
Pannenberg, Wolfhart, 75n., 81n., 86n.,
 89n., 96n., 119, 127n., 143-46, 169,
 184n., 205, 206n., 286n., 287n., 296n.,
 393n., 405n.
Papias, 98
Pauck, Wilhelm, 120n.
Payne, J. Barton, 333n.
Pelikan, Jaroslav, 98n., 101n.
Perpetua, 354-55
Perrin, Norman, 78n., 135n., 371n.
Peters, Karl, 180-81
Peters, Ted, 233, 237n., 331n.
Pieper, Francis, 258n.
Pike, James A., 262
Pius XII, Pope, 273
Plato, 2, 9, 264, 269-71, 277n., 279, 293-
 94, 303, 388n.
Plöger, Otto, 60n.
Praag, J. P., 242
Prenter, Regin, 278, 351
Prestel, Eduard, 198n.
Preuss, Horst Dietrich, 29n., 35n., 43n.,
 56n.
Probst, James, 5n.
Pyszczynski, Tom, 212

Rabbati, Persitka, 354
Rabinowitz, Celia Ellen, 340n., 341n.
Rad, Gerhard von, 12, 47n., 48n., 49n.,
 52n., 54-55, 274n., 293n., 401n.
Rahner, Karl, 259n., 276, 305, 357n.,
 359n., 360n., 362-63, 374n., 396n.
Ralph, Margaret Nutting, 336n.
Rasmussen, Tarald, 399n.
Ratschow, Heinz, 367n.
Ratzinger, Joseph, 153n., 277-78, 299,
 361, 362n., 363n.
Rauschenbusch, Walter, 156n., 204
Reicke, Bo, 38n.
Reimarus, Hermann Samuel, 112

Rhine, J. B., 262n.
Richter, Georg, 88n.
Ring, Kenneth, 264n.
Ritschl, Albrecht, 107, 108, 110
Robinson, James M., 68n., 112n., 164n.
Robinson, John A. T., 133-35, 138
Rochusch, Rolf, 345n.
Rohde, Joachim, 83n.
Rohnert, W., 258n.
Roloff, Jürgen, 98n.
Rosenstock-Huessy, Eugen, 6, 18, 207-8
Rost, Leonhard, 38n.
Roszak, Theodore, 227
Rowland, F. Sherwood, 198n.
Rowley, Harold H., 52n., 54-55
Rückerl, Hans, 318n.
Ruether, Rosemary Radford, 119, 163n.,
 165-66
Rufinus of Aquileia, 340, 349
Ruppert, Hans-Jürgen, 236n.
Russell, Charles Taze, 313
Russell, D. S., 52n.
Rutherford, Joseph F., 313

Sabom, Michael B., 249, 250n.
Sandmel, Samuel, 67n.
Santmire, H. Paul, 206n.
Sartre, Jean-Paul, 214-15
Sasse, Hermann, 294n., 295n.
Sauter, Gerhard, 223n., 258n., 327n.
Schade, Hans-Heinrich, 95n.
Scharbert, Josef, 39n.
Scherer, Georg, 269n.
Scherzberg, Lucia, 162n.
Schleiermacher, Friedrich, 341-43,
 360n., 361, 395
Schlosser, Jacques, 80n.
Schmaus, Michael, 299-300
Schmid, Rudolf, 186n., 187n.
Schmidt, Johann Michael, 66n.
Schmithals, Walter, 64n., 66n.
Schnackenburg, Rudolf, 71n., 72n.
Schneider, Inge, 310n., 313n., 314n.,
 317n.

Scholem, Gershom, 66n.
Schottroff, Luise, 162n., 163n.
Schreiner, Josef, 66n.
Schützinger, Heinrich, 34n.
Schwarz, Hans, 85n., 108n., 142n., 193n.,
    196n., 267n., 302n., 345n., 348n., 400n.
Schweitzer, Albert, 69n., 108, 110-15,
    120, 122, 128, 130, 142, 144, 148,
    208n., 281
Schweizer, Eduard, 75n., 288n., 122n.
Seeberg, Reinhold, 101n.
Segundo, Juan Luis, 153n.
Singer, Fred, 197n., 198n.
Smend, Rudolf, 45n.
Smith, Harmon L., 249n., 250n.
Soleri, Paolo, 168
Solomon, Sheldon, 212, 401
Spencer, Herbert, 15-16
Staehelin, Ernst, 341n., 350fn.
Stählin, Gustav, 383n.
Stahmer, H., 6n., 208n.
Stauffer, Ethelbert, 72n., 73n., 74n., 76,
    77n., 88n., 89n., 124n., 138
Steiger, Brad, 316n.
Stevenson, Ian, 267n., 307
Stock, Klemens, 336n.
Strack, Hermann L., 74n.
Strecker, Georg, 70n., 86n.
Strobel, August, 122n., 123n., 124n.
Ström, Ake V., 330n.
Stuhlhofer, Franz, 321n.
Suchocki, Marjorie Hewitt, 167
Swedenborg, Emanuel, 263

Tabor, James D., 315n.
Taylor, Vincent, 73n., 77n.
Teilhard de Chardin, Pierre, 179, 181,
    184, 188-94, 209, 227, 230-31, 233,
    253, 294, 342, 388
Tertullian, 103, 303-4, 327, 355
Thomson, William (Lord, Kelvin), 179
Tillich, Paul, 242, 248n., 279, 343-44
Tipler, Frank J., 182-85, 194n.
Tödt, Heinz-Eduard, 121, 122n., 149n.

Töpfer, Bernhard, 326
Toynbee, Arnold, 9-10
Traub, Helmut, 401n.
Travis, Stephen, 142n., 370n.
Trillhaas, Wolfgang, 351n.
Troeltsch, Ernst, 16, 120
Trypho, 99, 276
Tylor, Edward Burnett, 264
Tyrell, G. N. M., 262n.

Ussher, Bishop, 312

Valla, Laurentius, 386
van der Leeuw, Gerhardus, 276n.
Vanderwaal, C., 334n.
Veatch, Robert M., 251n.
Versényi, Lasyle, 211n.
Vielhauer, Philipp, 122n., 123
Vogels, Heinz-Jürgen, 349n., 350n.
Vriezen, Th. C., 29, 38n., 40n., 43n., 46n.

Walvoord, John F., 334n.
Weber, Max, 16
Weiss, Johannes, 108-10, 112, 120
Werner, Martin, 114n.
Westermann, Claus, 42n.
White, Lynn Jr., 204-5
Whitehead, Alfred North, 166-69
Wichmann, Jörg, 306n.
Widengren, Geo, 59n.
Wilder, Amos N., 118, 127-29
Wilder, Thornton, 250n.
Wilkens, Ulrich, 86n.
Wingren, Gustav, 292
Witby, Daniel, 330
Witherington, Ben, III, 123n.
van der Woude, A. S., 48n.
Wrede, William, 112
Wyclif, John, 386

York, Donald G., 184
Young, Edward, 49n.
Young, John E., 201n.

Zaehner, R. C., 59n.

Zaleski, Carol, 264n.

Zarathustra (Zoroaster), 56-59, 186

Ziegenaus, Anton, 279n.

Zimmerli, Walther, 11n., 37n.

Zimmermann, Heinrich, 96n.

Zinzendorf, Count Nicolas, 379

Zwingli, Huldreich, 273

Index of Subjects

Aeon, 65, 67, 79, 88, 93-95, 126, 259, 296, 347, 372
  coming, 67, 296
  first, 65
  future, 26, 88, 186, 372
  new, 53, 64-65, 93-94, 259, 323, 401
  old, 66, 93, 259
  present, 26
Afterlife, 59-60, 62, 360, 399
  life after death, 1, 24-25, 38n., 40, 131, 176, 219, 235, 256, 263, 267, 269, 279
  life beyond, 3, 6, 24-26, 36, 38, 247, 261-69, 272, 305, 314, 350-51, 360-61
Alienation, 55, 158, 258-59, 288n., 317, 386, 401, 403, 407
Alpha and Omega, 184-89
Anima, 25
Animal(s), 15, 23-25, 42, 163, 165, 178, 205, 227n., 248-59, 270-71, 354, 367, 404-5
Anthropic, 182
Anthropocentricism, 204-5, 248n., 369, 404
Anthropogenesis, 191
Anthropology, 13, 125, 160, 188, 204-5, 213n., 229, 274n., 292, 382n.
Anthropomorphism, 35n., 293, 395-96
Antichrist, 98, 101, 158, 333, 385-87
Anti-Christian, 173, 385

Anticipation, 2, 75, 80-81, 89n., 94-95, 143-46, 148-49, 153, 156, 161-62, 204, 222, 286, 296, 373, 375, 377-84, 389, 394
  of heavenly city, 370, 377-80
  Jesus', 96, 128, 137
  proleptic, 21, 206, 243-46, 260, 286-87, 296, 336, 370-87, 397, 405, 407
Anti-godly powers, 52, 55, 65-67, 70-71, 151, 162, 237, 258, 263, 274, 290, 310, 322, 333, 338-39, 341, 343, 346, 354, 358-59, 361, 368, 370, 381, 386-87, 390, 398, 400, 402, 405
Anxiety, 26, 38, 44, 210-12, 267, 291, 331. *See also* Fear
Apocalypse, 85, 247, 312, 315, 317, 329
  of John, 98, 162, 325. *See also* Revelation, book of
Apocalyptic (-ism, -ist), 26, 44n., 51-56, 59n., 64-67, 69-71, 74, 77n., 81, 88-89, 93-94, 96-98, 103, 108-10, 119, 121, 125-26, 130, 134, 137-38, 142, 144, 146-47, 150, 196, 222, 229, 233, 247, 286-87, 289, 309, 311, 313, 318-19, 322-23, 325n., 328, 330, 335-36, 348n., 383-84, 391, 395, 402
  age, 203-4, 209
  imagery. *See* Imagery, apocalyptic
  thought, 63, 66, 80, 134, 323
Apokatastasis, 338-52

Apokatastasis Panton, 45, 170, 337-52, 364n. *See also* Homecoming, universal
Asceticism, 5, 16, 199, 208, 225, 324
Assyria, 32, 42, 50
Astrology, 231, 310, 338
Atheism (-ist), 213, 237, 369
Atman, 8, 172
Augsburg Confession, 328n., 341, 386

Baal, 7-8, 29-30
Babylonia, 32, 41, 55-56, 333
Baptism, 94, 126, 260, 285, 305, 347n., 358, 372-73, 389
　Jesus', 110-11
Biosphere, 169, 184, 189, 198
Body, 25-26, 58, 62, 80, 96, 102-3, 113, 163, 175, 177, 192, 253-54, 260, 265, 267-70, 274-75, 288, 301, 304, 306, 316, 339, 341, 350, 372, 391. *See also* Resurrection, of the body
Body and soul, 24-58, 62, 80n., 96, 102-3, 163-64, 177, 232, 258n., 269-80, 287-88, 402
Body of Christ, 172, 335, 373, 375
Brain, 175, 182-83, 231, 250, 266, 268
Branch Davidians, 315-16
Buddha, 10, 170, 172, 302, 305-6
Buddhism (-ist), 8, 18, 169, 172, 234n., 303, 306, 374
Burial, 25-26

Calvinism, 16
Canaan (-ite), 7-8, 11, 29, 41, 303
Capitalism, 16, 218, 239
Carbon dioxide, 196-97
Caro. See Flesh
Christification, 190, 324
Christogenesis, 191
Christos. See Messiah
Christosphere, 189
Cloning, 5, 230
Communism (-ist), 217-22, 226, 239, 327, 329, 406
Conceptualization, 36n., 299

Confessio Helvetica Posteria, 341
Consummation, 65, 103, 113, 135, 138, 143, 169, 190, 291n., 303, 338, 386-90
Cosmic, 15, 26, 29, 44, 51, 59, 92, 94n., 97, 144, 150, 168-69, 189, 207n., 216, 229, 235, 259, 281, 283, 310, 388
Cosmology, 132, 181-82, 185, 316, 367
Cosmos, 9, 11, 26, 50n., 56, 88, 97-98, 158, 169, 180, 187, 189, 194, 230, 233, 389, 395
Covenant, 10, 12, 41-46, 63, 94, 128, 285, 326, 332, 344-45, 376
Creation, 11-12, 27, 53, 57, 65-66, 81, 93, 96, 99-100, 146, 148-49, 154, 158, 164, 169, 180, 193, 204, 211, 253, 256, 258-59, 273, 277, 283, 285, 291, 293-94, 302, 316, 324, 326, 339, 341, 373-74, 389-90, 397-98, 404-5
　New, 27, 44, 46, 80, 95, 103, 150-51, 158, 160-61, 180, 186, 204, 206-8, 245, 247, 278, 285, 288-90, 297, 318, 321, 360, 366, 371, 404
Creator, 10-12, 18-19, 29n., 56, 166, 213, 237, 257-58, 269, 294-95, 301, 369, 376, 404
Creature (liness), 13, 19, 145, 164, 188, 213-14, 219, 257-58, 277, 301, 372, 376, 405
Creed, 133, 282, 349
　Apostles', 102, 287-88, 347-49
　Nicene, 102
　Mormon, 330

Damnation, 16, 280, 284, 342, 396n., 400
Day of the Lord, 43-45, 91, 131, 313, 335, 355, 383, 388
Death, 4-8, 10, 32-40, 96, 149, 165, 169, 210-14, 241, 245, 249-61, 265n., 272, 276, 278-80, 285, 288-89, 296-310, 355-56, 360, 362-64, 368, 373, 384, 388, 394, 398, 402, 404, 407
　and resurrection, 83, 92-93, 123, 154, 162n., 290-301, 305, 348, 350, 368, 403-4

De-eschatologize, 114
De-kerygmatize, 114
Demons. *See* Anti-godly powers
Denomination, 227, 309, 319, 341, 374-75
Descent into Hell, Christ's, 346-52
Destiny, 26, 31-41, 346, 348n., 351, 359-61, 363, 373-74, 393, 395-96, 398, 404
    eternal, 343, 364, 402-3
    Jesus', 81-82, 86-87, 144, 287, 373
Devil. *See* Anti-godly powers
Dialectic, 94, 329
    theology, 27, 294
Disappointment, 50, 313
    over the delay of the parousia, 83, 95, 111, 115, 118, 130-31, 368
Disciples, 315, 349n., 374, 398
    Jesus', 77, 81, 83-85, 109, 123, 138, 140-42, 281, 286-87
    John's, 70, 111
Dispensationalists, 335
Doom, 45, 72, 84, 204, 207, 209, 318
Doomsday, 26, 72, 294, 311, 322, 336, 365
Dualism, 10, 56, 58, 126, 175, 189, 232, 270, 275, 279, 338, 345, 383n., 402n.
Dying, 213, 250-51, 256, 258n., 260, 263, 304, 390
    and rising, 367, 372, 392

Easter, 84-85, 116-17, 122, 138, 145, 148, 282, 286
Ecology, 20, 174, 194-206, 208, 228, 230, 238
Ecosphere, 196, 201-2, 207
EEG, 251, 266
Egypt (-ian), 7, 11-12, 26, 31-33, 35, 41-43, 46, 303, 319
Election, 16, 65, 333, 342, 344-46
End, 1, 27, 36-37, 40, 44, 53, 65-66, 71, 82-83, 86-88, 94, 96, 99, 101, 103, 113n., 116-17, 119, 125n., 136-41, 145, 150, 162, 174-75, 183, 188, 190-91, 203, 210, 235-36, 249-50, 254, 260-61,

276, 280n., 284, 287, 297, 299, 304, 309-22, 324, 332, 339-40, 381-88
    of history, 19-20, 64, 75, 86-87, 94, 125, 129, 133-34, 143-44, 159, 203, 365, 384
    of time, 75, 117-18, 167, 182, 284, 294, 300, 345, 376
    of the world, 2, 50n., 53, 72, 79, 82-83, 92, 100, 110, 113n., 116-17, 125, 137, 139, 144, 175, 179, 185, 188, 190-91, 209, 309, 321-23, 365, 368
Energy, 175, 178-81, 184, 199-202, 229, 233, 240, 270, 328, 388. *See also* Natural resources
Enlightenment, 14-15, 173, 236, 263, 328, 341
Enthronement, 7, 77n., 131n.
    festival, 28-30
Entropy, 179-81, 185, 194, 253
Environment. *See* Ecology
Eon. *See* Aeon
Eschatology: definition of, 25, 248
    Realized, 120, 130, 180
    Travelogue, 247-48, 298, 392, 399
Eschaton, 10, 21, 27, 48, 73, 79, 83, 85, 94-95, 103, 114, 118-20, 122, 125-27, 129-30, 132-33, 136-38, 145, 163, 167, 196, 207-8, 210, 217, 247-49, 256-61, 297, 309-10, 319, 336, 360, 372, 384, 387-89, 392n., 402
Esoterics, 228, 234
Essenes, 61-62
Essentialization, 279, 344
Eternal life, 1, 5, 37, 39n., 80-81, 84, 88, 127, 150, 161, 164, 166, 182, 219, 235, 268, 277, 279-80, 328, 343-44, 360, 368, 381, 394-96, 399
Eternity, 16, 33, 54, 57, 65-66, 101, 171, 276, 288, 293-96, 298, 333, 344, 347, 355, 382, 384n., 387-88, 393-94
Ethics, 57, 112-13, 128, 235
Eucharist (-ic), 101n., 102, 356-57, 371-73, 392
Eupraxophy, 241

Evil, 18, 56-58, 63, 66-67, 135n., 151, 160, 167, 180-81, 212, 214, 216, 233, 238, 242, 269, 274, 284, 297, 315, 324, 338-39, 342, 344n., 345-46, 350, 367, 372, 391, 397-98, 402n.

Evolution, 15, 18, 152, 185-95, 229-30, 235-36, 239, 273-74, 306, 382, 387, 390, 395

Existentialism, 118, 132, 146, 160, 170, 172, 210-17, 240-41, 259, 344, 351
Secular, 210-17, 241

Fear, 24, 87, 150, 178, 209, 261, 278, 311, 313, 318-19, 247, 351, 393, 400. *See also* Anxiety
of death, 210-11, 241, 259
of God, of the Lord, 37, 41, 166, 259, 326, 393

Feminist theology (-ians), 119, 162, 166

Flesh, 46, 62, 102, 126, 177, 274, 287-88
God as, 46, 91, 277, 385

Franciscan Spirituals, 386

Freedom, 14-15, 21, 95, 126, 146, 148, 153-55, 170, 214, 222-23, 232, 239, 317, 324, 329, 364, 377-78, 380
of choice, 10n., 242
God's, 149, 345-46
human, 15, 214, 333, 346, 349
personal, 146, 406
realm of, 217, 220-22, 329

Fulfillment, 12, 28, 40n., 41, 51, 81, 85, 90, 93-96, 100, 115n., 119, 132, 135-39, 142, 144-47, 154, 158-59, 166, 170, 178, 193, 208-10, 237, 261, 271-72, 280, 285, 297, 300, 316, 323, 325, 335, 339, 343, 346, 371, 383n., 398, 403-5
eschatological, 48, 94, 96, 136-38, 159, 207, 258, 260, 368, 377
future, 135, 382
of God's promises, 43, 56, 84, 92, 95-96, 100, 139, 147, 154, 158, 320-21, 325, 336, 338, 368
human, 18, 20, 189, 208, 237, 363

of time, 293-96

Fundamentalist, 322, 331

Funeral (-s), 24, 26, 32

Futurology, 333

Gehenna, 354, 402

Gilgamesh Epic, 32, 34

Gnosis (-tic), 54, 95-96, 101, 164, 233, 236, 275, 288, 365

Gnosticism, 60, 126, 275

God-confidence, 14, 16, 19

Golden age, 26, 222-23, 332

Gospel, 83, 85, 87, 90-93, 95, 103, 141, 147, 152, 154, 204, 258, 260, 285, 289, 328, 332, 346, 349, 374-75, 380, 383, 392, 395
of John, 88n., 90n., 58, 73, 75, 88-90, 126-27, 134, 138, 283, 296, 360, 381, 383, 395
social, 156, 204

Gospels, 83n., 62, 72-74, 76, 88, 124, 133, 163, 383, 400
synoptic, 82-88, 162

Grace, 6, 12, 14, 63, 72, 91, 94, 100-101, 109, 167, 194, 210, 213, 236, 260, 285, 305, 326, 333, 342, 344-45, 361-62, 364, 374, 391, 393, 397

Greek, 10, 33, 59, 96n., 275, 277n., 324
language, 47, 62, 64, 73, 76, 217, 251, 274, 282, 287-88, 322, 338, 340
people, 8-9, 11, 62, 352, 374

Greenhouse effect, 196-99

Hades, 102, 296, 338, 340

Heaven (-ly), 5-6, 11-12, 16-17, 26, 33, 38, 52, 56, 58-59, 67, 71, 83, 87-88, 92, 121, 131, 134, 138, 140, 147, 150, 155, 161, 177-78, 182, 190-92, 219, 235, 238, 247, 276, 284, 289, 292, 295-97, 309, 311, 323, 333, 338, 348, 360-61, 383, 388, 390-91, 398-404
city, 168, 370, 377-81
new heaven, new earth, 46, 57, 80, 97, 150, 180, 187, 193, 404

Heaven's Gate, 315-17

Heilsgeschichte. See Salvation history

Hell, 26, 57, 59, 72, 134-35, 214, 235, 247, 292, 296, 298, 338, 346-52, 361-62, 366, 380, 398-404

Hellenism, 9, 60, 70n., 96, 122, 137n., 169

Hereafter, 5-6, 26, 32, 34, 36, 40n., 166, 168, 178, 185, 220, 236, 242, 262n., 278, 312, 318, 353, 360, 366n., 370, 381, 399

History
cyclic view of, 9-10, 18, 27-30, 284, 338-39
linear view of, 18n., 20, 27

Holy Spirit, 57, 87, 90, 95n., 131, 133, 149, 159, 275, 291n., 326, 330, 332, 339, 352, 355, 378

Homecoming, universal, 133, 151, 309, 337-53, 364, 374, 394-97. *See also Apokatastasis*

Hominization, 191

Hope, 3, 9, 13, 19-20, 24n., 31, 33, 37, 39-40, 43-46, 48, 55, 66-67, 71, 77n., 80-81, 83-84, 87, 94-98, 101, 103, 105, 110, 119, 123, 125, 127n., 129n., 130-32, 136, 145, 154, 156-57, 161-63, 168-69, 170-241, 243, 245, 247, 254n., 263, 270, 273, 275, 278, 280, 285-87, 290, 295, 300-303, 305-6, 312, 316, 318, 320-21, 346-47, 351, 357, 365-66, 368, 370, 372-78, 380-81, 387, 389, 391, 397, 402-3, 405-7
for the millennium, 322-37
theology of, 146-52
secular, 105, 119, 173-240
universal, 119, 169, 323, 345

Humanism (-ist), 13, 20, 216, 227, 238-40, 243
secular, 237, 239, 241-43

Image of God, 100-101

Imagery, 45, 52, 59n., 70, 127, 130, 132, 138, 290, 301, 385, 391-92, 396n., 403

apocalyptic, 125, 392, 403

Immortality, 9, 26, 57, 165, 168, 176-78, 188, 241, 248n., 257, 261-80, 290-91, 299, 301, 331

Individual (-ism, -ity), 15, 26, 31n., 35, 40, 42, 54, 58, 60, 63, 72, 75, 78, 80, 82, 86, 88, 102, 113n., 115n., 120, 126, 131, 144-45, 148, 165, 169-71, 183, 189, 192-94, 203, 220-21, 224, 227-28, 230, 231, 234-37, 241, 250, 276, 279, 283, 290, 300, 302-3, 305, 316, 332, 343, 345-46, 360-61, 374, 381, 395

Indulgence, 353-59, 362

Industrialization, 16n., 218

Infinite (-y), 19-20, 185, 257, 272, 284n., 293, 329, 368

Injustice, 151-52, 154, 158, 215, 377, 379, 404

Interim, 82-88, 92, 95, 113n., 128, 136, 207, 273n., 378, 398
ethics, 112-13

Iran, 55-60

Ishtar, 32, 34

Israel, 7, 10-13, 28, 30-32, 35, 41-56, 59-60, 63-65, 73-74, 81, 85-86, 140-41, 143-44, 147, 158, 303, 319-20, 333, 347-48, 376, 395, 402

Israelites, 10-13, 29, 35-38, 40-42, 45, 47, 49-50, 53, 56, 67, 274
religion, 28n., 30, 35n., 56, 58, 147

Jehovah's Witnesses, 313, 330

Jerusalem, 11, 28, 31n., 43, 46, 48, 63-64, 74, 97, 111, 353, 383n., 402-3
destruction of, 43, 46, 383-84
new, 52, 99, 333, 377, 403
temple of, 50, 52, 76, 319

Jesus, 2, 27, 45, 48, 52-53, 60-62, 67-84, 88n., 90n., 79-93, 95-97, 100, 102, 108-13, 113n., 121n., 123n., 124n., 131n., 133-34, 135n., 136-48, 152, 156-57, 160-64, 169-70, 185, 190, 204, 206-8, 247-48, 258, 263, 265, 277, 280-83, 285-87, 295-97, 303-5, 309-

10, 313-14, 320-21, 326, 330, 334, 337-48, 351, 355, 360, 366, 368, 370, 372-73, 375, 381-85, 389-92, 394, 397-98, 403-5, 407. *See also* Proclamation
eschatological, 68-82
and the future, 79-82
historical, 68, 90, 114, 122-23, 282
of Nazareth, 1, 12, 27, 47, 55, 61, 68, 70, 79, 82, 91-92, 120-21, 123n., 133n., 143-44, 208, 283, 404
Jews, 59-61, 90, 92, 141, 238, 304, 333, 354, 374, 395
Judaism, 16n., 29, 30n., 53, 55, 59-60, 64, 67n., 74, 92, 110, 117, 356
Judgment, 4, 33, 41-46, 57, 72, 85, 88, 92, 97, 126-28, 130, 132-33, 151-52, 247, 259-61, 323-24, 333, 350, 360, 381, 390-96, 400, 402
Judgment Day, 5, 43-44, 52, 67, 100, 296, 298, 301, 311, 322, 392, 396n.
Judgment, final, 1-2, 26, 31, 41-47, 57, 65, 67, 85, 93, 98, 101, 115n., 130, 151, 167, 248n., 288-89, 298-301, 342, 346, 352, 359, 382, 387, 390-95, 398, 402
Justice, 50, 74n., 117, 146, 148, 154, 159, 165, 178, 180, 235, 242, 277n., 344, 355-56, 371, 378, 394, 397

Karma, 235, 303, 305
Kerygma, 68-69, 83n., 95, 114, 119, 127n., 367n., 368
Kingdom of God, 16, 43n., 53, 55, 69-73, 79, 83, 88, 101, 107-12, 116-18, 123, 129, 130-32, 135n., 137-40, 142, 146, 148-50, 156, 161, 163, 169, 171, 194, 204, 224, 287, 322, 327-29, 336, 355-56, 378, 382, 384n., 386-87, 397-98, 400
Kingdom of Heaven, 53, 85, 92, 110, 164, 226, 324, 397, 400, 401
Koran, 247
Kyrios, 282-83

Last things, 4-5, 25, 73, 107, 129, 146, 149, 151, 160, 186, 380-81
Law (s), 11, 41-42, 62-63, 67, 75, 84, 86, 94-95, 124, 129, 147, 174-75, 229, 285, 326-27, 333, 388, 395, 398
moral, 271-72, 337, 361
of nature, 174-75, 178-79, 181-82, 185-86, 237, 388
Liberal (-ism), 110, 112, 113, 115n., 239, 390
theology, 113-14, 121, 149, 280
Liberation, 57, 64, 149-50, 163, 225, 275, 319, 348, 377, 380
theology, 152-62, 206
Life after death. *See* Afterlife
Limbo, 348, 360, 364
Liturgy, 76, 101n., 371-73
Logos, 9, 168-69
Lord's Prayer, 371-72
Love, 115n., 145, 154-55, 166, 168-69, 172, 192, 224, 231, 233, 242, 257, 266, 326, 355-56, 405
God's, 134-35, 145, 158, 167, 280n., 342, 356, 362, 364, 371, 387, 394-97, 404

Marxism, 219, 222, 378, 406
Materialism, 174-85
Matter, 62, 101, 175-77, 181, 185, 189-90, 193, 221, 232, 234, 262, 273, 292-94, 387, 387-89, 406
Medicine, 224, 232, 249, 268, 317
Medieval period, 5, 14, 164, 264n., 319, 325n., 327, 357, 360, 376, 384-85, 392, 400
Memento Mori, 384
Mesopotamia, 31-32, 34, 56
Messiah, 27, 31, 44n., 47-55, 60, 66-67, 73, 90n., 123, 320, 323, 333, 385, 406-7
Jesus as, 47-48, 73-74, 76-79, 85, 88n., 90, 92-93, 97, 111, 121, 123, 283, 368, 376, 390
Messianism, 66, 327

Metaphysics, 216
Middle Ages. *See* Medieval
Millennialism, 309, 322-37
 dispensational premillennialism, 332-35
 historic premillennialism, 331
 postmillennialism, 181, 332
 secular millennialism, 150, 329
Millennium, 27, 32, 99, 101, 219, 313, 322-25, 329-33, 336-37, 365, 399
Millerites, 313
Mind, 56, 100, 169, 231, 234, 254-55, 262, 267-68, 272, 318, 340
Miracle, 40n., 70, 77, 87, 89n., 111, 175, 371, 382
Mission, 47, 84-85, 103, 112, 148, 159n., 282, 321, 332, 348n., 406
 of the Church, 101, 148
 Jesus', 112, 116, 134, 148, 282, 404
 Paul's, 91, 93, 276, 283
Missionary activity, 46, 101, 276, 313, 321
Monism, 303, 338
Monotheism, 56
Mormons, 330
Mortality, 174, 212, 256, 259
Mot, 7-8
Mysticism, 114, 171-72, 229-30, 237
Myth (-ologies), 9, 23, 32, 35, 115n., 125, 127-28, 129n., 161, 195, 236, 284, 398

Natural resources, 180, 194-96, 199-203, 318, 369
Near death experiences, 241, 261, 263-64, 265n., 267-68, 275
New age (movement), 227-32, 234-37, 261, 406
Nirvana, 294, 303, 305
Noosphere, 189

Occult (-ism), 261-62, 288, 302, 317n.
Old Testament prophecies, 92, 320
Oneida, 331

Optimism, 9, 15, 66, 178, 185, 187, 222-23, 240, 242
Orthodox Church, 352
Osiris, 33
Overpopulation. *See* Population
Ozone, 197-98

Paleoanthropology, 205
Paradise, 26, 81, 225-26, 296, 399
Parousia, 83n., 85, 87, 89n., 92-93, 96n., 98n., 103, 110, 133-34, 136, 138, 159, 190-91, 193, 247, 284, 288, 309, 330, 333, 371, 378, 390, 392
 delay of, 114, 118-19, 125, 139-42, 368
Parsism, 55-59
Penance, 305, 311, 357-58, 359n., 362
Pentecostal, 322
Pessimism, 9, 54n., 87, 128, 189, 192, 254, 318
Pharisees, 61-62, 78, 80
Pietism, 16, 127n., 341
Pleonexia, 199
Pleroma, 192-93
Pollution, 197, 199-201, 388, 404
Population, 5, 19, 189, 194-96, 201-2, 252, 318, 369
Predestination, 16, 343-44, 346
Proclamation, 44, 49, 56, 69, 82-92, 95, 114, 206, 286, 305, 344, 350, 374-75, 383, 397
 Jesus', 27, 61, 67-68, 70, 78, 80-81, 83n., 84, 108-10, 113, 118-19, 124, 127, 137-38, 142, 148, 156, 247, 348-49, 368
Procreation, 164
Progress, 6, 13-17, 19-21, 128, 156n., 178, 184, 186, 188, 192, 196, 205-6, 208, 237, 254, 320, 387, 404-6
 infinite, 272, 337, 361
 secular, 17, 20-21
Promise(s), 6, 20, 28, 31, 35, 41-42, 43n., 46-47, 49, 51, 53, 61, 70, 85, 90-91, 136, 145, 148, 152-53, 159, 161, 206-7, 209, 260, 280n., 296, 306, 314, 324,

333, 336n., 338, 371-72, 376-78, 391, 396, 403. *See also* Fulfillment, of God's promises
Promised land, 12, 35, 41, 43, 50, 147
Prophecies, 72, 310, 313-14, 320, 321n., 335
Psyche, 267-68
Purgatory, 223, 273n., 290-91, 303, 305, 309, 337, 341, 343, 350, 352-64, 395
Purification, 52, 57, 270, 280, 305-6, 338, 350, 352, 361-63, 395

Q-source, 72

Rapture, 33, 334-35
Rebirth, 8, 26, 270
Re-creation, 103, 158, 166
Reincarnation, 8, 26, 171-72, 235, 291, 301-7, 362-63
Redemption, 12, 20, 27, 167n., 184, 189, 275, 276n., 289, 294, 342-43, 348, 389
Remythologization, 398
Renewal, 26, 31n., 55, 58, 160, 207n., 232-33, 326-27, 333
Restoration, 46n., 49, 132, 284, 337-38, 340, 343
Resurrection, 8, 26, 28-29, 38-41, 55, 58, 81n., 88-89, 93, 96, 98, 101-3, 107, 117-18, 122, 126, 131n., 144, 148, 157, 162-63, 169, 176-77, 183-84, 223, 247, 260-61, 273, 275-76, 278-307, 322-23, 333, 335, 340, 350, 352-55, 360, 368, 394, 396, 402, 407
  of the body, 26, 58-59, 80n., 89n., 96, 102, 192, 275, 287-300, 403
  of the dead, 9, 46, 55, 58, 60n., 80, 93, 96, 98, 103, 115n., 144, 148, 152, 163, 182, 184, 235, 276, 280, 286, 328, 333, 350, 403
  of Jesus, 81-84, 87, 91-93, 96, 123-24, 131-32, 136, 138, 140-41, 144, 147-49, 154, 161, 176, 204, 206, 280-87, 296, 305, 348, 350, 373, 382, 389-90, 392, 403-4

universal, 40, 289-90, 300
Resuscitation, 39n., 117, 265-67
Revelation, 15, 40, 64, 77-79, 86, 92, 107, 111, 127, 143-44, 147, 159, 231, 314, 317, 325, 327, 358, 363, 370, 372-73
Revelation, book of, 8, 66, 97-99, 162, 247-48, 317, 320, 323, 325, 336-37, 380, 383, 385, 392, 395, 403
Revivification, 287
Revolution, 73n., 112, 145, 216-22, 224-26, 232, 239-40, 242, 284, 328, 330, 406
Righteousness, 57, 86, 111, 148, 306, 324, 382
Roman Catholic, 97, 153-55, 188, 259, 272-73, 275-79, 299-300, 305, 309-10, 314, 327, 343, 350-53, 356-59, 361-63, 377, 386, 395, 399
Russellites, 313

Sabbath, 62, 76, 122-23, 165, 323, 377, 405
Sacrifice, 186, 257, 283, 354-55, 371, 402
  eucharistic, 352, 356-58
Sadducees, 61-62
Salvation, 28n., 37, 39n., 41, 43-49, 51, 54, 58, 75, 80, 84, 86-90, 92-96, 98-99, 102, 126-27, 136-38, 154-60, 170, 172, 194, 219, 234, 236, 242, 266, 275, 278, 283, 295, 305-6, 311, 320, 323, 326, 329-30, 334, 337-38, 341, 346, 349, 356-64, 366, 381, 389, 393, 395-96, 400-401, 404
  eschatological, 27, 48-49, 52
  universal, 45, 170, 337-38, 341, 395
Salvation history (includes *Heils-geschichte*), 10, 13, 15n., 54, 65, 86-87, 115n., 160, 191, 326, 368
Sarx. See Flesh
Satan. *See* Anti-godly powers
Savior, 27, 57, 59, 67n., 92, 98, 121, 237, 311, 330, 392, 395, 404

Science, 105, 130, 157, 173-207, 229, 238, 242, 259, 267-68, 294, 388
Second Coming, 90, 116, 128, 130, 133-34, 190-91, 334
Sectarian, 328, 379, 399
Secular (-ization), 16, 18, 27, 63, 115, 148, 156, 203, 205-6, 211, 217, 230, 322, 407
Self-confidence, 14-16, 19
Self-disclosure (God's), 31, 75-76, 79, 82, 143-44, 158, 206, 238, 249, 274, 298, 321, 396
Servant (-hood), 26, 34, 91, 196, 373, 377
  of Yahweh, the lord, 47, 51, 84, 283
  suffering, 47, 51, 75
Seventh Day Adventists, 330
Shakers, 331
Sheol, 36-40, 59, 67, 274, 278, 401-2
Sicarii, 63
Signs (of the end), 111, 131, 319, 321, 330, 365, 371, 379, 381-87
Sin (s), 96, 151, 167, 193, 233, 258-60, 284-85, 298, 311, 314, 344, 353, 356-58, 371-72, 390
  forgiveness of, 6, 46, 75, 122, 124, 355, 357-59, 371-72
Sleep, 9, 25, 40, 59, 255, 296-98, 301, 354-55
Socialism, 217, 221, 224-25, 239-40, 374
Socialist, 224-25, 240, 374
Society, 4, 6, 8, 23, 119, 148, 151, 155, 157-58, 160, 163, 165, 171, 189, 211, 218, 220-21, 224, 241, 243, 306, 317, 322-27, 329, 332, 378, 406-7
  secular, 129, 318, 365, 370, 378
Solar Temple, 317-18
Son of God, 84, 90-92, 283, 297
Son of Man, 52, 66-67, 74-76, 84-85, 88n., 110, 112, 116, 118, 121-24, 131, 133-35, 140, 149, 247, 383, 388, 391
Soul, 9, 24-26, 33, 36, 39, 56-57, 62, 80n., 96, 101-3, 155, 164, 167, 171, 175, 177, 188, 193, 234-35, 262, 269-

80, 288, 290-91, 298-307, 316, 318, 332, 338-39, 343, 350-52, 355, 357-59, 362-63, 401. *See also* Body and soul
Space, 187, 264, 291, 293, 314, 333, 368
  and time, 132, 134, 178, 262, 271, 301, 309-10, 387-89
Spirit, 25-26, 34, 36, 38n., 56-57, 66, 91, 126, 164, 177-78, 189, 208, 226, 228-29, 232, 234-36, 239, 257, 262-63, 268-69, 271, 273-74, 287, 304, 326, 344, 348-50
  human, 8, 174, 229-30
  of the Lord, 50, 87, 233, 313
Spiritual, 38n., 43n., 102, 143, 159, 163, 175-76, 193, 219, 230, 233-37, 249, 260-62, 265, 269-70, 273, 275, 290, 299, 314, 316, 324, 326-28, 332, 335, 339, 342, 362, 379, 388
Spiritualism, 95-96, 263
Spirituality, 228, 230, 236, 302, 342
Spiritualization, 35n., 133, 159, 326
Suffering, 57, 66, 111-12, 122, 124, 151-52, 160, 163, 167, 208-9, 235, 251, 258, 281n., 295, 336n., 354, 357, 362, 366, 371, 377, 387, 403. *See also* Servant(hood): suffering
Suicide, 27, 215, 226, 266, 279, 313-16, 318
Symbolism, 12, 46n., 70, 117, 124n., 129-30, 163, 185, 213n., 222-23, 241, 248, 344, 353, 370-73, 376

Technology, 184, 195, 204, 231, 238, 387
Teleology, 204
Temporality, 94, 169, 210, 279, 295, 387
Theocracy, 10, 63, 150
Theophany, 76, 143
Theos Aner, 146
Third Reich, 329
Time, 3, 7-8, 19, 26-27, 32, 48-49, 52, 59, 65, 71, 75, 84, 89, 93, 95, 99, 116-19, 132, 136, 143, 146, 155, 167, 170, 182, 191, 222, 236, 245, 251, 286, 289-302, 313, 330, 345, 369, 376, 384n.,

381, 382, 387, 389, 394, 397. *See also*
Space, and time
cyclical view of, 7-8, 26
of decision, 70, 80, 95, 381
linear view of, 7-8, 27, 135n.
of salvation, 27, 46, 50-52, 70-72, 80,
    88, 99, 128, 371
Timelessness, 23, 293
Tomb, 26, 32-33, 35, 37-38, 285n., 298,
    348, 354
Totalitarian (-ism), 19, 216, 238
Transcendence, 190, 222-23, 229, 232-
    33, 303, 401, 404
Translation, 38, 304
Transformation, 17, 86n., 119, 151, 157,
    165, 167-68, 219, 232-33, 289, 316,
    332, 361, 387
    of the world, 21, 57, 82, 93, 110, 129,
    368
Transitory (-iness), 20, 65, 207, 268,
    279, 291-93, 296, 301, 336, 370, 389,
    394
Transmigration, 26, 301, 304
Transmutation, 363
Tribulation, 334-35

Universal (-istic), 10-11, 15, 40, 45, 47,

50n., 53-54, 61, 64-65, 72, 82, 115n.,
    119, 135-36, 144, 151-52, 166, 172,
    177, 211, 222, 229, 232, 235, 265, 269,
    272, 279, 289-90, 300, 323, 327, 338,
    340-41, 343-46, 353, 389, 392, 395,
    404
Universalist, 341
Universalism, 340
Universal salvation. *See Apokatastasis
    Panton;* Homecoming, universal
Universe, 23, 54, 92, 132, 134, 169, 174-
    75, 179-85, 188-90, 192-94, 228, 230,
    237, 241, 284n., 285, 294, 306, 388,
    404-5
Utopia, 47, 96, 132-33, 150, 156, 160-61,
    165, 207, 217, 221-24, 226, 322, 327-
    29, 331, 378, 403-4

World, end of. *See* End, of the world

Yahweh, 7, 10-13, 28-30, 36-38, 40-44,
    47-48, 50-51, 55, 61, 76, 147, 282-83

Zealots, 63, 73n.
Zoroaster, 56-59

Index of Scripture References

OLD TESTAMENT

Genesis

1:27	274
2:7	274
3	36
3:15	285
3:21	37, 285
5:24	38
12:2	35
12:2-3	49
14:19-20	11
14:22-23	12
21:33	293
23:19-20	35
25:8	35, 254
49:33	37
49:8-12	49
50:5-6	35

Exodus

3:14	35
19:6	41

Leviticus

4:5	48
11:44	41
25:8-12	165

Numbers

24:15-19	49

Deuteronomy

18:10-14	263
32:35	41
32:39	76
34:5-6	38
40:27	47
48:8	47, 283
49:14	47
50:6	47

1 Samuel

2:32	37
28	38

2 Samuel

1:16	48
7:12-15	49

1 Kings

8:27	401
17:17-24	39

2 Kings

2:11	38, 67
4:20-37	39
13:20-21	39

Nehemiah

2:1	312

Job

19:25-26	39
42:17	37

Psalms

1:2	42
2	43
2:7	50
20	43
21	43
37:35-36	100
46:8-9	99
49:15	39
73	73
73:24	39
89:11	295
89:48	401
90:10	18, 257, 306
102:25-27	292, 295
110:1	340
119:13-14	42
131	213
135:14	373

Proverbs

10:27	37

Isaiah

2:2	44
2:2-4	45

3–4	67	*Jeremiah*		*Micah*	
6	36	23:20	44	5:1-5	50
7:10-17	49	30:24	44	5:2	84
7:14	84	31:34	46	5:15	42
7:21-25	45	48:47	44	7:18-19	46
9:1	45				
9:1-6	49, 50	*Lamentations*		*Habakkuk*	
9:1-7	49	1:4-5	43	1:12	29
11:1-8	49, 50				
11:6-9	45, 405	*Ezekiel*		*Haggai*	
13:5	44	11	36	1:7-8	50
14:9-11	38	11:19-20	46	2:19	50
16:6-7	42	11:20b	46	2:20-23	50
26:14	39	16:63	46		
30:25	44	33:11	261	*Zechariah*	
34:8	42	36:23	372	4:6-10	50
35:5-6	70	37	46, 60	4:9	50
38:3	37	37:1-14	46	8:12	50
38:9-20	257	38:16	44	9:9	51
38:18	37			14:5-15	44
40:28	295	*Daniel*		*Malachi*	
40:31	295	2:1-47	59	4:1	44
41:4	76	7	52	4:1-5	67
41:18-19	46	7:1-28	59		
42:1-4	47	7:10-11	59		
42:5	283	8:14	312	**NEW TESTAMENT**	
42:6-7	46	9:24-27	312		
43:10	76	9:27	335, 385	*Matthew*	
43:21	46	12:2	40, 41, 59	1:1-17	326
44:6	283			1:22-23	84
45:1	48	*Hosea*		2:5-6	84
46:4	76	3:5	44	3:1-2	85
49:1-6	47			3:2	400
50:4-11a	47	*Amos*		4:12-15	84
51:9-10	46	2:1	36	4:16	85
52:7	71	5:4b	45	5–7	85
52:13–53:12	47	5:14-15	45	5:3	400
53:4	84	5:19-20	44	5:17-18	84
53:6	51	9	67	6:33	86
55:3	46	9:11	49	7:13-14	395
65:17-25	46	9:11-15	45, 49	7:21	397
65:20	37	9:13-14	49	8:17	84

8:22	69	2:28	122	17	88
9:17	70	4:11-12	84	21	88, 383
10	85	6:50	77	21:9	86
10:5	85	6:52	84	21:20	383
10:16	85	8:35	258	21:24	383
10:23	140	8:38	121	21:25-36	311
10:28	402	9:1	83	21:32-33	83
11:6	69	9:9-11	140	23:43	81, 296
12:28	381	9:11-13	303	24:21	81
13	80, 85, 289	9:32	84	24:37	287
13:30	397, 398	9:43	72		
13:49-52	397	9:48	402	**John**	
16:18	85, 380	10:45	75	1:11	90
16:27	392	12:18-27	80	1:14	9, 89
16:28	141	12:27	80	2:11	70
18:15-17	85	13	88, 383	3:18	381
22:13	402	13:6	76, 77	3:36	395
22:30	289, 360	13:10	83	4:25-26	79
24	85, 88, 383	13:22	385	5:24	88, 360, 381
24:5	77	13:26	121	5:24-28	297
24:14	141	13:30	140	5:25, 28-29	297
24:14-31	85	13:30-31	83, 383	6:19	89
24:27	383	13:32	71, 79	6:44	127
24:29-30	388	13:37	383	6:54	127
24:34-35	83	14:61	75	9:35-38	75
24:36	309	14:62	76, 77, 78	11:24-26	88
25	398			11:44	287
25:1-13	310, 346, 383	**Luke**		14:2	88
25:5	141	1:5-6	86	14:3	88
25:13	141	2:1-4	86	14:9-11	89
25:14-30	380	3:16	355	14:16-17	90
25:31-32	391	7:15	355	14:25-27	90
25:41	402	7:22	70	16:2	90
26:13	85	8:52	296	16:4b-11	90
26:64	77	9:62	69	16:11	89
27:51-53	348	11:20	70, 382	16:12-15	90
28:18-20	85	12:20	2	17:22-23	340
28:19	374	12:45	380	17:24	295
24	383	12:48	392	20:31	90
25	398	14:70	77		
		15:2	78	**Acts**	
Mark		15:3-7	78	1:7	309
1:15	71, 397	16:16	86	3:21	338
2:10	75, 122	16:19-31	296, 360	7:54-58	267

17:32	276	15:25	291, 340	*2 Thessalonians*	
26:23	287	15:27-28	340	22:3-4	385
		15:28	374, 403		
Romans		15:29	347	*1 Timothy*	
1:1-6	91	15:35-57	275	2:4	395
1:4	283	15:42-54	290	6:16	257
1:20	92	15:45	257		
5	283, 285	15:50	287	*Hebrews*	
5:12	259	15:52b	289	1:1-2	321
6	285, 381	16:22	392	1:10-12	292, 294
6:3	260			2:1-4	285
6:4	260, 372	*2 Corinthians*		12:2	405
6:4-5	287	3:6	94		
6:23	259	4:7-12	95	*1 Peter*	
7	285	4:14	94	1:7	356
7:14	274	5:2	96	3:15	245
7:19	160	5:7	94	3:19	349
7:24	275	5:10	350, 391		
8	285	5:17	321, 360	*2 Peter*	
8:11	275, 389	6:2	381	2:17	402
8:14	274			3:4	296
8:19-21	373	*Galatians*		3:10	388
8:19-23	389	6:7	391		
8:20	404			*1 John*	
8:23-25	94	*Ephesians*		12:18	385
10:9	282	4:10	401	12:22	385
11:12-26	376	5:28	164		
11:32	395			*2 John*	
12:12	163	*Philippians*		7	385
13:11	94	2:5-11	282		
		2:9-11	92	*Revelation*	
1 Corinthians		4:5	94	1:18	348
2:9	405			6:9	298
3:11-13	394	*Colossians*		11:15	97
3:15	356	1:15	284	13:1-10	385
6:12-20	96	1:16	284, 390	13:11-18	385
6:14	287	1:18	287	14:11	395
7:14	347			16:16	315
13–15	355	*1 Thessalonians*		20:1-15	331, 336
13:12	403	4:14	94	20:12	391
15:8	91	4:15	94, 291	21	403
15:14	286	4:16	390	21:1	97
15:18	296	5:2	93, 383	21:3	97
15:22	338			21:3-4	403

21:10	97	7:50	65	**Testament of Moses**	
21:22-25	380			10:1	53
22:20	372, 392				
				Jubilees	
		EXTRACANONICAL		22:17	354
		WRITINGS			
DEUTERO-				**Pseudo-Clementines**	
CANONICAL		**1 Enoch**	51	**Hom. II**	
BOOKS		6–36	52	15:1-2	65
		10:1	53		
2 Baruch	51	46:5	66	**Gospel of Thomas**	164
40:1-3	322	48:6	66		
46:7	38	48:10	66	**J. Taan**	
50–51	289	67:4-7	59	2:1	74
76:2	38	83–90	51		
				Mishna Sanhedrin	
2 Maccabees		**2 Enoch**		10:1	67
12	356	65:6-8	65		
12:38-42	353			**Yasna**	
12:43-45	354	**4 Ezra**		43:5.6	57
12:46	356	7:28-29	323	45:2	
				46:10	57
2 Esdras	51	**Sibylline Oracles**	324	48:11.14	57
4:9-49	38	3:652-43	322		

Printed in the United States
80184LV00003B/67-129